NOTHING STAYS PUT

NOTHING STAYS PUT

THE LIFE AND POETRY OF
AMY CLAMPITT

Willard Spiegelman

ALFRED A. KNOPF | NEW YORK | 2023

THIS IS A BORZOI BOOK
PUBLISHED BY ALFRED A. KNOPF

www.aaknopf.com

Knopf, Borzoi Books, and the colophon
are registered trademarks of Penguin Random House LLC.

Library of Congress Cataloging-in-Publication Data
Names: Spiegelman, Willard, author.
Title: Nothing stays put : the life and poetry of Amy Clampitt / Willard
Spiegelman.
Description: First edition. | New York : Alfred A. Knopf, [2023] | Includes
bibliographical references and index. |
Identifiers: LCCN 2022005036 (print) | LCCN 2022005037 (ebook) |
ISBN 9780525658269 (hardcover) | ISBN 9780525658276 (ebook)
Subjects: LCSH: Clampitt, Amy. | Women poets, American—20th century—
Biography. | LCGFT: Biographies.
Classification: LCC PS3553.L23 Z83 2023 (print) | LCC PS3553.L23 (ebook)
| DDC 811/.54 [B]—dc23/eng/20220520
LC record available at https://lccn.loc.gov/2022005036
LC ebook record available at https://lccn.loc.gov/2022005037

Jacket photograph (inset) courtesy of the Amy Clampitt Foundation.
Amy Clampitt papers, Berg Collection, NYPL;
(background) blue cornflowers, shapencolour/Alamy
Jacket design by Chip Kidd

Manufactured in the United States of America

First Edition

For Kenneth Bleeth

and

Mary Jo Salter

sine quibus non

Nothing stays put. The world is a wheel.
All that we know, that we're
made of, is motion.

—AMY CLAMPITT,
"Nothing Stays Put" (*Westward*, 1990)

It was all improbable and perfectly natural.

—AMY CLAMPITT,
letter to her family from Greece, April 30, 1965

Poeta nascitur, non fit.

—LATIN APHORISM

IOWA FLORA
(In Memory of Amy Clampitt)

We thought we were having an indigenous childhood
splashed with Indian paintbrush and grassy knolls
thickened by birdfoot violets and ordinary goldenrod,

but we kept finding noxious alien weeds in the hills—
quackgrass and thistle, European morning glory
that no state legislation could control.

We inherited pioneer grasses high as a prairie
schooner, but there were also fresh settlements
of bog flowers and refugees from the sea-

coast marshes, silky-leaved Virginia plants
and Texas marigolds, imported seeds and ornamentals,
weeds from the wasted villages of other continents.

Nature consists of immigrants and mongrels:
you showed us how to prize coincidence and impurity
in wayward fields, the deserted and marginal . . .

I went down to the swamp to mourn for you, Amy,
and it was as if Providence led me to the place
where I stumbled upon yellow swamp betony

and pink foxglove mingled with something nameless
(*unfathomable the mystery before us*, you said)
and the shining, cup-flowered grass of Parnassus.

—EDWARD HIRSCH, *On Love*

Contents

———

———

NOTHING STAYS PUT

PROLOGUE:

ASSEMBLING A LIFE

IN ITS ISSUE of August 14, 1978, *The New Yorker* published a poem by a writer previously unknown to its readers:

THE SUN UNDERFOOT AMONG THE SUNDEWS

An ingenuity too astonishing
to be quite fortuitous is
this bog full of sundews, sphagnum-
lined and shaped like a teacup.
                    A step
down and you're into it; a
wilderness swallows you up:
ankle-, then knee-, then midriff-
to-shoulder-deep in wetfooted
understory, an overhead
spruce-tamarack horizon hinting
you'll never get out of here.
                    But the sun
among the sundews, down there,
is so bright, an underfoot
webwork of carnivorous rubies,
a star-swarm thick as the gnats

they're set to catch, delectable
double-faced cockleburs, each
hair-tip with a sticky mirror
afire with sunlight, a million
of them and again a million,
each mirror a trap set to
unhand unbelieving,
                    that either
a First Cause said once, "Let there
be sundews," and there were, or they've
made their way here unaided
other than by that backhand, round-
about refusal to assume responsibility
known as Natural Selection.
                        But the sun
underfoot is so dazzling
down there among the sundews,
there is so much light
in the cup that, looking,
you start to fall upward.

The author was fifty-eight years old and had lived in virtual obscurity for thirty-seven years since she moved to Manhattan from her native Iowa, fresh out of college, in 1941. A manuscript of the finished poem among the author's papers is dated "5 January 1978." Beneath that date, in pencil, she has noted, "Accepted by The New Yorker, 3/78." Though not a youthful overnight success, she was now on a fast track with regard to publication. *The New Yorker* began to accept additional work.

Almost four years later (January 11, 1982), another poem—there would be a total of forty-eight in her lifetime, and two posthumously—appeared in the same magazine. The author used its title for that of her debut book, *The Kingfisher*, published by Alfred A. Knopf in 1983:

THE KINGFISHER

In a year the nightingales were said to be so loud
they drowned out slumber, and peafowl strolled screaming
beside the ruined nunnery, through the long evening
of a dazzled pub crawl, the halcyon color, portholed
by those eye-spots' stunning tapestry, unsettled
the pastoral nightfall with amazements opening.

Months later, intermission in a pub on Fifty-fifth Street
found one of them still breathless, the other quizzical,
acting the philistine, puncturing Stravinsky—"Tell
me, what *was* that racket in the orchestra about?"—
hauling down the Firebird, harum-scarum, like a kite,
a burnished, breathing wreck that didn't hurt at all.

Among the Bronx Zoo's exiled jungle fowl, they heard
through headphones of a separating panic, the bellbird
reiterate its single *chong*, a scream nobody answered.
When he mourned, "The poetry is gone," she quailed,
seeing how his hands shook, sobered into feeling old.
By midnight, yet another fifth would have been killed.

A Sunday morning, the November of their cataclysm
(Dylan Thomas brought in *in extremis* to St. Vincent's,
that same week, a symptomatic datum) found them
wandering a downtown churchyard. Among its headstones,
while from unruined choirs the noise of Christendom
poured over Wall Street, a benison in vestments,

a late thrush paused, in transit from some grizzled
spruce bog to the humid equatorial fireside: berry-
eyed, bark-brown above, with dark hints of trauma
in the stigmata of its underparts—or so, too bruised
just then to have invented anything so fancy,
later, re-embroidering a retrospect, she had supposed.

In gray England, years of muted recrimination (then
dead silence) later, she could not have said how many
spoiled takeoffs, how many entanglements gone sodden,
how many gaudy evenings made frantic by just one
insomniac nightingale, how many liaisons gone down
screaming in a stroll beside the ruined nunnery;

a kingfisher's burnished plunge, the color
of felicity afire, came glancing like an arrow
through landscapes of untended memory: ardor
illuminating with its terrifying currency
now no mere glimpse, no porthole vista
but, down on down, the uninhabitable sorrow.

Poetry readers—I remember, because I was one of them—scratched
their heads and asked, "Where did this come from? Who is this per-
son?" No poems like these had appeared on the scene in quite some
time, if ever. Curiosity was piqued. People wanted to find out more
about the new author, and to see more of her work.

In "The Sun Underfoot Among the Sundews," readers heard a
measured music that begins with the repeated, almost rhyming vow-
els of the title; they saw a rendering of a Maine landscape featuring
one "of several insectivorous plants of the genus *Drosera*, growing in
wet ground and having leaves covered with sticky hairs" (the author
helpfully supplied a note about this ordinary, enticing item when
the poem appeared in hardcover); and they were presented with
a modest, almost offhand philosophical inquiry into the nature of
creation, as well as Darwin's theory of natural selection. The diction
suggests that the poet wanted to update Robert Frost's ingeniously
cheery and vertiginously menacing sonnet, "Design."

Scholars, critics, and amateur poetry lovers would have noticed
that the second poem is full of literary echoes, and allusions to Greek
mythology, Shakespeare, Keats, Hardy, and Gerard Manley Hop-
kins; that it pays homage to more recent and important high culture
figures (Igor Stravinsky, Dylan Thomas, perhaps T. S. Eliot); that its
diction is mouth-filling, its imagery rich, and its luscious sentences
long and complex. It manages at least one cheeky pun—"a benison

in vestments"—about Trinity Church Wall Street. It is obsessed with birds not only as symbols or cultural artifacts but also as parts of our real, physical world.

The poem displays something that all art strives for: a unique style. And it is certainly not an easy poem. It does not even seem personal. It sounds distant and mannered. In fact, it is deeply personal, recounting a love affair gone wrong. It is a confessional poem masquerading as an objective third-person narrative, an extended series of vignettes, with birds rather than people as the central characters. Its author said of it, "The design here might be thought of as an illuminated manuscript in which all the handwork happens to be verbal, or (perhaps more precisely) as a novel trying to work itself into a piece of cloisonné." This is not entirely helpful to a reader of the poem, but the characterization derives in part from the author's unsuccessful efforts for about twenty-five years to write fiction, and then her distillation of narrative into lyric.

The poem is by, and about the life of, Amy Clampitt. Its origins lay in something from her life that had occurred more than a quarter century earlier. It is autobiographical, perhaps at second hand, but not revelatory. A biographer might understandably wish to associate it with the verifiable experience of its author, if he could ever connect it to matters in her life. But he would be foiled. Amy Clampitt was a retiring presence, a background figure, however flamboyant she was on the page and then, at the height of her celebrity later on, however visible. As Doris Myers, one of her oldest friends, said in an interview, "She wanted to tell the world things, but she didn't want completely to share herself." Poems that appeared in earlier, more personal forms became, as they were revised for publication in her five elegant volumes from Knopf, more impersonal. Revelation and concealment were partners in her psychological makeup.

In his inaugural lecture as the Oxford Professor of Poetry, W. H. Auden remarked that when he read a poem that moved him he asked himself two questions. The first: "Here is a verbal contraption. How does it work?" And the second: "What kind of a guy inhabits this poem?" By the latter he did not mean the sum of minute biographical facts about the author, but rather the kind of mind and temperament that we might infer, by reasoning back from effect to cause.

That said, we are always grateful, even eager, for additional information about the maker, the real person who "inhabits" the poem or novel or painting we admire. An artist's life is necessary, but never sufficient, to explain her art.

———

How does one measure an artist and her achievement? Can one define a person by her literary work? These are questions for critics and scholars. And a related question: Who deserves a biography? In an ideal world, everyone would get one, the written equivalent of Andy Warhol's fifteen minutes of fame. All lives can be made interesting. Every life, every biography, can give what Samuel Johnson most valued: something that "comes near to us, what we can turn to use." A poet's life is not intrinsically more compelling than anyone else's. Everything depends on the methods of the teller. And no biography can be complete, however, because all lives, even ones well observed and documented, are partial. All are replete with contradictions and unsolvable mysteries. No one is the same person to everyone in her sphere. People see one another through a unique lens or, often, through more than one lens. Some visions look clearer and cleaner than others, which may be muddy or opaque. But perceptions, memories, and attachments often overlap. We assemble a life from the shards of evidence and recollection that remain. A life in many pieces can be made to look whole.

Clampitt, who lived from 1920 to 1994, presents special challenges to a would-be biographer, and her life still warrants attention in the twenty-first century. Her visible presence on the American poetry scene lasted for less than two decades, and it will be for literary scholars and historians, as well as the general public, to determine her place in the pantheon. She bloomed late and then died too young, but her poems continue to generate both heat and light, and she still has fans, numerous and enthusiastic. Her poems evince a life engaged with books, and in political protest and religious struggle. They are not confessional outpourings. They open up to us a woman deeply connected to the physical world, who wrote about nature, landscape, and weather in the most detailed ways.

They mingle Keatsian lushness and Quaker austerity, an unusual combination and one evident in Clampitt herself. These poems, her artistic legacy, open a window onto their maker. This is one reason to examine that maker.

We should also have a written account of her life because we can regard her as one of the Patron Saints of Late Bloomers. It took her a long time to come into her own. The Latin proverb *poeta nascitur, non fit* (a poet is born, not made) is not entirely true in her case. Clampitt may have been born with a genetic predisposition and capacity to write. From an early age she was sensitive to language, first as a reader, and then as a schoolgirl who played around with words on the page. But she had to make herself a poet, and she did so only after many wrong turns and many years of failure.

And a third reason to pay attention to her life is that our current culture has begun to express appreciation for women who in generations past led exemplary lives, privately as well as publicly: "Overlooked No More," says *The New York Times* of its series of obituaries of previously ignored role models. Before she became famous, Clampitt was living eccentrically, but with aspirations to something grander. She had as many facets as a diamond, as great a depth as a cave of wonders. She sets an example. The last sentence of *Middlemarch*, the George Eliot novel that Clampitt read over and over because of her identification with its author and with Dorothea Brooke, its heroine, sums up Amy's status before she found fame, or fame found her:

> . . . the effect of her being on those around her was incalculably diffusive: for the growing good of the world is partly dependent on unhistoric acts; and that things are not so ill with you and me as they might have been is half owing to the number who lived faithfully a hidden life, and rest in unvisited tombs.

For almost sixty years she faithfully led a life that was mostly hidden, and certainly unhistoric. Then followed a coming out into the spotlight.

As I wrote this book, I fell gradually and almost unthinkingly into the habit of calling my subject Amy when portraying the woman who is now gone. I try to say Clampitt when I refer to the artist whose work remains. In the preceding paragraph, my reader has already experienced the liberty I have taken. I hope that reader will agree with me that writing a biography may permit an author a legitimate sense of intimacy with his subject, and allow him to use her given name.

———

The external shape of Amy's life before her two decades of renown (roughly 1978 until 1997, when the *Collected Poems* was published posthumously) is clear in its outline. Born in Iowa to a Quaker family of farmers on June 15, 1920, the eldest of five children, bookish and slightly eccentric from an early age, she was graduated from Grinnell College in 1941 and, following a summer working with European refugees at a Quaker establishment in Iowa, she made a beeline for New York. In her 1993 *Paris Review* interview, she said that "the happiest times in my childhood were spent in solitude," mostly reading, and that she felt like a social misfit. The absence of mountains or oceans in her native Iowa made her hanker for an entirely different landscape. She left the landlocked Midwest, although she never entirely shook the Iowa soil from her boots. She had a fellowship for graduate school at Columbia in English, but dropped out, perhaps before the year was up, and soon went to work at Oxford University Press as a secretary, and then rose to the post of promotions director for college textbooks. In 1949 she won an essay contest sponsored by OUP, for which first prize was a trip to England. I'd like to believe that she beat out dozens of other applicants for the prize, but we don't know anything about the competition. The anodyne assignment for the essay was something like "Why I Wish to Visit England." Traveling to a country that she knew of only through literature changed her life: "I believed that the past could be experienced as the present." The prize made her wish come true.

Postwar Europe possessed a magical appeal for Americans hungry for high culture, for poets as well as everyone else who was unable to get there during the 1930s, owing to the Depression, and

Amy with the head of Oxford University Press,
when she arrived by ship in England, 1949

the 1940s, owing to the war. Things began to open up in the late
forties, even though much of Britain and the Continent was still a
destroyed war zone. Recovery came slowly. England retained ves-
tiges of war rationing until 1954, but educated Americans were now
eager and able to see the real thing with their own eyes, and to
visit sites they'd experienced only in books, pictures, and university
classes, as well as movies and newsreels. The poets all went: Robert
Lowell, James Merrill, John Ashbery, Adrienne Rich, James Wright,
and others like Anthony Hecht, Howard Nemerov, and Richard
Wilbur who had served in the Army but were hardly at that point in
tourist mode. (Hecht, who was born into a family with some money
and considerable cultural aspirations, had visited Europe with his
parents as a child in the 1930s.) With the help of Fulbright grants,
awards from the American Academy in Rome, and especially the

generally favorable exchange rate, they took advantage of peacetime conditions. And Amy happily joined them.

After her return, she went back to work but then left the press permanently in 1951, to write a novel, which turned into several novels, and to travel through Europe more extensively for another five months. When no publisher accepted her novel, she got herself another job, this time as a reference librarian for the National Audubon Society. Birds, like cats, weather, and landscape, remained perennially fascinating to Clampitt, the woman and the writer: "She was galvanized by nature," remembered her oldest New York friend, Phoebe Hoss. Indeed, in her mature poetry nature often becomes— as it did in her life—a surrogate for the direct treatment of personal relations. (We can say the same thing about Henry Wadsworth Longfellow, another American poet equally alert to meteorology but reticent with regard to internal weather, and who often allowed the first to represent the second.) Thus, "The Kingfisher" and many other poems, in which outward data provide an outlet for guarded emotions. She was always reserved. We learn from people's reports about her that she often remembered the names of cats but not of their owners.

Is it coincidental that she took up poetry writing for the first time since adolescence when she began to feel the attraction of the Episcopal Church in the mid-1950s? Or that her major poetry coincides with her later abandonment of the church in the late 1960s and early 1970s in favor of political activism? Looking back, she allowed, "What I see in Christianity now is a kind of template of human nature—by which I guess I mean mainly human suffering." She left the church but rechanneled the religious impulse. In a letter to a friend who became the abbess of a religious order in England, she described "the dangerous qualities of faith, the destructive potentiality of faith, as well as its creative, constructive features." In 1977, having written poems for more than a decade, she took a creative writing class at The New School. It confirmed her sense of vocation, and it released energies that were previously pent up.

In the 1960s and '70s, she came into her own in several ways. She started working as a freelance editor, then went to Dutton Books, where she was known as the "Book Doctor," and began writing poetry with greater earnestness. She became involved in antiwar and other political pursuits. The other encouragement for writing poetry came in 1968. She met the man who became her life partner, Harold Korn, a law professor at New York University and later Columbia, through their shared political activity and work with the Village Independent Democrats. They were campaigning for Eugene McCarthy in his idealistic, perhaps quixotic drive to become president. She moved in with Hal in 1973, keeping this cohabitation something of a secret from her more conventional relatives, at least at the start, but she also held on to the small walk-up apartment in a Greenwich Village brownstone that remained the Woolfian "room of her own" until she was forced to give it up in the last year of her life when the building was converted into co-ops. She married Hal several months before her death. This long-deferred marriage is one of many parts of her life that are mysterious. According to some friends, she had always opposed marriage on principle. Other friends said that Hal would not marry a non-Jew while his observant Orthodox mother was still alive. The reality is always thornier, more complex than the facts.

Her poems began appearing in magazines, and she rose like a comet on the literary scene in the late seventies, praised by many and derided by some. A MacArthur Fellowship in 1992 gave her the first real money she ever had. "I know how to live poor," she told Doris Myers. Finally, she did not have to be poor. With her prize money she purchased a modest gray-shingled Cape Cod cottage outside Lenox, Massachusetts, almost adjacent to Tanglewood and close to Edith Wharton's The Mount. In the spring of 1993 she was diagnosed with ovarian cancer. She died in Lenox eighteen months later.

———

A biographer is left with various lacunae when he attempts to fill out Amy's life. Many people who might have helped me died before I could contact them. Clampitt's paper trail does not resemble those of Elizabeth Bishop, Robert Lowell, or James Merrill. Her friends did not realize that she would become "Amy Clampitt." But we have compensatory materials. Her papers are housed at the Berg Collection in the New York Public Library. Other materials remained in the Berkshires for twenty years, and have only recently been transported to the Berg, where they have yet to be catalogued.

Although there are gaps and omissions, Clampitt seems to have saved everything. There are mementos and writings from earlier stages of her life, going as far back as elementary school. The habit of hoarding, unlike the fact of renown, came early, even before she began to realize that she would become a person of interest. We have the manuscripts of her poems, as well as her novels and other unpublished work; we have her diaries, journals, and travel reports. We have her letters. And we have oral interviews with family and friends, conducted more than a decade ago. Nevertheless, much has disappeared. When I was in the process of assembling Clampitt's letters almost twenty years ago, her college friend Barbara Clark reached out to me and told me that she had many letters from Amy, all of which postdated 1968. Why not earlier ones? Because Clark's husband, eager to welcome his wife back home from surgery in 1967, had done a radical housecleaning and tossed away boxes of things he thought they would never want to look at. A quarter century of correspondence was disposed of. What revelations did the young Amy Clampitt make to her college roommate? How many other friends were there in similar situations? Every biographer confronts the inevitable losses that time inflicts upon him.

And he confronts mysteries as well as losses. In 2004, I saw a pen-and-ink sketch of a woman in profile folded among the papers at the Clampitt cottage. The sitter looked like Amy, or an Amy swiftly limned with artistic liberty. At the picture's bottom the artist had affixed her signature and the date: "Hartigan 1951." The autograph matches others of Grace Hartigan (1922–2008), the most extravagant of the few women who had joined the abstract expressionist movement that dominated the postwar American art scene. By the early fifties, Hartigan was shifting away from pure abstraction to experiments in portraiture. I phoned her in Baltimore, where she lived, and where she died four years later. Asked whether she remembered Clampitt, the contentious octogenarian dismissed me out of hand, sounding annoyed that I had disturbed her, and deny-

Amy in profile by Grace Hartigan, 1951

ing any knowledge or acquaintance. Might the sketch have been something quickly tossed off, at a party in the Village, or at a gallery opening, and then given to the subject as a memento? This seemed plausible to me, but Hartigan offered no reply, and it's unlikely that any answer will be forthcoming.

What of Amy's private life? And what about earlier lovers? We know she had them. As I mention above, the title poem of *The King-fisher* deals opaquely in a third-person narrative with a love affair gone awry. Friends say this was Clampitt's story. Amy refers to several "young men," and to serious love affairs in letters to her youngest brother, Philip, but there are no love letters per se, to anyone. She writes about Peter Marcasiano (1921–1984), a handsome painter she met on a park bench in Paris in 1951. He was born in Italy to American parents. He came to New York. She had an intense (but, according to her friend Mary Russel, platonic) relationship with him until

1958, when he returned to Paris, where he died. Other friends said Mary Russel was wrong about the "platonic" part. There were also other European men—one who married someone else, one who died—said Russel and Phoebe Hoss, but specific identities have been lost. Another friend from the OUP days, Janet Halverson, said in a 2002 interview that there was a lengthy affair with a married man named John Menapace from the OUP production department. Today's cultural climate would be unlikely to tolerate such office romances. At some point in the 1940s, she actually planned to marry a man named Howard, a painter who was both deaf and alcoholic. Amy's parents came out from Iowa, prepared to go to City Hall with the couple, and then the would-be bride backed out. Her brother Philip mentions a man named Raymond with whom there was an engagement, subsequently broken. (It's likely that his memory has played tricks; there was probably only one engagement.) Sister-in-law Jeanne Clampitt thought there was a blind man, although perhaps she mistook deafness for blindness. A biographer who wants to pin his subject down will meet with inevitable disappointment. He must rely on conjecture rather than certitude. For the most part, Amy Clampitt's amatory life remains unknowable.

Amy resolutely refused to breach confidences in her letters and even, as we have learned from those interviews with friends and relatives, in her conversations. She was often daring in her life, but never in her recording of it. A biographer would prefer more self-revelation, even self-advertising, but he must remain content with reflections, not stuff that is grist for gossip magazines.

———

Literature defined her, and it affected her work, her inner life, and her love life from start to finish. People in the twenty-first century may not understand a commitment of this sort. It might seem today unfashionable, perhaps even unimaginable. But for many thoughtful, quiet people a hundred years ago, books offered a special kind of release, escape, inspiration, and gratification equaled by nothing else. In a letter to Philip (March 17, 1956), Amy says with the confidence of the hopeful and untried, "I feel as if I could write a whole history of English literature and know just where to place everybody in it, with hardly any trouble at all. The reason being, apparently, that I feel *I am in it.*" The young John Keats ("I think I shall be among the English poets after my death"), Ezra Pound, W. H. Auden, and Robert Lowell, among countless others, would have said exactly the same thing about their place in literary history, although they all earned their places early in their lives. Few women would have been so bold to make this claim. It would take another two decades for her even to get her foot through the door.

Clampitt's sense of a literary calling ("a writer is what I was meant to be," she admits to Philip) coincided with, or was temporarily eclipsed by, her flirtation with the Anglican Church in her thirty-sixth year. She complemented her commitment to "the hidden power of language" with a religious zeal that led her, for a while, to find harmony and wholeness in spiritual observances, to find a place in a religious community, which she later abandoned in favor of political activism and more public engagement.

Almost sixty, coming out of obscurity well beyond the age when one might expect her to do so, she sounded a note of gratitude in her reply to the young poet Mary Jo Salter, who had just written her a fan letter: "I've yearned secretly for a poet I could write to." If she was born to be a poet, it certainly took her a long time to discover that fact. Her vocation was always clear, but the right genre was not. Not only did she try her hand at writing fiction when young, but near the end of her life, fascinated by the place of Dorothy Wordsworth in the circle that included her brother William, and Samuel Taylor Coleridge, Clampitt wrote and rewrote a play about the English Romantics, which displayed virtually no gift for the conflict and dialogue inherent in drama, in the same way her earlier novels, mostly about life on an Iowa farm, with some excursions back and forth to big cities like New York and Chicago, were thick with philosophical commentary and descriptions of nature but thin on plot and characterization.

From the start, Clampitt committed herself to her literary vocation as a consumer, that is, as a reader. In her letters and journals, we hear the voice of a custodian of literature, a keeper as well as a sharer of property. Her long life of reading came out of a dedication to learning, and to a solitary, contemplative temperament that looks increasingly old-fashioned in the third millennium. In a 1959 letter to Mary Russel she refers to "solitude, that dangerous luxury—or is it a necessity after all?" Earlier that year, to the same correspondent, she allowed that "I made a real try at not wanting to be a writer . . . The curious thing about this kind of voluntary relinquishment— or anyhow attempt at relinquishment—is that one emerges with renewed confidence: not in oneself, precisely, so much as in the nature of things." She was well aware of her "vocation"—which she admits "is a curious thing"—well before she experienced any success in it. But as a reader she was already permanently and deeply engaged. Books called to her, and she responded.

———

Many of the external circumstances of Clampitt's life, though hardly her personality or character, changed after fame and accomplishment caught up with her. She loved her laurels but never rested on them. The success of *The Kingfisher* made her work harder. She said yes to invitations to read, to give classes. She accepted teaching posts at William and Mary, Amherst, and Smith colleges. She continued to travel, by train or bus whenever possible, preferring to see the landscape from inside a Greyhound. (Her European trips, early and late, were managed almost exclusively by ship.) She had a paralyzing fear of flying. No other contemporary poet has expressed so keenly the complementary feelings of separateness and togetherness, selfhood and community, that one gets when traveling by boat or on a bus or train, as she does. (Elizabeth Bishop, in "The Moose," does the same thing. Clampitt did it many times.) Travel always brought out her congenital, almost giddy eagerness and joie de vivre: at forty-five, visiting Naples, she says she is mistaken for twenty-five and feels fifteen.

Once eminent, she offered suggestions about the work of friends and strangers alike; she accepted honors and invitations, from virtually everyone, everywhere. Part of her legacy is a series of recordings of her public readings. She sounds slightly high-pitched, littlegirlish, even seductive, like Marilyn Monroe if Marilyn Monroe had been an intellectual. To articulate the long sentences in her poems she had to develop stamina and breath control. She learned how to regulate her voice. In performance, as in life, she balanced exuberance with restraint.

In the flesh, she looked eccentric, but also as inviting and comfortable as a tea cosy. She was a tall woman, with a gap-toothed smile, and she had a way of accenting her body with a scarf, a skirt, a hat, often homemade or found in a thrift shop. For a *New York* magazine profile in 1984, Patricia Morrisroe met her at a Madison Avenue café. She noted that Amy's "hair is neatly tucked into a beret, [and she] seems out of place, like Wedgwood china in a high-school cafeteria." Life in the Village, rather than on the Upper East Side, suited her well. Because she never really felt at home anywhere, she was at home everywhere. Everyone who met her said she made an impression. Janet Halverson said that "nutty as she seemed to be, she was always, like, way ahead of me in everything, too." Her friend the actor Peter Kybart, who coached her before she did her first open-mic readings, said, "I don't think I ever saw Amy in bad spirits, never in a bad mood." She did, we know, suffer from a depressive strain that she inherited from her father, but she had no sympathy— this was part of her stern midwestern upbringing—for people who paraded their inner misfortunes, especially given her deep political attachment to people who suffered genuine economic and social privation, and psychological hardships.

In her years of eminence, she also knew when to say no. She had second thoughts about guest-editing a volume of David Lehman's *Best American Poetry*. She made a fuss in 1992 when William and Mary commissioned her to compose and deliver a poem in honor of the college's three-hundredth anniversary. Some of the college authorities thought that her "Matoaka"—a long poem about Pocahontas—might offend the sensibilities of Prince Charles, who would be on the same platform, and asked her to read it on a separate occasion. Her icy formal letter in reply shows the same steel in her spine that was evident in an earlier protest letter to Henry Kissinger and in her deeply felt, Quaker-inspired resistance to perceived injustices and social inequalities during her years of political activism. When she acted with indignation, she did so on behalf of a higher or impersonal cause, and never out of vanity or self-righteousness. Her fierce integrity matched her unsentimental generosity.

The literary culture had changed by the time Clampitt made her appearance in it. It was the era of poetry readings, degrees in creative writing, not to mention open-mic readings in coffee houses and church basements. Being a "poet" conferred a certain modest cachet. In a 1990 letter to her English friend Barbara Blay, Clampitt reports on a trip to the Midwest:

> There were several poetry readings, and at one of them half a dozen relatives from my hometown—the last ones I would have expected at a *poetry reading*—turned up. Another occasion brought out a group from my old college, along with a different crew of relatives. Times have changed, from when admitting to being a writer was an embarrassment. (What do you do? I'm a writer. What do you write? Poetry, said with a slow blush. What kind of Poetry? Oh . . . well . . . I don't really know . . . And so on.)

She was as surprised as anyone that she had become a success. The story of how she became that success is salutary.

———

A writer's life, like anyone's, is composed of interconnecting parts. Much of any artist's time is spent alone, working—painting, composing, writing—and this time is hardly the stuff of a derring-do narrative. Twentieth-century poets like Auden, Lowell, Rich, and Allen Ginsberg, who were vivid presences in the public sphere, became well known in part by virtue of their political work and other forms of social engagement. Some writers achieve more than poetic celebrity and become notorious *personnages*. Earlier than Ginsberg, we can glance back at Lord Byron, the Sitwells, and Dylan Thomas, all famous for theatrical shenanigans and bad behavior. Youth, too, counts for a lot. Lowell and James Merrill entered the public scene early, but more politely than Byron and Ginsberg. Their precocity and their social connections kept them alive in the eyes and minds of literary cognoscenti. But even they had lives of ordinariness: eating, sleeping, shopping, doing the dishes. All artists can make art out of the mundane stuff, the details of the lived life; thus, we have what Frank O'Hara called his "I do this I do that" poems. Although everyone's life is mostly banal, great poetry transcends its maker's quotidian habits.

The poet Stanley Kunitz observed, "It is out of the dailiness of life that one is driven into the deepest recesses of the self." An artist's life is supplemented by matters of will, decision, and serendipity. Flamboyant poets make good subjects for a biographer. Poets of dailiness, masters of the ordinary like Bishop, Wallace Stevens, Howard Nemerov, and A. R. Ammons, are in many ways a biographer's nightmare. These people led quiet lives of outward conventionality: they took walks between home and office, or they made daily examinations of the goings-on in the backyard. But rooted in routine, the inner life always flourishes, often in unpredictable ways. This was certainly true for Amy Clampitt.

———

An eccentric woman deserves an eccentric biography. In the following pages I shall not tell *all* the truth, because it is not available, but I shall tell some of the truth, and I'll have to tell it "slant." Emily Dickinson's word would, I think, resonate with Clampitt, a passionate and thoroughgoing reader of her precursor's poems. In addition to my narrative—a reconstruction of Amy's life—this book consists of shards accumulated from various sources. The first are the reminiscences and judgments of more than a dozen family, friends, and colleagues assembled in oral interviews. The oldest of these people are now themselves dead; I think of them as my informants, dramatis personae in an ongoing conversation.

A second trove of information is the diaries and journals that have been carefully transcribed from Clampitt's spidery handwriting (and later, her much cleaner typing), and that contain everything from ordinary laundry lists of things to be done to religious meditations during the years when she was deeply engaged with High Anglican theology.

The third is *Love, Amy*, the volume of letters that Columbia University Press published in 2005. Clampitt shines in them, and in other letters not included in the volume, as a prose writer whose deliberations, reports, and commentaries would be notable as energetic literary artistry even were their author not a distinguished poet herself.

And the fourth is the evidence of the poems. I have already offered my readers two exemplary ones. Amy knew how to live "poor," but she also knew, perhaps as compensation, how to write "rich." At a time when the cultural preference was for a plain or pared-down style (William Carlos Williams, Mark Strand, Robert Creeley, W. S. Merwin, Louise Glück), Clampitt went in the opposite direction. She brought extravagance and flamboyance back into fashion. Flaubert famously said that one must live a bourgeois life in order to become "violent and original" as an artist. Amy's situation is analogous: even when she had some money, her Quaker frugality and the congenital need to keep things simple would not allow her to live lavishly. Her work is another story, an intoxicated outpouring of language that can send a reader to a dictionary or an encyclopedia. Quoting from her letters, journals, essays, and especially her poems, I am allowing the poet to speak for herself. My biography willingly cedes partial authority to its subject. This book about a woman and her poetry is in large measure a portrait of the woman *through* her poetry as well as her unpublished writing.

Clampitt's self-presentations in poems and prose constitute a quite credible autobiography. A writer who is bookish defines herself by what she has been reading and thinking about. The inner life—the life of the mind—is as urgent, demanding, and constitutive as the lived life. The poet as a reader absorbs the musings of others. She then proceeds, as a writer, to create her own.

Although it gained in strength, Clampitt's work did not really "develop" through her five volumes, although her final book, *A Silence Opens*, suggests several new paths to follow. Her subjects and her various styles remained pretty much the same throughout the fifteen years of her creative maturity. I have used the poems as evidence of her life, but I do not deal with them in chronological order. Each of her five books has its own organization, but none necessarily represents the author's life at the time of composition or publication. Some of the poems speak about events in her life that took place well before she wrote them. Some were put in later volumes only because earlier ones were in fact already the right length requested by her editors. "Tepoztlán," for example, from *The King-fisher*, is based on memories of a visit to Mexico in 1944, where her parents were working with the American Friends Service Committee. "Losing Track of Language" (in *What the Light Was Like*, 1985) was written thirty years after the incident that it records. "Manhattan," a three-part reminiscence of Amy's early years on the island, might have appeared in *Westward*, her 1990 book, but was pushed forward into *A Silence Opens* four years later, in part for reasons of length and also because it fit better in what turned out to be her farewell volume. Other poems have origins in notes and fragments that she had tucked away for decades before bringing them into the light.

For all the simplicity of her daily arrangements, Amy was voluble and emotional, always an enthusiast. Her energy finally found an outlet in her work. Jack Macrae, her boss at Dutton, told me that Clampitt's poetry changed once she started learning Greek, but his memory is probably mistaken. She visited Greece in 1965. It was an eye-opening, mind-expanding experience. She began her Greek studies in the 1980s, after she had come into her mature style. It's more likely, as Mary Jo Salter has observed, that her "love of syllables"—lots of them—predisposed her to the long words and the long sentences that became her stock-in-trade. And in Homeric Greek, Clampitt found ample precedents for her exciting polysyllabic explosions.

Her poems are not to everyone's taste. Sitting down with her *Collected Poems*, according to a friend of mine, is like eating a meal composed entirely of desserts. The poems' richness owes a lot to their maker's earliest literary influences. This is the work of a woman who said, in her *Paris Review* interview, that her greatest debt was to Hopkins: "the delight in all things physical, the wallowing in sheer sound, in the extravagance of the possibilities of language." In another interview, she said that the first book she bought at the Gotham Book Mart in the fall of 1941 when she was struggling as an unhappy graduate student, was a volume of Hopkins's poetry.

Her poems offer a look into the woman who lived them as well as the poet who wrote them. "Iola, Kansas," for example: a thirty-two-line, single-sentence poem that opens us to the richness of a long bus ride, the kind of trip most sensible people would choose to avoid as tedious, uncomfortable, or even smelly, but which Amy loved. Or "The Woodlot," a stunning description of her childhood landscape that updates Frost's "Mending Wall" with a detailed investigation of barbed wire and what it does to the surround. Like Willa Cather, who left Nebraska as soon as she could, Amy was nurtured by her native soil long after she emigrated from it. In spite of her decades in New York, she was an Iowan through and through. Other poems, longer and more complicated (for example, "Westward" and "The Prairie," ingenious poetic constructions as well as investigations of culture and literature through the lens of landscape), explore their maker's political and historical concerns and obsessions.

She venerated European civilization. In the 1980s, some critics and scholars, as well as other poets, took issue with Clampitt's defense of the great Dead White Males of the Western canon. Some reviewers rebuked her harshly for her indebtedness to the old traditions. This happened during an age of cultural controversy (still going on today) that hollered for the dismantlement of canons, and demanded the expansion of university humanities curricula to include voices that had been formerly left out. There's an irony in this part of her critical reception. The naysayers either ignored or were unaware of Clampitt's commitment, as a person and a writer, to many political and social causes, and to the simple fact that she wrote some of the most powerful poems of political reportage, analysis, and protest of the late twentieth century. She was independent in her thought and her behavior; her poems open us to a mind not beholden to any contemporary pieties. She was always put off by being thought a "feminist poet," although she gladly accepted the feminist label with regard to her political and social stances. Her poems, along with details from the letters and the diaries, and the memories of the people who were part of her life, embody the coherence as well as the complexity of the woman and her work.

———

This book is divided into three parts. The first, "Iowa," covers the early years, from 1920 to 1941. The 2007 interviews with her brothers and sisters-in-law open a rich vein of reminiscences of Amy as oddball; as firstborn protector of younger siblings; a reader among readers; a naturalist from a family of people who knew the land; a young woman with a social conscience in a strong Quaker community; a daughter whose mother always worried that her eldest would not have the proper female fulfillment (marriage and children) but who would not direct her in any overt way; a fiercely independent and always enthusiastically playful free spirit.

Although her father, Roy, barely mentions his firstborn in his written reminiscences, she was the child who most resembled him. In 1971, he was awarded an honorary doctorate by Grinnell College, his alma mater, for his lifetime of good deeds with the American Friends Service Committee and other Quaker organizations. (Amy received her honorary doctorate from Grinnell thirteen years later.) An article in the *Des Moines Register* recounted his life, which sounds like a prediction of his daughter's. His parents were Iowa farmers who had migrated to California, where Roy was born in 1888. A year later they returned to New Providence and the farm. He graduated from Grinnell, Phi Beta Kappa, in 1911, with majors in Latin and Greek. He did a master's degree and tried teaching, but gave it up because "teaching used up too much of my nervous energy, and I went back to my father's farm." When his son Larry joined the Navy in World War II rather than become a conscientious objector, Roy observed that "he had many contacts with others at Iowa State, and I'm not surprised he discounted what he had learned at home . . . I never felt it was my business to tell the children what to do. I let them choose their own way." Amy inherited her father's intellect and his energy. In addition, she absorbed a Quaker sense of justice and a courteous respect for people who disagreed with her. She, too, chose her own way, leaving the farm and setting out for the city where, even when she protested against injustice, she never tried to force her views on friends and relatives.

"Obscurity," this book's second part, surveys the longest period of Amy's life, almost four decades of quiet anonymity that began in 1941. A paucity of details from those years will leave much of her life shrouded in uncertainty. That period began to wind down in 1973, the year of her chapbook *Multitudes, Multitudes*, poems that barely resemble what was to come from her several years later, but that evince her growing commitment to a poetic vocation. These are also the years without incident, at least without public incident, but they are the necessary cauldron for the explosion that lies ahead. Having met Harold Korn in 1968, taking an active political role and leaving behind her earlier commitment to High Anglican religion and its rituals, Clampitt came into her own as a new if not "young" poet in her late fifties.

The book's final part, "Fame," concerns the years of success and honors, the two decades of rich outpouring, and the public life that was the exact antithesis to everything Amy had previously known, but to which she adjusted rapidly, giddily, and happily. Her emergence was one of her own doing, although she was encouraged and abetted by others. She gained confidence from having taken a couple of writing courses, but regardless of her intellectual and literary temperament, she was always an outsider, never part of an institution or a group. Poets of today almost universally have to earn university credentials. Clampitt did not. (Her contemporary May Swenson had a similarly independent career trajectory.) For her, there was no Master of Fine Arts degree, and only a modest history of "workshopped poems" in the single poetry workshop she took in 1977.

Doris Myers described her old friend as "a person who walked alone." But her stepdaughter, Amy's goddaughter, said that, for a child, being in Amy's presence was "like eternal spring." This is an image of happy fecundity, not lonely inwardness. Myers's husband, Tom, said Amy "was a very private person, but she didn't have a false self. You were dealing directly with her. One knew that right off the bat." In the last chapter of her life, Amy was less alone than ever. At the end, she was walking, still herself, but now in the company of admirers. The woman who seemed, according to what her partner said to one of her editors, as if she were "sixty, going on three" had a "true" self that was compounded of high seriousness and flights of ecstasy.

Clampitt would be happy, I think, to have a famous phrase from

John Keats, whom she venerated, applied to the "mysteries, uncertainties and doubts" that confront someone attempting her biography. These uncertainties also give the writer an advantage. My frustration at not knowing all the facts means that I must accept uncertainty and mystery. In life, I met Clampitt a half dozen times during the decade of her renown. As a scholar, I wrote about her poetry. As the editor of a literary quarterly, I corresponded with her, and I published her work. I admired her from afar. Distanced now in time, I admire her even more. Some biographers, working their way into and through the lives of their subjects, come to dislike them. Others lose their identities in the person they've spent so many hours with. I became closer to mine, but not as close as I might wish to.

A biography is always an invasion of privacy. I hope my reconstruction or reimagining of my subject's life does not constitute a violation of her reticence. A writer who saves all of her papers must want someone to read them. I have done so. And I have made it my job to get as close to the poet's true self, the flights and the depths, as I can.

Some kinds of finality are difficult to bear, let alone understand and accept. Writing about Amy's last few months—the illness, the pain, the late, hastily improvised marriage, the confusions, frustrations, and anxieties—and her far from easy death, was an arduous business. I didn't want Amy to die. I wanted her to go on, confident, upbeat, and exuberant, to write more poems, and more prose. I was hoping she might have at least another ten years. Her editor Ann Close said Clampitt called her head "the poetry factory," and that when she was on a roll she could not stop: "The poetry factory is in full gear. It's just cranking things out." To some unsympathetic or skeptical readers, this self-appraisal may suggest the limitations of the poet's energetic expansiveness. "Cranking things out" sounds like an excess of exuberance, an almost hysterical compulsion. But it's the same kind of manic energy that Sylvia Plath, whom Clampitt admired, demonstrated in the lyrics that make up *Ariel*, her posthumous masterpiece. And Clampitt's other heroes—Wordsworth and Keats—also had spurts of intense creativity. Plath, like Keats, was young when she died; Clampitt was not young, but she was still working with the passion of a young poet. I did not want to see the Clampitt factory shut down. I was hungry for more work.

We can call no biography definitive. Like translations, biographies are of a time, not merely the time of the subject, but that of the author and the audience. They are all provisional. Everyone's life is lived forward, but it is remembered, reimagined, and reconstructed backwards, and in circles. The recollected life grows piecemeal, as a series of discrete details that, when assembled, may try to reproduce the original although it will never succeed in doing so. Individual pieces seldom slip neatly and exactly together. Nothing stays put. The entirety, as we look back on it, may look more like a mosaic: individual tiles that have been found or created are then placed artfully together to make an original design. And yet something will always be missing.

◀ IOWA ▶

TO SOMEONE WHO PEERS OUT from the window of a plane descending into Des Moines, the state capital, Iowa in mid-June can look Ireland-green, especially after a late, wet spring. Heavy rain has made the soil sodden. It has delayed the planting season. The landscape is "plotted and pieced," as Gerard Manley Hopkins would have called it. The predominantly rectilinear fields are neatly geometric, with alternating quilt-like blocks of green and brown, as though Cézanne had painted them. Occasionally, roads break through the boxy squares on a diagonal. And one also sees from above some meandering rivers and streams, refusing to be controlled or contained.

Like those streams, Amy Clampitt refused to be contained. She would not stay put.

Her birthplace, New Providence, appears pretty much the same today as it did a little more than a century ago when she was born. The population, approximately 200, has remained steady. Small and medium-sized farms here still rely primarily on family members, many of them with agronomy degrees from Iowa State University in Ames, forty-two miles away, to do the work. Seasonal help is not really needed. New Providence Hardware, Iowa's oldest hardware store (est. 1863), along with several other modest shops, stands on Main Street. Inside, there's a wall plaque that bears the slogan of an 1882 temperance campaign: "A schoolhouse on every hilltop, and no saloon in the valley." The brag still remains a living truth, at least in part. "Neither a tavern nor a saloon has ever existed within the borders of New Providence," the plaque continues, although the schools have long since been consolidated with others in deep red Hardin County. Among several claims to fame, New Providence boasts the residency of Mildred (Ghrist) Day, who attended a one-room school here, and invented the Rice Krispies Treat in 1939. Nearby is Eldora, the county seat. This was the birthplace of another Iowa poet, Clampitt's contemporary who was for years much better known, Mona Van Duyn (1921–2004). And here, as in other small rural towns in the county, many houses abut fields and farms, not backyards. This is not suburbia. Everything is green to the very door.

It was into this community and a family of self-reliant, pacifist, literary and intellectual Quaker farmers that Amy Kathleen Clampitt was born on June 15, 1920, the year that American women—courtesy of the Nineteenth Amendment to the Constitution—were granted the right to vote. Her life was shaped by the major events of the twentieth century: the Depression, World War II, postwar prosperity, and then the unleashing of political unrest in the wake of the civil rights movement. She belongs to that century. And she also belongs to Iowa. Many things have changed in her native terrain, but much has remained the same in farm country. She would surely recognize the place today.

When I visited in June 2019, it was unclear whether there would be enough sun and warmth to guarantee a good autumn crop. For farmers, there is nothing to do but wait and see. They have suffered worse. They have inherited or developed patience. They know that human effort can go only so far. After that, one relies on larger forces, perhaps on divine grace.

New Providence residents, like people everywhere who are of the land, tend to be straightforward, unironic, but verbally adroit when they choose to be. Farmers are conservative in the best sense. They are vigilant, circumspect, frugal, and self-protective. Asked about their reactions to weather, economic changes, governmental policy, tariffs, and taxes, one man repeated what he said was a standard, because true, adage: "Farmers always suffer first, suffer hardest, suffer longest." A fact of reality.

There's a paradox in small-town life: people seem to mind their own business, but there can be no privacy where everyone knows everyone else, and everything about the community. As Willa Cather, wedded to but separated from Nebraska, understood, there's no hiding on the prairie. And local history always runs deep. Late in her life, Amy referred to this paradox as "the mentality of townships, where there is no getting away from being known about and, ipso facto, classified."

In an interview with the novelist Jean Hanff Korelitz, she made her point more harshly. She was labeled from the beginning as someone who did not quite fit into the place she called home: "Everybody who is ambitious is called selfish . . . that's the term for somebody who goes off someplace . . . I was a misfit from the start." How did this come about? For one thing, when Amy entered school she already knew how to read and write; she became isolated—in her memory—and had no friends. An early grade school teacher thought she was showing off. She skipped a grade. At the same time, she "realized that life at home was fraught with something I didn't really understand. My parents were both feeling very frustrated about being where they were. And you absorb that. I didn't have exactly a carefree childhood."

Looking back, she allowed that by the time she'd reached adolescence she had also begun to refuse standard roles, a refusal that came to dominate her social life as a career woman in Manhattan in the 1940s and '50s:

> I thought I had to know how to keep house. It wasn't that I didn't want to get married, I just didn't *exactly* want to get married, so I always managed to be connected with unsuitable people who were already married or something. It was as if I played a sort of trick on myself to keep from settling down. I know other women who have done that, although they will say that they're very sorry not to have had a child. This is something I never was interested in. I knew very distinctly from the time you first talk to people about what you're going to do that I didn't want to have children. I knew that. I just saw that it was such a drag and I knew I wouldn't be a good mother and that's one thing that's always been clear to me all my life.

She *sort of* wanted to get married; she *sort of* did not want to get married.

And with regard to offspring, from all reports about Amy as an adult, as an aunt ("Amy Aunt"—not "Aunt Amy"—as her brother Larry's children always called her, with an appropriate quirkiness) she was a fairy godmother, a combination of big sister, Dutch uncle, and bohemian host. She was something of a midwestern Mame Dennis. She said that after the bomb fell on Hiroshima she did not want to bring children into the world. But she adored and was adored by children. Her nephew Peter, second son of Larry and Jeanne, recalled that when they got to be twelve, he and his siblings would each be treated to a visit with their "hippie" aunt in Manhattan. For him, a fledgling drummer, the trip included a visit to the Five Spot on St. Mark's Place to see jazz legend Art Blakey. Amy Aunt knew exactly what would give pleasure, excitement, and a momentary escape from the conventional suburbs of Boston. At forty-five, she thought nothing of climbing to the top of the Statue of Liberty—354 steps, twenty stories—with her nephew. The writer Cynthia Zarin, a friend during Amy's final years, recalled taking her two-year-old daughter on picnics in the park with Amy, who had made dolls for the toddler: "She was like a fairy."

Paradoxes seldom go away. They multiply. In a late poem, "Homeland," Clampitt, now advanced in age and confident in her poetic craft, looks back, with what begins as nostalgia, to the apple trees—and their crop—that dotted her Iowa farm. The poem is rich in details borrowed in part from John Keats's "To Autumn" and Robert Frost's "After Apple-Picking." And it offers a reminder that in Amy's midwestern landscape, an orchard of apple trees offered protection against the elements: it was a "windbreak" and a "shelterbreak."

Harvest and fall come not only with the fulfillment of nature's bounty but also—here's the turn—with the menace we might associate with the ghouls of Halloween:

> . . . out there the old gods

> slithered and swam uncaught,
> and though we knew that no one
> knew when one of them might next

flatten a crop or set a barn afire,
or worse, the bagged winds' black
archangel, even, had no proper name.

Homelands possess unease, forebodings, and their own "black /
archangel." The apple bin contains the peculiar "long-dormant reso-
nances / of an oncoming winter." The farmer knows the grim truth:
destruction is always possible. The sensitive child can feel the chill
of weather, and of an internal climate as well. She remains both in
and not quite part of her family, her community, her landscape.

———

Outcast in one way, in others Amy was known and classified, boxed
in like the landscape. Her great-grandfather Thaddeus Clampitt
(1835–1912) had come to Iowa, an illegitimate child, from Indiana
in 1859. New Providence had been settled earlier in the decade by
Quaker farmers from North Carolina who were unwilling to live
in a slave state. Latter-day family members told me that their fore-
bears were also smart enough to realize they could not compete
with southern slaveholders on large plantations. They had business
sense as well as moral principles. Amy's grandfather Frank (1860–
1943) wrote a memoir when he was seventy-two describing with
clarity and common sense what life on the farm was like. Her father,
Roy (1888–1973), did the same.

Amy lived, successively, on two family farms, one of which is still
in family hands—the first until she was ten, the second until she left
home for college at her father's alma mater, Grinnell. She left again,
for Manhattan, following her 1941 graduation, but returned home
dutifully and frequently to visit family. She considered herself a New
Yorker for the rest of her seventy-four years, although she never felt
quite at home anywhere. But it was Iowa, as well as determination,
character, and genetics, that made her. And the genetic inheritance
from her grandfather and father included strong doses of indepen-
dent thinking, literacy, and occasional depression, manageable and
seemingly modest by today's standards.

Frank Clampitt privately published *Some Incidents in My Life: A Saga of the "Unknown" Citizen* in February 1933. He describes the drudgery of farm work with an acknowledgment of Hamlin Garland's *A Boy's Life on the Prairie* as an inspiring predecessor. By his own admission he was "a nervous, sensitive lad" who at fifteen or sixteen suffered "a period of spiritual depression and gloom," which, after he mentioned it to his parents, disappeared on its own. Life before psychopharmacology seems inconceivable today. Skeptical readers may laugh at the immediacy of a self-help cure, but there it was, just as John Stuart Mill, earlier in the nineteenth century, had talked himself out of an existential crisis by reading Wordsworth. For Clampitt, "the load *was gone!*—and a certain lightness, a buoyancy, a radiance filled my being." "Gone," yes, but not permanently. That buoyancy did not last forever.

Frank's decision to spend time in college—unusual for a farm boy—came from and led back to a bookishness that continued to offer sustenance throughout his life. His youthful reading included the essays of Bacon, Lamb, and especially Emerson, Whittier's *Snowbound*, poems by Sir Walter Scott, and Longfellow's *Tales of a Wayside Inn*. Moving into a new house, the young man was thrilled with an upstairs library, which contained "a large walnut bookcase and little desk." Everything seemed sumptuous compared to the previous house: "this room with its magazine tables, its single bookcase, and dictionary stand was to my book-obsessed fancy a veritable literary paradise."

Reading inspired writing: "I later practiced composing sonnets as I guided my plow through the long stretches of prairie sod . . . I wrote sonnets to the lark trilling its morning song from a fold of sod near-by." Consider "Voices of the Wind," an Italian sonnet whose octave is:

> I sit alone within this cotter's door,
> While whispering round it comes the lonesome wind,
> Breathing in cadences though undefined
> A story I have heard, oh! oft' before.
> Its tone suggests to me a mystic lore
> Sublimely wild and sad; there crowd my mind

Vague fancies of Aeolian harpings, twined
With weird oaks' murmurings on the Epirian shore.

This is a schoolboy's studied, formulaic effort, amateur but honorable. Still, even at a time and in a culture that prized verse-writing, most ploughmen did not write sonnets. A heartfelt poem, even if trite, stands out.

The need for bodily labor to offset his depressive spells led Frank to drop out of college after a year. He taught school for a while, and then returned to the farm but remained unsatisfied. Thinking to try his hand at other vocations, he moved to California (where Roy was born), but found Pasadena dusty and barren compared to Iowa. So he came home, but his headaches and "nervous dyspepsia" resumed. He discovered that he actually liked farming, especially the business management part of it. Until the end, he maintained a farmer's frugality, but he also remained extravagant with regard to books.

In 1906, he was again threatened with a nervous breakdown, headaches, low spirits, and "gloomy foreboding," but he strove to remain useful for his final thirty-seven years. Apparently he succeeded. For the rest of his life, he lived with his ailment, whatever we might label it today. Steadfastness, seriousness, and commitment—what used to be called Yankee virtues—are in evidence on every page of his memoir, as is shyness with regard to self-analysis or confession. When his best and oldest friend lay dying, Frank wrote him a letter "in which I tried to say some things his life had meant to me which natural reticence would have prevented my ever saying to his face." Intimacies are acknowledged but neither defined nor explained. What was their relationship like? Mutual respect, passion tamped down? Like his granddaughter much later, he said some things, and he remained silent about many others.

The impulse to write never abandoned him. In the summer of 1923, he made an automobile trip west, camping out with his wife. Merely driving along small, dusty rural roads in a rattling car constituted an adventure in itself. He recorded the details, just as, decades later, his granddaughter, having inherited the desire to describe traveling adventures, but with far greater gifts to do so, meticulously recorded her vacations, explorations, and treks in Europe and the States.

Amy inherited as well her grandfather's agnosticism and—sometimes but not always—his reluctance to belong to anything. In a chapter called "Matters Religious and Spiritual," he admits that he was never much of a joiner and was uninclined to be churchy. He had, however, a devotion to a greater spirit. He uses the word "evolution" to describe the human urge "to something higher." Amy, too, felt an aspirational principle. It would lead her briefly to the rituals and practices of High Anglicanism, but she ultimately rejected these, replacing them with political engagement, and then the full-fledged satisfactions of a literary life, which her grandfather neither desired nor attained.

Throughout Frank's life, New Providence remained a quiet backwater, temperate, indeed chaste, and without anything in the way of sophisticated cultural activity. It relied on the efforts of its residents: "We have no movie theater, the community in the main providing its own entertainment. A choral society, under the leadership of a well-trained local director, has occasionally put on programs of high class music." Frank and his wife, Eva, read aloud to one another (as did Amy and Harold Korn decades later). Reticence prevailed at the end: they burned their letters as being "too private and fervid" to be shared.

At the end of his book he looks back. He says he finished his work each day "so that I could have the time for my *very own*," not in idleness "but with my books and periodicals . . . I have found joy in the perfected expressions of thought and feeling of our great writers, our poets, our novelists, and often in the stray gems of verse appearing in our current magazines. Such words oft times inspire like great music." His memoir is full of standard but deeply believed-in clichés: "a broadened horizon and enlarged interests in new things. I have tried to learn some of the secrets of expression from these sources, and felt something of the joy and the pain of trying to build my own dim perceptions into acceptable English, just as I suppose my wife has joyed or fretted in trying to fit her scraps together into some new quilt pattern."

He rejoices that "life with its family ties and its friendships and its books, and with its unresolved problems continually beckoning on, has been a rare experience." We can flash forward almost a half century. In a 1982 letter to her friend Mary Jo Salter, as fame is beginning to come to her, Amy writes that she regards herself "as one of the fortunate people who happen to be around." It seems likely that she would have been a happy woman—notwithstanding the occasional period of depression or anxiety—even without her literary success. From nature or genetic inheritance, and from training and character, she possessed an unaffected enthusiasm for the things she loved, and an un-self-contained ardor the world could not quash.

———

Her circumspection constitutes part of Amy's heritage not only from her grandfather but from her Quaker parents as well. Roy J. Clampitt also wrote an autobiography, *A Life I Did Not Plan*, in 1966, and like many people of his generation he is equally reserved on certain matters—the private life in general, the sexual life in particular. His daughter eventually came to share what she referred to (in a 1984 letter to Helen Vendler) as his "shy eminence." And his orneriness as well: both father and daughter maintained a midwestern mistrust of authority. Roy Clampitt repeatedly voted for Norman Thomas, "not so much because he was a Socialist as because of his opposition to authority in general," according to his daughter (who in her days of political resistance voted for the comedian Dick Gregory in the 1968 presidential election). His son Philip remembered that Roy grew a handsome pair of sideburns when the Iowa attorney general in the late 1960s banned lawyers from wearing them in court. He was not a lawyer; he never appeared in court; he merely wanted to perform a gesture of solidarity.

The genetic strain of reticence ran wide as well as deep. In the 1990s, Amy exchanged letters with a distant cousin, David Hammer, a lawyer in Dubuque, who used to visit New Providence in summers. He wrote:

I'm afraid I have very little information about our shared great-grandfather. My only knowledge comes from my grandmother, and true to her Clampitt genes, she was seldom revelatory. I don't know whether it was Quakerism or the pioneer spirit which was abundant in our grandparents (wash rag, shoehorn, tough as boiled owl) or whether it was part of the Reece-Clampitt tradition, but her personal thoughts were not often shared and the more deeply something was held, the less it was discussed.

Amy receives less attention in her father's book than almost anyone else in the family. Roy joyfully announces the birth of his firstborn; soon we learn that she is off at college, then in New York on a fellowship; she makes periodic visits home, especially when she moves back to Des Moines for six months in 1960 to live with her sister Beth (1928–1994), who was diagnosed with schizophrenia during her senior year at college and who then spent most of her adult life in health care facilities; she takes up photography; the parents see her occasionally in New York or at the house of her brother Larry outside Boston. We have little idea of what she does or of who she is. Rather like Anne Elliot in Jane Austen's *Persuasion*, Amy seems to be taken for granted. Being ignored, however, is not the worst thing that can happen to an artist. Even a person who seems to have support from the community of a family can experience the profound isolation that inspires creativity as self-expression, compensation, or even—although infrequently in Clampitt's case—revenge.

Amy's first memory of life at Cedardale Farm was of the day her brother Larry was born, but it is nature rather than her baby brother that harnesses and then releases her energies. In her essay "Providence," she looks back more than sixty years:

> It is the twenty-sixth of April, 1923, I am not yet three years old . . .
> My father's sister Edith . . . is leading me past barns and through
> feedlots to the outermost grove. What holds these details in place
> is the sight, out under those trees, of a bed of violets whose hue
> I cannot reach except by way of a later metaphor: the contained
> intensity of a body of water. It is as though I became in that
> instant aware of edges, shores, boundaries, limitations. The shell
> had cracked: an exodus, an expulsion, was under way.

The writer may be recollecting her life accurately, looking back wistfully, or even recreating and embellishing it. The passage suggests that a poet's memories, genuine or confected, work with images that then become leitmotifs, tools of the trade in a creative process as well as in a lived life.

Those "edges" and "boundaries" that the adult remembers have literary equivalents. In writing, what separates poetry from prose is the insistent presence of lines. Borders are everything. Was Amy born a poet? She was certainly articulate, given to language very early. Her brother Philip remembers a family story about Amy, who, knowing the word "drink," looked down at the Mississippi River on a car trip and said, "Big drink." She was two. Naming things was important to her even at that age. And bodies of water—rivers, lakes, the ocean itself—were to remain a source of wonder and inspiration for her entire life.

Clampitt herself has answered my question about being born a poet. She makes the connection in "Providence":

By the time my own memory begins, shrubbery and shade trees, neatly fenced and gated, enclosed the place with what amounted for me to a charm, in the etymological sense of a spell against harm from without; and in the sense that the word derives from *carmen*, a song, my earliest consciousness is rooted in the stuff of poetry.

Her poetic roots have been grafted onto the living plants of her environment.

As she was entering the years of her fame, she wrote to Robert Quint—a college friend of David Clampitt, her favorite nephew—about her lifelong attachment to native soil:

There had been a drought, so the cornfields were browner than usual at that time of year, but even so I found the countryside beautiful in its own peculiar, amorphous and elusive way. I've been puzzling my head over the nature of that landscape for years, and have just lately begun writing about what it means. And it now occurs to me that possibly the reason I've been drawn to

the ocean as long as I can remember has to do with the notion of
the prairie—"half sea half land," as Charles Olson calls it—which
over the eons has so often been under water, and unlike some
other parts of the continent has never once been lifted and folded
under again. Rather than archaeological, in other words, it may
be that roots I have there are *geological*. Which might explain,
also, why it's so hard for a Midwesterner to find out who he or she
is. (October 25, 1980)

"The Prairie," her longest poem, was already under way in her
imagination, waiting to be written. In addition to the land and the
weather, Clampitt also folded into her poem a sympathetic portrait
of her grandfather, beleaguered, hardworking, unhappy, and stoic,
a victim and a survivor of circumstance. A decade after the letter to
Quint, "The Prairie" appeared in *Westward*.

Life in what seemed like Eden was short-lived. Cedardale belonged
to Amy's grandparents; in 1930 her father, who had been working
with Frank, decided to get his own farm, about three miles down the
road. The landscape must have been similar, if not identical, but to a
child the difference was enormous. Cedardale had been surrounded
by abundant shade and fruit trees. Pioneer Farm seemed by com-
parison barren and burdensome. It had not yet become a genuine
home. Amy lived here with six other people. She shared a room with
her sister. The boys had their bedroom: Larry and Richard shared
a double bed, and baby Philip had his own. This is how Americans
used to live. The actual farmhouse, modernized but otherwise little
changed, and still containing three bedrooms and only a single full
bathroom, is now occupied by collateral Clampitt relatives.

The child felt exiled. The adult writes about this in "Black Butter-
cups" (in her second book from Knopf, *What the Light Was Like*),
more than a half century later. She did not merely move. She was
expelled:

> Exile to raw clapboard,
> a privy out in back, a smokehouse
> built by the pioneers, no shade trees
> but a huddle of red cedars, exposure

on the highest elevation in the township,
a gangling windmill harped on by each
indisposition of the weather,
the mildewed gurgle of a cistern
humped underneath it like a burial.

The child has learned about menace, about danger. She discovers that "*There is no safety*." Having known "for the first time forever what it was / to be heartbroken," Amy would be in many ways unsure of herself and her surroundings for the rest of her life, and equally eager to make for herself a home in even the most modest circumstances.

As in her memory of her brother's birth, Clampitt projects her feelings for human beings onto nature, and gives her attention not to people but to blue spruces, "the bluebells / and Dutchman's-breeches my grandmother / had brought in from the timber / to bloom in the same plot with peonies / and lilies of the valley." The grandmother is known by what she has done and given. She is the active, feminine principle of growth. And in the field, there is the "perennially / resentful"—masculine, needless to say—bull, who "stood for the menace of authority / (no leering, no snickering in class)." Clampitt calls herself, at the end of this elegiac poem, "the child who wept to leave" and who "still sits / weeping at the thought of exile."

In her 1993 interview for the *Paris Review*, Clampitt pictures herself as, from the beginning, both out of place and part of a community:

What I most enjoyed was the order of the seasons and especially the arrival of spring, which, when you are small, comes from a great distance. In the late summer there would be the threshing season, which totally vanished once the combine came in. In those days the grain had to be cut and tied into bundles, and the bundles put into shocks to keep the rain off, and then the day came when the entire community would be involved in bringing in the grain and feeding it into the threshing machine and taking away the threshed grain and stacking the straw. This is something I've written about. The boys in the family would be out bringing water to the men in the fields, the girls involved in the kitchen, cooking a huge meal at noon for all the crew; and this was something you looked forward to. Then at the end of the season there would be what they called the "settling up," when the balances were arrived at—so and so contributed so much labor and so on, and that would take place at somebody's house, and there'd be ice cream for everyone, games of hide-and-seek in the shrubbery outside, that sort of thing. Those are the pleasantest memories. I have some winter memories, too, of riding in a sleigh, of an evening of bobsledding on a steep hill; the whole community turned out. There were a lot of relatives, a lot of cousins, and at Christmas there would usually be a huge family gathering— pleasant in a way, yet I remember being miserable. I couldn't deal with all the people who sounded so sure of themselves when I didn't feel sure of anything.

Simultaneously present are a ten-year-old's self-appraisal as an exile and a grown woman's recollection of her awkward, alienated status. These feelings became prominent strands within the artist's work.

Even by her own acknowledgment, however, life after the exile and before the subsequent departure for college was not unrelentingly grim or traumatic for this sensitive girl. And her brother Larry recalled farm life and school life in which his sister participated as helper (not quite strong enough to milk a cow, but feeding the chickens, getting the eggs in, assisting in the garden) and, more important, as mentor to the younger siblings. Pioneer Farm had 120 acres—an average size—with corn and hogs the principal products. Money was in short supply, but food was not. The family never went hungry. During the Depression, they burned corn to keep warm. Coal was more expensive. Cedardale had a root cellar, where fruits and vegetables could be put up for the winter. Both of the elder children had home births at Cedardale (the younger three were delivered in the hospital), a place without rural electricity but with a bank of batteries in the basement, probably charged by a windmill. These provided water as well as power. Later, Larry rode on the school bus with his older sister into town, three miles away:

> I remember Amy in high school. I think I was becoming aware somewhere there that she was different from most of the high school girls; their interest in boys and interest in finding the one they were going to marry, and settle down on the farm, and have children, and clearly that was not what Amy had in mind.

Adolescence can produce a self-image that will last throughout life, no matter what other changes and choices intervene.

If Amy felt like an outsider, she also felt the need—if only subconsciously—to prove to her neighbors and classmates that she had amounted to something, or might amount to something. At some level, she never got over being the bookish eccentric, different from her classmates who managed to marry and settle down quickly. In a journal entry (June 19, 1951) from her long European tour when she had quit her job at Oxford University Press and sailed for the Continent, she recounts a troubling dream that opens with a lover, and ends with another lover, between whom are "distorted members" of her own American family:

> Martedi il dicianove—I'm having lots of dreams again. A vivid one about Charles, brought on by conversation with English girl—[but] uncomfortable, going off to make love someplace and being followed by people who seemed to be distorted members of my own family, and the frantic feeling of being pursued and finally closed in upon by my own mother. Slept most of the afternoon, and had a dreadful dream of being three-legged, all three feet neatly shod, and the necessity for apologizing to people about same. Woke up in a heavy sort of panic, saw myself as still the frustrated little girl wanting to show the people back in New Providence, Iowa, uneasy over the Pope's Palace piece, and frantically wishing for John. Anybody would have done at the moment—Bennett, [name illegible]—but mostly it was John [probably Menapace].

At thirty-one, she is still the frustrated outsider, tormented in her imagination by her family and peers, and eager for the sweet satisfactions of revenge. These would come, in time, but not quite yet. (She has also adopted the habit of dating her journal entries in the language of the country she is visiting!)

In a poem dated "Spring 1969," published in her 1973 chapbook *Multitudes, Multitudes* and never reprinted, Clampitt takes a backward look to her schooldays, in tones that combine the nostalgia of A. E. Housman with heavy-handed references to Greek mythology. Her subjects: three classmates dead before thirty, two boys during the war, one girl in an accident on a mountain slope in winter. You wonder whether Amy didn't share some traits with this girl, her opposite in many ways:

> The third was always tomboy-restless;
> ballgames with the boys at recess;
> fame dreamed, far off: "Don't you just
> HATE your folks?" late at night, under
> the quilt, she'd cry, confiding.

What Clampitt still hears, decades later, "that un- / stilled will of hers," is the determination that Amy brought with her from Iowa to Manhattan, from girlhood to maturity.

Her brother offered yet another memory, solicitous and loving. He recalled Amy as teacher, doing

> what I sort of assumed at the time [was] what big sisters did, and that was read to her younger siblings. She read Dickens, she read Milne. We had moved to Pioneer Farm [1930] . . . we had a furnace in the basement, and there was a big register that warm air came from, and we would sort of huddle around that on a cold winter night or evening. I just assumed big sisters did this.

Most people remember being read to by parents. Larry remembers not them, but his older sister, for whom reading aloud to siblings was one form of communication and attachment.

There were other forms as well. Amy had pen pals, as was customary in the States before communications systems became more sophisticated. The Clampitt files contain letters to Amy, at ten, from a schoolboy in Manila, and three years later from a girl on a farm in Brazil. Dulcie Ross from Queensland, Australia, became a correspondent in 1934. Megan James, a London nursing student, wrote letters in 1936. When Amy was thirteen she also corresponded with Desa Bünning, a girl her age in Altengamme, near Hamburg. In a letter dated November 3, 1933, Desa says, "Now I write to tell you that in Germany is peace, and the horror-baiting against Germany is untrue. Our leader and Emperial [*sic*] Chancellor, Adolph Hitler, makes enormous speeches. Everywhere he comes, there is an exultation . . . In the next letter I shall tell you more about Adolph Hitler and about the other great man [*sic*]." The following February, among other formulaic details about school and family, nature and holidays, Desa writes in German about the construction of stadiums for the 1936 Berlin Olympics. She mentions the Hitler Jügend, of which she seems to be a willing, innocent member. A tiny swastika and a "Heil Hitler!" are drawn on the top left corner. In February 1936, she ends with a request: "Please write me in the next letter what you know about the World-war [*sic*] 1914–1918." Every story, every issue, has many sides. Perhaps Desa, inquiring and credulous, wanted Amy to offer an American perspective on current events and recent history.

Desa's last letter is dated December 9, 1936. We know what lay ahead. The girls did not. Another German pen pal, Annemaria Rohatsch, writes on July 31, 1934, about life at school: when the teacher enters the classroom, "we must greet him with raising our right arm and say 'Heil Hitler.'" At the end of class, the students perform the same salute. This girl survived the war: the Clampitt files contain two letters from 1957–58, but we have nothing from the intervening years.

Reading letters—reading anything—offered Amy the chance to reach beyond her Iowa farm. Her life was, in this way at least, an enchanted one, spent with *Grimms' Fairy Tales* and *Robinson Crusoe*, in a home without too many other books but ones borrowed from the library of her literary grandfather. On Sunday afternoons, Larry said, the Clampitts would drive into town and "Amy would be closeted with Grandpa, and he was introducing her to another book he had read." Larry liked Grandpa's stereopticon; his big sister went for the books.

The bookishness began early—through genetics, choice, and habit—and lasted for her entire life. In a letter dated January 16, 1990, to three schoolgirls who have asked about her literary life and her favorite poem, Amy, almost seventy, writes:

> Since I first encountered it at the age of four or five, one of those favorites has always been "Jabberwocky" from *Through the Looking-Glass*, the second of the Alice books by Lewis Carroll. It is one of the few poems I can recite from memory without stumbling, and that is strange since it is studded with words that come out of nowhere and mean nothing in particular. As Alice herself put it, "it seems to fill my head with ideas—only I don't know exactly what they are." Anyhow, the sound of those words is somehow magical and ridiculous both at once. And the sound, after all, is what makes a good poem worth remembering.

Like many poets, Clampitt was entranced, intoxicated by the sounds of poetry. We have evidence of its early effects. Here, from the family files, is a poem from Amy at thirteen, transcribed by someone else (perhaps her mother) into a notebook:

O cold, darksome travel
Past boulders moss-grown,
Where your wild song is hushed
As you glide on alone;

[As?] onward you journey
Unwearied, unstayed—
Still dashing, still dancing
Through sun and through shade.

Your journey unceasing;
No wonder you're gay—

Who wouldn't be, free,
Seeing new things each day?

This combines bookish sophistication (how many thirteen-year-
olds knew words like "darksome" and "unceasing"?), lilting rhythms
(it sounds like "On Dasher, on Dancer . . ."), and the child's envy of a
person or animal who has become free by running away.

Reading poetry engaged the girl in many ways. In a 1990 inter-
view for the *North Dakota Quarterly*, she remembers reading Keats's
"The Eve of Saint Agnes" for the first time in junior high school:

> I think the reason I loved the poem so much, without knowing
> why, was that it had to do with being cold. I knew about that. In
> a farmhouse it's hard to get warm when you sleep in an upstairs
> bedroom and you wake up and there is frost all over the window.
> I liked the frost on the window, but I didn't like to get up in the
> morning in an unheated room. And so all that imagery of cold,
> and the imaginary warmth it frames.

Harold Guthrie, her much-esteemed high school English teacher,
lived long enough to take notice of, and to delight in, his student's
late successes forty years following her appearance in his classroom.
A handwritten note in a copy of *The Kingfisher* says, "For Harold
Guthrie—who opened the excitements of English poetry for me so
many years ago, and whose friendship I treasure—with thanks and
best wishes always."

Art offered escape from and recompense for quotidian dreari-
ness, but not to everyone in the family circle. In an unpublished
essay, Amy recalls vividly the anxieties of her father and grandfa-
ther, but her mother remains a more subdued, unexplained figure.
On one side is Frank's "poignant record, whose importance to me
can scarcely be exaggerated, of anxiety amounting almost to terror."
But on the other:

> It may be that my mother and grandmothers suffered no less;
> but if so, they set down no such record. For my mother there was

the recourse of tears, which made everybody feel guilty, whereas for the men in my family, whatever feeling was openly expressed took the form of anger. Setting things down could make a difference, as I seem to have known from an early age; but the legacy of self-doubt remained.

Even with her own college degree (and with *Little Women* as her favorite book, from which she borrowed the names for her two daughters and her eldest son), Pauline lacked, or never thought to explore, the same habits that provided outlets for her husband and father-in-law. She apparently wanted both of her daughters to have conventional lives as wives and mothers. One irony is that, according to recollections of the younger Clampitt cousins who own the farm today, Pauline was neither a particularly good cook nor a careful housekeeper, at least in her later years. Perhaps she had tired of her burdensome lot as homemaker, mother, farmer's wife. (Another cousin, Marjorie Clampitt Silletto, said that *her* mother, Pauline's sister-in-law, always thought that Pauline never wanted five children. She suspected Pauline envied Marjorie's mother, who had only a single daughter.) When Amy was young, unmarried, and discovering herself in Manhattan, she cooked extravagant but low-budget meals for friends in her bohemian studio apartment. By the time she had settled into her creative maturity in her sixties, and was living with Hal, she poured all her energy into writing. Chinese take-out became a staple of life on the Upper East Side. And dusting was never a feature of her domestic routine at any stage.

In 1976, Pauline wrote a note "For My Grandchildren." She wanted her progeny to know something about her. She is modest, straightforward, and accurate, but hardly forthcoming with regard to anything personal. When she graduated from high school in Michigan, she "had no ambition for college, or self-confidence either." She had fallen in love with music, and she began giving piano lessons for twenty-five cents, driving over dirt country roads in a horse and buggy. She attended the Michigan Agricultural College (now Michigan State), where she studied "Domestic Science and Domestic Art," what later came to be called Home Ec. Then she went to Iowa, where her brother and sister were living. She taught school. She met Roy. She married.

Talented, bookish, artistic, lacking self-confidence: does this sound like her first daughter? Out of an expected combination of gratitude and devotion, when Clampitt the poet had her first *New Yorker* publication and received a check for an important poem, she sent flowers to her mother in Iowa. Earlier, after visiting Des Moines for Roy and Pauline's fiftieth wedding anniversary celebration, Amy had written (September 5, 1969) to her parents following a trip that took her—by bus—to her friends Doris and Tom Myers in Colorado and then back. In miniature, it juxtaposes her present life and her gratitude for her roots:

> Last evening I went to a cocktail party for Fannie Lou Hamer, the Mississippi Freedom Democratic leader, which was also a sort of kickoff for a new registration drive, and from there I went with Hal, my friend who teaches law at NYU, to a concert in the East Village by the Incredible String Band, the Scottish group who were the original reason I decided to buy a record player, and who are even better in person than on records.

She remarks that friends have congratulated her on being part of a large, enthusiastic family whose members all get along: "I can certainly say that I wouldn't belong to any other family for anything." This is the voice neither of flattery nor of mere filial duty.

Roy died on December 16, 1973. Three days earlier he had stopped eating. He dictated a farewell: "The time is ripe for the end. When such a time comes there is no point in stretching it out a few days longer. My love for all of you has grown as this end has become more evident." Notice the word *love*. This was never part of a Quaker's secular vocabulary.

The following year, Clampitt wrote a poem ("The Snow-Shoveler") about her father, which she never published. She recalls him, "schooled by rigor," with "a diffidence immense / as icebergs," having few words, and little "feeling for places / or for voyages." He was "a diffident patriarch." He did not express, or at least vocalize, love. But when it came time to make his peace, he composed, orally, the note above:

> . . . it was
> the youngest of us fittingly,
> he asked to set it down—
> saying he was ready,
> hailed his friends, and sent—
> three times, in the constricted
> cadence of rapture the syllable
> he'd been too shy to use recurred—
> and sent his love.

That almost stuttered interruption at the end—"and sent . . . and sent his love"—shows the poet's breathless hesitance. Reluctant, she is almost incapable of uttering the very word he, too, has been too shy ever to say, and she has been waiting to hear, for a long time.

Roy, a man of few words (unlike his daughter), had much earlier written a charming poem about himself, which was read at his memorial service in Des Moines:

> When I am gone, please do not speak
> of me as one who studied Greek.
>
> I much prefer the world should know
> I kept the walks well cleared of snow.

Such epigrammatic dignity is worthy of Leigh Hunt and Walter Savage Landor, those nineteenth-century English poets who became staples in many early-twentieth-century American classrooms; the little poem proposes its self-eulogy in an easy, jaunty tone that Robert Frost would have understood.

In her unpublished poem, Clampitt recorded her father's wishes in her words, not his. Later she wrote something longer and more complex. She eulogized her father in a poem called "Beethoven,

Opus 111." The surprising title names the composer's final piano sonata, which Clampitt heard played by her nephew David's friend Norman Carey, and which had literary associations for her because Thomas Mann, E. M. Forster, and Milan Kundera all invoked it in their fiction. Beethoven and Roy Clampitt make an unlikely duo: the strong-minded, deaf composer, embodiment of nineteenth-century Romantic angst and aspiration, and the mild-mannered, deeply repressed, stalwart Iowa farmer. But according to Clampitt, in mid-America, "my father / might have been his twin," vigorously, obsessively at his work, naïve and revolutionary at the same time, thinking "he might / in some way, minor but radical, disrupt / the givens of existence." Instead, the well-meaning do-gooder, trying to rid his fencerows of poison ivy, managed only to get "a mist of venom" and "a mesh of blisters" from which he writhed for a week. There was no high Romantic agony for him, just an itchy, painful skin rash. Nevertheless, his daughter the poet allies him with a figure from the European canon. She wants to unite her midwestern heritage—both genetic and cultural—with her drive to live in the high culture of the Old World. This pairing—hoped for and finally achieved in her mature poetry—stuck with her. She made it work. She made her work out of it.

Aspiration and compulsion join the poet, her father, and her other model, the genius Romantic composer. Beethoven, deaf, tries to hear himself. Roy, driving back to Iowa from the West, stops his car to dig up a flower he hopes to transplant in his home soil. This effort brings his daughter to tears in the poem, even as his dying does not. We might ask why. The answer is not hard to find. Death, however painful, is inevitable; life, on the other hand, is sad, even tragic, especially when effort does not meet with satisfaction. Amy knew that her father suffered. And there was nothing she could do to help him.

Is it merely coincidence that Clampitt's great flowering occurred only after the deaths of her parents, Roy in 1973 and Pauline in 1979? She had achieved the final independence that all children strive for. Perhaps part of Amy's inheritance as a WASP female was her struggle, a battle really, between selfhood and the desire not to embarrass anyone, especially one's parents. She could not disappoint or startle her parents after they had died.

The Beethoven poem is matched in *The Kingfisher* by an even stronger and longer one, "A Procession at Candlemas." It brings together descriptions of a final trip to see the poet's mother, dying in Iowa, with allusions to the pastoral movements of Mediterranean shepherds; to plains-dwelling Native American hunters; to the peplos woven every four years in Athens and presented to the statue of Athena on the Acropolis; and to the Christian holiday Candlemas, celebrated on February 2 to commemorate the purification of the Virgin and the presentation of Jesus in the Temple. Birth and death, history and time and distance all come together.

Like much of Clampitt's mature work, this poem is not easy. It is deep and complex, but it begins simply:

> Moving on or going back to where you came from,
> bad news is what you mainly travel with:
> a breakup or a breakdown, someone running off
>
> or walking out, called up or called home:
> death in the family.

Pauline and Roy Clampitt, c. late 1960s

Those clear, directional words—"on," "back," "to," "from," "with," "off," "out," and "up"—may remind us of Robert Frost's monosyllabic opening in "Directive": "Back out of all this now too much for us."

And after several pages of divagations, the poem returns at the end to its beginning, "down the long-unentered nave of childhood" . . .

> . . . the mother
> curtained in Intensive Care: a Candlemas
>
> of moving lights along Route 80, at nightfall,
> in falling snow, the stillness and the sorrow
> of things moving back to where they came from.

Amy buried and then mourned her parents. Clampitt commemorated and revived them. She found materials for her poetry in many places, but home was where and how she started.

——

Amy was always drawn to language, read and spoken. Pauline recalled saying to her children, "When the day is over I feel best when I have finished some particular job." Amy—who began talking early, but did not walk alone, unassisted, until she was fifteen months old—added, "I feel best when I have finished a book." Loquacity went, in part, against the genetic grain. Quakers, like farmers, tend to be concise in speech, even if, like Frank and Roy, they can commit themselves easily to writing. Amy was never that way: "I grew up in a family who had difficulty in expressing themselves, and it was a great nuisance to be very talkative, sometimes—very objectionable. I didn't feel at home anywhere, it seems to me now, until I crossed the border from France into Italy, and found myself suddenly surrounded by expressive people, all talking with their hands. I felt in a way as though I'd found a home." Talk, language, expression, all foreign: they offered a sense of belonging, even if at one remove, elsewhere. At a writers' conference, she confessed, "I'd rather read than talk, but I talk a lot."

Her brothers, and the next generation of Clampitts still in New

Providence, have suggested that Amy had another role model, her father's younger sister Edith (1890–1970), the spinster aunt who led her out into the fields when Larry was born in 1923. She worked as a seamstress or milliner in Chicago during the Depression, making hats and dresses. Later she returned home. A prairie hostess or Iowa *salonnière*, she entertained Amy and other younger relatives in her Ames apartment. She proved that a single woman could exist actually supporting herself as an artist of sorts. And that a woman could live happily without a man. She always kept a cat, and she knew everything about birds. She must have inspired her niece in ways neither would have consciously predicted. In a late poem, "A Whippoorwill in the Woods" (*Westward*), Clampitt, thinking back to birds and their "cheekily anarchic / dartings and flashings, their uncalled-for color," remembers herself at five, and also her aunt, "a noticer // of such things before the noticing had or needed / a name." This woman "believed her cat had learned to leave birds alone." She died of cancer. Brought back to her childhood by the sound of whippoorwills, Clampitt establishes her own nodes of contact with the past: Aunt Edith told her

> of how her father, my grandfather, by whatever
>   now unfathomable happenstance,

> carried her (she might have been five) into the breathing night.
> "Listen!" she said he'd said. "Did you hear it?
> That was a whippoorwill." And she (and I) never forgot.

Those knots of connection stayed with her, as did the sonic memories.

We use the phrase "daddy's girl" for the daughter attached to her father more than to her mother. Amy was, perhaps more than anything, a grandpa's girl. A tiny copy of *Mother Goose* with Kate Greenaway's illustrations was inscribed "To Amy, from her grandpa Clampitt" and dated Christmas 1922. It was probably her first book. The stage was set. In a piece of writing (intended for what or whom it is unclear, but probably for a family newsletter or an Iowa gazette) that Clampitt executed in 1941–42, her first year in Manhattan, she recalls her grandparents from her perch on Morningside Heights with the affection of the dispossessed and the homesick, and with the confident grace of a mature writer:

When there were rehearsals and such after-school goings-on I sometimes used to spend the night in town at Grandpa's House, since we lived a couple of miles out. The composite recollection of these overnight visits is one of a serenity almost awesome, for in a houseful of children going to school somebody is always in a hurry, and at Grandpa's nobody ever hurried. This impressed me, though I doubt whether I ever put my awe into words. There was nothing sepulchral in the quiet of the place, punctuated though it was by the unhurried tocking of the big clock which hung in the dining room . . . It served as a kind of genius of the place.

They had things to do, on the nights I spent there; they kept a cow, even in town, and there was the furnace fire to be attended to, and the eggs to be gathered; but all this was a routine so mellowed by long practice that it seemed to me at least to require no effort. I used to wander desultorily around the house, look at the pictures in the *National Geographic*, and finally curl up with a copy of the poems of Oscar Wilde. It seems a little curious now, perhaps, that such a book should have been in Grandpa's library, but I saw nothing curious then; the luxurious fantasy of the poems had somehow absorbed, for me, an air of serenity which had no relation to my subsequent ideas of Oscar Wilde . . .

When the dishes had been washed and put away Grandma would get out the book they were currently reading together. It is fortunate indeed that their disabilities are complementary; for while Grandpa's eyes are not very good, Grandma has been totally deaf for as long as I can remember. She could usually read Grandpa's lips, but I usually had to write everything down on the scratch pad she kept always by her for such purposes. Even so, I scarcely recognized her deafness for the misfortune it must have been, because even approaching the age of eighty she has kept a somehow childlike pertness and spontaneity . . . her characteristic attitude was a playful one of mock horror with laughter on the heels of it. Little and thin without being fragile, she came scarcely past my shoulder even while I was still in high school, and her eyes were unfadedly blue and bright. I think what she resented most was to be recognized as helpless, because helpless she was not.

They read book after book together, new books and old favorites, brought from the shelves of the room we used to call the office because of the big official-looking desk in it. There were a great many books in Grandpa's collection, and he was always happy to lend them to us or to the people in town; but not without being sure that the borrower understood the almost sacredness they had for him. Grandpa had discovered books as a youth in pioneering days, really discovered them for himself instead of growing up surrounded by them as I did; their existence meant something to him that I probably do not quite understand. And there is of course the love of words, their mystery and importance, of which he would often speak to me. Grandpa too I never quite thought of as being old, as other people are old; with the certain quiet disillusion which comes with having lived a long time he seems never to have lost a kind of boyish earnestness of manner . . .

It is scarcely my place . . . to call their serenely sunlit house anything so literally banal as a sanctuary. In winter the south bedroom window was full of heliotrope and geraniums and delicate crimson hothouse roses, and in summer the garden bloomed with phlox and poppies and bachelor's buttons; and all year long I used to look forward to the coolness and fragrance of the place as to a retreat. Even to remember is to be refreshed.

"The love of words, their mystery and importance": what better inheritance could a writer have imagined for herself? And Frank's "boyish earnestness" repeated itself, translated into a higher key, in the exuberant seriousness of his grown granddaughter, in Manhattan, for the duration of her years there.

Grandmother Eva, wife of Frank, also offered womanly guidance, if only antithetically. Clampitt remembers her in "The Christmas Cactus" (dated November 1972, and published in *Multitudes, Multitudes*) as the deaf one, "who could domesticate / just about anything," and who kept her Christmas cactus waiting all year until finally, miraculously, and against the naysaying of nature and relatives and relatives and weather, it burst into "hummingbird rockets / succulent as fruit / pure carmine, color of scandal." The poet herself has tried (but presumably failed) to make one open in Manhattan. Looking back, she now remembers with wonder and gratitude an Iowa hothouse, with plants breaking into bloom in December.

And there was music, sometimes with words, for the most part without them, but which, like poetry, elicits feeling through sound. Roy made sure to give Pauline—an educated woman trapped in the never-ending chores of a farmer's wife—a piano as a honeymoon gift. In high school (twenty students in her graduating class), Amy was Pitti-Sing, one of the three little maids in a production of *The Mikado*. In central Iowa a century ago, the operettas of Gilbert and Sullivan, now both unfashionable and politically problematic, were part of the normal, living cultural heritage. The farmers' sons and daughters wore "Japanese" makeup and tried to look exotic. Amy's music teacher from sixty years before, Hattie Zoe Short Shoesmith,

New Providence High School class of 1937.
Amy is the second from the right in the second row.

wrote to her with reminiscences (June 12, 1993) and said—here is where a biographer regrets what has been lost—that she still had a photo album with pictures from the school productions of *Mikado* and *Pinafore*. Amy sang. She acted. In her senior year, the school also did a production of Shakespeare's *Measure for Measure*, a work hardly suitable for farmland adolescents. She played in the school band. The family had a Victrola, with scratchy old discs and not very good sound. That was sufficient.

In the last year of her life, Amy, belatedly famous, received a letter (April 24, 1993) from Paul Franzenburg, "a voice out of the past, and I trust you may remember your New Providence band director. The year I was with you, originally, was 1936 and I continued as your director into 1937. I do recall that you were one of our outstanding band students and that I relied upon you, among only a few others." What did she play? We have two memories. Her brother Philip remembers a soprano saxophone, which he attempted and failed to master after Amy had left home for college. Shirley Mayo, a school classmate who moved away, wrote to Amy (January 1, 1937) asking whether she was still playing the French horn. Amy marching down the football field with either of these instruments: it's a scene hard to picture but worth cherishing.

Music also contributed to a young girl's unconscious awareness of difference, snobbery, separation, and social class. The Clampitts had a piano, but their neighbors down the road, recently arrived from North Carolina, had a banjo: "I seem to recall a sneaking fondness for that uncultivated sound; but [that] an assurance as to what is vulgar might in itself constitute a greater vulgarity did not occur to me until long afterward." The nascent aesthete and the future Quaker activist are one person.

———

By the time Roy and Pauline's family had settled in New Providence, its Quakerism was different from what George Fox and William Penn might have imagined in England or Philadelphia. Anyone who has attended a silent meeting at a Quaker meetinghouse in

Honey Creek Meeting House

this country will stop cold, in wonder—as I did—when entering the Honey Creek Meeting House in New Providence.

The forty-four North Carolina Quakers who reunited with their families here in the spring of 1852, having made their long trek west, built a log meetinghouse. This burned in 1854, and was replaced five years later by a frame building, which itself was superseded by a brick building in 1916. Regular services were held here until 1973, when the church united with the New Providence Monthly Meeting several miles away.

The 1916 building still stands. Its interior is exactly as it was then. But anyone familiar with plain Quaker meetinghouses, with rows of benches facing one another, and with nothing resembling the apparatus of a house of worship, will have a shock. Honey Creek Meeting House is a church. It has a pulpit; it has an organ; it has pews facing the front. It has a minister, who gives sermons. Meetings are not silent. Interviewed, Philip said Quakers use the phrase "a well-gathered meeting" to mean an hour of perfect, concentrated silence. But that was not what Honey Creek had, or has. They have music and hymns. What became of silent meditation and a focus on the inner light?

Honey Creek Meeting House, interior

The Quaker population in Iowa was never especially large. A newspaper article (May 23, 1971) about Roy and Pauline, who had moved to Des Moines and had been living for eighteen years at the American Friends Service Committee headquarters there, pointed out that there were five thousand pastoral Quakers, and only one thousand non-pastoral (silent) Quakers in the state. But like Quakers everywhere, they made their presence felt.

Amy wrote:

The Great Revival in the latter part of the previous century had dislodged the Quakers of the township, as elsewhere, from their habit of silence into a pastoral and evangelical one. What had been meetinghouses were now churches. The one we attended, on the site above Honey Creek, was (and is) of brick, squarely built with a bell tower and mollified about the entrance by a growth of Virginia creeper ... During my earliest years the pastor was a Reverend Mr. Culbertson, a young man of moon-faced earnestness, who had a growing family and with whom my father carried on, directly and indirectly, a sort of running debate. His sermons being thus questionable, I could not see why we had to go to church at all. My grandfather, a lifelong skeptic, went out of deference to my grandmother. His younger brother, my Uncle Ralph, stayed away (though his wife and family went) until his later years. I believe it was the perpetuation of intolerance they both objected to. I objected to what I saw, arrogantly, as sheer compulsory nonsense.

Looking back, Amy acknowledges her freethinking status. She also acknowledges the defiant arrogance of her stance. Hardheadedness can lead people like her to new modes of rebellion and discovery. In 1996, years after Amy had left, a poet named Mark Schorr returned to Grinnell College—his alma mater as it was Amy's and Roy's—for his thirtieth reunion, at which Betty McKibben, an emerita lecturer in Classics, mentioned an Iowa Quaker who, not allowed to sing songs, "would memorize poems and recite pentameters as an accompaniment to plowing fields." Amy, her father, and her grandfather who composed his own sonnets while plowing, not to mention earlier poets like Clampitt's beloved Wordsworth, would have understood both the rebellious impulse and the poetic products of such cunning sublimation.

In an essay that appeared at the end of her life, "The Poetry of Isaiah," Clampitt remembered what seemed like the constant, nagging bad news of Isaiah the prophet, as opposed to the more hopeful news she heard in Elijah and Jonah. She called him inseparable "from the most forbidding of the Old Ones who sat there, Sunday after Sunday, nodding dour agreement. Isaiah is unmistakably for grown-ups; and I was myself exceptionally and protractedly resistant to my elders and all they stood for." In a kind of compensatory revenge, the rebellious adolescent dreamed of going to a nightclub, where she saw "the figure, in a beautiful, wicked décolleté, of Lena Horne [emerging] from a sodden blur." The call of the wild, the seduction of New York: "this was the world, I was in it, at the drunken heart of it." Amy's time—traveling in Europe, experiencing sophisticated enchantments, flirtations, and other fleshly pleasures—would come soon enough.

Her brother Philip also remembered:

My grandfather was something of a skeptic . . . he attended church with [his wife Eva] but he, until later in life, didn't join . . . he didn't want people who knew him to think that he thought he was better than other people that weren't members of the church . . . Some time in the late nineteenth century . . . a wave of evangelism came through. There were revival meetings . . . people got saved. After they're saved, they have to join the church, and the only church there was the Quaker Church. So the Quaker pacifist tradition wasn't a part of the evangelists' message, and the Quaker tradition just got lost . . . And that was the kind of thing that Amy and I grew up with. They didn't have baptism, they didn't have communion, but they did sing evangelist type hymns, and they had a minister . . .

My father had a college education, and after sermons were preached by the minister at Honey Creek . . . he would criticize the sermon at home at Sunday dinner. So Amy had this kind of rebellious streak, and I had some of that myself. Why go at all? Why bother if it's a bunch of nonsense? That's not quite what my father said, but there were some implications like that. So Amy was really not religious at all.

As things progressed, a nascent spirituality drove Amy, years later in New York, to the Episcopal Church, eager for order, for submission, and for a way of harnessing her love of music and language, even of abstract thought, to a mechanism that would give her an outlet as well as stability.

Philip adds:

Whatever Amy got involved with, whatever she got engaged with, would get her full attention. It was like she would go in with both feet, and she certainly did when it came to religious conversion. I think my parents felt—certainly my mother felt—you know, my mother had a lot of anxiety about a lot of things, but one of them: When is Amy going to settle down, get married and be a normal person? And Amy, knowing this anxiety on my mother's part, wouldn't share, with either of our parents, very much of what was happening.

But back in Iowa, as a child, Amy felt a double pull. Church received "her full attention," but a complicated attention.

At church, she joined in, lustily singing the hymns, some of which—"When He Cometh" and "Oh, Beulah Land, Sweet Beulah Land"—she recalled toward the end of her life with a kind of manic glee: "For sheer inanity there can't have been anything to surpass it before the advent of the sung commercial . . . a few of the hymns I remember best provided a foretaste of the commercial's rollicking glibness." She went on, "it sounded to me like a travesty of something I didn't believe a word of. What I did believe, crassly and from an early age, was that out in the real world, religion—i.e., having to go to church—was already obsolete."

"Out in the real world" was where she yearned to be, and she knew somehow that a prairie church was not part of that real world. She wanted liberation. Feeling uncomfortable and hemmed in, eager to be released from any societal or parental expectations of normality, and intellectually receptive and curious, Amy was no different from countless other brainy adolescents who seek to escape.

———

As a poet inspired by and committed to landscape, Clampitt never forgot what Iowa looked like, or how it nourished her imagination as well as her body. In a poem from *Archaic Figure* (1987), her third volume from Knopf, she makes the unlikely equation between Venice, with its "mirrorings and masquerades, / brocaded wallowings, ascensions, levitations"—all the riches and complexities that travelers have always relished about La Serenissima—and its diametrical opposite, a prairie landscape. Both are equally but differently vertiginous. A "homesteader's wife,"

> . . . numb
> in the face of the undisguised
> prospect of the place she'd come to, drove
> a post into the yard outside the sodhouse
> to have something, she said, to look at.
>   ("VENICE REVISITED")

In a letter to Helen Vendler, Clampitt recalls this story as having been passed down from her grandfather. The woman here was actually in North Dakota, a more treeless and windswept landscape than Iowa. The poet has taken legitimate poetic license. Later in the poem she compares the reedbeds of the Venetian lagoon to the tall grass of the actual Iowa prairie. Whether scrubby, arid North Dakota or more fertile Iowa, it does not matter. Venice shares something in the imagination of the mature poet with Amy's childhood memories of Pioneer Farm, when she and her family arrived there in 1930. The earliest Venetians were like the American homesteaders and plains settlers, all coming to treeless locations. Having to make thoroughfares where there had been none, they transformed treacherous, desolate muck or seemingly infinite expanses of prairie into habitations.

Another poem, from *The Kingfisher*, "On the Disadvantages of Central Heating," is set mainly in England, but it starts, and perhaps ends, with recollections of an Iowa childhood. Unusually for Clampitt, it is written in a kind of free form—no capital letters—a long streaming sentence that enacts the connections among disparate things. Here is the opening:

> cold nights on the farm, a sock-shod
> stove-warmed flatiron slid under
> the covers, mornings a damascene-
> sealed bizarrerie of fernwork
>   decades ago now

And it ends—several farms and several experiences of cold having merged together—by evoking what has been lost or forgotten, and what retained and remembered: "what's salvaged / is this vivid diminuendo, unfogged / by mere affect, the perishing residue / of pure sensation."

This poem seems to float on its page. Other poems about Iowa, written decades after her departure, recall the sense of openness as well as the efforts to contain things that stayed with Amy for her entire life. Consider "The Woodlot," with its note telling us that "according to the Iowa Guide, the anonymous inventor of barbed wire was an Iowa farmer." The wire

> taught, if not fine manners, how at least to follow
> the surveyor's rule, the woodlot nodes of willow,
> evergreen or silver maple gave the prairie grid
> what little personality it had.

Like the grids and plots one sees coming into the state, the fences and other enclosures represent at least partial efforts at mastering nature. (Lines of poems exert their own control over unruly imaginations.) As the poem ends, Clampitt brings it all home, to herself and to Cedardale, recalling herself to her own earliest memory. She imagines an "enclosure," within which, "under / appletrees like figures in a ritual, violets / are thick, a blue cellarhole / of pure astonishment." This memory of nature's delicate bounty and of human effort, of protection against the elements, precedes even the fact of other people, and of human relationships:

> Before it,
> I/you, whatever that conundrum may yet
> prove to be, amounts to nothing.

So much for philosophical or psychological theories about an infant at a mother's breast, or any future kind of human intimacy. For Clampitt the poet, and perhaps to some extent for Amy the woman, Mother meant Nature.

And if Nature is Mother, it is also both the occasion for, and the site of, artistic creation. One of several poems in *The Kingfisher* devoted to Clampitt's native soil is "Stacking the Straw." Decades of nostalgia, the recovery of memory, and periodic reminders of home in the form of family visits enabled the poet to look back to the cornfields and see the Iowa landscape as a work of art, and its resident farmers as not only tillers of the soil but also arrangers of its produce. That these arrangements were a joint effort (as she remembered in her *Paris Review* interview) only adds power to her recollection. Everyone worked together, cutting the grain by hand, tying it into bundles, and putting it into shocks. The community would then bring in the grain and feed it to the threshing machines.

For at least two millennia, poets have declared that life is short but art is long: writers from Horace to Shakespeare asserted that their work would outlast the monuments of princes, and outlive bronze and marble. Things have changed. Contemporary artists like the British Andy Goldsworthy make pieces designed to decay rather than survive. Clampitt was onto something very much of her moment, which is also ours. Although the mown hay will ultimately come down "to toaster-fodder, cereal / as commodity," with nothing permanent about it, she finds something wonderful in the farmer's handiwork:

> Strawstacks' beveled loaves, a shape
> that's now extinct, in those days were
> the nearest thing the region had
> to monumental sculpture. While hayracks
> and wagons came and went, delivering bundles,
> carting the winnowed ore off to the granary,
>
> a lone man with a pitchfork stood aloft
> beside the hot mouth of the blower,
> building about himself, forkful
> by delicately maneuvered forkful,
> a kind of mountain, the golden
> stuff of mulch, bedding for animals.
> I always thought of him with awe—
>
> a craftsman whose evolving altitude
> gave him the aura of a hero. He'd come down
> from the summit of the season's effort
> black with the baser residues of that
> discarded gold. Saint Thomas of Aquino
> also came down from the summit
> of a lifetime's effort, and declared
> that everything he'd ever done was straw.

What to Aquinas was an admission of insufficiency in the face of God's bounteous mysteries and those of His creation, to Clampitt and her farmer is a promotion of petty human efforts to the level of heroism, even divinity. Rightly seen, everything man-made can be considered as art.

A cheerful but corrective remark in a letter (February 28, 1983) from Amy's cousin Marjorie Silletto reminded her that she was romanticizing a bit, or at least stretching the facts for the sake of her own artistry: "I didn't think my father thought he was a craftsman when Stacking the Straw! He usually did the job because he knew how to do it the way he wanted—but it was a dirty and very hard job! It was tiring—I remember that."

"He knew how to do it the way he wanted": the farmer shared with any artist a sense of the proper way to go about his work. At a reading in Des Moines in the late 1980s, with her supportive English teacher Harold Guthrie in the audience, Amy admitted she could not remember how many straw bundles her father needed to make a full stack. According to a report in the *Des Moines Register*, the husband of one of her classmates saved her by holding up nine fingers. Amy was delighted: "There comes a time when you find that there is something you have in common." And when she visited the Greek island of Thasos in 1983, the annual communal harvesting of the olive crop put her in mind of Iowa's own traditional seasonal rituals.

Clampitt as a writer could harness the lessons that Amy learned as a midwesterner, converting straw into literary gold. Looking back allowed, even required, some degree of romanticizing the past. In a piece about the now forgotten novelist Marguerite Young, with whom she studied briefly in New York, Clampitt identifies with her mentor as both a Greenwich Village neighbor and a midwesterner. She might be describing herself:

> Self-consciousness is . . . the beginning of estrangement; but as one who fled the region, I cannot but attribute the widespread lack of confidence out there, the apologetic inability to believe one is anyone worth notice, to the nature of the landscape—to there being so little to hold onto or to be glued by. It seems to me hardly less axiomatic that nobody can begin to understand this

country, if it even is or can be thought of as a country, without taking account of that interior setting and the effect it has on its inhabitants.

———

At seventeen, Amy left home and moved sixty miles southeast. Grinnell College was her base for four years. Her interviewer Jean Hanff Korelitz asked whether she had ever considered going farther away, but Amy said such a move would not have been possible, because the Clampitts were, in the middle of the Depression, so poor. But in 1937, only 15 percent of the American population of eighteen- to twenty-two-year-olds, most of them men and most of them from privileged backgrounds, experienced higher education of any sort. Amy was lucky to have had parents who valued college for their daughters as well as their sons. They were not as poor as she thought, or, rather, their values had not been impoverished. At the end of her first year, however, the student got a shock. Farm conditions had worsened. Roy Clampitt wrote to the college registrar in April saying that unusual operating expenses made it impossible for him to contribute anything toward his daughter's education as a sophomore until the end of the calendar year at the earliest. In July, the Grinnell dean of women offered a $100 scholarship stipend, to be applied to the annual bill ($300 for tuition and fees, plus $146 for nightly dinner). The stipend was supplemented with a contract for ten and a half hours of weekly work. This aid package assured the student's return, not to mention her successes over the following three years.

During the summer of 1937, Amy exchanged letters with her future roommates and with an upper class "big sister" or adviser. The letters show how things have changed, and also remained the same, in the past century, as adolescents prepare for a major rite of passage. Cecilia Kinsley wrote from Sheridan, Wyoming (June 23, 1937), introducing herself: "I was wondering if you would like to make our room at school Western. I have been given a number of western things for my graduation. I would like to know what you think of my plan rather soon as the dude season starts soon and the nicest things will be picked over before the start of September." And then, "I imagine you would like to know some of my hobbies? Well, I like swimming, golfing, shows, and things like that in general." Another soon-to-be roommate, Gwen Corbett from River Forest, Illinois, seems to have been more literary: she wrote to Amy announcing they will "get along splendidly," at least in part because of her recently developed passions for Carl Sandburg and Countee Cullen.

In August, Charlotte Carman, who had probably also been assigned to Amy as some kind of adviser, responded to some questions Amy had posed in a July letter about what was to come. She offered pointers for Amy's arrival at Grinnell. Amy had asked about dancing. Charlotte says the lessons, one hour a week, cost one dollar for the term. Charlotte has an allowance of $1.50 per week. Amy also—was she serious, or just trying to fit in?—asked whether she should bring her sports equipment. And what, she wondered, about ankle socks? She sounds like a typical college coed (as female students used to be called), eager to fit in, not a sulky intellectual misfit. Charlotte tells Amy about gym classes and what sorts of things to bring from home: "Bring your own golf clubs. The kids like golf heaps. And your own tennis racket." The first week will involve a formal reception that will require a long dress: "Probably it will depend upon what color and material your summer formal is as to whether you want to wear it or not."

She ends, "Write again if the spirit moves. It will be good practice for our English courses."

Amy, who did not like golf heaps, did not need to practice for her English courses.

———

We have evidence, written and photographic, of Amy as a college student. She did not bring golf clubs with her, and probably not even a tennis racket. College offered something better than sports. She finally found herself among people with intellectual aspirations equal to hers. Fifty years after graduation (April 29, 1991), crossing the Atlantic on the *QE2*, Amy wrote a piece of sweet doggerel for her classmates at their reunion:

> O innocent wickedness at the heart of things
>   that sustained the S&B
> with its Doric column, the League Board,
>   the intramurals, the Honor G!
> From Read to Mears, from Langan to Gates, such
>   hotbeds of iniquity:
>
> of sleeping through chapel, of cutting class
>   and sneaking off for a bite
> at the Dixie, with its aura of grease; the illicit
>   beer at the Maid-Rite,
> the ultimate, the aspired-to pinnacle
>   of staying out all night!
>
> Times change; sanctions dwindle, like the clatter
>   of the southbound M & St. L.,
> the Doppler chord of the westbound Zephyr; like the mating
>   urge that was so powerful,
> come spring, one wonders, reminiscing, that we ever
>   went to class at all.

This hardly sounds like the musings of a serious intellectual, let alone the famous Amy Clampitt who had been winning prizes and gaining a national spotlight. She had sounded that other note in 1984 when she received an honorary degree from her alma mater. At that event she gave a three-minute speech: "I talked about our society and how we are fast becoming a country of analgesics and soporifics. We watch television so much that we are conditioned to believe whatever nonsense comes out of that box . . . As a poet, I'm trying to sort out values, to discriminate between the authentic and the phony—to preserve what's worth preserving."

A reader might think that the commemorative light verses about cutting class were the joyful nostalgia of someone who was a cheer-

Amy, on the right, with Grinnell classmates, 1940

leader, or the prom queen, a lighthearted party girl. Amy was, of course, none of these. Her poem gives little indication of who she was to become. But along with it, she contributed a more somber note to the class book, in which she said that her main goal in life had always been a protest against "a conspiracy to stamp out singularity, to do away with everything that can't be commodified, and in the process to make ordinary day-to-day living as boring as possible." The editor of the reunion book wryly, perhaps enviously, observed of Amy's account of her past fifty years, "I ask, is this an account of a *boring* life?" The answer is clear. A life is interesting in proportion to the care one takes with it, and to the care one gives to explaining it.

Amy's files contain school report cards and early poems from New Providence, as well as dozens of college writing assignments. For decades, until educational changes swept through in the 1960s, college students had to take two or four semesters of "Composition," and these required weekly themes that went through many forms of discursive and "creative" writing: short stories, character sketches, book reports, description, argument, local color, journalistic reportage, and position papers. The topics touched on matters from philosophy, economics, religion, literature, and history. Not many college undergraduates in the twenty-first century are writing reports on André Gide, Greek tragedy, George Meredith, *La Princesse de Clèves*, Milton, Rousseau, and Walter Savage Landor. Amy was interested in practically everything. Her work, some of it typed, some of it handwritten (when her handwriting was still legible), was flawless with regard to grammar, spelling, and diction. An exemplary handwritten fifteen-page term paper, complete with bibliography and footnotes, dated December 17, 1937, on a childhood favorite, Edna St. Vincent Millay, opens us to a young writer confident in her opinions and already eager and grateful to do "research."

As the twig is bent, so is the tree inclined: Amy's confidence bore fruit decades later. She wrote a review of a centenary selected edition of Millay's poems in which she recalled liking the words, the music, and the borrowings of this famous Jazz Age poet when she was fifteen. Millay and Swinburne were her favorites. "In the work of both, pretty sounds were what attracted me—pretty sounds being literary ones." Millay at her best generated "a sensuous freshness that slips in and out of her work as regularly as the tide, inundating the formal music of her work with a vigor and a specificity beyond itself."

Even at the beginning, Amy the student showed the stylistic habits that would come to define the mature poetry of Clampitt decades later. In her sophomore year (March 7, 1939), her instructor comments on a short piece called "Prelude on a May Afternoon": "This is very fine, extremely natural description. Could you end with another reference to your mood and the effect of the rain on it? If you could, this might do for the *Atlantic*." She wrote a short piece about the American humorist James Lane Allen. The wise professor says, "Good analysis. You show a tendency to write involved, puzzling sentences . . . Try for sentences that are instantly intelligible." (If only he could have read her poems fifty years later!) Of another piece, he says, "This is all excellent, but I think if you ever wanted to use it—in a short story or a novel—you would have to shorten it. The concentration of description is pretty high." And a month later, he asks, provoked by an evocation of the scent of a cherry blossom,

"This would be better as a poem than as a piece of prose. Why aren't you writing poetry incidentally?"

Why indeed? Clampitt remarked, looking back, that once she arrived in Manhattan she thought that to be a serious writer meant writing fiction. She was wrong. She had her blind spots.

Amy's correspondence contains fan letters from classmates who found her during the years of fame at the end of her life. George Wayne Bowman, who dropped out during the war and returned to graduate from Grinnell in 1948, wrote:

> I saw your picture in the last issue of the Grinnell College magazine. I couldn't resist writing to you to see if you remember an incident one evening back in about 1939 when you and a friend walked from a play rehearsal to downtown and back to the Dixie Inn with your eyes closed. I worked there part time as a student and got "coffee" for you. I told you that I could make you open your eyes but you said "you can't." I served you plain water and you drank nearly all of it without detecting that anything was different. Then you suddenly yelled, "what's in this coffee?" You opened your eyes and we all laughed.

Oh, those college high jinks! The days were innocent, or at least seem that way through the prism of time. Kay Madison Fiester, another college friend, wrote (March 10, 1988) with a more serious memory:

> Do you know that for fifty years an analogy of yours from a "Tanager" story (it must have been in a 1938 or 1939 edition) has come back to me every time I start recovering from a fever—feeling limp and vulnerable and reborn, like your wet-, crumpled-winged moth emerging from its cocoon? So you see you have been adding a little style to my mental life since long before "The Kingfisher" caught fire.

And another classmate, Elsa A. Diggins, remembered presciently (in 1985) that Amy "directed a one-act play, *Mary, Queen of Scots*, and I played the part of the ill-fated queen. Even then I was sure your career would be in the creative arts."

A final reminiscence was sent by David Matlack, two years Amy's junior, to Harold Korn when he heard the news of Amy's death in the fall of 1994. He and Amy had stayed in touch, but they never saw each other after their Grinnell years. He wrote to Hal:

> Since I lived off campus with my twin brother and mother, Amy loved to come to our little apartment where my mother would serve jasmine tea and the raisin biscuits Amy liked. In the evening she & I would walk to a tavern down by the Rock Island railroad, named the Brotherhood of Railroad Trainmen, and talk and drink a quart or two of beer. She taught me "Joe Hill" and "Cocaine Lil" among other songs . . . Recently I had a letter from Mary Lee Theobald, a classmate . . . She wrote "Amy was assigned to me as a big buddy when I was a Grinnell freshman, and the sudden impact of this tall person with the fresh lovely skin and the swan-likeness was quite overwhelming."

Amy thought of herself as an ugly duckling. It turns out she was really, perhaps always, the swan.

———

Amy Clampitt, a shy college junior with a Phi Beta Kappa key, spent the 1940 summer (June to August) at the Cummington School in western Massachusetts. She applied to and was accepted by this avant-garde, progressive place, which also granted her a much-needed scholarship. Cummington's working philosophy combined insights from John Dewey and Rudolf Steiner. Two of Amy's Grinnell contemporaries had been there: Harry Duncan (1916–1997), who went on to establish the Cummington Press, and Margaret (Currier) Boylan (1921–1967), whose one novel, *The Marble Orchard* (1956), became known as a kind of midwestern *Catcher in the Rye*.

Other visitors to and alumni of the place established by the harpist Katherine Frazier as "an environment congenial to creative activity" include Helen Frankenthaler, Willem de Kooning, Diane Arbus, and Marianne Moore. Whom Amy met there remains a mystery. But we know a lot about what she did, and how she was changed, although there's no evidence from her letters and papers that she ever mentioned the experience again. A prospectus for the 1941 summer session lists writing workshops with Delmore Schwartz, Katherine Anne Porter, Allen Tate, and R. P. Blackmur. In Amy's summer, the primary literature instructor was Sidney Cox, friend and biographer of Robert Frost.

Amy's letter of application, written when she was nineteen, is both typical (of her) and astonishing (for someone of her age). It shows how well she understood her situation, her gifts, and her needs. It reads, in part:

April 18, 1940
Dear Miss Frazier:
    Ostensibly it is for help with my writing, and essentially it is for the expansion of my own boundaries, that I hope to attend Cummington School this summer. I believe I have talent, and I know I have something to say; whether or not mine are qualities which will "stack up" into tremendously good writing I have yet to determine. I have lived nearly twenty years, have studied and thought, and, I believe, achieved a certain integrity; and I feel that if now it were possible to devote a summer to consistent effort, with the companionship of others of similar aims, I should be able more fully to discover myself, and to fill out what now seems to be lacking to what I have written.
    My father is a farmer, and I have been accustomed to a poverty which for all its limitations was not unpleasant. Nevertheless I was unhappy, as I suspect most children are; growing up in pieces, I came to college amazingly immature, my knowledge still insufficient to balance a prevailing interest in generalizations and abstractions; I did not understand people, and I clothed myself in a sentimental imitation of my father's intense and rather narrow idealism . . .
    [She goes on to discuss her reluctance to identify with a cause. She calls her temperament "classical." But she still thinks that "the idea" will be fundamental in the novels she intends to

write. Abstraction is still a flaw in her work. She realizes that she is insufficient in many ways, and with limited experience in observation and emotion. She is unsure of structure in both her life and her work.]

What I know of painting, music, and the theater has been acquired mostly at second hand; I have never visited an art gallery, and I have seen only a few plays. Since my own ideal of perfection places art at the summit of human achievement, I hope to gain my understanding of our civilization chiefly through an acquaintance with art in all its forms.

Finally, it is for companionship that I should like to go to Cummington. Until not so long ago I cherished romantic ideas, which I of course never entirely believed, of the sterility of social intercourse; but those ideas are quite gone now, and I have never been so fully happy as during this year, spent in the companionship of a small group whose first serious concern is art. I have been slow in reaching social maturity . . .

As I widen my own experience my eagerness to abstract and over-simplify should disappear, and as I see things happen I should rid myself of the last vestiges of an adolescent belief that nothing really happens. I have seen the processes of change in an agricultural community, processes which are part of a long cycle, a static rather than a dynamic thing. I have seen too the beauty which exists so wonderfully incomplete and essential in the midst of ugliness; and I have known that other limpid beauty of field and sky, which is so perfect and inarticulate. When I have detached myself from my own small and rather unhappy connections with the rural Middle West, it will perhaps be in the language of these two aspects of beauty that I shall speak.

This is the work of a serious young woman alert to her strengths and shortcomings, eager to forge a path for herself and to find companionable souls who are not midwestern.

In 1940, the ten-week Cummington summer session included workshops on music, writing, painting, sculpture, stage studies, dance, crafts, and education. No one took all the courses, but everyone dabbled in several. Art was the basis for everything: "The Cummington School relies on the intense drives of the creative type of student for results that are honest and lasting," read the confidently utopian brochure. Everyone participated in "dramatic readings." In 1940 the plays were William Saroyan's *My Heart's in the Highlands,* the now forgotten Angna Enters's *Love Possessed Juana,* Eugene O'Neill's *The Emperor Jones,* Shaw's *The Devil's Disciple,* Sheridan's *The Rivals,* Molière's *The Miser,* plus *As You Like It, Macbeth,* and Euripides's *Alcestis.*

Among the trustees of the school was Grace Hazard Conklin, a professor of English at Smith College; almost a half century later, an endowed professorship in Conklin's name would enlist as its first holder one Amy Clampitt, distinguished poet. Conklin and the others were all educators who valued "community" as much as self-enrichment and self-fulfillment through art, and the one class required of all students was something called "General Appreciation . . . in which all members of the school participate, a symposium on the fundamental problems and values in the life of an artist." The school also had its own Town Meeting (which must have struck a sympathetic chord in the Quaker Clampitt) "to settle certain practical concerns of the school by democratic procedure." On the cooperative plan, everyone worked, did dishes, served in hall, ushered, and emptied ashes from the fireplaces. The school sounds like a glorious, artsy, left-leaning summer camp for nervous intellectuals and brainy misfits.

At the end of the session, the instructional staff filed long reports about each student, paying more attention to general psychological assessment than to purely academic accomplishment. Reading Amy's today, one is struck by the now quaint and sometimes incomprehensible pigeonholes the school used for diagnosing the students. The psychological and performative evaluations have subcategories like "Predominating Sanction," "Productiveness," "Blocked Segments of Mind" ("still reluctant to grow up, but well aware that she has to," wrote Frazier). Despite the quirky terminology and the procrustean categories, one is impressed by the accuracy of the teachers' sense of Amy: "a little girlishness that most adults find charming, but which doesn't give play to her wisdom, except in observation." For "Social

Insight in Personal Relations," the evaluator types "extremely sharp, hard, clear, yet toned by pity." Among "Indices of Development" we read "awkward, sometimes gawky, concealing womanhood." In the cumbersome category labeled "Relation to Span of Time and Space, Matter, and the Universe," Frazier pencils in: "the maturest aspect of her being, rich and brave." These "Indices of Development" make the place sound like a psychological Petri dish more than an artistic cauldron.

There are categories for everything from Adaptability to Leadership, Sense of Humor, and Spontaneity, as well as physical things like Posture and Energy. Under "Sensitivity to Values" we learn that Amy is "strong, tough, delicate, but unconscious of many values present in those she examines"; that she is not inclined to "domination" but is aware of her own limitations; that she is "over-anxious to be liked"; that there are "discrepancies between the little girl with high voice and facile enthusiasms, and the ironical and perceptive woman." Under "Sensory Specialties" the grader notes her "visual and auditory senses [as] very active and sharp. Strong sense of weather, and of darkness and light." The teachers could never have predicted how that strong sense of weather would come into full play decades later in her poetry. Under "General Interest in Human Relations": "considerable, but of brief life." This was still a very shy girl. "Boys are afraid of her," wrote Frazier (as Amy was clearly afraid of boys), and the "sloughing off of childishness" that her teachers hoped for was a feat she never fully accomplished, much to her credit. Finally, acknowledged in the culminating evaluative category, "General Integration": "she is one of the best integrated certainly, one of the most profoundly honest people in this school." To which the censorious Miss Frazier penciled in: "her own integration constantly upset by conflicts."

We shall probably never learn what happened to this provincial girl that summer, nor why she avoided commenting in later years on what might have been a major life-enhancing experience. Did she find the companionship she had been eager for? Did she read her teachers' reports? If so, was she discouraged? She filed her own end-of-term self-evaluation. She seems to have had fun: "I came to Cummington to write, and I came to be with people." She felt respected: "I have found myself less afraid of disliking and being disliked"; "I think I am a little tougher"; "I am less hypersensitively shy than at the beginning of the summer."

We don't know much more about Amy's responses to her first extended trip away from her home state. In the fall, she returned to Grinnell for her senior year, earnest, ambitious, untried, but more confident than she had been earlier in the spring. She had left Iowa for the summer. The following year she would leave permanently.

———

From an early age, Clampitt was never not a writer, but she also harbored other dreams: "My earliest ambition was to be a painter. I never saw any real Old Masters . . . but I knew there were such things, and I wanted to paint Old Masters: I had this notion of what painting was, it was a Madonna-and-Child kind of thing, it was Italian painting. There must have been some books in the family library, although I can't remember what they were, that had pictures like that."

We know that while at Cummington, Amy visited the Smith College art museum, where she saw for the first time some Old Master paintings, and work by Corot and Courbet. More important, Edith Sternfeld, a Grinnell art history professor and another female role model, imbued Amy with a sense of "the livingness of the past," lessons she took with her when she went to Europe years afterwards. She fooled around with watercolors, but couldn't really draw. When she returned to her desk, the drawing board became a writing board.

As her grandfather had written adolescent sonnets, so did she. *The Husk*, the literary magazine of Iowa's Cornell College, published a pair of them in its March 1937 edition. Second prize, in the Midwest High School Creative Writing Contest of the 1936–37 year, went to the star pupil of Harold Guthrie, who is mentioned along with the author. There were 409 manuscripts submitted. One wonders, naturally, who wrote the first-place poem, and where it was published, and what became of the poet. Here's the first part of young Clampitt's "Transition":

> I saw the warm, swift spell of autumn done,
> Swept by on twilight winds with eerie crying,
> Bright leaves had drifted down one after one,
> More lovely even than their life, their dying;
> And never seemed the world so rich as when—
> Boldly the cold portent of change defying—
> Fall marshalled up her forces once again,
> And flung forth this last shout ere life went flying.
>
> With awful suddenness her glory fled,
> Pursued by wind and cold and whistling rain;
> And now with earth I stand and share her pain,
> Seeing the leaves shattered and lying dead,
> To know that splendor which had seemed so strong
> Was but a hollow bauble crushed ere long.

The sixteen-year-old fledgling had been reading and absorbing Shakespeare, Shelley, and Keats, all of whom, especially the last, would stay with her, reappearing fifty years later in the author's maturity. Clyde Tull, from the college, extended his congratulations in a letter that also included a check for five dollars, the first payment that put Clampitt on the way to becoming a professional poet.

Keats and Shelley, everything we might label a "Romantic" as well as a romantic impulse, never disappeared from Clampitt's imagination. They were soon rechanneled into prose, which Clampitt considered the proper literary stuff of adulthood, more serious than the poetic effusions of adolescence. Through her postgraduate years in Manhattan, she contributed occasional prose pieces to *The Tanager*, Grinnell's literary magazine. Some are sketches, like "Faithful, in My Fashion," full of Ernest Dowson and late Victorian decadence, heavy with description and longing, spring rain and unrequited love. Or "At Gunderson's Bar" (1946), an effort to reproduce the kind of sketches of louche characters and squalid quarters that Joseph Mitchell was writing for *The New Yorker*.

The longest piece is a two-part story called "The Envious Night," an outpouring of existential angst about Iowa kids, first in the playground, then growing into adolescence, anguished sexuality, and religious doubt, reading Keats's *Endymion* and "The Eve of Saint Agnes," and Shelley's "The Indian Serenade." The hero, Billy, who goes by William as he matures, sounds like a midwestern version of someone from a Thomas Wolfe novel, or Joyce's Stephen Dedalus: "Then suddenly the universe trembled into torrents of song; and dissolved in its transcendent harmony he rested his head against a stone which marked the sleep of death, and looked out upon the transformation of the world." The prose is as predictable as the situation: "He lay shaken by an agony of dry and ineffectual sobbing . . . he was alone and without significance." Adding a daring dose of realism to her stylistic outpourings, the young author has the protagonist's sister die of a botched abortion. Clampitt would require decades to recover from these false starts.

———

After graduation from Grinnell, Amy spent the summer of 1941 at the Scattergood Hostel for European Refugees in West Branch, Iowa. Alert to what was going on in Germany since Kristallnacht three years earlier, Iowa Quakers had volunteered to accept (mostly Jewish) refugees at Scattergood, which had been a Quaker boarding school. The Scattergood Hostel operated between 1939 and 1943, when Jews were no longer allowed to leave Germany. A total of 185 people came there. They were subsequently resettled throughout the United States, with jobs made available to them.

Roy had been active on the Scattergood committee, and was a leader of the work camp there. (Later on, he also worked under the 1948 Displaced Persons Act and the 1953 Refugee Relief Act.) Midway through her three months, Amy wrote an essay that she called "Impressions of a Summer Volunteer." Always on the qui vive, she remarks that "spontaneity and surprise"—hallmarks of her own disposition—were the elements of the experience that most impressed her. While struggling with laundry, cleaning and handling pots and pans, and preparing large family-style meals, she is charmed by the "evenings of singing on the lawn, the practical jokes, the conversations which made of tutoring something more than the giving of lessons." This young woman, who had been nowhere, would in another decade have been to Europe twice, soaking up culture and reveling in the delights of the Old World. But even here, in her home state, she is experiencing both cultural difference and a Whitmanian sense of America's infinite variety and its easy absorption of immigrants:

> For an American there is of course a certain superficial glamor surrounding those whose backgrounds are so different from his own, but the really unforgettable qualities go deeper than that; and at Scattergood, where there exist a freedom and informality which are really democratic, there is an opportunity to know these people well.

Her brother Philip attributed to Amy's Scattergood summer a reaffirmation of her native Quaker resistance to violence, and her lifelong opposition to warfare and other forms of social injustice. In retrospect, we can also discover one source for the energy that she eventually unleashed, decades later, in her mature poems that confronted political issues.

(In a coincidence, Philip's future wife had associations with Scattergood. Among the first "guests" at the Scattergood Hostel were Emil and Regina Deutsch, Austrian Jews who arrived in 1939 with their two young children, Michael and Hanna. As an adult, Hanna taught at an elementary school in Des Moines. She and Philip met there in 1955. At an event called "Scattergood Day," the Saturday after Thanksgiving in 1959, with Amy back home for a visit, Philip decided that Hanna was the woman for him. They married on June 12, 1960.)

By her own account, Amy began to think of herself seriously as a poet during a 1971 protest against the Vietnam War outside the White

House. She had returned to her strongly pacifist, Quaker principles, rooted in childhood and Scattergood. Protesters sprawled in front of the White House gates to symbolize the number of Vietnamese killed that day: "We all wore Vietnamese hats and [had?] to designate our occupations on banners. I chose 'poet.' It was the first time I thought of myself that way." (See "The Dahlia Gardens," in *The Kingfisher*, inspired by the self-immolation of a thirty-one-year-old Quaker named Norman Morrison in front of the Pentagon in 1965.)

Amy always felt different from her New Providence peers. At Scattergood, she came to realize something that everyone eventually learns, especially poets, whose stock-in-trade is the language of metaphor. She recognized how people have points of contact as well as points of separation. In "The Burning Child," the last poem in her first book, which follows "The Dahlia Gardens," Clampitt compares the plight of the relatives of Harold Korn, her longtime partner, with that of her pioneer forebears. The poem's language and syntax are difficult and tangled: this is the kind of poetry that the mature woman came to write. She thinks of the concentration camps, the cattle cars, "the shunted parceling—*links, rechts*— / in a blaspheming parody of the judgment / by the Lord of burning." This is the only poem in which Clampitt refers to the automobile accident that left Hal maimed for life, a "dim phoenix-nest of scars." Fires, and deaths by burning, are very much on her mind. His mother's people perished in the camps. The travels of Amy's American ancestors— Frank and Eva Clampitt—were by comparison modest and of their own devising. The grandparents made a different kind of journey, from Iowa to California, "where, hedged by the Pacific's lunging barricades . . . they chose / to return, were free to stay or go / back home, go anywhere at all."

Years later, replying to a woman who'd written her a fan letter, Amy says (March 6, 1987), "I don't myself feel like an exile: I just don't seem to live anywhere in particular, anymore." She has just quoted W. H. Auden on Henry James: "It is sometimes necessary for sons to leave the family hearth; it may well be necessary at least for intellectuals to leave their country as it is for children to leave their homes, not to get away from them, but to re-create them." It is the language of "A Procession at Candlemas" with a different inflection. Traveling, or creating and then re-creating a home, the poet remains conscious of her place and her time.

By necessity, by chance, by choice, people are on the move. Some relocate freely, others against their will. This is the story of the whole world, but it has a special resonance for an American girl. Following her three months working with European refugees even before the hideous machinery of the Holocaust went into high gear, young Amy Clampitt enacted a pilgrimage of her own, a distinctly American one. She alit for Manhattan. She became one of the countless eager young people, fresh from the country, the farm, the small town, the university (not to mention millions of immigrants from abroad, sailing by the Statue of Liberty as they entered New York harbor), whom E. B. White was to describe in his classic essay "Here Is New York," written in the hot postwar summer of 1948.

The United States had not yet entered the war that was already raging on the European continent. Nothing would be the same again. Amy was twenty-one. She wanted to become a New Yorker. And she did. She, too, would never be the same, but she carried Iowa with her on her journey. In a long, rambling poem from the mid-1970s, "Crossing the Jersey Meadows," she remembers her father and her native landscape, pairing them:

> I think
> of my father, in so many ways
> the best of men,
> bottled up all his life
> by constricting notions of perfectability,
> an ambuscade against animals, against the dread
> of emptiness, the prairie space, of the
> nameless: the dread that dries up sorrow.

Vastness and emptiness become synonyms and antonyms. The first, considered as plenitude, offers the possibilities of richness to counter the threats of the second. And Clampitt's poem continues, recalling the "roving anomie, the quiet / cousin of tornadoes' devouring suction, / archetype of prairie terrors."

One understands that the richness of available things, even the fact of merely listing or articulating them, may protect against emptiness. Such lists will become a hallmark—troublesome to some of her later readers—of Clampitt's mature style. She says that "names" can appease the terrors:

> . . . rosebreasted
> grosbeak, tanager, cedar waxwing;
> vervail, dogtooth, hickory, walnut,
> locust, osage orange—currency of names
> passed from hand to hand, from one generation
> to another, pledge and token of
> community.

Amy knew plants and birds. Her lists of these things and others gave her a way of staving off or rebelling against the threats and unnamed fears that haunted her. She finds emptiness; she fills it. Both her anxieties and her accumulated, compensatory *things* belonged to her Iowa childhood. And the need for at least a "token of community" adds a link to the chain constructed from Amy's strong Quaker spirit. Feeling herself an outsider, she also craved and frequently felt a sense of belonging: a Quaker meeting and a long bus ride in the presence of strangers are two versions of the same thing. They combine intermittent speech with more extended silences. Toward the end of her life, when she was conducting workshops and classes all over the country, Amy received a letter from Ann Knox in Hancock, Maryland, one of her students in a seminar at Florida's Atlantic Center for the Arts. Knox wrote gratefully (February 16, 1992), "You gave of your time and thought with unstinting generosity, you created a cohesive community among the writers and set high standards of craft and criticism." "Cohesive community" is the phrase that shines.

In *The Kingfisher* Clampitt includes a charming but gritty sonnet that, in its brevity, condenses many of her feelings about her home state. "The Local Genius" (the Latin phrase *genius loci* means "the spirit of the place") roots everything Iowan in the soil itself. The author's note offers her indebtedness to two predecessors, the poet Charles Olson and the prose writer Glenway Westcott, who had differing but complementary takes on the Midwest. And she salutes the inventor of and, until early in the twenty-first century, the manufacturer of the washing machine:

> SPACE (spelled large) the central fact:
> thus Charles Olson. For Glenway Wescott,
> the state of mind of those who never liked
> to live where they were born—all that
> utilitarian muck down underfoot,
> brown loam, debris of grassroots packed
> thicker than anywhere else on the planet—
> soil, so much of it that the central fact
>
> must be, after all, not SPACE but DIRT,
> forever present as the sense of guilt
> washday alone can hope to expiate.
> With what Will Voss of Davenport
> invented, the Maytags of Newton built
> a dynasty on getting rid of it.

As if to drive her point home, and into her reader's ears, Clampitt makes sure that all fourteen lines end with a hard "t" sound: DIRT is the poem's leitmotif, thematically and phonically. Everything Iowan emanates from "muck down underfoot" and "grassroots packed," which cry out to be, like "guilt," expiated. Can one ever be free of sin, of filth?

In her interview with Jean Hanff Korelitz, Clampitt borrowed a formulation from the essayist Bill Holm describing two kinds of imagination: Woods Eye and Prairie Eye. The first sees small things in great detail; the second sees things in broad focus. She realized that, born to one landscape and one kind of eye, she later came to require the other. Larger spaces and panoramic vision; smaller spaces and closer focus: the woman and the writer would come to know both.

In an unpublished poem from 1975, "The Arrow in My Mind," Clampitt tries to retrieve from memory her sense, as a child during the Depression, of both poverty and relative privilege. She calls herself "a hippie / before her time," and remembers wanting only

> . . . a little space to be free in, to enjoy the view
> of where I came from, to understand what I could
> of that wrinkled cuneiform—trade routes and saltlicks,
> the frayed interweave of watersheds and genealogy—so many
> sad wheelbarrows trundling upward
> to nowhere but the cemetery.

She got her wish—a little room on West 12th Street with a view that allowed her to look back and look out—and she came both to accept and understand her native soil and genetic inheritance. The wheelbarrows of her country girlhood would indeed lead uphill, not to a prairie cemetery but to an artist's lifework.

———

I like to imagine that Amy's departure from Iowa in 1941 bore some similarities to mine, more than three-quarters of a century later, after my short visit to New Providence. She would not have left her home state by air but by automobile (if her parents drove her) or, more probably, by train. On that early Sunday morning in late spring, I drove along back highways to the Des Moines airport. On a thoroughly deserted road, I stopped my rented car about a hundred yards from a snug farmhouse that looked like an advertisement for cozy domestic comfort, in a landscape with nothing but farms and more farms, punctuated by barns, silos, and wind turbines—lean and stately, gleaming and unmoving. No people were in sight. Perhaps they were sleeping in, or getting ready for church. Amy would not have seen modern wind machines, although in her day many Iowa towns still had nineteenth-century wooden windmills. Cedardale Farm had one to pump water. Everything else would have been familiar to her. I stepped out of the car. There was no sound but the wind. The clean air smelled of meadow grass and hay, with a lacing of horse manure.

As I surveyed prairie that had been converted to farmland, I felt a

grateful appreciation for a wide, formerly pristine beauty now culti-
vated and plotted. I looked with a Prairie Eye. That was also Amy's
eye, or so she might have thought, until she made her escape east.
In a kind of reverse irony, Clampitt the poet admitted late in life
that she could not write about the Midwest until she had written
about Maine. She needed both spatial and temporal separation from
her native spot in order to retrieve and then use it. The similari-
ties between the two populations in Iowa and Down East Maine—
hardworking and unpretentious people both—combined with the
differences between the two landscapes to open up something in
her that had been tamped down for decades. She had not realized
that she already possessed a Woods Eye as well as a Prairie Eye. In
1941 she made a getaway from her native soil, but the precise details
of childhood, farm, and nature remained in her mind until the end.

◄ OBSCURITY ►

PART 1: 1941–1951

Amy arrived in Manhattan to attend graduate school in the fall of 1941. University classes began, traditionally, after Labor Day. She attended Columbia University, in some sort of master's degree program in literature. We have no information about what courses she took, whom she met, what else she did. (Decades later, when she began publishing in *The New Yorker*, she discovered that her editor, Howard Moss, had been at Columbia around the same time. Like her, he had found the whole experience—with the exception of the Yeats scholar William York Tindall—entirely uncongenial.) She dropped out, dispirited, after one or possibly two terms.

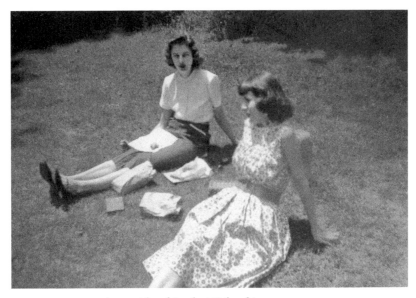

Amy with a friend at Columbia, c. 1941–42

Something else also happened before the first term ended: the Japanese attacked Pearl Harbor on December 7. The nation then began to prepare for war.

We have two addresses for Amy in Morningside Heights near Columbia, rooms she occupied in graduate school and shortly after. And we also have a letter, dated October 1943, to Amy from a Grinnell friend named Jack Wilson, announcing his graduation from flight school at Childress Army Air Force base in Texas. It is addressed to her at 161 West 10th Street. She had moved downtown. She shared the apartment with her friend Cecile Starr (Boyajian), a southerner whom she met at Columbia. This place is today a shabby apartment building next door to Julius', the Village's oldest bar. Gordon Kahn and Al Hirschfeld in *The Speakeasies of 1932* described Julius' as "a madhouse without keepers . . . jammed to the squirming point every hour of the night." Ten years later it was pretty much the same. Amy wasn't in New Providence anymore. For reasons we do not know, she did not stay on 10th Street too long. She moved two blocks north and farther west. At some point in the late fall of 1943, Amy took occupancy of the small studio apartment at 354 West 12th Street, near the Hudson River, that would be her home for more than three decades, and which she held on to even after she moved in with Harold Korn on the Upper East Side in 1973.

When I was preparing the Clampitt letters for publication two decades ago, I asked myself many questions. Many of these stayed with me as I was writing this biography. What was it like to be a young, anonymous "career" woman with literary dreams in Manhattan, and with World War II going on, as soldiers and sailors shipped out and then, in 1945, returned to postwar American prosperity? Did Amy ever meet Madeleine L'Engle or Leonard Bernstein, both of whom lived near her on West 12th Street in the early 1940s? Or Djuna Barnes and E. E. Cummings on Patchin Place, down the block from her louche West 10th Street digs? I wonder whether she ran with the Village crowd described by Anatole Broyard in *Kafka Was the Rage*: "Nineteen forty-six was a good time—perhaps the best time—in the twentieth century. The war was over and there was a terrific sense of coming back, of repossessing life. Rents were cheap, restaurants were cheap, and it seemed to me that happiness itself might be cheaply had." What was her version of Wordsworth's "Bliss was it in that dawn to be alive, / But to be young was very heaven"?

Amy's motives for getting to Manhattan were the obvious ones. She wanted to be in a city. She wanted a large cultural mecca and a major university. She hungered for things she had only studied or dreamed about. The prairie dweller wanted to live near the ocean. And she also wanted what all the young people who have set their sights on Manhattan have wanted: the excitement and pleasures not to be found on some version of (in her case) a farm in the middle of America. In a late poem ("The Halloween Parade," *Westward*), she mentions the thrill of being

swept away, caught up in a spate
of appearances, gorgeous, gorgonish,
déraciné—O saturnalian
    anonymity of cities!

Let it be said: though our grandeurs
were tacky, at least we were honest:
what we looked for was no more
than a license to be silly
    about what matters . . .

She wanted displays of flamboyance as well as intellect. She wanted to let loose, to abandon herself and find herself, rollicking as well as studying, opening up, letting go in the multiple directions of which idealistic and energetic youth is capable. She was as high-minded as Henry James's Isabel Archer, but with a streak of hedonism.

Amy was aware of her own eccentricity from early youth. She wanted companionship or at least evidence that she was not unique. If she was a misfit, she wanted to be around other misfits, with whom she might, paradoxically, fit in. She needed to experience the abundance of human weirdness that she thought was unavailable among the Iowa farmers she knew. In an interview she allowed that "the Midwest may not produce any more misfits than any other region, but just about anyone with small confidence but large imaginings is going to be a misfit out there. New York is, of course, full of such misfits—which makes it not the most comfortable place for any of us to settle in to."

In another poem from *Westward* she describes an odd neighbor in the Village, whom she met during her religious and political periods in the 1960s. This woman became a friend of sorts. Like so many lonely obscure people, she died at home and vanished from the scene. She was a cat lady, an alcoholic, "Old? Young? She was of no age." The woman was of her time, but also of no time, "impervious to trends," and in the poem she has no name. Amy, at this point a middle-aged New Yorker with no particular accomplishments, could identify:

> Unclassifiable castoffs, misfits, marginal cases:
> when you're one yourself, or close to it, there's
> a reassurance in proving you haven't gone
> under by taking up with somebody odder than you are.
>   ("A HEDGE OF RUBBER TREES")

The poem is set in 1968. The West Village was changing but it also resembled what it had been a quarter century before, when young Amy moved to it. And Amy, too, had changed, but she could still sympathize with the woman who was inside "getting gently blotto." Had she met the woman in 1943, she might have been fascinated and enchanted rather than saddened and threatened by her anonymity and gradual decay; by the glimmers of an exotic past erased by the loss of hope; by the diminishment of expectations; and by a mandolin the woman took down from the mantel, and on which she played Italian airs "through a warm fuddle of sauterne." The poem is layered in time: first the events themselves, in the past, and then the recording of them twenty years later. Clampitt must have realized her good fortune in not having turned into an alcoholic cat lady, living behind "a potted hedge of / rubber trees," with a profusion of cockroaches, memories, and unrealized dreams.

Mostly, we must infer what Amy was doing, what she was up to in her early twenties. We have little evidence of her comings, goings, and doings between 1941, when she moved to Manhattan, and 1946, when she was firmly established at Oxford University Press, having started in 1943 as a secretary/receptionist, as young women did in those days and for decades afterwards. Her first job was clerical, in the Bible Department. She helped with *One Fourteen*, the monthly OUP newsletter (the address of the press was 114 Fifth Avenue). In 1944, we know that she visited her parents in Mexico. They were working with a Quaker public service project. During her two weeks there, she also traveled through the country with her brother Philip, ten years her junior. By 1946 she had become promotions director for college textbooks at Oxford. Her studies at Columbia, her jobs and friendships before OUP: all of these particulars will probably remain lost in the abysm of time. After leaving the university, she worked for a short time at Cyanamid, a chemical company. Doing what and for how long? Something boring in the office, probably. An undated letter from her friend Joe Wall, writing from Bogotá, Colombia, congratulated her on her new Oxford position, and for "getting out of the Cyanamid game."

We have a sheaf of letters from Roy and Pauline to their daughter in her early Manhattan years. These are models of stylistic clarity and efficiency as well as expressions of parental concern. They also confirm conventional gender relations. The always-frugal parents saved postage costs by including their separate letters in a single envelope. Sometimes they even shared paper, Roy typing on one side, Pauline writing by hand on the other. Roy was typically high-minded. On March 7, 1943, he worries that his eldest child may be too invested in the "froth" of *The New Yorker*, and urges upon her more serious pursuits:

> It is no excuse to blame surroundings of other people, or circum-
> stances of wealth or the lack of it. It seems to me, as I've sug-
> gested to you before, that grandpa's life is evidence of the fact
> that the greatest achievement in life is in becoming a personality
> of significance—just *being* the kind of individual God intended
> one to be. In the case of my grandfather Clampitt it seems to me
> that it would have been quite easy for him to have blamed his
> stepfather's cruelty to him as sufficient reason for his never get-
> ting anywhere. Instead, he left home at fourteen and went out to
> make his own way. In his case it was not so much the material

wealth he accumulated as the type of character he developed that really counted.

Good old American self-confidence is at the heart of Roy's cautionary hopes.

For the most part, the Clampitts' weekly letters overflowed with the details of rural life: there's much talk of threshing, sowing, pig slaughtering, family and town gossip. These were also the stuff of their earlier letters to Amy at Grinnell: the rhythms of the seasons and the work of the farm, weather reports, the latest church doings, the growth of the younger children.

The same year—1943—that Amy was leaving Cyanamid for OUP, Pauline wrote with cautiousness that matched that of her husband, referring to a beau of her daughter's who is otherwise unmentioned in Amy's letters or journals:

> Howard may be a perfectly fine person, and his paintings equally fine, and it's all right to be friends, but it's my opinion one should be a little careful about accepting gifts and attentions from such a person, under the circumstances. At best, I'd go a little slow . . . Hasty love affairs are the rule now in war times, but the same should be guarded against, unless one expects to try marriage four or five times like some.

In the same envelope there's a note from Frank's wife, Grandmother Eva, to Roy and Pauline, which mentions Amy's deaf boyfriend (presumably Howard, but unnamed). Grandma says, "I would advise her not to get too intimate with a deaf person."

Roy and Pauline visited Amy in Manhattan in September 1943, six months after she had begun her work at OUP. Was this the trip that some family members remember as the time that Amy was to be married, only to back down on her way to the altar? Probably. The strongest, virtually inescapable, candidate for the role of Amy's New York fiancé is the man whom Pauline mentions by his first name, Howard Mitcham (1917–1996), a writer and artist from Mississippi, who was a childhood friend of Shelby Foote and Walker Percy. He made his way to Greenwich Village before decamping later for Provincetown and New Orleans, where he became a chef and cookbook writer of note. A piece from the *Mississippi Sideboard* in 2014 refers to him as "a brilliant, stone-deaf, hard-drinking bohemian, raconteur and bon vivant." There could not have been too many deaf and alcoholic bohemian artists named Howard on the Village scene in the 1940s. Mitcham was a difficult man. Assuming he is the right Howard, he certainly would have appealed to several sides of Amy's youthful and enthusiastic personality. For one thing, he was a provincial outsider, like her. In addition, he was an artist—and her first ambition as a child was to become a painter. He was the director of the now legendary Jane Street Gallery, New York's first artists' collective, which lasted from 1943 to 1950. Nell Blaine and Larry Rivers were among the young painters there, many of whom had studied with Hans Hofmann. It is not inconceivable that Amy met Mitcham at the gallery, virtually around the corner from her home, or in the company of other artists they both knew.

Or Howard may have come to her through Cecile Starr and other southern contacts, perhaps Lieutenant Patrick Quinn, a college friend of Amy's with connections to LSU in Baton Rouge, who corresponded with Amy during the war about books and art. Or by way of another man, from Shreveport and New Orleans, whom apparently she never met but only corresponded with in 1941–42, mysteriously signing himself Jpsiv, or "Your love slave, John." Maybe the southerners in Manhattan banded together, with their ranks extending to other folks back home.

Because of his deafness, Howard must have struck a chord in Amy's nascent Quaker capacity to root for the underdog. He would have been powerful, exotic, and needy in equal measure, a cause she might want to take up. In order for them to understand each other, Amy might have had to learn to use sign language, and Howard to read it. He might have also needed to learn lip-reading. The enterprise of signing might have appealed to her: it was as if Eros were to be bound to language. But reading lips or signs, according to reports from family members decades later, would not have been congenial to Howard. He lacked the patience. He merely bellowed at other people and expected them to respond to him. Those same reports suggest that he was also cantankerous, rowdy, and exuberant to the point of dangerousness when drunk. He was more than a merely charming eccentric southerner. Amy was quickly disabused of her infatuation, perhaps by other people, but more probably by her own nagging internal doubts. We do know, from a remark she made decades later to her friend Karen Chase, that she called off the wedding at the last minute, saying that she had come to her senses. Her prudent, cautious parents were relieved.

So much for the earliest Manhattan years of an Iowa transplant, years tentative and exploratory for her, and shadowy for anyone hoping to assemble pieces from her past.

———

Once Amy got to OUP, however, and began making her way up the ranks, we can learn a lot about what she was doing, professionally if not privately.

The Clampitt papers include a sparkling trove of ordinary work reports that Amy wrote during her five years in a managerial capacity at the press. These took the form of a "Weekly Bulletin" (later called "The Weekly Bugle"), the OUP in-house newsletter to the press's sales representatives and other staff members. Each one, a page or two long, was composed on a manual typewriter, mimeographed, and then distributed to the staff. Each is dated and addressed "TO The Representatives," and "FROM ac." (The minuscules remained until the end, perhaps a tongue-in-cheek acknowledgment of her lowly status.) All of them include facts and figures about what was going on in the office and in the field. They serve up tidbits of office gossip, and vignettes of the world of books in an energized New York. Each contains glimpses into the greater cultural life of Manhattan as it settled into postwar normality. Each showcases the style and the quiet wit of its author.

On September 26, 1946, Clampitt observes, "The Oxford dinner is not the only event this week. The Rodeo is in town. If you had been here yesterday morning you would have seen us hanging from the windows for a glimpse of Gene Autry, riding a white horse at the head of a parade down Fifth Avenue." Two weeks later, she has finished *All the King's Men* and breezily observes of Robert Penn

Warren that "there is no doubt that he can do something besides understand poetry" (a waggish reference to the man who with Cleanth Brooks coauthored the money-making textbook *Understanding Poetry*, a staple of classrooms for decades). The English major is coming into her own as a literary critic. She also tells us what's playing on Broadway, what she has seen, and what she has regretfully missed. She is putting an old-fashioned liberal arts education and a lifetime of reading to excellent use. This is cultural reportage by a young woman just beginning to feel at home in the metropolis and eagerly taking advantage of whatever she can afford to see on her modest salary.

The newsletters open a window, actually several windows. They show us Clampitt as a natural writer, growing in confidence as she began to loosen up the style of her reportage. All of them display insouciant, unofficial authority. (Think of what most typical office memoranda, today as well as yesterday, sound like.) As the years go by, the letters contain more weather reports (a subject always dear to her Iowa farmgirl heart) and personal observations. Culture starts to predominate over facts and figures. It's as if Amy has begun to treat her job as a source of self-expression, of fun. At the start, she even makes a prescient commentary, as though unknowingly predicting her future as a published poet: "This is volume 1, number 1 of a limited-edition bulletin which is to appear each Thursday, just like *The New Yorker*, in an attempt to keep you all informed on matters of current interest. I can't promise that there will be any cartoons, at least not *regularly*, but we'll hope at least to keep you fairly well up to date." *The New Yorker* is on her mind from the beginning.

The bulletins are lists, accumulations of data, preludes to the verbal plenitude that we find in Clampitt's poems forty years later. From both the banality of office life and the material deprivation in her lived life, she could turn facts and figures into lively, life-enhancing writing. In this sense, she resembled some of the poets who became her literary models. John Keats, whom she loved in junior high school, was poor. Gerard Manley Hopkins, whom she discovered in college, lived a life of Jesuitical self-abnegation and artistic, verbal extravagance. Emily Dickinson, not materially deprived, willfully isolated herself from the world, even within the bosom of a close, loving family. These poets were all enamored of words, which they poured forth (in the case of Keats and Hopkins) or used more restrainedly but with equal force and mystery (as Dickinson did). Deprivation—whether inflicted or elected—engendered gestures of compensation.

Amy had fled from the farm to make a new life, but that life always included those she left behind, to whom she wrote frequently and at length, in an age when a letter, stamped and mailed, was the major means of personal communication. Her coworkers, recipients of her bulletins, came to constitute another audience. Decades before she published anything, she always had her readers.

Here's some of what we know she was able to see and hear, on her limited worker's wages, during the five years at her office post: Rodgers and Hammerstein's *Oklahoma!*; Lotte Lehmann singing Schubert's *Winterreise*; Elisabeth Bergner in *The Duchess of Malfi*; Gian-Carlo Menotti's *The Medium* and *The Telephone*; Eva Le Gallienne as the Queen of Hearts in a production of *Alice in Wonderland*; Arthur Miller's *All My Sons* and *Death of a Salesman*; Katherine Cornell in *Antony and Cleopatra*; John Gielgud in an adaptation of *Crime and Punishment*; the world premiere of Balanchine's *Orpheus* at City Center, and other Ballet Theatre (precursor of New York City Ballet) performances with Maria Tallchief and Tanaquil Le Clercq; the harpsichordist Wanda Landowska ("that ageless musical institution, dressed in purple velvet with a train"); Sadler's Wells at the Old Met with Moira Shearer; *Gentlemen Prefer Blondes*; and countless movies, museum shows, and the occasional grand opera at the Met. And this is only the stuff she chooses to mention. It may come as a modest surprise to learn that, according to brother Philip and his wife, Hanna, Amy's favorite performing art was the ballet, the one that most inhibits or silences language, and the one for which she had the least aptitude. But perhaps this should not be at all surprising. A woman whose primary resources were linguistic was searching for comfort and stimulation, part of the time, far away from language.

She also tells her workers what she's been reading: Arthur Koestler's *Thieves in the Night*; Arnold Toynbee (a big OUP bestselling author); E. M. Forster (who's in town to visit the office—might she have caught a glimpse of him in the corridors?); *War and Peace*; Lionel Trilling's *The Middle of the Journey*. Of Malcolm Lowry's *Under the Volcano* she observes, "He can describe a cat catching a dragonfly, or set down an uncomfortable conversation, or get inside the mind of an alcoholic, in an uncanny way, never seeming to lose track of exactly what he wants to do, and there are few enough people that get books published whom you can say that of."

We also watch Amy making a literary judgment that shows how even the savviest people in publishing occasionally get things wrong. Consider the following, dated April 25, 1947:

> I am filled with sadistic glee at the moment because Simon and Schuster have at last produced a book which appears to be a real turkey, and Book-of-the-Month, what is more, took it as one of their May selections. I refer to a thing called AURORA DAWN, and I have yet to see a review which didn't pronounce it unbearable. Perhaps the revolution has occurred, the man has bitten the cur, and the BOMC can no longer be sure it is the oracle. All of which is extremely impolite, as befits the state of bookmen's tempers these days. But I wait eagerly to see what the irrepressible people at S&S will do; I'm sure they'll think of something.

The book in question was the first novel of Herman Wouk. It launched his immensely successful commercial career. A bit later, in a letter to her brother Philip (November 28, 1955), she refers to Wouk's latest bestseller, *Marjorie Morningstar*, as "a soggy and frowzy tale which arrives at no better conclusion than that none of it should ever have happened." So much for literary judgments. Thousands of book buyers didn't share this sentiment. Amy was decidedly highbrow and high-minded in her tastes, at least until the 1960s when barriers, along with tastes and various kinds of classifications, began to break, change, merge, and get rearranged.

In addition to weather, culture, literature, the goings-on about town, Amy found time to comment on real estate, that perennial Manhattan phenomenon. In a report dated May 18, 1950, she depicts the changes wrought by the postwar building boom with an eye for detail, a wry wit, and a poet's gift for metaphor:

All over town buildings are coming down and new ones going up, so nobody should be too surprised to learn that the landscape around Fourteenth Street is likewise being altered. A large chunk of fairly antique brownstone just across from the Thirteenth Street Schraffts' on Fifth Avenue is the latest to submit to the demolition contractors. One by one, Sheed and Ward [an important publishing house], the Country Dance Society of America (whoever *they* were, anyway; they had several pairs of antlers on their wall, for one thing), a basement luncheonette, an art supply store, and one of the unique Fourteenth Street emporia specializing in bridesmaids' attire have disappeared. The bridesmaid place was the last to go; it hung on tenaciously until one side of the building had actually started to come down. Now at lunch time there are crowds lined up in front of Hearn's watching the large-scale termite activity. The men engaged in it, perched fearlessly along the top of the façade, look at the first moment rather like a row of figures along the roof of a classical temple. I am going to miss them, I expect. So far, nobody seems to know what they are making way for.

It was ever thus. As she says in "Real Estate," a poem from her second volume, *What the Light Was Like*, "Something there is that doesn't / love a Third Avenue tenement, / that wants it gone the way the El / went." Or, more cosmically, consider the title of a poem in *Westward*, her penultimate volume: "Nothing Stays Put." In Iowa, barbed wire could contain the livestock but not the wind; in Manhattan, nothing can overcome the force of human greed, however much one tries to resist it. One must never expect constancy, let alone permanence. Commerce always wins, as it did at the end of Amy's life when her beloved West 12th Street studio apartment was converted into co-ops and she had to give up her long-held lease.

Although Amy was in part a homebody, she also refused to stay put when she had the money or opportunity to get away. Travel was relatively cheap. The poles of her life started to come into focus as she reached the age of thirty. Home and abroad, domesticity and travel, staying put and moving on: she had already made one great move, from Iowa to Manhattan, but a new rhythm now began. Hav-

Amy with Barbara Blay, one of her hosts, London, 1949

ing experienced the pleasures of England for a month in 1949, after she won an essay contest sponsored by OUP, Amy was eager to return for more. That first trip brought to life everything the eager American midwesterner had been reading about for years. The past became real, and actual. On April 26, 1951, she bade farewell to the office and the staff:

> This was going to be one of those elegantly phrased valedictories I suppose everybody plans to toss off some day or other—at least that was the way I planned it, but no such luck. For one thing, there are all sorts of shirtless, singing men (I never saw such a cheerful lot of builders) banging around with a lot of galvanized metal pipes—very mysterious, but not a bit quiet—and they make the collecting of ordinary thoughts, not to mention the composition of elegant phrases, rather more than I am capable of. Anyhow, that will be my excuse. Besides, I have been hopping around all day from typewriter to typewriter, and in my usual fashion, only more so, starting half a dozen things without finishing any of them.

Her "hopping around" defined much of Amy's animated, often impulsive manner throughout her life. And that hopping was now to take on a larger meaning as she embarked on larger journeys.

———

Before we accompany Amy on her European trips, we should take a look at her at home on West 12th Street, out of the office as well as in it, through the reminiscences of her friends and coworkers. One acquaintance, Lorraine Wheeler, knew Amy through OUP. She wrote to her in 1990 after Amy had become a famous poet:

> We saw one another only a few times after we met in 1947, but I thought about you over the years and remembered you vividly. That was why I wanted to know if the Amy Clampitt in the New Yorker was you. I remembered you as kind and sensitive and very attractive in a distinctive way, a way I liked and envied. I was very much a theater buff in those days, went to see everything . . . and you had a quality and a look I associated with the actresses I admired. And I learned at the reading . . . that you are indeed an actress, who holds and dazzles an audience.

Wheeler could still remember her coworker decades after she had last seen her: thin, tall, striking, birdlike. Everyone else remembered her that way too.

Another friend, named Carrie, wrote Amy a letter in 1983 after seeing her poems, which she said she did not understand. We know nothing about this woman, neither her last name nor how and when she met Amy, but here's what she wrote about their meeting in 1949. She thought at the time:

> I may never see Amy again, but I'll remember her . . . Somehow I knew that pretty little head was filled with ideas—beautiful, loving ideas that would express themselves one fine day. And the words would sound like music.

"That pretty little head" may be a cliché, either unintentionally dismissive, or unlikely as a depiction of Amy, but the writer's sentiment and prediction are entirely accurate.

There must have been other Carries who came and went. More

important were the people who remained in Amy's life. The oldest of those friends was Phoebe Hoss (1926–2017), who met her in 1946 or 1947. Everyone was living on thirty-five dollars a week, more or less. Amy was in publicity at OUP, and Phoebe worked there as a copy editor until 1949, but stayed friends with Amy until the end of her life. She remembered her colleague as "always so excited about things." And yet, for all the closeness, there was still secrecy:

> She didn't talk about herself, her own feelings, although her feelings were always flying out for flowers and nature. What was going on inside her in respect to other people was a mystery, largely . . .
>
> I took her and a friend up to Bennington, where one of my sisters was graduating. It was May and it was absolutely gorgeous, and it was as though spring had been sprung, and Amy was just all over like a bee or a butterfly.

Amy could open up like a butterfly; Amy could also close down. The two comments above show two facets of her being.

As it always has done for lucky New Yorkers, spring signals the chance for release and escape to the country, the shore, a mountain greenery, any place that counters indoor urban life with outdoor pleasures. Amy knew the names of flowers, of birds. Central Park, at her doorstep in the 1950s when she worked at the Audubon Society on Fifth Avenue, always brimmed with the flora and fauna that she held dear. The park, like the country, meant freedom. Indoors, she held her feelings in check. Outdoors, she blossomed.

The urban life meant not only culture. It was also a setting for the private life, a room of one's own, Amy's domestic space, her apartment: a one-room studio that became a world, encompassing everything she valued. The space must have grown cramped during her decades there. Even at the start, it never possessed a Zen-like or modernist austerity. In a letter (May 14, 1982) to her old friend Rimsa Michel, a coworker in the 1950s at the Audubon Society, Amy, now cohabiting with Hal for almost a decade, is in a flurry because her apartment must be repaired and tidied up in preparation for its planned conversion to a co-op: "I've just taken everything out of the closet for the first time since I moved in." There must have been surprises waiting for her. Luckily, the co-op conversion was delayed for another decade.

The fifth-floor walk-up was a typical New York brownstone arrangement. It had two windows, looking south over a courtyard with a catalpa tree that Clampitt watched for decades. The tree became part of her West Village life; it became, we might even say, part of her. In "A Catalpa Tree on West Twelfth Street," a late poem dispatched as a Christmas card, she wonders about the enduring tree, referring to its growth as "the resurgence of this / climbing tentpole, frilled and stippled / yet again with bloom / to greet the solstice":

> What year was it it over-
> took the fire escape? The
> roof's its next objective.

She could measure her own growth, and her long tenure on West 12th Street, through the years of watching this hardy survivor, her arboreal twin. It became for her the equivalent of the ailanthus tree in Betty Smith's 1943 novel *A Tree Grows in Brooklyn*, a sturdy symbol of flourishing in the least likely of places.

Between the windows was Amy's dropleaf table, a place for both eating and writing. She had a manual typewriter. A working fireplace faced the all-purpose table. A single bed occupied a space underneath many book- and record-filled shelves. By day it doubled as a sofa, seating for guests. Her brothers also remembered a "camp cot" or a "daybed," perhaps a second couch stored underneath something else, and pulled out for the occasional overnight visitor. An old-fashioned corded rotary phone was never replaced during almost fifty years of occupancy. Beneath a wooden counter were other shelves, unsteady at best, for clothing and the storage of miscellaneous items. A single large closet, a small four-burner stove, a tiny fridge, a bathroom: that was all anyone needed.

Throughout her life, Amy always preferred to write in front of a window, looking out at and taking in her surroundings. A window frames a scene and grants access to the world beyond. It also invites the world to enter the apartment and the soul of the writer. She loved being near the water, with tugboats hooting on the Hudson. And she loved, equally, crawling onto the fire escape to watch the ocean liners come in. In a famous letter, Keats once wrote that "if a Sparrow come before my window, I take part in its existence [*sic*] and pick about the Gravel" (to Benjamin Bailey, November 22, 1817). His careful twentieth-century reader always kept him in mind: Amy's friend Karen Chase remembered her saying that, watching from her studio apartment window, she would see a sparrow that "used to come around all the time and she would look for the sparrow . . . she talked about it as if she was totally friends with the sparrow, and then one day the sparrow stopped coming around and she said, 'I knew it couldn't last.'"

Her brother and sister-in-law Larry and Jeanne remembered this apartment—its layout, its haphazard, inexpensive furnishings, the catalpa tree—and their time at West 12th Street, from visits that extended over decades. Jeanne said there was a balcony with plants, but she was mistaken: it was only a fire escape. (To some Manhattan real estate agents and promoters today this would count as "outdoor space.") For the family, both this apartment and the "bigger" one—a genuine one-bedroom she shared with Hal after 1973—reflected Amy's character and her behavior. Domesticity, energy, and perpetual enthusiasm defined her hospitality, creating a kind of eternal youthfulness, until the very end:

> She was really sort of ageless. She always looked to be Amy and young, and the littler girl was always there . . . probably it's the face but partly the giggle and the excitement about whatever it was that had just happened that really appealed to her. I never thought of her as being old, maybe unless it was seeing her after . . . chemo, a month or so before she died . . . My memory of Amy is a very lively person with limitless energy when it came to getting something going someplace or creating a meal. She somehow, with very limited resources . . . created some delightful meals for us right there in her apartment.

For her relatives or friends who when they visited Manhattan would sleep on the army cot (or later on the fold-out living room couch on

East 65th Street), she made even a tiny studio a world in miniature. The apartment was a place of self-contained merriment.

Hanna Clampitt, wife of Philip, also remembered her sister-in-law as a skillful seamstress and as an improvising cook who never relied on recipes. In many ways she had absorbed her mother's sense for home economics, or, rather, economies. And as a counter to the reticence of the father and grandfather whom she venerated, she seemed to have developed—perhaps as a result of the liberation offered by Manhattan—an exuberance that never abandoned her. After a decade as a sophisticated New Yorker, in a letter to Philip (February 16, 1953) she seems exasperated by the buttoned-up side of fearful, timid people:

> Why are people so afraid of being enthusiastic? I don't think it's so much laziness as the fear of turning out to be wrong. But who knows what is right, anyway? If one only feels the *right* things one might as well not feel anything. Of course one is usually wrong. I've been being enthusiastic and getting knocked down and proved wrong for some time now, so that I'm practically used to it.

Later in life, academic literary eminences like Harold Bloom and Helen Vendler said that in their rare in-person dealings with Amy they found her quiet, deferential, respectful, perhaps a bit intimidated by the attention of such august admirers. At home in the West Village, on her own turf, Amy could allow herself to be unencumbered.

Between Amy's death in 1994 and today, the West Village has undergone the kind of predictable, perhaps inevitable transformation that has made living there all but impossible for young people who want to get a toehold in downtown, bohemian Manhattan. A 2019 description of her old property, written by the real estate people, gives a sense of the new style:

> Situated on a cobblestone segment of West 12th Street between Washington and Greenwich Streets, 350–354 West 12th Street

is a row of three contiguous walk-up apartment houses, joined together both in their design and as a single cooperative. These three buildings were built in 1875 by architect William Joel, with detailed beaux-arts elements from stoop to sky. The first floor windows and doors appear as part of an arcade, while the second floor windows are topped with ornate pediments. 350–354 West 12th St are crowned by a matching unbroken cornice punctuated by carved scroll brackets, bringing them all together in a wonderful ensemble which remains much the same as it was a century and a half ago.

For residents, the rear of the buildings are [*sic*] joined together by a well-manicured private garden. With these building [*sic*] standing 5 stories each, some higher floor apartments can enjoy the feeling of being "above the view break," since neighbors across the street stand just two and three stories high. Many apartments feature decorative fireplaces and quaint six-over-six windows that take in great light. The buildings do not allow pets, and there is a full-time super on staff.

The inflated sales pitch would have repelled Amy the woman and Clampitt the writer. When she was on West 12th Street, "quaintness" was not a bankable, advertisable commodity, and fireplaces were not merely "decorative." On a practical front, air-conditioning was certainly not part of her life, as it was not for most Manhattanites until window units became popular, well after the war. During the summer, many New Yorkers routinely slept on fire escapes in the row houses and tenements that constituted the bulk of the city's housing units. Late in her life, Amy recalled to her friend Karen Chase that during a typical sweltering Saturday afternoon in midsummer, "I'd open all the windows, pull my bed into the middle of the room, take off all my clothes, lie down and read *Anna Karenina*."

Only a person who leads a life steeped in literature will find physical relief from torrid heat by reimagining herself back into the snow of nineteenth-century Tsarist Russia.

Amy entertained. She cooked. She was part of an ever-changing circle of artists and literary people, some men (including a gay male couple, unthinkable in Iowa) but mostly women, and she felt eager, as young people do, to try on new roles, finding out who she was while making herself anew. In a letter to Barbara Blay (March 5, 1950), the English woman who was her unofficial host during her 1949 trip to England, Amy is delighted to report a Christmas gift from her parents, a sewing machine: "at least I did launch the thing with something of a flourish—one evening I had a sewing machine warming, like a house-warming, you know, to which everybody was required to bring something to sew on. And though a good deal of the work was done by hand, since only one person could use the machine at a time, it seems to have been a success." How many seamstresses could squeeze into her flat? Even before the move to West 12th Street, she provoked a kind of envy in her former college roommate, Libby Parks Braverman back in Iowa, who wrote in the spring of 1942, "You do have the makings of a very efficient *Haus Frau* in you. Perhaps you could find a job as housekeeper somewhere. Would that appeal more than graduate school? . . . Your apartment sounds darling and I am envious because every year at this time I begin to feel the urge for domesticity—and don't say it is just part of the old sex urge."

According to Phoebe Hoss, a much-used feature of Amy's apart-

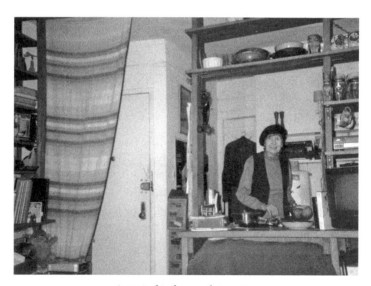

Amy in kitchen, c. late 1980s

ment was a full-length mirror mounted on the rear of the front door. When talking, Phoebe said Amy would "stand staring at herself in the mirror . . . She was very proud . . . and she really didn't recognize failings easily . . . She was a tall, rangy woman. It was as though she was talking to somebody, because she would move her head and gesture." She was, Phoebe remembered, practicing, or performing. Looking back, we might say that she was actually practicing for a performance, years before she had any professional occasion to do so. She was growing into her own as woman and as artist, creating several kinds of self.

Janet Halverson, another friend from the early days at OUP, also remembered the mirror:

> I'd be invited for dinner, and I'd sort of sit on this cot bed that was under some bookshelves that I always bumped my head on . . . And she would be across the room, where there was a sink and some sort of kitchen surfaces, and probably cooking up [a] kind of soufflé or some such thing. And all the time she's doing that, she's talking to me and looking in the mirror which is right in front of her. She's always looking in the mirror and making a soufflé, and talking to me, who[m] she can't see because she's concentrating elsewhere.

Looking at herself and concentrating elsewhere, Amy was capable of a kind of double consciousness, one rooted in the self, the other in the world.

Her friend Tom Myers said in an interview that she did, in fact, move from dramatizing herself, with friends, to dramatizing herself for the benefit of her audiences years later. He called this transformation a step in the direction of full maturity, however late in coming. In her interview with the *Paris Review*, Clampitt said that at the height of her creative maturity she required an audience to "hear" her poems as she recited them. That audience was always, initially, Hal Korn, once he came into her life. Such sharing extended to their reading aloud at home, or on vacation in Maine, the novels of Dickens or Balzac or anything else that caught their joint fancy. Things began to come together that were initially, at the start of her Manhattan life, separate: reading, writing, speaking, listening, performing, and sharing. Selfhood and solitude struck a working balance with relationship and community.

Amy's life at home was in some ways not like that of most other people. Phoebe recalled that "she really did not know how people got on, get on in real life, sort of ordinary domestic life. She was lucky enough to keep herself in a kind of cocoon for a long, long time, and have friends, but live in a very cheap apartment in the Village and live according to her principles. I think she was impatient with human frailty." We know from her letters to Philip that for most of her life she resisted the idea of psychotherapy, relying instead on the power of independent thinking, will, and guts to negotiate with the world. Phoebe saw the same obdurate resistance to matters therapeutic: was this resistance really denial, fear, or just plain midwestern stubbornness? Unworldly in many ways, Amy also found it difficult, according to her friend, to act as a nurturer in her relationships. And "there was a period when she just sort of kept herself away from the smudges of the world."

Any person can give different signals to different people, depending on circumstance and relationship. Phoebe remembered Amy as both unworldly and stern. (She also remembered her friend as rather prudish, and recalled that she did not drink much.) Family members, however, recalled a more open-spirited, open-minded person. They claimed that she never tried to impose her will, her ideas, her principles on anyone. Consciously or not, she imitated her father's respect for his oldest son's decision to join the Navy rather than join second son Richard (1925–1981) as a conscientious objector during World War II. Amy was gentler with her family, less patient with her New York contemporaries.

———

Amy was one person at home and a somewhat different one when she traveled. When one reads her travel journals, one sees that—at least when abroad—she had an impressive capacity for both alcohol and other physical pleasures.

Perhaps it all began at the office. In her office memo dated April

22, 1948, she mentions her first meeting with the man who, as far as we can ascertain, is the unnamed lover in "The Kingfisher": "Mr. Charles Johnson, a member of the Oxford younger generation, who is the son of John Johnson, retired Printer to the University, and who has been here learning how the place operates." One year later, having won the OUP essay contest, Amy went to England, returning in late May and in great high spirits. On February 23, 1950, Charles revisited New York from his perch as the new manager of the Toronto branch of the press. In between, the two spent time together in England.

Crossing the Atlantic by boat, in April 1949, Amy wrote a month-long journal of some twenty-four thousand words. A year later she took a first stab at a travel book, which she sent to Stuart Gary Brown, one of her OUP authors, for his reading pleasure. It contains her enthusiastic responses, some predictable, some original, to everything she saw. (She expanded her jottings after her second trip, two years later, and tried to publish it as a travel book, *Gargoyles, Campaniles, and Clichés*. No press accepted it.)

In the journal, she is alert to everything, beginning with herself and extending to an entire world she has known of only through reading. College has begun to pay off. The Old World is about to welcome a recent worshipper. John Keats and Henry James are on her mind, the first owing to his early death, the second to his exacting representations of Americans in Europe. Amy's writing is that of an excitable, eager tourist, taking it all in.

The journal begins on board, April 22, 1949:

Death, death, death—booming like a great bell, I heard it through the headache that came on again this morning. Half asleep in my deck chair, cradled airlessly in my bunk, I heard it throb in the motors; and in the wet dark of the empty dock I felt it wash against the ship. Probably it is the isolation of being at sea that makes it possible to breathe deeply, almost joyfully, of an air that has always been [brushing?] the poison of sorrow. Or is it simply the romanticism of thinking on the early death of a beautiful boy, death, moreover, of tuberculosis, that moist romantic disease, a death that seems to come as if wooed?

There is no privacy in tourist class except in one's own bunk. Everywhere there are befuddled old ladies, and I am not sure whether my nearness to tears, alone or with other people, is true sorrow or simply frustration at finding life on shipboard pretty dull. A great space of sleep and sorrow—endless time to dress carefully for dinner, sweep in wrapped in calculated mystery and a black cape, and find that a downy puffy old lady has one's seat at a table one is horrified to be at, since it consists entirely of puffy old ladies with the exception of one lorn young-middle-aged couple who also frantically wish themselves elsewhere.

You can tell the English girls by their complexions and their long-faced prettiness; their rather ravenous animalism. I watched two at the next table—one had sparkle, one a beautiful profile, and both faces fell when they found out that the boy who had sat down was there only because I had his seat at the table where he belonged. I found myself regarding the young men at nearby tables with perhaps an even more hungry air. There isn't much to choose from, evidently, especially if one is looking idly as for a chocolate with just the right flavor. Now it seems just a part of a scheme in which very little goes right . . .

And the next day:

I still don't know what to do if I really want to make the acquaintance of an officer—even the assistant purser, who is so accessible. But the fact is that the Irish lady and the wonderful old seafaring gentleman are probably more rewarding anyway. It's only a convention that one must have flirtations on shipboard, so it is probably one more convention I must ignore.

Is it any coincidence that she is reading James on board the ship? Or that the aspiring novelist regards all her shipmates with a satirist's gimlet eye and a psychologist's probing curiosity?

Life begins to imitate art. Lessons from books might have their payoff. Four days later she admits, "Henry James, you have served well":

As my reward for putting a Lambert Strether screen before everything, I have leaped the breach of shipboard flirtation and discovered that the assistant purser is not merely beautiful and uninteresting. He has a range of cultivation which in an American of twenty-two would seem merely precocious, but which—unless I have conjured up an entire hypothesis—in him seems a natural development. Is he a type, or not? I suspect still that he is, since no other explanation appears possible. Besides this, the vulgarity of the American [illegible; perhaps "fairies"]—there are at least four aboard—is the more appalling. Perhaps, indeed, Henry James will have served too well. Am I to end up with discontent, only, at the process I have gone through so painfully, since it can never substitute for the inborn grace of the [illegible; perhaps Binnets?] and the assistant purser? Well, at least that was one thing I came to find out.

"I came to find out": Amy is herself an almost quintessential Jamesian character, whether Isabel Archer, Daisy Miller, Christopher Newman, Lambert Strether, or Chad Newsome. She has come to find out things about herself, the world, and all the points of contact between the microcosm and the cosmos.

By the time the coast of Wales comes into view, Amy's imaginings have begun to overwhelm her, and she is grateful for landscape and scenery. She is ready to put her Jamesian desires aside: "Maybe the Lambert Strether screen should go out the window after all":

In avoiding one form of vulgarity I have only fallen into something more painful and scarcely less vulgar. My only salvation is to swallow it, vulgarity and all, like inhaling a cigarette, and trust the vertigo will pass. Must new experiences necessarily arouse the old forms? If so, I shall have to be on my guard in all kinds of ways.

And then a witty undercutting: "What would have happened if I had brought along Faulkner?" One wonders.

On land, moving from Liverpool to London, and arriving on

May 1, 1949, Amy is ready for everything that her life so far, especially her book learning and her imagination, has bred into her. Castles, gardens, landscapes and cityscapes, country lanes and city buses, churchyards and the "fragrance of lilacs in gusts," teas and biscuits, cobbled courtyards, local pubs, Oxford spires, Victorian music hall shows, food of all sorts, and, even more, humans of all sorts: the vigilant, indeed greedy eye, ear, and mind of the ever-hungry tourist take in everything. Henry James's famous advice to an aspiring novelist—"Be one on whom nothing is ever lost"—could hardly have found a more receptive, willing student.

Charles Johnson then pops up again. Amy remains baffled, and says he "constitutes the most unsettling aspect of the trip so far," even more than the assistant purser. She observes, she analyzes, all the while suppressing her own feelings in favor of concentrating on him as an object of study:

> He found me, I suspect, as hard to decipher as I did him—as baffling and fragmentary, as full of hiatuses. Certainly that is his effect on me. He adds up to three different people: first, with his head-on forward [illegible], his odd clothes, the redundant scarf and waistcoat, his breezy manner, he was the rather grubby grown-up, small boy he seemed in New York; then, when we were both a little drunk beyond the fire at the Dog, he suddenly blazed with charm, and I realized how truly beautiful his eyes were, how dazzling his smile, and the excitement for both of us, I think, seemed something more than drunkenness; then, before the electric heater in his flat, when the initial fascination had passed and we found each other [illegible] to the point where we were almost quarreling, I saw in the structure of his face, with its strongly defined features (the beautiful eyes in shadow), not only the upper class English gentleman but something very nearly sinister, and he was suddenly a person I didn't know at all, and couldn't possibly ever know. So, during the whole day Sunday, I was being brought up short, watching him snap from one aspect or mood to the other. His politeness can be as slippery as any English snob's; a moment later he would be all deference, and I basked in the luxury of being admired in a new way that

seemed at moments worth giving up independence—humanity first, womanhood second (which he said was nonsense so firmly that I was confused)—all my shining book-culture, for.

Alert to her beau's multiple self-contradictions, Amy is mining him, looking for some essence that she never finds. She wonders implicitly whether her "shining book-culture" may have led her astray after all. She never uncovers the essential Charles. Instead, she works through details, scads of them, just as she will, later, when making her poems, accumulate objects and phrases through which to amass a whole thing, to re-create a scene or subject through its constituent parts.

She sees a character by way of the items that mark him; she measures a relationship by its outward circumstances. (Literary critics call this the technique of metonymy.) Charles's Oxford rooms, filled with blue-and-gold-bound scholarly books from the Clarendon Press, enchant her perhaps even more than he does:

> I was in love with the room from the moment I entered it, and under its spell, without knowing what I did or how defenseless it was to leave me, I rejected all New York had given me as if suddenly it were only so much tinsel, of no value.
>
> If the room embodied all I had for the first time become conscious of lacking, it also hinted at a new aspect of its tenant. His manner, however, in no way altered. In the midst of this asylum with its throngs of shades and echoes he said merely that as we were to visit the pubs via motorbike and I had brought no suitable clothes, I had better accept the loan of a sweater and trousers from his wardrobe. That I looked a little peculiar thus attired disturbed me not at all, nor did the thought that to anyone who did not know Charles the whole transaction would be impossible to explain. I climbed aboard the motorbike feeling, in fact, younger than I had in years and as innocently scandalous as if I were on a college escapade.
>
> Riding through the late dusk on the back of the motorbike, in Charles' trousers and sweater, I saw as in a dream almost unimaginably beautiful country—whole villages with thatched roofs,

fields of gorse (Winnie-the-Pooh), black rows of evergreens, the water rushing through the lock at Godstow, the ruined nunnery in the background. A bitter at the Trout, at Godstow, with fresh-faced Oxford students at the next table; a visit to the ladies' convenience, penny clutched in hand, and the recurrent talk of this fascinating institution. Then the little Awful Pub, with its billiard table and fireplace screen, its new beer with mush in the bottom of the glass. Hills and peaceful cows in the thickening dark, then the Dog, with its wing chair before the fire, the guffaws in the hall, my failure at locating the convenience among the corridors upstairs, growing crowd at the bar and increasingly lively dart game as the evening progressed; well-dressed people, the ease of drinking without the drive to get drunk, in cretonne-and-dark woodwork surroundings. The ride back to Oxford in the moonlight, here and there masses of trees crowding overhead, curving walled roads, the lights of the town twinkling out below us as we reached the crest of a hill. All is quite hard to remember, because none of it seemed real . . . Scrambled eggs in the cold, cement-floored kitchen of the flat, another drink, more and more awkward pauses in the conversation, attempts to start over, and somewhere the admission of a kind of failure.

What happened? What did not happen? Have they made love? Does it matter? What kind of failure, and what kind of admission? Reading through the diaries, one gets a sense of a woman who is ready for anything but unsure of everything. She is hungry for experience, bold and timid simultaneously. Such is the nature of Amy, the woman; Clampitt, the would-be writer of fiction, will be able to capture the details, to look at the trees while missing the forest, building toward a narrative climax that never arrives.

As for Amy the woman who did not drink much—according to Phoebe Hoss—consider the following excerpt, which is far from unusual:

I consumed one and one-half gin-and-lime cocktails, one glass of beer, two scotches, part of another beer, and a gin-and-orange between Saturday noon and midnight without getting quite drunk or quite sick—not to mention the baked beans, fried eggs and bacon at eleven p.m.

It is probably a good thing she never learned to drive. Do we attribute such gusto to the custom of the times? Or to the woman's being almost twenty-nine but still girlish? Or to travel itself, to throwing caution to the winds when abroad, and acting on impulses that, at home, one normally keeps in check?

By May 17, the holiday was over. It had changed Amy's life.

To her college chum David Matlack—whom I have cited in the previous chapter—Amy wrote a long letter (April 15, 1952) that encapsulates in a single paragraph everything about England that affected her. The letter omits any reference to lovers, although it mentions a "we" (this probably means Charles Johnson) who are traveling through the countryside:

You asked about England. I've been there, twice, the first very briefly in the spring of 1949 when I was still with the Oxford Press, and the other last fall. I have some wonderful friends there, and while they haven't the irresistible grace of the Italians, they have more durable qualities and are perhaps the only civilized people left in the world. They put up with so much, and they are still, under that stiff upper lip, so warm-hearted. It was amazing to find this out, because before I went there I had thought all English people rather horrid. They say themselves that the experience of the war has changed them. But there is that wonderful past, which seemed to me more alive there than on the Continent. Especially in Oxford, which I love wistfully and insatiably. The country is beautiful, especially in Oxford and the Cotswold country round about—a green the like of which doesn't exist on this side of the Atlantic . . . It's hard to say what it is about the rural landscape that makes you want to cry with delight—it's the opposite of spectacular, modest, lived-in, civilized, a place where you can settle in a stone house on the edge of a village and be happy for the rest of your life.

"Wistfully," "insatiably," "cry with delight," "modest," and "civilized": these are the characteristic tones that will persist in Amy the woman and Clampitt the writer-still-unknown.

Two years later, after her first trip, she left the press permanently (May 14, 1951), and her travels resumed, as did her travel writing, now more extensive. The next journal—more than one hundred thousand words—follows its author through France, Italy, Austria, and back to France. She is preparing for something, but neither the author nor a prospective reader can figure out exactly what. The writer demonstrates an enormous appetite—for food, drink, culture, reportage, adventure, romance—and fills her reports with countless details, any one of which might be the germ for an entire story, or even a novel. As Amy the woman moves from place to place, absorbing the details, so Clampitt the writer takes down data and makes observations, and then continues her creative journey.

Reading Clampitt's travel journals, I pictured Walt Whitman, a less unlikely American model than one might imagine. Both poets look with an expansive, even undiscriminating eye at everything. Every line in a Whitman poem ends with punctuation, either a period or a comma. No line ever runs into the following one. Every item in a Whitman catalogue could become, if the author so chose, the germ of something bigger. Whitman gathers his "leaves," his pages, from the individual blades of grass that he accumulates, democratically giving his attention to everything for a moment, but to nothing for too long. Like him, Clampitt writes with a feeling for inclusive, democratic plenitude. Is she nodding to him, at least obliquely, in the title of her 1973 chapbook *Multitudes, Multitudes*? (The two-word phrase comes originally from the book of Joel 3:14, in the Old Testament.) Like him, she is "large" and "contains multitudes." In her 1993 *Paris Review* interview, she in fact acknowledges an affinity for Whitman that she developed late, proving not only that one's tastes and preferences change with age but also that Whitman was one of those "predecessors" every writer needs.

Amy is eating and drinking and flirting. She is also reading as she goes: *Romeo and Juliet* in Verona; Aldous Huxley, Conrad, Ford Madox Ford, and probably unmentioned others, en route. She

looks at paintings, scenery, and architecture. She is especially atten-
tive to the people she encounters who share her literary enthusi-
asm. Through her American friends Joe and Connie Goodman, she
meets, in Venice, the American poet Horace Gregory (1898–1982)
and his wife, Marya Zaturenska Gregory (1902–1982, herself a Pulit-
zer Prize–winning poet), "a family literally unable to live without
books." They enchant her:

> . . . it was a relief to be with people who wrote and dealt with
> books but were not intellectual about it—no professional pride
> that must be maintained before all comers, but an almost hum-
> ble simplicity. Horace seemed to me one of the nicest people I
> had met in a long time. He is [ashily?] pale; his hair must once
> have been red, but it and his eyebrows are now an ashy gray.
> He is troubled by what must have been a partial paralysis, and
> indeed looks so unwell that his energy was surprising. He has
> bright blue eyes, and a delightful, vigorous way of saying "Ye-es,
> ye-es," when you mention something you like that he likewise
> approves.

Amy was, after all, a woman whose role models included her father
and grandfather, bookish "but not intellectual about it." She must
have been relieved to find another midwesterner (Horace was born
in Wisconsin) who could inspire her.

As in her first trip abroad, she looks at people. She is trying to
figure them out, and mostly failing in her efforts. In Venice, for
example, she finds herself in new company and surveys the scene.
Here's one man among several, Imbre Buffum, with whom she
spends time:

> His manner of speaking is so mild, his appearance so pleasantly
> unprepossessing, that the adjective *smug* never occurred to me
> until after he had mercifully departed. He had dirty fingernails
> and the casually ill-fitting clothes of the college professor; his
> fair hair was getting a little thin, and I finally decided that he
> was probably younger than he looked—possibly, even, not much

older than I. His impassivity—and I suppose his total lack of susceptibility toward me as a female, since I was so much in his company—in the end nearly drove me wild; yet in his presence I was never irritated, only afterward. He never argued, he only pronounced. I saw him show curiosity only once, when he was prompted to ask Joe about his philosophy of the function of the arts. But he must have had a great deal of curiosity, or he would not have bothered to read the *Gazzettino* so faithfully every day. But he gave the impression that for him everything had been examined, judged and completed a long time ago, so that I felt that coming to Europe every summer could only be an exercise, not an exploration.

A man, in other words, lacking Amy's drive to examine and explore, to be as demonstrably alive as an innocent American in a James novel, as wide-eyed as she herself is.

Part of her vibrancy is sexual. Every man seems a possible creature of erotic interest, until proving himself or being proved by Amy to be otherwise. Her enthusiasm and her desires occasionally verge on the adolescent. And they also seem to have been influenced by her reading. She is Madame Bovary without the tragedy, Don Quixote without the unhinged pathos. One has the impression through the Clampitt diaries of a young woman eager for adventure, but adventure formed by literature. She is developing as a woman. She has been a reader first and foremost, but now she is also a budding writer, placing herself as a character in a narrative of her own creation. She moves from one hotel, museum, or church, or man to the next. She is a character compounded of lived events and parts from books that she has absorbed, a heroine in search of a hero and a story.

I am reminded of William Butler Yeats's lines from "Adam's Curse" (1904):

There have been lovers who thought love should be
So much compounded of high courtesy
That they would sigh and quote with learned looks
Precedents out of beautiful old books.

Amy was probably one of these. In one entry, she recalls how one morning she tossed and turned, like any confused lover. She dreams of John (Menapace?), in Paris:

> Awoke just as it was growing light, before anything was stirring, thirsty and with a thumping hangover. Lay awake happily for hours, remembering back, scene by scene, times with John as I hadn't been able to since I left New York: the way his tweed jacket felt on the last Tuesday when he arrived without Maria, just as I was putting the soufflé into the oven; and saying goodbye to him on the *Île de France*, and his hand on my wrist; but not, I think, ever, quite his face. Again composed all kinds of ecstatic messages, ending with Darling, Darling, which would not get mailed or even written. It was a long time until nine and the breakfast tray, by which time the excitement of wakefulness had worn off and I was simply a bit vague and unsteady.

Swerving from hopefulness to disappointment, Clampitt leans heavily on the "literary," filtering what were doubtless honest feelings. It also sounds like something from a 1930s woman's movie or a romance novel. "Precedents out of beautiful old books," indeed.

Amy traveled, read, reported, and wrote. However important these efforts were in preparing her for future work, they came to nothing at the time. In a letter to her uncle George and aunt Ruby Felt, she wrote in August 1952 that she had finished her book of travel sketches, and was beginning work on a novel. Writing proceeded, aggressively but helter-skelter.

———

Back home, several years later, Amy wrote to her brother Philip, tacitly acknowledging her discovery that one could not base one's life on examples from books. Art and reality cannot be compelled to intersect:

> I wanted a great romance; I wanted to know what it felt like to be tragic; I wanted the impossible. And the extraordinary thing

Beautiful, mysterious man, late 1940s, early 1950s

is that without calculating in the least, I got it. I got two big romances, plus a number of small interludes that were in various degrees exciting, amusing and painful, plus a couple of more extended involvements that were none of these and were the hardest to get out of.

People, she realizes, are not interchangeable. She has just put her "uninterchangeable young man" (perhaps Charles Johnson) on the train at Grand Central:

I thought I knew all there was to know about farewells on station platforms, and all about being tragic, and all about love; but by this time we had even got past the tragedy and the histrionics. I don't understand it at all. There is nothing quite like it in any of the books I have read.

Amy was growing up slowly. Her ideas about love, formed by reading, were chastened by the sometimes implausible, always unpredictable uniqueness of real people. Those people—those men—will probably remain mysterious to us. Amy's friends and family recalled some of her lovers, or at least love interests. There was, for example, Emil, a German neighbor on West 12th Street; it is perhaps he who survives in old pictures, in the kind of bathing suit that only Europeans wore, on a boat, and on a dock, perhaps in the late 1940s or early 1950s. He is a sepia revenant from the past, captured in a picture with no label, packed away in a box, the kind most families still have somewhere in attic or basement. So much has been irretrievably lost.

———

To return to Amy as a traveler: not just literature but also the visual arts—everything she sees, everything she has studied in illustrated art books and museums—comes into play when she deals with people. Here, for example, from the 1951 trip, a description of two brothers she has just met in Florence, the first a Sienese sculptor:

> ... an exquisitely handsome, almost beautiful young man, but with a luxuriantly hairy chest showing at the open collar of his shirt: put together lightly and perfectly, with a jaunty carriage but a face of great seriousness and even intensity. His coloring was not spectacular—rather fair skin, curling brown hair and the gray-green eyes I have seen so often in Italy ... but the contours of his face seemed modeled rather than carved, and the way his lips fitted into the planes of it, neither quite parted nor quite compressed, was so delicious that I could scarcely take my eyes off him ... The new young man proved to be his brother, and he again was so wonderful to look at that I found myself fairly bewildered. He had the same light, jaunty build, though he was not quite so tall, but his face resembled his brother's only in being beautiful: whereas the older one might have come from a Mannerist painting, this was a face out of Pietro Lorenzetti—the long, slightly slanting eyes, a dark brown instead of the ambiguous, troubled gray-green, the simple flat modeling across the cheeks, the narrow but beautiful mouth that carried out the same scheme of horizontals.

We hardly need more proof of the truth that life copies art (until it no longer can), especially the life of a woman who has raised herself through acts of reading and looking.

Amy the traveler openly confronts the likelihood that her upbringing has affected her points of view. Like James's Isabel Archer, Amy learns to revise her ideas in the light of her experiences. She wonders whether she is "going to be forced or cowed into relinquishing, as too silly and perilous, too aimless, my own tiny bark and single oar for some large majestic vessel—in short whether I [am] not going to find tradition a lot bigger than I had yet supposed it to be."

Supposition would have to give way, eventually, to revelation and readjustment. Precocious in her intellect and her bookishness, Amy did not yet have an experiential sense of life's truths. Neither the lover nor the writer in her had yet matured fully. Perhaps the "lover" never did. It is curious, even predictable, that in her dealings with Harold Korn, her permanent adult partner and finally her husband (about whom different friends made different reports), Amy retained a giddy girlishness as well as an adult woman's understanding of how domesticity might operate. In the few surviving pieces of correspondence between the two of them—they were not apart frequently or for long—as well as in Hal's copy of Amy's *Multitudes, Multitudes*, she addresses him and refers to herself as if they are characters from *The Wind in the Willows* or something by Lewis Carroll, thus: "To dearest Lion / from / ever grateful Cat." Amy finally learned how, and when, to purr. A decade later she inscribed a copy of *The Kingfisher* to Hal:

> To her critter without a peer
> the other feline finds she
> can only say—words fail her.

One doesn't know whether to be more surprised by what seem to be conventional gender stereotypes—Hal as lion, Amy as kitten—or by the charming fact that, for once, words have failed a creature of self-admitted garrulousness.

———

When she returned to New York after months abroad, she returned as well to her literary pursuits. From her undergraduate days more than a decade before, Amy had committed herself, misunderstanding her gifts, to becoming a writer of fiction. It took her a long time to discover where her true talent lay. She was toying with genres, just as she was trying out various roles for her life.

The 1952 letter to David Matlack, quoted above, continues with a reference to its writer's personal and professional circumstances. It mentions her completed travel book, ten essays on all the subjects Amy was recording and considering during her European adventures, ideas about religion, a kind of summa or perhaps an explosion of everything going through her brain:

> . . . a literary agent with whom I have been playing peek-a-boo has read it and sent it back, confirming my suspicion that it was a hodge-podge, though he used politer words. For a man who sends things back he is terribly encouraging. He mentioned several times doing a novel—they all do, of course, you can sell a novel, sometimes—so here I am, by God, on the second chapter of one.

PART 2: 1951–1960

For Amy, the 1950s was the decade of the Audubon Society, novel writing, religious cravings, and a moment of grace the fruits of which would not become evident until decades later. Poverty was a constant, although $42.75 a month for a good studio apartment would not have been burdensome. The average annual income for a man (women, of course, made less) in 1955 was $3,400. At home, Amy Clampitt, unknown writer, began her literary work in greater earnest, although as early as February 1952 the would-be novelist confronted roadblocks. In a letter to her brother Philip, she admits that a literary agent to whom she has sent three chapters says that the novel "was well written" (the damning-with-faint-praise every writer dreads to read) "but there was no market for it."

Amy is living without employment but not, for the moment, worried:

> It would be nice to make some money, of course, but I have gone ahead writing [her novel] and having the time of my life. I haven't

gotten a job and haven't even looked for one, but though the money is beginning to run rather low even that doesn't bother me. I can always go to work at Macy's or something, and probably will, because the idea of a good job in which I have to work hard chiefly at flattering people and pushing them around now seems too awful to contemplate, and I have discovered that I am really happier with a very little money than when I could buy things just for the fun of buying.

She persists in her hopefulness. After all, she has proved to herself that she can hold a job if she wants to; her needs are few; and she is convinced she will write a good book. She remains contented with her bohemian life: evenings at poetry readings, recitals, meeting a White Russian journalist with a wonderful collection of Turkish fezzes, Persian shoes, and maracas. A woman entering her thirties but not going anywhere too quickly is enjoying a kind of measured hedonism. Soon, however, with "holes in my shoes and approximately twenty-five dollars to my name," she has taken a job at the Audubon Society.

At least at the start, the Audubon job had its charms. During her time there, dissatisfied with what she found in the standard Library of Congress designations, she designed a special classification system for bird books. She writes to her parents (August 10, 1952) that visitors to headquarters have included a man who trains hawks for hunting; a man rumored to be a Communist who has made contacts with fellow travelers by means of pamphlets on birds that he has written and sent all over the world (this one was too complicated even for her to figure out); a little boy with a bow tie and braces on his teeth who knows more about the whereabouts of the library's collection, both on the shelves and in the card catalogue, than she does; an ancient Italian priest with whom Amy and the librarian converse in his native tongue. Plus, much to her delight, all the weirdos who show up claiming sightings of birds virtually extinct. For Amy, because the society is not a profit-making venture, "I can bother to look up such things just to please people." Pleasing people without the profit motive was an assignment she could readily accept.

An additional pleasure was the location of Audubon House—1130 Fifth Avenue—near the Metropolitan Museum of Art. In good weather, Amy could enjoy her lunch hour by eating a sandwich on a park bench and then wandering through the museum itself. She wrote to her brother Dick (September 30, 1954), "There's no place like Central Park—it has everything, from seagulls to maniacs, in short it is the world in miniature." The maniacs included an adolescent mugger who the previous year attacked Amy in the park with a stick and demanded her pocketbook. Fast-thinking Amy whipped a dollar bill from her purse, which seemed to satisfy the acne-pocked girl and also made Amy wonder what muggers wanted: "They don't want pity. They want to have their revenge. What can one do? Of course, if we knew the answer, then wars could be stopped, and Senator McCarthy could be stopped." It was like her to begin a two-page, single-spaced letter (May 14, 1953) with an account of seeing people off on the *Queen Mary*, then move to the mugging and the reflections it inspired, and end with a return to ordinary life. As in the poems she would write in her maturity, twenty-five years in the future, nothing is beneath consideration. Everything is interesting.

To David Matlack she wrote similarly, and without pain or fear, in her 1952 letter about her travels, her writing, and now, her daily situation:

> . . . there's the matter of my financial resources which are now down to something like two hundred dollars, and I still haven't faced squarely, or even with trepidation, the problem of what I shall do when that runs out. Everybody I know, practically, is either more worried than I am or rapidly coming to the conclusion that I am being kept or into the smuggling racket. Which isn't surprising, for I never would have believed that my savings could stretch so far. I live in the most magnificent parsimony—it suits me better than spending money on things to console me for not doing what I thought I wanted to do, namely, write books, ever did in the days when I got paid every two weeks. Yesterday I splurged: I spent twenty cents to go uptown and back on the subway—it was a little far to walk, as I sometimes do—walked across Central Park with the magnolias just coming into bloom

around Cleopatra's Needle, went inside the Metropolitan Museum to look at a Cézanne show which is free on Mondays and costs fifty cents on other days, and which is limpid and blazing with such color as I never dreamed was really Cézanne's.

That parsimony can be magnificent is an idea that will please only the young and the hopeful. Amy was both.

Poverty was a choice. It appealed to many sides of the hungry artist. She wrote to Beth in 1953 that her poverty was a voluntary test to prove what would suffice. She calls it a wonderful escape from "the pressures of prestige, and appearances, and doing things according to a pattern. One can think so much more clearly, not being part of any group. For me, it's necessary to feel free, and I never felt more so." The giving up and letting go—a combination of Buddha and Saint Francis of Assisi—allowed Amy to feel free. This was one side of her character. The other, at this moment in abeyance but soon to appear, was a desire for community, which she would discover in submitting herself to the discipline and order of the Episcopal Church, and after that to the communities available to her in public political activism.

Three years later, even more convinced of her own brand of nonconformity and her willingness to live close to the bone, Amy unburdens herself again to her youngest brother. She is glad to have left her job at Oxford, if only because she has decided she doesn't want to be a boss to other people. And as she would not be a boss, so also would she not "want to do what I'm told unless I myself see a reason for it." She has, she confesses, a horror of turning professional. (Indeed, she remained for the rest of her life an amateur—a "lover" of knowledge—in many fields until the point when she could take pride in becoming a professional poet.) As a thoroughgoing nonconformist, she can do pretty much whatever she wants to: "For instance, I like being poor, relatively speaking; and it is a great victory not to have been made to find a job where I would simply be pushing other people around for no reason except the money and the prestige attached." She considered herself an oddball but not a rebel—an important distinction—and she always remained, in her work as well as her life, committed to order, but always of her own choosing. What will become Clampitt the poet's signature style—an abundance of verbal richness—is the other side of Amy the woman's life of abnegation, a kind of compensation.

A professional is a person who earns money for her efforts. Amy enjoyed a foretaste of her years of success a quarter century before Howard Moss at *The New Yorker* published her. At the end of a letter to Philip (October 2, 1954), she announces amusedly that she has sent to her favorite magazine a remark she overheard while seeing some friends off to Europe at the pier: "He keeps oysters. He puts in a thing so that it doesn't come out pearls, it comes out diamonds." And then, "*The New Yorker* has sent me a check for five dollars. And this seems to be a most satisfactory achievement." The squib appeared anonymously at the bottom of a page in the magazine. At almost the same time, she's written seventy thousand words—nine chapters of her novel—and says she is almost halfway through, and moving ahead strongly. In 1955, publishers reject her: "Scribner's turned it down with the most lukewarm half-praise ('intelligent and sensitive, but needs something to give it urgency'), and now there is a letter from Knopf which says the same thing, although with a more percipient editorial conscience: they wish it had more pace, more of an outward story line; as it stands (and no doubt for the author's purposes it is right as it stands) it is not likely to engage a sufficient number of readers to encourage them to take it on."

———

What was Clampitt's prose fiction like? What did she attempt in her novels, and in what ways did they fail? Why did no publisher accept her work?

If much of what we know about Amy shows her practicing roles for a life, modeling herself on figures from books, taking what she had learned in college courses and trying to fashion an identity, the literary ventures of Amy Clampitt similarly indicate a woman committed to looking about, recording impressions, analyzing and speculating. Her troves of travel observations imply that she was gathering material for some larger project. But what? That is the question for which she was groping, consciously or unconsciously, to discover an answer. She was making herself a writer by constantly writing. When she became a successful poet, decades later, she found an appropriate form for her observations and vast lists of things. For all their lush texture, individual Clampitt poems maintain a discrete, compact wholeness. But in her prose, the details merely accumulate. They do not cohere. When Clampitt took an informal writing class from the novelist Marguerite Young—who was to become a friend of sorts—her fellow midwesterner was the first person to tell her that her gifts did not direct her toward fiction. It was Young who urged her to return to poetry. But this was a lesson that Amy did not learn until later. She had to be told again. Obdurate, she persisted for decades with her fiction. By the time of her *Paris Review* interview, Clampitt could barely remember her novels—three of them, as she recalled—and dismissed them as the misbegotten efforts of someone who had virtually no idea what she was doing.

Clampitt's papers include the manuscripts of two full (undated) novels, *The Sound of a Bell* and *The Parapet of Choice* (an earlier version, unfinished after 240 pages, whether by choice or because the manuscript has been unintentionally cut off, or additional pages lost), plus dozens of stories, fragments, and synopses of other works. Her friend Doris Myers remembered another novel, perhaps merely a retitled version of the previous ones, and still undiscovered, called *The Tribes Go Up* (the title comes from Psalm 122). Clampitt was working on this in 1957–58 and finished it in 1960 but kept revising. *Parapet* has the same cast of characters as *The Sound of a Bell*, with the story line plotted a bit differently, and it rearranges the focus. Clampitt was writing these things, large and small, for more than two decades. No one really ever knew what she was doing, because she didn't discuss her work with friends. Doris Myers said she never heard anything about other novels. "That's one thing about Amy: she would tell you what she wanted you to know, and the rest of her life was just a closed book."

Her books, as well as her life, were, if not exactly closed, then not widely shared. In May 1961, she ends a letter to Philip and Hanna with a teaser: "Did I tell you that I have started a new novel? A first draft of a first chapter is now extant." She provides no other facts.

The last mention she makes of fiction writing in her letters is dated 1966. And the last mention of her travel writing is a reference in a letter (December 31, 1967) to a book on Greece, "still in the same publisher's hands." Having resigned from the Audubon Society, and having returned from an extended European trip that includes her first visit to Greece, she writes to her old Audubon colleague Rimsa Michel:

> My agent entered the novel I finished last fall in a contest sponsored by Putnam, McCall's, Fawcett Publishing, and Warner Brothers—total guaranteed at about $210,000. I told her I thought it was pretty silly, but to go ahead. I was right. The ms. came back; so did thirty-five hundred others. Nobody won the prize. Can you imagine a novel that would satisfy all those customers and still sound like literature? So my heart isn't broken.

Of course her heart is not broken: she has become wise.

Her Greece trip resulted in a travel book—or so she hoped—which she assembled hastily, 165 pages, and submitted to various publishers, all to no avail. A letter from Joseph A. Maurer at *The Classical World* (an academic wing of the Classical Association of the Atlantic States) was sent to Clampitt's new literary agent, T. Carter Harrison in Philadelphia. He rejected a section called "Apollo, Daphne, and The Python" saying that "the article is not suitable for a scholarly journal . . . it belongs rather to a magazine such as *Atlantic Monthly*." Not only did Clampitt have trouble finding the right genre, she also couldn't find the right outlets. She was never not writing; she was always writing intensely and speedily. She was just not writing the right thing.

———

During these years, Clampitt the would-be novelist was simultaneously working hard and flailing about without purpose. Like many young writers, she started with what she knew, or thought she knew. Anyone familiar with Amy's life, her family, and her Iowa upbringing will find more than mere traces of them in the long prose ruminations that sound like compilations of stories and character sketches along the lines of Sherwood Anderson's 1919 *Winesburg, Ohio*, laced with some sensational situations and dilemmas imitated or borrowed from Theodore Dreiser and D. H. Lawrence (whom in a letter from 1954 she refers to as "that dangerous, often tiresome, and often superb maverick"). The subjects predictably include the richness along with the stifling sameness of rural life; the allure and danger of the big city; the Madame Bovary–ish need to escape; the mysterious nervous energy of young love; and the predictable angst and fatigue of adolescent rebelliousness. Characters come and go; stories interweave. Because everything exists at the same level of urgency, nothing stands out. Instead of six (or more) characters in search of an author (the dilemma in Luigi Pirandello's absurdist 1921 meta-comedy), we find, in Clampitt's novelistic forays, one author in search of a story.

Phoebe Hoss said that Amy told her she was writing a novel, or perhaps several, about New York, but the available evidence argues otherwise. New York settings appear, but not extensively. Clampitt was an Iowa writer. Just as James Joyce fled Dublin for the Continent in order to re-create his homeland at a distance, and as Willa Cather left Nebraska but was never abandoned by it, composing her novels about the Midwest from the safe eyrie of Manhattan, so Clampitt's attempts at novel writing brought her back to New Providence, which never relinquished its hold on its eccentric, nonconformist daughter.

———

Lurton Blassingame (1904–1988) was a southerner who came north for college at Columbia, worked as a writer in Hollywood, returned to New York, and established himself as a New York literary agent in the 1930s. Clampitt had dealings with him for about eight years. He took her on as a client, at first with enthusiasm and then with increasing frustration. In January 1952, he rejected a collection of essays (perhaps travel work; perhaps something else, now lost) she had sent him, and encouraged her to send fiction. So she sent stories. Every time he made a request, she replied virtually immediately. (She was just as speedy decades later. Making her rounds as a poet, if an editor returned a poem, she sent it elsewhere straight-away. Whether in failure or success, she was not going to stop.) On February 7, he told her that the trouble with her stories was "they are not plotted strongly enough for the popular magazines, and they are not quite polished enough for the intellectuals . . . My feeling is that your real métier would be the novel." She complied. The following day, in a letter, she enclosed outlines for two novels. The first, set in London, is about a girl in her early twenties, "high-spirited, intense, disorganized, and frivolous," who falls in love with a young married man. (Except for "frivolous," the author might be her own heroine.) Into the picture comes an older man, also married, "whom she per-mits to seduce her." Then follows an unsuccessful suicide attempt. Her mother swoops down and takes her back to Yorkshire. Clampitt returned to this scenario shortly afterwards, now placing the action in New York.

The second scenario: a novel about American Quakers in an iso-lated Mexican village with a dizzying cast of eccentric characters. This idea must have been provoked by Amy's recollection of her 1944 month with her parents and brother Philip in Mexico. Nothing ever came of this one.

Clampitt was looking for a genre and for an audience. In March, Blassingame rejected the travel pieces she had accumulated during her European trip the previous year: "It just does not fall into any category. It is a combination of ideas, art criticism, travel experi-ences, and personal experiences—yet it does not give a satisfying enough picture of any of them." He continued to encourage a novel.

Clampitt's initial letter to Blassingame appears in a folder with a synopsis of one of her novels, called *Stranger, Tread Light* (a phrase from John Crowe Ransom's "The Equilibrists"). The manuscript of the novel itself has vanished. In April, Blassingame sent sample chapters from *Stranger, Tread Light* off to publishers. A month later, having seen subsequent chapters, but still trying to sound encour-aging, he says that "the story seems to have lost a great deal of its early pace." Press after press rejected it; Blassingame himself called it "rather rambling" and told her he could not imagine a market for it. This back-and-forthing went on for months. On July 9, 1953, writing about we can't be sure which manuscript, the frustrated agent repeated his main point: "I'm afraid the story itself is not tight enough and that you do not show enough real motivation for the climax that arises in these people's lives . . . Do try for a little stronger plots." He continues to praise the writing. But the author was still in search of a story.

———

By this point she was already "thinking of another novel," about a rural pastor and his family in Iowa. She was also writing a long short story about Italy "and its effects on several Americans." In the Clampitt papers, her letter about it is bunched together with a short story called "A Bundle of Keys."

The synopsis of the unfinished book, a remake of the story originally set in England, reveals a great deal about what the real Amy was doing as she entered her thirties. Clampitt writes about what she (presumably) knows. As a writer, she is spinning her wheels, repeating herself. In the novel, a twenty-four-year-old Tess Armstrong comes to New York from a small New England town "to get a job and find out who she is and what she wants." She falls in love with a young married man in her office. Their relationship is spiritual rather than physical but it has enough power ("Feelings of guilt and awareness of power to hurt are new to Tess") to force her to quit her job. Like her predecessor in Clampitt's "English" novel, she meets another married man, this one somewhat older, who seduces her. She feels even more guilt, and yearns for some kind of religious salvation. There is despair, and thoughts of suicide. Her mother comes down from Vermont, takes her daughter home. Then Tess returns to Manhattan in search of a new job. Clampitt writes, "On the realistic level the novel is intended to give some picture of the life led by nice young people who come to New York, without roots and without money, not so much to find success and recognition as to find themselves." She says she wants to give the flavor of Manhattan in 1950–51. She calls her narrative method cinematic—"a progression of carefully focused, set and lighted scenes." And she claims to borrow an underlying spirituality from the theology of Reinhold

Niebuhr, and a theme that leans "upon the literary tradition of Haw-thorne and Henry James." "It is," writes its hopeful author, "to be first and last a love story—not of sex, avarice or dependence in love's clothing, but of love as the search for a spiritual reality."

Ten major publishers had rejected Clampitt's fiction by Novem-ber 17, 1953. The last letter from Blassingame's office is dated August 3, 1960, to Clampitt, then living with her sister in Des Moines. It rejected a story called "The Shell," which his agency had tried and failed to place with distinguished little literary quarterlies. The com-plaints were the standard ones. On April 3, 1959, Margaret Hartley from the *Southwest Review* wrote to the agent that the piece had too much going on; that there were too many elements, which the author was trying to compress into a story; that "it's pretty much an outline for a novel . . . it is too long for us, we feel, too complicated for its own good as a story."

"Too complicated for its own good" rings true. Clampitt could not figure out how to give publishers what they thought fiction looked like. She did not know where and how to compress, or where to expand. She never learned how to adapt to her editors' expecta-tions and recommendations.

Clampitt's real success in prose came in the intelligent critical essays that make up *Predecessors, Et Cetera*, prepared after she became famous. Before that, and for more than a third of her life, she never stopped writing fiction. Her college literary magazine published some of her work after she had left Iowa. Two early sto-ries in manuscript are headed by what was one of her two Columbia University addresses: Box 295, 411 West 116th Street. They antedate her move to West 10th Street a year or so later. Nothing else came of her efforts.

———

Let's return to *The Parapet of Choice* and *The Sound of a Bell*, two tries at a single story, with an eye to their strengths. The most strik-ing thematic aspects of both books are the author's unshakable obsession with Iowa, the appearance of figures who come straight from her family, and the recurrent motifs of belonging and alienation, the girl (or sometimes the boy) from the provinces who goes to the city and who (in some versions) returns. Rudy Piper, an oddball artist even in elementary school, "hovered, an erratic planet, at the furthest reach of that magnetic field which drew his classmates increasingly towards its center." Even a conventional minor figure, Olive Curry, one of the daughters-in-law of Gifford Curry, Frank Clampitt's stand-in here sketched by his favorite grandchild, has a modest dose of the eccentricity that her creator understood deeply: "if there was anything that curdled the vast sensitive surface of Olive Curry's wish to think well of other people, it was the refusal to be allied."

The best things in the novels are the memories and the re-creation of farm life, the life of nature, the details of agricultural rhythms, the planting and the harvesting, that remained with Clampitt throughout her years in Manhattan. Just as in "The Kingfisher" and other of Clampitt's poems, botany, animals, and the whole range of the natural world produce a sense of bounty and specificity (Darwin as a presiding deity?), so do the novels come alive when people are either banished or reduced to figures in a landscape. The chapter "Sunday Noon" from the manuscript for something called *Blue Vervain*, tucked among other fiction manuscripts, begins deliciously— "In that region of memory it is always summer"—and the excerpt contains affectionate reminiscences of, for example, "those golden, sculptured loaves," the straw stacks that Clampitt would return to as a subject in a poem years later.

In *The Parapet of Choice* and *The Sound of a Bell* we find a thinly disguised Amy Clampitt in the figure of her protagonist, Selena Corey. One two-page paragraph describes the nature of Selena's homesickness for her old house. The prose moves outward in space and time, from the window seat (as I mentioned earlier, Clampitt always wanted to write while looking out of a window, preferably with a tree or two in view), to the green north light in the parlor, where Selina reads or practices the piano, and then outside to the lawn, in which she counts the flowers, to the garden, the woods, the pasture, the hillside with "the long grass full of crickets and the thump of windfalls." She mourns for every tree she can recall and name. Two lengthy sentences exemplify the grace and rhythmic pacing in her writing. It would take several decades for her to take advantage of these gifts in her poems, not stories:

> She missed, finally, even the sense of missing something—she ached for the loneliness of the sleigh that stood locked under a mantle of cobweb at the back of the furthest barn, an ache out of the past; for the pussy-willow windbreak stretching like a sigh along the western horizon, where the world, or at any rate the farm, came to an end; for the melancholy spires of the blue vervain, for the bright and almost extinct prairie phlox (once, her father had told her, it had been everywhere) and the nameless flowers that straggled along the roadsides, misbegotten stars that filled a straying child with a vast, smothering, tearless sorrow. Her homesickness came full circle and she knew exactly what her mother would miss: her hollyhocks, her climbing rose, the woodpile, the cats, the well-house with its stone jars and cream separator; the kitchen window that was right for begonias, the living-room that was right for ferns and the Christmas cactus; the pantry shelves on which everything had a place so immutably fixed that Susan Corey could find it in the dark; the old black cookstove whose habits she knew perfectly, having shaken it down every morning for so many years.

The tone is elegiac. The list of items helps a daughter counter the loss of her mother by enumerating the things that each of them loved. Each one has a place. And writing puts, and keeps, things in their place.

Clampitt could write this way with ease. Feelings of loss and efforts at restitution came almost naturally to her. From *The Sound of a Bell*, here is another attempt in the same vein. Selina, having banished an ardent suitor named Ted, tells her father that the young man will not be coming around any longer. It is Christmas. She thinks of something she will never find again in her waking life— "it waited now, that orchard of the past"—and as though responding to an invitation, Selina and her author allow themselves the luxury of reminiscence. We the audience also participate in the reverie. The orchard waited unvisited through all the snows and the thaws and through the dusty fragrance of the plum blossom that whitened the first warm nights of April. She would never find it again, that region of uncut summer grass that tugged about one's ankles, alive with winged grasshoppers and the possibility of snakes—things peculiar to a time long submerged by the denser grasses of forgetfulness. How long since she had so much thought of the vanished cider-press!—thinking of which, now, she felt once more the season drawing in, the day-warmed, night-cooled air rich with decaying apples, the grass rank and hoary with gossamers, the voices of the crickets everywhere: heard first out here in the orchard, they moved houseward with the season until they spoke from the darkness at every doorstep, minutely strident on the eve of the great, final, silencing frost. And then once again, its boughs disburdened, the yellow grass laid flat by the vanished pyramids of apples, the orchard stood unvisited, unthought-of until the day of the pilgrimage into the remote country of its midwinter solitude, to choose a Christmas tree.

This is the prose of someone who has immersed herself in English Romantic poetry, in Keats above all. These two passages are like bel canto arias, set operatic pieces in which a singer onstage steps forward and unleashes a soaring melody. Clampitt's descriptions do little to advance the story's plot, but her command of imagery and sentence rhythms gives its own pleasure and foretells the poet-to-be.

Clampitt had trouble with any narrative longer than a stand-alone vignette or an anecdote. When she tried to write a sex scene, she lost all stylistic grace and authority. Here is a character named Agnes, giving herself to Rudy the painter, now grown up:

And now when they came together her lips from the very start were not like paper, they were like petals, and drinking at them he felt how by degrees her untaught body awoke and dissolved in answer. It did not take long. Though she did not respond, neither did she resist while quickly, with no joy and little pleasure, he deflowered her.

She lay so still, with no sign of reproach except the tears that slid soundlessly from under her eyelids, that he began to be frightened and a little sick. Indeed, the entire machinery of physical contact so disgusted him that he could scarcely lift a hand to wipe the sweat from his own forehead. He said sincerely, "I don't know how it happened, Agnes, I didn't mean for it to happen."

This sounds like an adolescent's attempt to imitate D. H. Lawrence, with Rudy and Agnes as the American prairie versions of Paul Morel and Miriam Leivers in *Sons and Lovers*. Perhaps she is also remembering her European romances, but rendering human action and advancing a plot were not Clampitt's strong suits. She had no trouble with the arias, but had to force herself to develop, in recitative, human characters; to allow us to understand them; and to let us watch their interactions. It would take her another two decades to discover how to let the songs stand alone.

Years later, Clampitt's editor Alice Quinn recalled a story told by Mary Russel. For an evening at home, with several friends, "Amy would make something lovely, we'd all have a couple of glasses of wine, and then she'd read a chapter or two from her novel. And we would all leave and be shaking our heads, saying 'Amy's a poet.'" Others knew the truth before she did.

———

By the mid-1950s, Amy was settled in her job at the Audubon Society, not entirely happily. She was writing amusingly pithy book notes and reviews for *Audubon* magazine. She had met Rimsa Michel, who became a lifelong correspondent when she left her job at the Audubon Society as Amy's assistant, and then left Manhattan itself; and the painters Mary Russel and Peter Marcasiano, with the latter of whom she had a difficult, fraught friendship and who was possibly a lover. And she was deeply engaged with her never-to-be-published fiction.

In 1954, when he was sixty-six, Roy Clampitt had largely stepped away from his farming work. Like many men transitioning between an active life and semiretirement, he entered a period of mild depression, the condition that both his father and several of his children also suffered from. In a letter dated June 13, addressed only to her father, Amy reflects on the familial predisposition to nervousness and unhappiness, and then opens into a moving self-analysis. She acknowledges the long time it took her first to recognize and then to accept her own peculiarities, those genetic traits stemming from a "more than usually intense inner life." And she goes on, complimenting the parents who raised her "to believe that there were things more important than how much money one had . . . Values are not manufactured on the assembly line, and character is not to be found in the department stores."

If we follow the letter's train of thought, we learn how Amy's mind worked associatively—one idea or emotion suggesting another—and we can see, retroactively, the various facets of her character. From a consideration of values, she moves on to a sense of the infinite suffering in the world, then to her own limitations, pride being paramount: too proud to acknowledge problems and too proud to seek advice from others. She then makes a seamless transition to matters of vocation, and then of learning. One of her biggest questions,

> which I may never solve, is how to set down what I know about human happiness and misery in a form that will make sense and also get published. My life is not going to be ruined if I don't, since it is a colossal task and I prefer an honorable failure to a meaningless success, but I haven't given up yet.

One thinks of Keats, in a moment of combined hesitation and headstrong ambition: "I would sooner fail than not be among the greatest."

Because she was an intellectual at heart, Amy's way of dealing with, or learning about, suffering was to systematize her ideas, so she set herself the task of learning enough Greek to read Sophocles. (For ordinary people, ordinary suffering offers its own lessons, sufficient unto the day. Amy goes to books.) Roy, the Classics major, had taught his firstborn the Greek alphabet when she was seven. She says she can't forgive herself for not taking a Greek course in college. She spends a weekend boning up on the alphabet. Then come declensions and conjugations. (Her papers include helter-skelter worksheets of her Greek exercises.)

The letter unites several strands that make up the fabric of its writer's life: acknowledgment of oddness; stubborn pride; gratitude to parents; ethical principles; vocational aspirations; empathy for human failings; literature as lived experience; and, finally, a genetic replication of the person whom, as it happens, she most resembles.

Three months later (September 30), Amy wrote to her brother Richard, who had turned from physics to psychology as a course of study and then as a career, about the ways in which her rebellious ego was reduced "to that condition of humility which now seems to me the only source of real self-confidence, as well as something like peace of mind." She was thinking of the intersections between science, religion, and art, and about how "the cathedrals and crucifixes of Europe," everything she had visited during her breathless travels, still "represented something far grander and nobler than anything my silly intellect was capable of."

Pride and humility, knowingness and doubt are the poles between which Amy was living her inner life. The fluctuations soon led to a radical change of behavior and commitment, both predictable and transformative.

———

In her midthirties, Amy underwent a new existential crisis. Nascent religious impulses were moving her away from her home-nurtured Quakerism and toward something more doctrinally conventional. She began to spend time at an Episcopal church in the Village, and also at a convent in New Jersey. At one crucial moment, however, religion, music, the visual arts, and literature itself came together in an epiphany, an experience of what some people might label "grace," whether spiritual or secular. In an extraordinary letter to her brother Philip (March 17, 1956), she refers to something "quite astonishing." She moves slowly into her subject. She says she has not fallen in or out of love; she has not changed jobs; she has not received a contract for her novel. A self-confessed "garrulous creature," she begins to feel that she may have a talent for happiness. And she then recounts a visit to the Cloisters, the Metropolitan Museum's outpost in northern Manhattan, its repository of medieval art.

Looking at the Unicorn Tapestries, listening to medieval music, taking her place within an audience of like-minded aesthetes, and sitting on a stone, she loses and then seems—in a different register—to find herself:

> I had—perhaps for no more than an instant, but there is no measuring this kind of experience—entirely forgotten my own existence. It is the sort of thing that has happened to me a few times in my life, but always before in moments of great excitement and with a kind of incredulity surrounding it like an iron ring. This time there was no iron ring, no excitement, no surprise even, but a serenity so complete that I hardly thought about it just then, I simply took it for granted. Possibly this is what is supposed to take place at baptism—but if baptism it was, it wasn't of water, but of light. By this time it was late afternoon, and with the reflection from the river so bright that you could barely look at it directly, the whole hilltop, the whole world was fairly brimming with radiance. I walked around for a while, looked at the people, and walked to the subway, rather tired, and yet rested, too, and pleased with everything.

The effect of the trip to the Cloisters extends beyond the mere visit itself. Amy at home is reading Keats, and then Katherine Mansfield—both of whom died young—and she begins to contemplate mortality and our responses to it. She says she feels no fear, and begins to write down her feelings in her journal. The writing starts out as though it might become a short story:

> And then something happened which I could absolutely never have predicted: I have not altogether recovered yet from the surprise, though I suppose I shall get used to it in time. Quite as though they had a will of their own, the sentences broke in a way that was not my usual style at all. Rather frightened, I must admit, for the moment, I let them break. The next thing I knew, they had begun to reach out for rhymes. This frightened me almost more,

until I discovered that finding a rhyme could be almost as natural
a process as the resolution of a dominant chord: I didn't have to
look for them, they simply came.

Writers sometimes say that a character has run away with a story; or
that a plot has spun off on its own in unforeseen directions; or that
a poem—I am thinking of Elizabeth Bishop's nineteen-line, elegiac
"One Art" ("The art of losing isn't hard to master")—might start in
a prosaic way and then become something different, say a villanelle.
Clampitt's experience is one of many such. Her epiphany has three
parts: an initial shock, an attempt to record it, and the subsequent
discovery that the writing has a mind of its own. Art comes to sur-
prise, even overwhelm its maker. She will not find her true poetic
voice for another two decades. Indeed, she doesn't even keep up
with the writing of poetry for a while after this, but here she finds
the impulse, and plants the seed.

The result is a rambling effusion of faith called "The Sun on the
Stone," which Clampitt's friend and correspondent Mary Jo Salter
called "an everything-but-the-kitchen-sink" kind of poem. In man-
uscript it is eighteen single-spaced typed pages. Salter also points
to the fortuitous resemblance, at least in their titles, between this
poem and Clampitt's first *New Yorker* acceptance, "The Sun Under-
foot Among the Sundews." A score of years counts for a lot.

The moment of grace coincided with Amy's decision to go to
church. She never did anything tentatively, and when the religious
impulse overtook her, not only her spiritual life but also the con-
tours of her daily life began to change. Following her epiphany at the
Cloisters, she opened herself up to organized religion in ways she
had never done before. As so often happened to this woman suscep-
tible to literature, this time the turn to religion coincided with what
she had been reading, in this case William James's *Varieties of Reli-
gious Experience*. A 1956 Easter letter to Philip outlines the shapes
of her inner life. She thinks she will join a church—not knowing
yet which denomination—and she recognizes the oddness of such
a push in a person who is a "professed believer in science and ulti-
mate human progress." She has stepped tentatively into strange
waters:

I have noticed a faint wish to observe the fasts and a kind of thirst for liturgy, which is no doubt partly just from being around people like Monica [a French woman, and her boss at Audubon], who is a devout Roman Catholic, and the Goodmans [Joseph and his wife, Constance, musician friends; Joe had been a volunteer in Mexico with Amy's parents in the 1940s; she visited them in Venice, and stayed friends with them in New York], who are equally devout Anglo-Catholics; one respects their observances, after a while, to the point where one would like to share them. Last Sunday afternoon I went to St. Luke's, the little Anglican church a few blocks south of me, where Joe's mass—specially composed for them—was being sung, along with one of Mozart. I was in rather too exultant a mood, the lingering effect of having finished the poem apparently, to listen in the proper spirit to this mass of Joe's, which is a very tense, difficult, I would say almost painful composition; I have listened more worshipfully to recorded masses, such as the Mozart Requiem.

In short, I was a little, and quite unjustifiably, puffed up with my own accomplishments. But since that afternoon I have been to church five times, not counting dropping into a couple where no services were going on, yesterday. I don't know what all this means, if anything. It might not have happened at all if I had not found myself involved in a terrible and totally unexpected new argument with Peter [Marcasiano]. Just when I thought an equilibrium had been reached! One never knows, that's all.

Amy's tone combines eagerness and uncertainty. Pride mingles with humility. Above all, she is willing to venture out, not even knowing the path or where it might lead. Like Dante at the beginning of the *Commedia*, she is in the middle of her life. In May, again writing to Philip, she says she's started a new poem, in Dante's *terza rima*. That poem has not (yet) shown up.

As with her European travels, so with her religion: Amy is coming to everything fully equipped as an aesthete and an intellectual. She is reading Dante. She listens to masses and other religious compositions. She has discussions with English friends about the differences between Catholicism and Anglicanism. She begins to think of herself as a proto-Catholic. She confesses to Philip that she is still involved with a "young man" (never naming him: perhaps still Charles Johnson?). Of this involvement all we know is that she has been seeing him, several times a year, for some time. And she comes to understand prayer, by which she means not vocalized language, but inward meditation, as the key ingredient to faith, "an attitude of mind, of waiting and hoping." She finds, she says, what she has been looking for, in the liturgy; she feels that joy will come from pain and suffering. In a capping gesture of self-understanding she acknowledges, "I don't do things by halves."

Looking back, in 1980, Amy wrote to Robert Quint that being drawn to a life according to rule had been prepared for "as much by the esthetic side of Christianity, the paintings in European churches, the music of the liturgy, as by anything doctrinal." Luckily for her, she landed at St. Luke in the Fields, the Episcopal chapel founded in 1820 on nearby Hudson Street, and famous for its music. Here, for a while, she was happy "simply because my personal affairs had come unhinged and I was grateful for the grand predictability of the liturgical year."

By November 1956, Amy has been confirmed. She has also, not coincidentally, made peace with her friend Peter, a few months earlier. They have called a halt to their quarrels. Things have settled into a new rhythm: "We can't be friends any more on the old pagan terms, but at least I have stopped feeling indignant with him and he has stopped trying to battle with the Holy Spirit; so far as I am concerned, the Holy Spirit has won and he will let it be so." Do "pagan terms" refer to the differences between their belief systems? Or to physical intimacies that they have outgrown and put aside? We can only speculate.

The conversion and confirmation coincided with the move toward the writing of verse, however awkward the resulting poems seem to us today. But they also perhaps inhibited or at least retarded the full flowering that would come two decades later. In a late letter to Philip Clampitt (March 16, 1998, after Amy's death), Phoebe Hoss wonders whether [Amy's] conversion, however sincere, wasn't significantly a product of her discomfort with the strong "pagan" feelings she evidently expressed in the last two thirds of that religious poem ["The Sun on the Stone"]. Her conversion postponed her really getting to poetry. Perhaps she—like so many of us—wasn't up to accepting those strong feelings then and let religion assume them, a ready vessel. Her speaking of her religious experience is moving, but also reminds me of other writers on spiritual experience—where her passages on nature do not, they reflect her own fresh self.

Hoss was right: whether in her prose or her poetry, Clampitt was always most herself when looking out at the world. Her ambition to tell a story, like her ambition to live a purer, religious, or merely a contemplative life, took her away from doing what she came to do best and most subtly when she put aside both prose fiction and religion in favor of poetry alone.

Her life away from work now began to focus and settle on St. Luke in the Fields. The church was under the supervision of Trinity Wall Street, the church she mentions in "The Kingfisher." One of its early wardens was Clement Clarke Moore, author of "The Night Before Christmas." It was here that she encountered James H. Flye (1884–1985), who had been the teacher of James Agee in Tennessee, and who for years officiated at St. Luke's. In a letter to her sister, Beth (October 20, 1959), Amy wrote that she encountered Father Flye one Sunday morning after church at St. Luke's, and he left her "feeling so cheerful, in spite of its having started out a gray, sullen sort of day," that she felt she owed the uplift in her spirits to the geniality of this kindly, generous man. For much of its history, St. Luke's has been a place of architectural beauty, gorgeous music, and political activism as well as holiness. It made a perfect home for a woman looking for spiritual sanctuary, religious uplift, and aesthetic stimulation. It also offered the chance for a community beyond the secular, intellectual and cultural crowd Amy had grown into. It was here that Amy met two women who not only shared her spiritual cravings but also became lifelong friends: Anne Marshall and Doris Thompson (Myers).

Doris Thompson (1934–2019) had been living in Washington, D.C., and teaching English to Marines at Quantico when Amy met her. She was an Arkansas native who, having read an advertisement in a church magazine, decided in the summer of 1957 to volunteer with the Sisters of St. John the Baptist in Mendham, New Jersey. The sisters assigned her to their small house on Barrow Street, in the West Village, not the main convent in New Jersey. On June 16, 1957 (Trinity Sunday in the church calendar), she participated in a procession of the nuns at Trinity Wall Street. The Sisters put Amy, who at this point had been visiting them for less than a year, in charge of the new recruit. Amy invited Doris for lunch, then for dinner. Thompson said that "we just talked and talked . . . all of a sudden it was after eleven. So she walked me home to Barrow Street and then she took off as fast as she could, to get back home before she got mugged or something. The sisters of course were very perturbed. They were really afraid something had happened to me, because they could see how ignorant I was and how completely unguarded."

The friendship was immediate and long-lasting: "We're both kind of like cats, you know, we walk alone. She was a very friendly person. She was always so interested in everything. I loved her enthusiasm . . . I was kind of the sister that she wanted and didn't quite have, because Beth's life was so problematic." In an interview years later, Doris (now Myers) thought of Amy as ageless: "She never had a birthday and she never talked about age, and she never complained." And Amy was Doris's escort not only in the church, every summer, but in secular New York as well: a guide to the Cloisters, the Empire State Building, Chinese restaurants, the entire gamut of cosmopolitan experiences that both women from the provinces had come to Manhattan to taste.

Thompson continued her work with the sisters, in Manhattan, Jersey City, and then in Mendham, until the fall of 1959, when she entered graduate school at the University of Nebraska. She later became a professor of English at the University of Northern Colorado in Greeley. In 1960, she visited Des Moines, where Amy had come to live with Beth. (The troubled younger sister had begun showing signs of schizophrenia while she was in college. Following other treatments, she was given a partial prefrontal lobotomy.

Amy with her parents at Grinnell, 1941

She never lived alone again.) To Doris, as to many other observers, Amy embodied her father's youthful appearance, but she manifested a gushing enthusiasm where Roy retained a Quaker austerity. Roy seemed to be forty-five, while Pauline "looked like *his* mother . . . like an old lady of seventyish." Stubbornness and seriousness were obvious parts of Amy's genetic makeup. Doris and her husband, Tom, recognized a homespun Iowa sturdiness. Tom said this put him in mind of the jaunty opening song in Meredith Willson's 1957 *The Music Man* that mentions an "Iowa kind of special / Chip on the shoulder attitude." The folks are "so by God stubborn," they can "stand touchin' noses / And never see eye to eye."

Amy was Iowa-stubborn to the core, but neither Doris nor Tom ever quite understood where her very un-Iowa exuberance came from. Earlier, I quoted the estimate of Liz Campbell, Doris's step-daughter and Amy's godchild, who said that being in Amy's presence was like "eternal spring." That enthusiasm, remarked on by everyone who ever knew her, could also get her into trouble. By the 1960s, Amy would be in full outrage against the Vietnam War.

After she had left the Episcopal Church, she tried to encourage the Quakers to send her to Vietnam. They rejected her, thinking she was too unstable.

The third member of the young Anglo-Catholic novices at St. Luke's and Mendham was a teenager named Anne Marshall (b. 1939), the younger daughter of John Marshall (1903–1980) and his first wife, Mary Crandon Gardner Marshall (1903–2000), old-fashioned, high-thinking, vigorous New Englanders. In 1959, John Marshall became the first director of the Rockefeller Foundation's Bellagio Center at the Villa Serbelloni near Lake Como in northern Italy. It was in this glamorous setting that Amy, in September 1960, would bid farewell to her younger friend, who was about to take the veil and enter the convent of St. Mary's Abbey in West Malling, Kent. Amy, like Doris, remained a practitioner at least for a while, but had given up any plan to become a nun.

Having stepped down as the abbess of her English order in 2008, the former Miss Marshall, now Sister Mary John, recalled to me with enthusiasm and precision, in 2019, her younger days with Amy. She remembered herself as something of a rebel from a family whose members were all upstanding Brahmins and Ivy Leaguers. The adolescent Anne was searching for something—she did not know

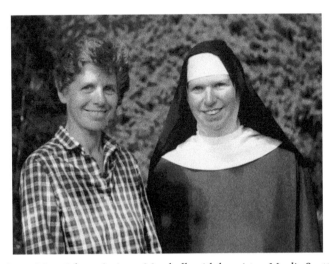

Sister Mary John, née Anne Marshall, with her sister, Maylie Scott, mid-1980s

what—that might bring a different kind of stability and harmony to her life. Like Amy and Doris, Anne approached the church as a "visiting Christian," someone searching for a path. She was as dazzled by Anglo-Catholicism as she was attracted by Amy's appearance at first sight. She finally found her path by entering a religious order. (Amy found it differently, through her writing.) After boarding at the Buxton School in Williamstown, Massachusetts (1954–58), she briefly attended college: Marlboro in Vermont, then Barnard in Manhattan. Three semesters were enough for her. She met Amy at a Sunday service at St. Luke's Chapel, as it was then called, in 1956, while she was still at boarding school. Amy always managed to turn heads, to draw people to her. Anne noticed her and, like Doris, took to her immediately. Amy seemed both sophisticated and otherworldly. Like Doris, Anne was also looking for a big sister, and said that Amy, especially by 1960 when she had lived with, and then left, Beth in Des Moines, may have been looking for a younger one. Anne was struck by this fey creature, utterly different from the inhabitants of the high WASP world in which she had grown up and into which she never fit, but who had created for herself a life full of high culture, book learning, resourcefulness, and spiritual aspiration.

Anne went with Amy to the Cloisters for the art and the music, and to the New York City Ballet, which they both adored, and where the ballerinas Tanaquil Le Clercq and Maria Tallchief became heroes for her. Like everyone else in Amy's life during this period, she, too, remembered the 12th Street apartment, even sixty years later: its narrow bed shoved against the teeming bookcase and doubling as a sofa for visitors; the get-togethers in the studio that were always tête-à-têtes ("I knew a little corner of her life"); Amy's "birdlike" physicality enhanced by her depth of intellect and fierce enthusiasm. "Basically, she was a contemplative, but she was [also] connected to everything. In Naples, when we were traveling there, Amy would notice something—a flower, a building—that grabbed her attention and she became transfixed by it. We almost missed our train." Amy's powers of concentration amounted to compulsiveness in their intensity. Girlish giddiness enhanced the intensity. On that, all her friends agreed. She could seem as jittery as a butterfly and simultaneously fiercely attentive. Within a decade the poet would find a formal outlet for these qualities.

During this phase of her life, Amy filled her journals with deeply felt observations, following the monastic custom called *lectio divina*, divine reading. One reads scripture, then meditates, prays, and contemplates, in order to commune with God. The purpose is not so much to formulate an accurate commentary on a text as to consider scripture as a way to understand Christ. Amy's entries never employ a first-person voice: the "I" is always absent. The would-be believer is an Everyman or Everywoman. A generalized identity takes precedence over an individual personality. Amy's reflections in these entries give us a glimpse of the person who has been striving—for something—for forty years, and offer a foretaste of the attentive poet who will emerge some years later. Throughout, she calculates, contemplates, and wonders about the relationship between the world and the spirit.

Two entries in the diaries—one on meekness, the other on obscurity—are especially revealing of its Christian reader-writer. Amy picked her Bible passages with care. She was aware of herself as both timid (in spite of her confidence) and unknown. Having just returned from Europe, she dated one entry November 6, 1960:

"Blessed are the meek; for they shall inherit the earth." They demand nothing; they expect nothing; they inherit—everything. False meekness, temporary meekness, is not meekness at all, but avarice in sheep's clothing. To be truly meek is to be meek without interruption. It does not take the lowest place in the hope of being called to come up Higher; it takes that place out of its very nature, not so much as lifting up its eyes in vanity. True meekness is totally unself-conscious; it rejoices in whatever is good, with no thought of its own desert. To be wholly meek is to be wholly naked—naked of affectation, of expectation, of every prospect, of every advantage; it is self-effacement without a single sidelong glance. It gives its back to the [smiters]; it makes no answer on its own behalf. When it speaks, it is the transparent speech of the intercessor and the intermediary. True [meekness] is fearless; it needs no badge of [rule], no assurance of status, to armor or bolster it before the world. It asks nothing in the way of reputation, favor, or even experience; it accepts grace with grace, it accepts deprivation too with grace. And it is thus, in that grace of being even without grace, that it inherits what it never asked for, never expected. Having nothing, it becomes the heir of all things.

And from January 1, 1961:

"The voice of one crying in the wilderness, Prepare ye the way of the Lord" . . . The wilderness: solitude and desolation, the death of comfort and of human society: and out of that wilderness, a prophet: a figure without charm, not pleasing or cultivated, repellant, even frightening; and a voice: Prepare ye the way: echoing the call of prophecy from the ages . . . And when that prophesied and looked-for One appeared, it was from obscurity, to be part of the preparation of His own way. From obscurity He appeared, and into obscurity He returned: into the wilderness, into solitude and desolation, the dearth of comfort and of human society: into the rigor of absolute honesty, of withdrawal from the world in order to know where, when he returned to it. His mission lay: into the clarity of rigor, the searching light of the [desert] sun, into the company not of men but of animal nature which is [crossed out: part of] man's nature. In that solitude He would have seen that nature for what it was; perhaps it was there that He [stored?] up His parables and aphorisms—the fowls of the air, the budding of trees, the fading of lilies, the eagles gathering about a carcass. He became one with nature, with the wilderness, in confirmation of the supernatural, after that symbolic death-by-water which is also the beginning of a new life.

Despite the absence of an "I," we can read between the lines and infer something like an autobiography. The writer is a woman aware of herself as naked but unselfconscious, both fearless and all-accepting. Having nothing, she can nevertheless identify with Jesus, the man whose mission possesses "the clarity of rigor," and who is storing parables and aphorisms for future use. A woman living in obscurity finds solace in a man equally obscure before he burst upon a scene. Looking back, we see how Amy here unconsciously sets the stage for her future emergence into a new life several decades later, from cocoon to butterfly, from supplicant to creator, from prose writer to poet.

Amy stayed in touch with Sister Mary John for the rest of her life, visiting her when she went to England and writing letters to her. Most of these do not survive, owing to the rules of the order, which dictated that a letter once read had to be destroyed. How several of these still exist we can count as accidental.

By 1960, Amy's life was divided into three parts: the religious one, centered around St. Luke's, and the sisters in Mendham; the secular, artistic, and social one; and the work life. Much of the 1950s was spent at the Audubon Society, but by the end of the decade, Amy had had enough. As she had done almost ten years before, she decided to quit her job. As early as 1957, after five years at Audubon, she was getting restless. She wrote to Philip that with more responsibility she has learned to give directions, but she really does not like being an administrator. She consults with her boss, with a doctor (who prescribes a mild sedative) and a priest. She has to hire an assistant, a process she finds onerous. The bosses want to promote her, but she resists the extra responsibility: "I am not a born administrator; I'd even rather write my own letters than dictate them. I'm pretty good at needling a superior, and at keeping calm while she gets upset; but I now see that that doesn't mean I wouldn't find myself getting just as upset in her place." In the interview that appeared more than two decades later in *New York* magazine during her years of renown, Amy admitted that her seven years at the Audubon Society were not a happy period. She didn't much like being a librarian, although she loved learning about biology. "I felt like a misfit. Everybody was married, and I didn't want that. But I didn't want to move up in the business world, either. So I didn't have a husband *or* a career. Ultimately, I became a recluse because I didn't have a niche. I'm not saying I'm to be pitied. It's just that I was an anomaly." Her self-confidence was at a low point.

But she learns something about herself: she can resist authority but she does not wish to possess it. This is her version of Abraham

Lincoln's "As I would not be a slave, so I would not be a master." It is an important legacy of her contrarian Quaker heritage. Protest and principled outrage came easily to her. Controlling, even confronting other people did not. Doris Myers recollected, "I don't think she got where she was going in life by explaining herself to people who disagreed with her. It might have been nothing more than just not being able to face hurting their feelings." In January 1959, she writes to Philip that she is considering leaving ("the old urge," she calls it), in order to finish her novel. The job has become too easy, "and there is beginning to be just enough prestige to spoil me a little." Her religious advisers remind her that "too much solitude is unwholesome, frivolous, and even downright wicked." Now, having a community within the church, she feels that she can avoid the life of a total recluse.

Beth, diagnosed six years earlier with schizophrenia, and now about to be permanently hospitalized, wrote to her older sister in 1959 about pessimism and boredom in her job. Amy replied with "a little secret: all jobs are boring. The odd thing is that when you just take it for granted that there isn't any job in the world that *isn't* boring, what you happen to be doing begins to be interesting. I suppose it's partly a matter of not expecting it to sweep you off your feet, and sort of meeting it half-way—something like that. I know that I once thought pessimism was an interesting thing—but not anymore. *It's* more boring than anything else." Her decision to move for a while to Des Moines in order to help her sister strengthened her resolve to quit her position at Audubon. She wrote to Mary Russel, now traveling in England, that she planned to leave in November.

———

The Des Moines residency did not turn out well, and the doctors eventually suggested that the sisters, for both their sakes, should not live together. Beth would spend the rest of her life, until her death several months after Amy's, in nursing facilities. According to her nephew David, Amy always insisted that Beth "was the most gifted of all" the siblings. Amy's months in Iowa allowed her to continue her writing and also to renew a fondness for the land she had left almost two decades before. Des Moines, a mid-size city, required adjusting to: it is neither the rural landscape that nurtured Amy nor the Manhattan in which she came to feel comfortably, in part because anonymously, ensconced. The lack of bookstores disappointed her. So did the lack of good public transportation.

Amy was never without an Emersonian capacity for optimism. The place had its compensations:

> We are living in a three-room apartment above a garage, overlooking a wooded ravine which in turn slopes down toward the Raccoon River. Through the trees—mainly oak, ash, and catalpa—we have a view in three directions towards the hills on the opposite bank. Rock Island trains pass through the valley, and to me they sound almost invariably like tugboats on the Hudson, hooting before one is quite awake on a foggy morning in New York.

By May, she joyfully reexperiences the Iowa springs of her childhood, lawns carpeted with blue flowers, and a multitude of birds—veeries, white-throated sparrows, whicking flickers, in addition to more ordinary species—and she has been able to spend a week with Doris in Lincoln, Nebraska, and to fall in love with Kansas City, where she eats and drinks well: "I never ate a better filet mignon, and the whole dinner came to two dollars. Also, one can order cocktails in a restaurant—and the exhilaration of that fact can be appreciated by one who has been living some three months in a dry state: you feel civilized and cosmopolitan, a certified adult." Even the tornado warnings add a piquant touch. While the streets go dead, pedestrians scurry indoors in an "ominous dead calm, and one sits drinking a brandy, quite calmly except for a queer feeling at the pit of one's stomach." When, finally, the all clear comes through, and no tornado has struck, "one had all the excitement with none of the discomfort of disasters and acts of God."

———

Perhaps Anne Marshall's greatest gift to her yet-to-be-published poet friend was the inspiration for "Rain at Bellagio," in *The King-*

fisher, written almost two decades after the events it describes, events recorded in Clampitt's journals at the time. In September 1960, free from family and work responsibilities, Amy traveled with Anne in Italy. They arrived at the Rockefeller villa in Bellagio in a pouring rain. She spent two days there. Years later, she wanted to dedicate her poem to her old ecclesiastical comrade, now Sister Mary John, living in Kent. The Reverend Sister demurred, saying her order would not look kindly on such a sign of pride, so the dedication went to the third member of the Manhattan trio, Doris Thompson Myers.

Like many Clampitt poems, "Rain at Bellagio" is a story—in this case a travelogue—that suppresses at least as much as it reveals. Clampitt has here found a way to bring storytelling alive by framing it within the tight confines of a poem. It is also the poem of hers that is closest to its prose original, a distillation of events and a transformation of them into a poem. The twelve individual sections range, with only seeming haphazardness, between the Italian landscape, history, and geology; the weather; the elegance of the Villa Serbelloni; the dinner guests at table; and the story of the unnamed, soon-to-be-swept-away daughter who wants to become a nun. The villa's servants, manners, flawless cuisine, and well-stocked cellar offer no temptation to the daughter with religious aspirations, although we can sense the poet's infatuation with her surroundings. Years before she wrote the poem, in a letter to her family dated September 17, 1960, Amy singles out with wonder the three glasses for mineral water, red wine, and champagne at the dinner table. She's in a place of controlled, elegant hedonism, and she loves it. The following day at lunch they are served corn on the cob from the villa's gardens, in honor of the Iowa-born wife of a Mexican agronomist, both of whom are also in residence. Another detail for her to relish.

Both Amy and Anne hunger, but for different kinds of sustenance. Amy has never stayed in any place so magnificent, so much better than what she experienced as a young first-time traveler to the Continent a decade earlier. Anne is eager to leave for England. She wants to escape the world. Amy wants to embrace it. The poem tells their stories decades after the fact, and in its center opens us to the personal crisis at hand:

My friend is twenty,
blond as Lucrezia Borgia, her inclinations
nurtured with care since childhood.
She speaks three languages and has had
six proposals. Since January
her existence has been an exercise
in living like a Principessa. Her father
still cannot fathom what has happened.
He points, appealing, to a letter
on the hall table, overhung
by the tuberoses' extravagant love-death,
addressed to an abbess.

And will she be free to leave if she should wish to?
He, for one, does not believe it. They will wear her down
in that enclosed community, those Anglican Benedictines.
She will become nothing other than a model prisoner.
That, as he understands it, is the long and short
of what they call *formation* amounts to.

One might have said by way of a response (but did not)
that living under vows, affianced to a higher poverty,
might likewise be an exercise in living well.

The last phrase summarizes everything that both women were seeking. Anne found wellness in her vows. Amy took a separate but parallel path.

Clampitt traces those two paths in the poem's two final sections. These fork away from but also reflect each other, like the two women themselves. The friends have long since made their choices. Memory remains.

XI

Sometimes since, in dreams I find myself obliged
to assume, without previous instruction, control

of a plane I have no memory of boarding. I wake
without ever having learned the outcome. Or,
in another region, I find myself
face to face with the transparent strata
of experience, the increment of years,
as a wall of inundation, the drowned mosaic
glimmering above the flood plain. Waking,
I hear the night sounds merge, a single rustle
as of silk, as though becoming might amend,
unbroken, to one stilled, enclosing skein.

XII

At the Abbey, between the shored-up Norman church
and the trefoiled oak of the pilgrim hostel,
running liquid and garrulous through a life of silence,
cushioned and tended between banks of tamed wildflowers,
the sound of water: indivisible, unstilled,
unportioned by the bells that strike the hours.

First, we see the poet forced in a dream to fly and take control, and
then looking back over the years and waking to the sound of waters.
Next, by contrast, we have the silent life of the nun, who is not even
mentioned, but who, like her friend, is surrounded by garrulous
waters that flow unstilled. One life is open, the other enclosed: both
are exercises in living well. The poem tells several stories, as we see
Clampitt learning to reduce the need for confessional or even clearly
personal details in her writing.

The habit of rearranging and reimagining details from her lived
life remained part of Clampitt's creative process in her maturity.
She often blurred identities or changed names: "My Cousin Muriel"
(*Westward*), for example, is a poignant reminiscence and elegy
about her first cousin Margaret Clampitt Carter, dying in California.
Personal details frequently appear, of course, but they are never the
poet's sole focus. Names can often be incidental or irrelevant. "Rain
at Bellagio" shows how a writer can become increasingly impersonal

in her reports about life and people, even as she becomes more herself as a stylist.

A longer, later poem that recalls the past in semi-anonymous terms is "Manhattan," from *A Silence Opens*. The book, like many other last volumes, is obsessed with death and with backward looks. In three parts, "Manhattan" is a valediction, part nostalgic reminiscence of the old Village days, part rueful acknowledgment of the way of all flesh. Phoebe Hoss—to whom Clampitt dedicated this poem—gave the names in her 2007 interview of the individual friends who are described but never specified in the poem: bohemians, writers, eccentrics, part of Amy's crowd, dispersed, dying, dead. "Like kids," Clampitt says, "unwilling, sent back to school, / we learn how our own history has its exits / and its entrances, its waning phase." They are all characters in a play, but she recalls them now anonymously, as if to suggest that death takes away even our names from the mouths of the survivors. Clampitt wants to write elegies but refuses to tell her readers whom she is writing them about. In presenting her life this way—withholding much of it—she is working against the grain of those poetic contemporaries who wish to speak of their lives, their loves, their relationships, as openly as possible. Secrecy, as she once admitted in a letter, is part of her life. Perhaps it is also a sin, perhaps evidence of sublimation, or refusal. Whatever she wished to conceal, and for whatever reasons, the poet came to make an art both deeply individual and objective—or as objective as any art can be.

Her unnamed friends were all at one point like her: young new arrivals to Manhattan, looking for adventure and fulfillment. She offers them as specimens more than as actual persons. Her subject is humanity, Everyman and Everywoman, particularized but not unique. She remembers the giddiness of youth, "shipboard trysts," "tinkling / martini pitchers," "sunsets on Great South Bay; birthday / bashes, welcomes home."

The poem begins with a section called "Grace Church," site of the funeral for the unnamed Hight Moore, who was one half of the gay couple in the old circle that now reassembles, "the loose, patched, decades-frayed / half-accidental, half-willed Old Crowd." Clampitt omits the date (October 1983), which Phoebe Hoss offered in her interview. The poem glances even further back in its second part ("Charles Street"), to the time when all these transplants—from the Carolinas, the Berkshires, Pittsburgh, Appalachia, and Iowa—had come to the walk-ups and "the ginkgo-shaded side streets" of the Village

> to claim the privilege
>
> of ignoring one's next-door neighbors, of
> getting drunk in bars, of being sick in
> hallways, of fornications in strange beds.

The third part ("The Staten Island Ferry") is a homage to Norman Hoss, Phoebe's former husband (also unnamed), a seaman with a fondness for the Manhattan harbor. Clampitt then moves to the Brooklyn Bridge, Hart Crane, Ellis Island, the Statue of Liberty, now the symbol "of the possible, the yet-, the never-to-be- / ventured on." The eternity of myth absorbs us all. This three-part survey of the poet's crowd is a celebration and a lament. Its last line—"the mind gropes toward its own recessional"—implies that all looking back is an awkward defense against a sober looking ahead.

———

Following her time in Des Moines, Amy returned to Manhattan and spent a week in New Jersey with the Sisters of St. John the Baptist, toying with the idea of actually becoming a nun. Then came the trip abroad. She alit for Europe, where she visited Bellagio and other Italian sites. She took her leave from Anne Marshall. She went to Salzburg, Paris, and England. She returned to New York in November, unpublished and unemployed, and disabused of the notion of taking religious orders. On June 15, 1960, she had turned forty. She was doing freelance editing, an on-and-off makeshift employment that paid her enough to get by. Her most important supporter and client, from 1967 on, was the journalist and historian David Schoenbrun (1915–1988), who relied on her attentive editorial expertise to guide him through several books, who thanked her generously and publicly, and who lived long enough to witness her rise to fame in the 1980s.

At home, politics soon began to compete with religion as a primary focus in her life. Even on picket lines and protest marches, attending zoning meetings with the likes of Jane Jacobs (February 7, 1962) and palling around with Grace Paley and other Village lefties, Amy managed to maintain what one old comrade-in-arms, Myrna Berase, recalled in a letter from 1992 as her "elfin, serene presence." Her otherworldliness only heightened the grit and fierce determination that she had begun to put to use.

PART 3: 1961–1973

On February 4, 1962, Amy notes Beth's thirty-fourth birthday in her journal. Then she continues, without any obvious transition, to a reminiscence of the (perhaps still modestly ongoing, perhaps long passed) romance with Charles Johnson. Trouble has given way to resignation. Such resignation is what will lead her down other, more public paths:

> Twelve years compounded of one great [catastrophe] and of successive small miracles have passed. Something has been salvaged, just as something was salvaged of that furious, snatched, law-defying counterpoint that had its beginning with incalculable [and] fortuitous simultaneity with that other, undeliberate madness; but just what, how much, it is impossible to know. I fear no more the heat of the sun or the furious winter's rages; but on the other hand, Out of the day and night a joy has taken flight; Fresh spring and winter hoar move my faint heart not even, indeed, with grief, but certainly not with delight—although the mood of Shelley, barely thirty, is not mine at all. But as Charles once complained, and I would not understand him, the poetry is gone.

Amy here knits a complicated patchwork quilt of literary and personal references. Her sister's madness has led her to think of her own situation. She invokes both Shakespeare ("Fear no more," the song from *Cymbeline*) and Shelley ("A Lament") to measure her distress. Almost forty-two, she cannot avoid fashioning her life as a literary artifact, but she goes beyond the example of her cherished English Romantic predecessor. Amy is numb to both delight *and* grief, whereas Shelley, who died when he was twenty-nine, could take some consolation from unhappiness: "Fresh spring, and summer, and winter hoar, / Move my faint heart with grief, but with delight / No more—Oh, never more!"

In August, Amy set out for the Midwest, first to visit her family and then to meet up in Omaha with Doris and her fiancé, Tom Myers, for a camping trip to California. She arrived by bus in Omaha from Lincoln, with a sleeping bag on her lap. In a letter to Barbara Blay, her host during the 1949 trip to England, Amy describes this unique western-bound expedition in a Chevy Bel Air as a "wedding trip before the wedding," she as a bridesmaid and duenna to the chaste young couple, and all three of them camping out in city parks; tucking sagebrush for fragrance into their pillows at Amy's suggestion; freezing one night in Colorado, and configured as spoons in their sleeping bags with Doris in the middle between her friend and her boyfriend; picnicking during a dust storm in Nevada. She has never done anything like this before. In her letter she says it's just the kind of weird and unexpected traveling she loves.

In her journal of September 1962, Amy, having arrived in Berkeley, comments on the behavior of Tom and Doris: "By now I could scarcely remember Tom's name—not because I felt a stranger but rather because I had become so interwoven with his and Doris's existence (in fact I could scarcely remember her name either) that my own identity seemed to have melted into theirs." For the woman and soon-to-be poet, this statement seems a version of the Keatsian loss of individuality that comes from melting into other souls: as he took part in the existence of the sparrow at his window, so Amy could blend—spiritually? metaphorically?—with her engaged friends.

The wedding was a success. Amy then set out for a circuitous return to the East, via Los Angeles, the Grand Canyon, and Santa Fe.

She kept notes in a journal. At a restaurant in a bus station in Taos, she meets a man from Colorado whom she misidentifies as a

Texan. Just as everyone she sees is a potential figure of interest, so she, too, is a figure who provokes curiosity. He inquires, "What y'all writin' in that book?" Fascinated, he says he has mistaken her for a detective, owing to the trench coat she's wearing. She stops in Iowa once more, for a family reunion that reunites all five siblings, plus her brothers' children, for the first time in two decades.

Back in Manhattan, Amy continued her life in an even more piecemeal fashion. There were occasional freelance editing assignments. In April 1965, she set sail for Greece. The trip was part confirmation, part transformation. She could now witness at first hand the ancient land of myth, history, culture, and philosophy that helped to form her imaginative life as a student and reader. Like all of her travels, the experience produced intellectual stimulation and spiritual uplift.

She comes equipped with her typewriter, of course, but mostly she maintains a combination of hawklike vigilance and charitable neutrality: eyes and ears are open and she takes in everything, first on shipboard, then on land.

She is eager to be pleased:

> We have a delightful cabin steward named Giorgos, who speaks English and is very encouraging about one's stumbling efforts in Greek. ("Kalimera-sas," for Good morning; "Efkaristo" for thank you, "Ti kanis?" for How are you? "Poli-kala," for Very well, and so on.) And every afternoon there is a half-hour Greek class where we learn phrases and are being taught to sing "Never on Sunday" in Greek! I never saw a ship so organized: there is even something called Social Discussions—and an Iowa-born man and his wife told me they went, and the first one was about the benefits of the unpolished-rice diet!

Amy's mates in a small, cramped cabin include a Greek grandmother, with no English, returning from visiting her children in the States; a Russian exile who also speaks no English; and a chic Neapolitan lady with whom Amy communicates "in a wildly haphazard mixture of French, English, and Greek phrases when they happen to come out." With a smattering of Orthodox Jews headed to Haifa (the

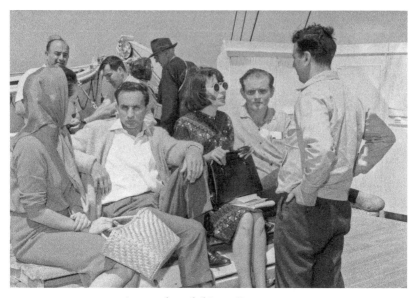

Amy on board ship to Greece, 1965

ship keeps a kosher kitchen for their needs), and a Greek Orthodox patriarch with black cassock and silvery beard (conducting services for his coreligionists), the boat is a sailing experiment in cultural variety, a floating United Nations. A delicious fact takes even Amy by surprise: because she travels with a typewriter, people mistake her for a traveling stenographer, just as the Coloradan thought she was a detective.

As eager as she is to be pleased, she is equally willing to please. She obliges her shipmates' requests and writes letters on their behalf: some for a multilingual Israeli to friends in the States, others for a striptease dancer from Dallas. She is always writing. Two years earlier, she wrote to Mary Russel that "vocation is a curious thing." She had tried not to want to be a writer, but she has kept coming back to the only thing that makes sense to her. On board ship, or traveling inland, still with no publishable proof of her supposed vocation, she is steadfastly proving it, if to no one but herself.

No matter that the author is a nobody: Amy's travel letters and journals make for engaging reading. Throwing herself into fun that does not begin until midnight on board ship, with a Greek band playing and the native Greeks doing what Amy calls a blend of

"English country dancing and Russian gymnastics," she turns in around three and is up at eight before breakfast the next day. They pass by or through Lisbon, Naples, Stromboli, and Messina, but Amy is hungering for something bigger and better. She has instructed the night steward to awaken her at five so that she will not miss the first sighting of the isles of Greece: "at half-past five I was looking at a sunrise that explained all those repeated references in Homer to Rosy-fingered Dawn." Reality is indebted to mythology, as is life to literature. Finally, the harbor of Piraeus comes into view, and Amy picks a hill she is sure is the Acropolis (a mistaken notion, as it turns out). Reality disappoints. The first sighting of the Parthenon "was far too remote and dim to be at all spectacular." Nevertheless, she can hardly eat. They pull into port.

As a single American woman traveling alone (with a hat box, too!) and speaking a little Greek, Amy is something of a sensation, and "an Athenian hairdresser had transformed me into something or other; also, nobody could see very well, and I'm afraid once again I was being taken for twenty-five, if that!" In Athens, five young swains begin to pay attention to her. One is a shepherd from Mount Parnassus, or so he brags. She is carried through back streets to her hotel. The young man prefers traveling by donkey to cars or buses, he says, but he was "one of the most elegantly groomed young men I ever saw." She finds it charming to suppose that herdsmen on Mount Parnassus "would carry on the cult of Apollo. My friend the desk clerk assured me 'He thinks he *is* Apollo.' At this point the Greek consciousness becomes a total mystery." Why should she not give in to the phantasy?

Amy's fifteen-page, single-spaced typed letter to her family shows how she constantly meets and happily fraternizes with people of all ages and types, from everywhere. It's no wonder she finds herself constantly "exhausted to the point of stupidity" or "limp with fatigue." "Excuse the long-winded ecstasy," she begs, after raving about Delphi, the most beautiful place she's ever seen, "but that is why I came here, to see and exclaim."

One entry might stand as a representative of her entire trip, her entire life. There's a final party. Amy stands among students, toasting and singing. They have pushed the tables together, many students from Salonika and a guest from America, "and someone gave me an enormous pink and yellow rose; and then they began singing, and from the singing they went on to dancing . . . it was all improbable and perfectly natural."

This excitement does not fade. It lasts, perhaps even more strongly, in memory, replayed in a higher key. She writes to Rimsa Michel from New York (August 28, 1965) that her return to America on a smoggy July day made her think that the red Manhattan dawn "looked like Sodom and Gomorrah." Everything at home, she says, pales in comparison to Greece, where knocking about "in reckless disregard of danger to life and limb on . . . wild mountain roads was a form of taking one's life in one's hands that could also be enjoyed. I expected to be killed from minute to minute, and I never was happier anywhere in my life." Delphi, Parnassus, Mykonos, Delos, Naxos: "it was all wild, improbable and romantic."

Like the party, like the entirety of her Greek adventure, Amy's life—improbable, and "perfectly natural"—goes on. Equally important, the trip has planted seeds that will bear fruit two decades later in the poems of her mature years, heavily inflected by her love of this country's landscape, literature, and myth. Clampitt's Greek poems had a long gestation, as did much else that was nurtured in her imagination.

———

Clampitt's persistent failure to market her fiction made her reluctant to keep plying this particular trade after 1966. A quarter century was more than enough time to persuade her that her novels were going nowhere. And now politics, history, and American cultural unrest all added to her reluctance to keep writing them. As early as 1961 she was involved in local politics: protesting housing policies, condo conversions, and other large-scale real estate developments. By 1967 she began to supplement her local political work with efforts in a more intense register: the Vietnam War had captured the national attention. Amy became fully engaged. In 1970 she did fundraising for the Black Panthers and the Cesar Chavez grape boycott to help migrant farm workers. She told her oldest and always favorite nephew, David Clampitt, a college student in the late 1960s, that "novels—they're for peacetime, when people have time on their hands."

Amy was not only throwing herself into protests against the war; she was also entering what her family referred to as a dark period of nervousness and unhappiness. David recalled the Christmas visit to his parents' house in the late 1960s or early '70s, when she was prone to "vehement rants." His mother, Jeanne, said she was reluctant to deal with these in a house with children around her: Amy "was in turmoil . . . she was tense. Her misery made everyone else miserable. She was like a drum, she was so tight."

At its most extreme, Amy's agitation spilled over into fear, even mild paranoia. According to Mary Jo Salter, there were moments when Amy thought the government was stealing her mail. Salter also suggested that were she alive today, Amy would be timid of the Internet for the ways in which it might allow the government to surveil ordinary citizens and to betray their privacy without their consent. (On the other hand, Amy would welcome the speed with which anyone might find facts on the Internet—a perfect tool for a researcher and editor like her.) Besides, technology never appealed to her: "Her idea of really challenging technology was switching from a manual typewriter to an electric one."

Her unhappiness in the late 1960s, however, had an upside. Political engagement made Amy part of a community, something she was trying to find during the earlier years at the Audubon Society when she had sought refuge from her professional life in organized religion. Political causes spoke to her pacifist nature and to the righteous indignation she could muster when she felt provoked. She channeled her natural exuberance into participation in public affairs. Such activity both complemented and offered respite from the freelance editorial work she had begun in order to secure a modest income. In March 1968, she went to Washington to protest in front of the Internal Revenue Service building, having deliberately filed an incomplete tax return. She wrote to her college classmate Barbara Clark, "The penalty, should the Government choose to enforce it, is up to a year in jail and/or ten thousand dollars fine. I took my text from Thoreau, as being a part of the American tradition." She has "gone into politicking," has joined the local Reform Democratic Club, and begun canvassing throughout her Village neighborhood. Terrified at first, she finds the committed political life a great adventure. She has thrown in her lot with Eugene McCarthy's run for the presidential nomination, and she follows the war "with a horrified fascination." She has reluctantly forgone opera and ballet; even cooking, she says, has been tossed aside for the moment. Art has given way to more timely incitements, a striking change for someone who as recently as two years previous (May 1966) could describe happily waiting in line for five hours at the Metropolitan Opera House box office to buy tickets to see the Bolshoi Ballet. The chapter of Amy as a cultural consumer was temporarily fading into the background, or being put on hold.

In June 1968, Amy describes to Rimsa Michel a young man named Bill, who has enchanted her (we know nothing else about him), "an authentic flower child" whom she also mentions in a December letter to Barbara Clark as "the great love of this mad year, with whom I rang doorbells in the spring but who has since defected from the whole thing—very, very young, but articulate as the young seldom know how to be, and likewise gentle, and at the same time radical as only the young are, perhaps, even nowadays. In short, I never felt more alive."

———

Whoever he was and whatever he meant to Amy, Bill quickly vanished from the scene. Then someone better for her showed up. At some point in the late spring of 1968, Amy met Harold Korn. Before the end of the year they had become a couple. Like her, he was a member of the Village Independent Democrats, and was canvassing for McCarthy; like her, he lived downtown, but at the Brevoort, on more glamorous lower Fifth Avenue near Washington Square, farther from the noise of the West Side Highway and the expanses of the Hudson River. He was a professor at New York University's law school. He was almost a decade her junior.

Born in the Bronx (June 25, 1929), raised in Brooklyn, an only child, Hal attended James Madison High School, one of four secondary schools worldwide to have educated five or more Nobel laureates. Other alumni include Garson Kanin, Ruth Bader Ginsburg, Chuck Schumer, Bernie Sanders, and Chris Rock. The school was a cauldron of intellectual activity, a place filled with immigrants or the children of immigrants, who were destined for advancement in what appeared in the first half of the last century to be an America of opportunity and promise. Hal was the valedictorian in a class of seven hundred students. He was also popular, handsome, charming, witty, and modest.

Jacob and Nettie Korn, Hal's parents, were both Polish Jewish immigrants who had arrived in New York right after World War I. Nettie's extended family were murdered by the Nazis during the next war. Jacob ran a series of barely viable grocery stores, at the last of which—in Harlem—he had a Black partner. Hal was the revered intellectual among nine first cousins on the Korn side. The family called him Hesh or Heshie.

According to Margot Honig, who knew him as early as 1961, and who became his accountant, "his parents were afraid he was retarded" because he didn't really begin to speak until he was close to four. And when he did speak, Yiddish, not English, was the mother tongue. The language of the New World came second. The family remembered the story of little Heshie's first day in kindergarten. He came home in tears, having been bullied by the other children. "Why do they hit me?" he cried.

His mother, a natural although untrained psychologist, asked, "Why do you think they did?"

His thoughtful, measured answer: "Maybe because they can't understand me, and I don't understand them." At Hal's memorial service (May 23, 2001), his cousin Helen Korn Atlas suggested that "reason, not revenge, was to be the solution for meanness and injustice." His course was set.

After high school, Hal went on a scholarship to Cornell, the first person in his family to pursue a postsecondary education. His closest college friend was another native Yiddish speaker, the even more eccentric Harold Bloom from the Bronx, equally out of place in a country setting. This second Harold sailed through Cornell before becoming an institution himself: a distinguished, sui generis Yale literary critic. Bloom described for me a drive home from Ithaca one vacation. The two Harolds, both with New York accents, stopped for food in a small hamlet. Bloom could recall the scene even after seven decades: at a roadside diner, talking with some of the local rustics, neither pair could understand the other. The college boys were speaking to each other in a combination of Yiddish and English, but even when chatting with the locals, their thick accents made it impossible for their interlocutors to follow them. The city mice and the country mice—the Jews and the goyim—dealt with one another, guardedly but amicably.

After law school at Columbia, Hal clerked for Judge Stanley H. Fuld at the New York Court of Appeals from 1954 to 1956. Standards were intimidatingly high. He became painstakingly slow in finishing his work (Bloom said that even in college Hal agonized over his writing), for which reason his publishing record during his academic legal career was skimpier than it otherwise might have been. His articles were significant, however, and are still quoted in the fields of criminal law and evidence. The first volume of *New York Civil Practice* (there would be sixteen in total), coauthored with Jack B. Weinstein of Columbia Law School and Arthur R. Miller of Harvard, was published in 1963. His final project, *Modern Conflicts of Law and Jurisdiction*, which he took with him to the hospital as he lay dying in 2001, was on civil and administrative procedure, according to his obituary in *The New York Times*. Most lawyers agree that "conflicts of laws," Korn's last major field, among the most esoteric, most challenging of legal subspecialties, was perfectly suited to an intellectual always on the lookout for nuance, contradiction, and unforeseen problems. One lawyer told me that "resolving conflicts of laws questions has been analogized to looking into a barbershop mirror . . . just an endless set of further reflections to infinity." Hal did not make things easy for himself. He sought out difficulty rather than avoided it.

Jack Weinstein was both Hal's colleague at Columbia Law School (where Korn went to teach in 1971) and a longtime friend. In 1967, he became a U.S. federal judge for the Eastern District of New York. Like Bloom, Weinstein was aware of Hal's perfectionism as a writer. When *The Kingfisher* appeared in 1983, he wrote a congratulatory letter to Clampitt (a late publisher although never a slow writer) with a note about her partner: he told her that Hal "should not really be depressed by the Columbia article. It is just great, although it does not meet his impossibly high standards." In a memorial note about Hal in the *Columbia Law Review*, Judge Weinstein remembered—as did Bloom in conversation—that his college classmates found Hal charming. Weinstein used words like "modest," "funny," "princely," "generous," and "whimsical" to describe him: "Hal, like Amy, was in a sense only three years old. He had the capacity to the end to look with wide-eyed wonder at the law and ask, why is it the way it is, and how can it be better."

Elizabeth Bernhardt, a Columbia Law School student in the 1980s, said that when she was considering taking a government job and a huge pay cut, with two daughters to put through college, Hal "blithely" said to "take the job. So you'll eat spaghetti for a few years." She heeded his advice and took the job, realizing that a daily pasta diet alone would not save her enough money to pay the tuition, but knowing also that Hal was always on the side of his students, doing favors for them, cheering them on.

Honig said the same thing: "He had a compassionate, open spirit. He listened to what people said, and was exceptionally appreciative of things. He wasn't at all somebody who was uniquely focused on his career or puffed up. He was interested in everything in the world around him." In spite of ups and downs (Hal became envious when Amy won a MacArthur prize in 1992, and a temporary rift opened in their relationship), Honig allowed that "it was kind of a match made in heaven." Bernhardt used the word "jealous," in its authentic sense: "he adored Amy. When I first went to his apartment, she was away, teaching somewhere. He was jealous, wondering what she was doing when she was away from him. It was not a mean jealousy—it was sweet and sad, the jealousy of someone who thought no one could be more irresistible than Amy." Harold Korn was a mensch. He brought or offered stability to many people, Amy above all.

John Sare, another Columbia law student from the late 1980s, remarked that Korn parted ways with his colleagues in many respects. He was not a charismatic lecturer. He didn't grandstand. He was shy, not self-promoting. His kindness made him even more appealing to students who did not take easily to the coldly professional and competitive zeitgeist that used to be the norm in law schools. He played with words, slyly. Take "seminal." It is a word that lawyers use a lot ("the seminal case" on some legal principle or another):

> Hal studiously, consistently, would not use it. He always said "the ovular case," and I loved him for that. It seemed to be at once a command for us to wake up and pay attention to what words mean, a statement about the capacity of metaphors to become denatured clichés, and a tribute to the creative capacity of women, perhaps the famous poet who was his spouse but whom I don't recall him ever actually mentioning. I often use the term in my legal practice, as a tribute to him, and obliquely to Amy, and always with attribution.

For some years, Korn was one of two professors of Civil Procedure, a course required of all first-year law school students. Hans Smit was the other. John Sare remembered, "Professor Smit and Professor Korn could not have been more different." Smit was tall, bald, Dutch, cosmopolitan, multilingual, amusing, and intimidating. He was also an accomplished water polo player. He owned the twelve-thousand-square-foot Schinasi Mansion, in French Renaissance style, on Riverside Drive. He collected fourteenth- and fifteenth-century art and furnishings, and had a spectacular wine cellar.

Hal's European-born colleague lived in splendor, like a grandee. He made lots of money as a consultant. Hal, the Bronx *yeshiva bocher*, lived, by contrast, modestly in a one-bedroom apartment with spartan furnishings and everything helter-skelter. Material things seemed to concern him not at all. His spirit was princely although his style was not.

That princely, whimsical, generous nature served him well with people. Indeed, it became indispensable to him after the fire.

In 1957, in a car driven by his first wife, Korn was involved in a freak accident with a drunk driver one morning in Wellfleet on Cape Cod. Both Korn and his wife were seriously injured. The marriage ended in divorce shortly thereafter. Hal sustained horrible

Harold Korn in middle age

burns that required considerable reconstructive surgery. For the rest of his life, his disfigured face looked like part of a grotesque mask designed to terrify small children. His friend Rachel Brownstein, a CUNY literature professor, said he had such beautiful blue eyes that "once you noticed them you forgot everything else about the face." Doris Myers said the same thing: "You look at a picture of him and it's like a Halloween mask. You'd be with him for five minutes and you [didn't] see it any more. He had such a winning personality."

After the accident, he would never sit on the passenger side of a car if he could avoid it. He did all the driving himself, never wanting to relinquish control. He disliked flying almost as much as Amy did, even though he understood how much safer a plane is than an automobile. And in Manhattan he avoided public transportation and city streets as much as possible. First downtown, and then at 160 East 65th Street, he always kept a car, which he drove between home and his university offices, at NYU and then, after 1971, at Columbia.

Reticent, as usual, about private matters, Amy brought Hal to the attention of her friends and family only gradually—both in correspondence and in person. She revealed his presence and introduced him into her circle circumspectly, even slyly. (For his part, Hal was equally private. He kept Amy out of the family circle for a while, and his first cousins recalled meeting her only years after she and Hal had become a couple.) Her first mention of him to her family came in a letter of November 18, 1969, which included a long description of participating in the March on Washington. She refers to him as "the gentlest and most unflappable person I know." In the early years of her fame more than a decade later, she would often refer to him in letters and interviews, anonymously and objectively, with words like "my best friend, a lawyer."

Phoebe Hoss recalled that Amy first introduced Hal to their friends at a party in 1968. There is a weird irony in the fact that it was not a masquerade party, although held close to Halloween, but when Amy and Hal arrived, "none of us were prepared for how he looked. His face softened out in later years, and I got sort of used to it, but it was a shocker." One ear was more than a little peculiar, and Hal's translucent skin was creased and folded like ragged paper.

Hoss pointed out that Amy had a principled obliviousness to other people's feelings. In her high-minded way, she evidently thought that a man's physical appearance was not something to be discussed, or perhaps even mentioned. This might seem odd in the woman who, when traveling in Europe a decade before, could not avoid commenting on the beauty—or lack thereof—in men she saw, admired, and flirted with.

Another kind of woman might have felt an opposing ethical impulse, namely, to forewarn her friends that her new beau might shock them at first sight. One principle won out over the other. All along, Amy was a woman of standards, sometimes competing ones. In a lengthy letter to Philip in 1954, other parts of which I quote throughout these pages, Amy at thirty-three gives a list of these standards, squeezed out of the welter of her still young life:

> . . . never to exert power for its own sake; never to cultivate anybody or anything for the sake of a possible future advantage; never to blame anybody without assuming a share of the blame myself; never to make claims on anybody else; to yield gracefully and with equal grace to be firm, and not to be swayed by other people's ideas of what is important.

Amy as a child

Amy, high school senior class photo

354 West 12th Street

354 West 12th Street, interior overlooking courtyard

Amy on board ship, 1949

Young Harold Korn

Corea, Maine

Amy and Hal at home in the Berkshires, 1992

Amy and Karen Chase, Berkshires cottage, 1993

The Berkshires cottage

Mary Jo Salter, 1979

Alice Quinn, c. 1983

Ann Close, 1994

Peter Kybart, c. 1994

Phoebe Hoss, 1994

Reading at Bellagio, 1991

On the train to Key West, 1994

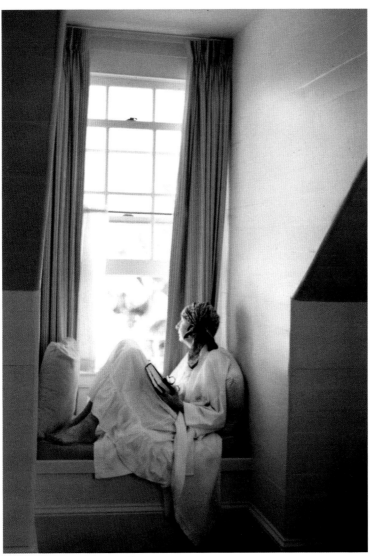

Reading in the hotel window, Key West, 1994

In the backyard, summer 1993

Amy and Hal, wedding photo,
June 2, 1994

This is high-minded thinking, bearing the stamp of Emerson, and of both Henry and William James. It endowed Amy with a credo of independence and responsibility.

For the next twenty-five years, most people were charmed and gratified by the ways in which Amy and Hal supported each other. Looking back, however, Hoss considered that they did not really communicate as intimately as other couples did. The relationship had a darker underside. Much was unexamined: "Amy was often distressed and didn't know how to deal with [adverse feelings, her own or others'], but she was not in the habit of talking about it, and she disliked the whole idea of therapy." She had never lived with a romantic partner before, so she had difficulty when Hal came into her life: "she had been able to avoid the prickles of living closely with people." Hoss thought that in spite of his pride in Amy's rise to fame, Hal also harbored some envy, slight but inevitable, because she had become better known than he: "they each had an undeveloped emotional aspect. They were not fully emotional partners, really, and I think Amy said once they got along together like children, you know, happy children."

There was a conventional part of Amy, remembered Doris Myers, that countered her uncontainable exuberance and bohemianism. Myers said "it was painful to her not to be married, even though she had another side of herself that ran like crazy away from commitment." Amy herself had confessed in her letter to Philip fifteen years earlier, quoted above, that she "very much wanted to make a fairly impressive marriage, in order to have seemed to have arrived, in the eyes of other people—and what other people thought has always been of great importance, odd as it may seem." She credits, or blames, the standards of "others," but she clearly had internalized these to the point of wanting for herself some symbol of normality. From the surviving, almost purring letters that Amy wrote to Hal during their occasional times apart, we get the sense that gentle affection rather than raw sexual urgency was the physical sensation that registered with both of them. Most of Amy's old friends had the same sense. "Dear Critter [or Crittur]" begin many of the letters. He's the lion, she the purring cat. (Clampitt inscribed a copy of an unpublished 1977 poem, "The Perils of Channel 13," to Hal: "For

Lion / with a hug / from Snuggle-Cat.") Karen Chase, a friend at the very end, thought otherwise: "She never talked about sex, but I always had the feeling that sex was probably a very important part of their relationship . . . you could tell sex was important to [Harold]. It wasn't something they talked about."

It took Amy seven years to open up about Hal to Rimsa Michel, who'd left the Audubon Society and New York for Alabama. In 1975 she says her friend is right to ask for explicit details:

> How to categorize what's going on isn't easy, though, partly because we're both just wary enough of institutionalizing not to have settled on a category. I guess we mainly think of ourselves as Best Friends.

She says she doesn't want to be a wife, but she has accommodated herself sufficiently to a Jewish partner to talk about "the mishegass" of Hal's Orthodox parents and their expectations for him. She has settled down. And as the relationship developed, she became close to Nettie Korn, a woman who everyone said shared Amy's general enthusiasm for life but lacked her intellectual precocity. Phoebe said that Nettie had the same "ardor" and "inner fire" that Amy possessed, but in a different register. Ann Close, Amy's second editor at Knopf, called Nettie a "game girl." Hal must have sensed that his new lover possessed the same energy his mother had always embodied.

It took a decade for this quasi-in-law relationship to deepen and thrive. In a letter of December 16, 1979, Amy says she has been invited for the first time to celebrate Hanukkah with the Korns on West End Avenue. And she adds, "There was a small flurry a while back when his father got into his head that I might be persuaded to convert, and then they could have a proper daughter-in-law; but they have since been set straight on that, or so Hal says. They're dear people anyhow."

Hal's first wife, Ann, was a gentile who—according to one family memory, which may be unreliable—converted to Judaism for her husband's sake. Hal had lived as an undergraduate in some kind of boardinghouse run by Ann's family in Ithaca. She was at the time of the marriage a librarian at Columbia Law School. The accident

Jacob and Nettie Korn, probably early 1970s

did not bring the couple unity in suffering. It drove them apart. After the divorce, the entire Korn family either banished her from conversation or forgot all about her. Amy's presence in Hal's life was in at least one way a repetition of his first marriage (the inevitable shock to his parents of his bringing home another shikse), but in more important ways it was a move away from it. She was not about to convert, for the sake of her lover or his parents. Her kindness and her high-minded stubbornness managed to coexist, and the quartet of family participants gradually became less wary of one another. She referred to her all-but-in-name in-laws as the Elderkorns.

———

In 1969, Richard Nixon having been elected president the previous November, Amy threw herself even more fervently into anti–Vietnam War protests. On October 15, an all-day, widespread Moratorium to End the War in Vietnam sponsored events all over the country. This was followed one month later by the March on Washington. Amy was at both. In Manhattan, she squeezed herself into one protest venue that featured Senator McCarthy and Mayor

John Lindsay, the cast of the rock musical *Hair*, and the folksingers Judy Collins and Peter, Paul and Mary. To Beth in Des Moines, she wrote:

> At the end of that rally I came downtown and joined a sort of straggling procession into Washington Square Park, with everybody carrying lighted candles. Under the arch, people were reading the names of American soldiers killed in Vietnam. It was very quiet and strange, with a little sliver of new moon just about to go down in the background. After a while the whole procession started uptown to Rockefeller Center, carrying candles and pretty much stopping traffic.

A bit later, a Black and Brown Caucus appeared at St. Mark's Church in the Village with a list of demands, and calling for the support of the congregants. Many of them answered the call and walked out of the service to signify their shared resistance to various forms of oppression. Meetings, phone calls, noise, and anger ensued. People were confused, not knowing how far to go, and in what direction. This was the point at which, according to Philip Clampitt, Amy's frustration with the church began to simmer. In a few more years, that simmer began to boil over. In the spring of 1971, she met with Paul Moore, who the following year would become the Episcopal bishop of New York. She demanded that the Episcopal Church take a stronger antiwar stance. Moore, an outspoken liberal, did not satisfy all of Amy's demands, even though he had led a peace mission to South Vietnam in 1970. She wrote to her family (April 2, 1971) that she had left the church in anger. In a later essay, "The Long, Long Wait: The Epistles to the Thessalonians" (1990), she offered another reason for her flight, colored of course by her long relationship with Harold Korn: the Christian church's age-old "callousness toward the Jews." She had come to the realization that Anglo-Catholicism had better music and art—those rich, medieval stained-glass windows, the Renaissance pictures she had always admired, more beautiful architecture—and all around "better taste" than the enthusiastic, Low Church Protestant sects she had grown up with in Iowa. But at the core of Christianity, going back to Saint

Paul, was antisemitism, not so pure and not so simple: "The accretions of history, of its folly and turpitude, stare us down."

In middle age, Amy was readjusting to changes in her life. These led to changes in her understanding of religion, politics, and society. And she became more aware than she ever had been of how language reflects and creates our political consciousness. The woman who was an exuberant and hedonistic traveler when younger, but who called herself a "prude" later in life to a group of students in Florida when discussing four-letter words in poetry, came to understand the meaning of obscenity. In a letter to her family (March 11, 1970), she says her eyes have been opened:

> I think we've all been anesthetized to the things that are really wrong, in part by an undue concern with what is "nice" or "not nice." For myself, I know that this is true. I refused to see or read *Who's Afraid of Virginia Woolf?* because of the four-letter words, as much as anything else. Not that I necessarily missed very much, but it was symptomatic of my own hangup over being *above* things like gutter language. It was the Chicago convention that turned me around finally. Abbie Hoffman using obscenities, Mayor Daley using obscenities—it was no use hiding from the language, when the real obscenity was the management of the convention, and above all Hubert Humphrey quoting from Saint Francis and going all misty-eyed about getting the nomination. It was *that* obscenity that kept me from voting for Humphrey in November.

She was as high-minded as her father and grandfather, and although she would never resort to those four-letter words in either speech or writing, she was learning that unethical deeds, not distasteful or vulgar language, were the proper object of her animus. She may have been overheated in her political commitments, but she was also capable of refining or tempering her responses to provocation.

Hal's presence coincided with Amy's ongoing political activism. The combination of a new domestic partner and a life of public engagement could result in the occasional contretemps. These emanated from, and fed back into, Amy's nervous energy and her anxieties about matters private and public. One letter to Barbara Clark (September 25, 1970) mingles, perhaps unconsciously, the two spheres. It begins with an excited account of getting locked up, for the second time, in a protest for tenants' rights, and the thrill of encountering, and then being jailed with, people this middle-aged intellectual would not run across in her normal life. The experience energizes her. But the letter then segues quickly into a description of the kind of incident that occurs in the lives of any couple, especially one just getting to know each other. Hal and Amy were heading to dinner with Shale and Rachel Brownstein: he was a psychiatrist friend of Hal's and she an English professor. During a political conversation on the street, Amy became heated; the psychiatrist, supported by Hal, called her biased; Amy felt cornered and angry but said nothing, preferring to simmer. Sensing something amiss, Hal admitted his failure to stand up for her, and the quartet went into dinner, but the unpleasantness and uncertainty hung on for days, especially because Amy was upset by what she took to be the other couple's condescension: they applauded her unrealistic idealism while implying that their own hardheaded realism was preferable or more mature. The following day, the effects still lingering, Amy uses the word "camouflage" to explain how her depression over the state of the world might be a cover-up for unassuaged anger, even though Hal has finally come around, as he did for the remainder of their domestic life, to understanding and supporting her. He recommends as delicately as possible psychotherapy of some sort, but the patient has been smart enough to analyze herself and to confront the forces and the feelings overflowing from within. Hal, she comes to realize, has the remarkable capacity to be both sorry and undefensive about it, offering support when she needs it.

As Amy details her complicated responses in the letter, she is in the process of both understanding herself and reaching for greater truths. Even with infinite reserves of goodwill, she allows that it is difficult to remain truthful, even—or especially—with the people one feels closest to. Anger festers within, just as political rage is in the air we breathe, or at least the air that she was breathing in the late 1960s. She continues:

... the reason truthfulness between people is so rare is that it is even harder to be completely honest with oneself. I never really expected to meet and be close to anyone who made truthfulness easy, the way Hal does. This isn't to say that we don't quarrel, or that it isn't painful when we do; but thus far the quarreling has been bearable because there has been some way of resolving it other than mere armed truce.

Then, with a pause of forty-eight hours and a change of typewriters, Amy Clampitt the woman moves from a description of domestic strife and emotional uncertainties, from coming to grips with herself as part of a serious couple, and from an acute articulation of her own self-understanding, back into the persona of Amy Clampitt the engaged activist, who has returned from a Sunday expedition to Queens to picket in front of the houses of "five bad brothers," the landlords of the buildings in which her homeless friends had been squatting.

Although Amy sometimes fell into despair—headaches, depression—over the events of these years, when one reads her letters one also sees another side of her character. Participating in groups conferred a feeling of solidarity, even elation. Of the first Washington march, in November, she calls the mood and ambiance a strange "funeral march that was also a celebration, lighthearted on the surface but with a solemnity that went down, down." She wanders into a local church for some rest and finds it crowded:

> It was like a vision of paradise; it was also like rats or refugees taking over—from a catastrophe yet to come. What I mean to say is that no questions were asked, nobody was subjected to any ordeal of acceptance or rejection, there was no ego any more. Outside, in that freezing weather, roses and camellias were still in bloom. I came back to New York and wept, telling Hal about it. It's the kids, I kept saying—what is to become of them?

Describing the same event to another correspondent, Amy again compares the scene at the church to something heavenly, in this case Giovanni di Paolo's version of Paradise at the Metropolitan Museum. It was a paradise and a refugee camp at once. "No ego any more": what Amy achieved a decade before, during her period of religious commitment, she now finds in political camaraderie. Losing herself, she is finding herself. And being with Hal, she finds ease and harmony that amount to freedom even though the two partners spend most of their time together. Both kinds of community—as a public political persona among like-minded colleagues, and as a member of a domestic partnership—consolidate her sense of self.

The Clampitt files contain the manuscript of a short talk Amy gave—we cannot be sure where or when, but probably in the mid-1970s to an audience of concerned left-wing religious people—in which she explains, well after the event, her reasons for switching allegiance from the organized church to more secular forms of participation. She still identifies herself as an Episcopalian, having become a convert sixteen years earlier. Before that she'd been "an unbelieving pagan, but I'd come to believe, through my own experience, that the Body of Christ really did exist—and I still do, even though I've stopped going to church on Sunday mornings."

Her rejection of organized religion had its origins in what, looking back, we might identify as nascent feminist impulses. She had volunteered at her local church:

> I remember that in my enthusiasm, as soon as I joined I asked if there was something I could do—and I was put right to work polishing brass and laying out vestments in the sacristy. I loved doing that, and for a while it was enough. But then I began to be uneasy. I'd been told about something called the Priesthood of All Believers, but I never found out quite what that meant. The clergy knew exactly what they were supposed to do, and for me it was very comfortable for a while to call a priest Father, and go and make your communion and feel that everything had been taken care of.
>
> But after a while it all began to seem too comfortable. It was as though we were all being lulled to sleep. And meanwhile there were people outside who didn't understand what made us feel so comfortable inside when there was so much wrong outside that

we weren't doing anything about—were even being reassured that we weren't expected to do anything about, that we just had to have faith and go on making our communions, God didn't ask any more of us. It began to seem more and more as though the clergy were the only ones in the church with a job to do—that they *were* the Church, and the Priesthood of All Believers was just a myth. The strain between their work at making us comfortable and what was going on outside got to be such that I changed parishes, hoping that things might be different somewhere else.

Ecclesiastical organization was not going to give the sense of community she had expected. At the same time, she was getting involved in a political club, knowing it can be "a rough place," with dirty fights, too dirty for a Christian to mess with:

But after a few months I found more of a sense of community up there than I ever did at a church coffee hour—and that doesn't mean that church people aren't friendly. They are, in a way that clubhouse politicians often aren't. The reason for that sense of community—and I first noticed it after I'd been in the midst of a real fight—was that we'd been doing things together. And I realized that this was what I'd really been looking for in the Church, and never quite found.

So then I began to ask more and more questions about what the Church was and wasn't doing, and to feel more and more uneasy about it. I remember saying half seriously that maybe going to church on Sunday mornings was just a habit that ought to be kicked. And one day that is just what happened. I was sad about it. But I'd gradually realized that I hadn't found a way of contributing anything through being there, and I suppose for that reason I wasn't getting anything out of it either. Because by then I'd rejected the notion that you go as a lay person to receive something that can only be given by the clergy.

Where does one belong? Where does one feel at home? These are questions that this woman would begin to explore in poetry as well as prose.

Amy got an additional sense of community during her high political phase: being locked up in jail, at least three times, in her protests against unfair New York City housing policies. The Iowa ingénue who had come to Manhattan in search of truth and beauty as well as romance and escape more than a quarter century earlier now confronted the nasty, gritty facts of capitalistic greed, bureaucratic heartlessness, and a national war machine.

Amy spent more than a decade doing rugged political work. She went into this ambitious activity with a page-of-swords purity of spirit based on her firm conviction that personal integrity was the key to societal transformation. She always fought for the underdog. A *New York Times* article dated February 22, 1971, reported a major protest event. The headline announces, "Squatters Seize Uptown Building," and the piece describes the symbolic but mostly quixotic efforts of two hundred welfare clients to move their beds, food, televisions, and modest possessions to a new but unoccupied twenty-six-story apartment building at 65 West 90th Street. A six-year-old boy, Tyrone Holland, had died after falling down an elevator shaft in one of the dismal hotels—the Kimberly—that were housing the poor. During the late sixties and early seventies, more than eleven hundred welfare families were being housed in various of these so-called welfare hotels, at the cost to the city of eight million dollars. John Lindsay was a sympathetic mayor, but conditions in the hotels remained squalid. Families that had been staying at the Kimberly were reluctant to return, so they took up temporary residency at the new place. They did not stay long.

On February 26, as a member of the Village Friends of Welfare Rights, Amy joined a procession that took the body of Tyrone Holland back to Brooklyn. Further action ensued. Amy boarded a bus along with several welfare families and other supporters. Their destination was the same hotel previously occupied by the protesters. Eleven arrests were made there; five of the people were welfare mothers, and the rest were staff people or other supporters, of whom Amy was one. In a letter to "The Episcopal New Yorker," an agency of the Episcopal Church, she wrote that she chose "to be arrested as an expression of solidarity when I realized that the mothers themselves had made up their minds to stay."

Amy was one of only two white women at the protest. Maxine Phillips, a journalist turned social worker, was the other one. Phillips recalled that when the police would start to rough up protesters— any protesters, anywhere—they tended to go easy on white women, reserving the weight of their force for people of color. She, a relatively naïve young woman with ideals, found this shocking. Like Amy, decades her senior, Phillips became savvy quickly enough. The welfare mothers vowed to stay "forever." By early afternoon, most of them had already left, finding temporary housing elsewhere. The women were afraid that their children would be taken from them and placed in foster homes.

According to Phillips, Amy went through all this commotion with her "bird-like" pride intact, and her high-pitched but steady voice able to calm her allies. "It was," she said, "a long afternoon and evening at the 100th Street Precinct House" for the protesters who got booked there. Amy phoned Hal, who came over, picked her up, and took her away. Until that point, Phillips was totally unaware that Hal, or indeed any man, was a part of Amy's life. She kept her spheres separate. She knew she had it easy. She soldiered on. She had, perhaps, "no ego anymore," but she certainly had achieved a sense of identity that came from membership in a larger community. The previous fall (September 26, 1970), she had written to her family after meeting four prostitutes and helping homeless people on welfare settle into vacant apartments, "Jail is the great leveler." And she was thinking ahead to her next cause: "If I could think of some way to go about it, prison reform is the next cause I'd like to take up." Where the church had begun to fail, politics took over. But politics, too, would soon fail.

———

Something more momentous than protests and jail occurred during these turbulent years. Simultaneous with her meeting Hal, and several years before their cohabitation, came the unexpected eruption of Amy's poetry writing. In her 1968 Christmas letter to Barbara Clark, with its reference to the mysterious "Bill," Amy describes her progress from being a quasi-recluse the year before, from read-

ing, taking notes, and helping with a book for the journalist David
Schoenbrun; to becoming a "nighttime gadabout" and McCarthy
supporter; to casting her presidential vote for the Black comic and
political renegade Dick Gregory; to cohosting a big party with Hal
(still referred to only as "another member of my team, an N.Y.U. law
professor").

And then:

> But that isn't all. In the midst of all the running around at night—
> which goes on even now, with the election all but forgotten, but
> things like the grape boycott and rent control rising up in its
> place—I'm also on the biggest poetry-writing binge in my his-
> tory. Behind it all is the great love of this mad year . . .

Something here is mysterious. Perhaps Bill, "the great love," pro-
pelled Amy erotically into a creative frenzy, but by December he was
also gone from her life. Hal's presence in that life was quietly expand-
ing. Bill might have sparked a flame. He seems to have ignited some
kind of passion in her. Hal, with greater attention, kept the flame
burning, and it never went out. This was no coincidence. Despite the
political turmoil of the late sixties, and despite—or perhaps because
of—her gradual disillusion with the Episcopal Church, Amy was
experiencing domestic contentment as part of a couple for the first
time in her life. The relationship with Harold Korn was unconven-
tional in many ways. Two people beyond middle age had set up
housekeeping like a young graduate student couple. But with Hal,
Amy had won the support of a person who believed in her. Had he
appeared earlier in her life, one wonders whether she would have
been prepared to take a chance on him. An intellectual equal, albeit
a man who came from a different cultural and professional station,
had begun to encourage her. The results astonished even Amy.

Clampitt's chapbook *Multitudes, Multitudes* is the first product of
these flames—the erotic one begun by Bill, the domestic one stoked
by Hal—and of the shifting of the writer's imagination from the
realm of prose to that of poetry. Published by Washington Street
Press in 1973, the little book contains poems written between 1966
and 1973. One of them, "The Existential Choice," dated May 1969,

appeared in *The New York Times* when poetry was still a feature, however faint and fading, of many daily newspapers. It's an odd sonnet, earnest and thoughtful, provoked by the poet's sense of reaching a turning point in her life, when "at peace within the existential choice, / astonishment runs deeper still than fear." It brims over with references to an "unaccustomed gate" that "gives way"; to Charon, the ferryman in classical myth who transports souls across the river Styx; to an immovable stone (at the tomb of Jesus, presumably) that moves. The sonnet invites its reader to pause with the speaker "on this threshold of the will," at a moment when "unmapped, unentered ways unfold before us."

Other poems in the book touch on other matters that Clampitt had experienced in the 1960s. For no particular reason, "At the Welfare Hearings" uses mythic images of women—Hera and the Virgin Mary—to represent the victimized welfare mothers she sees in court. The longest poem, "The Eve of All Souls," rambles haphazardly and addresses an unnamed British lover (Charles Johnson?), now dead, who was always a religious skeptic; it attacks and laments the current international political turmoil; it refers to Christ and his sacrifice on this November holy day, but it fails to cohere. Other than a fondness for the occasional formal, or even arcane, word, and a commitment to book learning, nothing in these poems signals what will happen in the next unfolding of Clampitt's poetic flowering.

Although she never reprinted any of these poems in her subsequent volumes, we can see with hindsight how her public activities were increasing her self-confidence. It was in 1971, as I mentioned in the previous chapter, that she took part in the "daily death toll," in which protesters sprawled in front of the White House gates to symbolize the number of Vietnamese killed that day. She chose the banner that said "Poet," to designate her occupation. Public outrage had produced or at least coincided with inner certainty.

———

If we jump ahead for a moment we can see how Amy's experiences in protesting, marching, petitioning, getting arrested and sent to jail for squatting in abandoned buildings, plus the excitement and ferment in group action of all kinds, resulted in the major poems of Amy Clampitt, the self-confident, strong-voiced enthusiast and sometime ironist. Consider, from *The Kingfisher*, "Amaranth and Moly," an exuberant character sketch of one of Amy's revolutionary comrades-in-arms from the days of protests, rent strikes, sit-ins, and welfare hearings. The landscapes of Rikers Island and ancient Greece mingle easily. Colloquial diction and classical allusion march together. The former novelist now turns her astute eye to sketching a vivid person in appropriately vivid language. Where the poems in *Multitudes* were frequently leaden and lugubrious in tone, this one is celebratory, even witty, in part because it is communal. Clampitt has found a voice by blending into a group.

Here is the opening section, of three:

The night we bailed out Jolene from Rikers Island
tumbleweeds in such multitudes were blowing through the dark
it might almost have been Wyoming. Built like a willow
or a John Held flapper, from the shoulders up
she was pure Nefertiti, and out of that divine
brown throat came honey and cockleburs.
She had nine children and no identifiable husband.
She wore a headcloth like a tiara above a sack dress
improvised from a beach towel. She'd turned larceny
against the bureaucracy into an art form.
When they raised the subway fare and simultaneously
cut back on Human Resources, Jolene
began jumping turnstiles as a matter of principle.
The police caught up with her at approximately
the fifteenth infraction, and the next thing
anybody knew, she'd been carted off
to the Women's House of D.

"Jolene" is a pseudonym for a real welfare mother named Jennette Washington, who was actually thin enough to slide through subway turnstiles. She taught Amy several lessons: "From what Jennette told us, in her ebullient way, about the experience of being detained out there, it is easy enough to understand what happened at Attica. The letters of George Jackson likewise."

"Amaranth and Moly" laces energy with outrage and high spirits: a John Held flapper joining an Egyptian empress; a tiara paired with a sack dress; larceny becoming delicious art. Clampitt's tone is jubilant, her style vigorous. She brings together her book learning and her newly acquired street smarts; or high culture and the tribal culture of *Hair*, the musical that changed Broadway. What she called, in a letter to her family (December 20, 1970), "my life of crime," including pleading guilty to Class Four trespassing, as well as her multiple efforts to join in solidarity with the homeless and the impoverished, turns out to have inspired, years later, major poems.

In the middle section of her poem, Clampitt—in her inevitably scholarly way—offers vocabulary and geography lessons, as she and her comrades take a "backhanded kind of joyride" in a beat-up Volkswagen. They cross the East River as if it were the Styx or the Little Big Horn. With her keen scientific eye, she identifies "desiccated *Amaranthus albus*," in the States known as pigweed. She wants us to hold this detail in our minds when she returns to it at poem's end, where she brings together the detritus of modern America and the undying glory of classical Greece.

Stephen and Regina Banks knew Jennette Washington. The Bankses were a couple who had befriended Amy during their days at the Village Independent Democrats. In a 2002 interview they remembered their shared political experiences: ringing doorbells, collecting signatures, marching, and sitting in. They looked back nostalgically to their youthful fights for housing for welfare families, the squatting in abandoned tenements, the citations for disorderly conduct. "It was fun . . . it was exciting," Stephen said. But, he added, appearing in court was something different. "Breaking and entering was a serious felony . . . suddenly we weren't so cute." They could still picture Amy with buckets of Kentucky Fried Chicken for the welfare families squatting in the new building on Columbus Avenue. They didn't even know that she was a writer until several years after they met her through the Village Independent Democrats circa 1968. They knew her only as a fellow soldier, the "lunatic friend," decades their senior.

Stephen suggested that Amy changed her heroine's name to Jolene not merely to offer her a pseudonymous cloak but also because in the South and the Midwest (he had moved east from Indiana some years after Amy arrived from Iowa), Jolene would be associated with "poor white trash country types." Dolly Parton's plangent "Jolene" had come out right between the actual event in the poem and the poem's composition. Could Amy have been swayed by this song? It seems plausible. We can see and hear her heroine as belonging to more than a single place and time.

Jennette, the real Jolene, was at last released in the middle of the night. Amy called Stephen and they drove to Queens to get the bus to Rikers. The vignette continues. Jolene emerges,

> the same beautiful outrageous gingersnap
> with a whole new catalogue of indictments.
> On the shuttlebus, while a pimp was softly
> lecturing his sullen girl on what to do next time,
> Jolene described how at the precinct
> they'd begun by giving her a
> Psychiatric Assessment for which the City
> then proceeded to bill her.
> By the time the van arrived to take her
> to the House of D., the officer
> who'd brought her in in the first place
> was saying, "Jolene, I love you." And she'd
> told him, she told us, exactly what he could do.
> All around us in the dark of Riker's Island
> the tumbleweeds scurrying were no pigweed,
> I was thinking, but the amaranth of antiquity.
> And Jolene was not only amaranth and moly, she was poetry
> leaping the turnstiles of another century.

Moly was the herb that Hermes gave to Odysseus to help free his men from Circe's captivity. It's also related to ordinary, garden-variety garlic. Clampitt has here turned mock heroism into something like genuine epic grandeur. Jolene is a divinity in our midst, prose turned to poetry, an outrageous outlaw who can remind us that nobility and joie de vivre are compatible forces.

Clampitt's poetic education began in childhood. It received three major supplementary pushes in her maturity. The first was the sudden baptism by light at the Cloisters in 1956; the second was the ongoing, solicitous encouragement offered by Hal Korn beginning in 1968. The third came a decade later, when Amy returned to school. Clampitt's forays into poetry in the late 1960s were energetic, heartfelt, and awkward. They produced nothing as spectacular as the tour de force of "Amaranth and Moly." But the testing ground that produced the early poems was more fertile than anyone, perhaps even the poet herself, could have imagined.

In September 1973, Amy wrote to her family during the Watergate hearings: "for the time being I've lost my taste for activism, and look forward to spending more of my time just writing instead." *Multitudes, Multitudes* was in preparation. She was transferring her fervor out of the public sphere, into her imagination and onto her desk, into her poetry.

◀ FAME ▶

PART 1: 1973–1983

Amy Clampitt's public success as a poet arose from a combination of talent, perseverance, and luck. She was a born writer. She worked hard. She had the good fortune of finally being recognized by important people in high places. Most of all, her new confidence and her rise to prominence would not have been possible without the presence of a lover, a teacher, and a landscape. I have already introduced Harold Korn. The other two appear below.

Achievement and fame came to Amy late. By 1973, her dark cloud had lifted. A period of repose and hopefulness followed a time of agitation and despair. She had found stability as well as contentment in her relationship with Hal. Poetry was consuming as much of her energy as political protest, and would soon come to monopolize her attention. Domestic comfort is one explanation for the literary flowering. Although they did not marry until very near the end of her life, Amy and Hal lived as a couple for the next twenty years, and were rarely separated. A certain kind of respectable conventionality—if not quite the kind that Pauline had imagined for her older daughter—descended on her.

Although political work still engaged her, it was mostly as a writer rather than as a marcher. She was involved in the South Manhattan Committee for Neighborhood Government, and she wrote articles for the *South Manhattanite* through 1973 on subjects like the West Side Highway renewal project and local public transportation. At the beginning of the decade, moderate public officials like Nelson Rockefeller and John Lindsay offered her and other lefties the hope that good government and enlightened, respectable elected leadership were not impossibilities, and that equal opportunities and economic fairness were within reach.

On the home front, as someone congenitally committed to solitude and domesticity, Amy held on tenaciously to her lease at 354 West 12th Street for both personal and political reasons, but, her jail days over, in 1973 she took up residence, at first gradually and somewhat secretly, in Hal's apartment at 160 East 65th Street (#4F). He had moved in shortly after its 1968 completion. It is a typical East Side, postwar high-rise, designed by Emery Roth, and with a central garden by Paul Rudolph. Like many Manhattan apartment buildings, it has a name: The Phoenix. This seems an appropriate residence for a writer about to be reborn from the ashes of past failures, as well as for a man who literally arose from an almost fatal conflagration.

The new apartment was an easy subway ride, only a few miles away, from her old haunts, but the symbolic distance was enormous. From the charms of West Village row houses to the antiseptic modernity of a glass-and-concrete building, Amy had gone uptown in more ways than one. The Upper East Side was a quarter for respectable grown-ups. And at fifty-three, she had to learn to accommodate herself to a roommate.

On January 18, 1973, Amy wrote to her college classmate Libby Parks Braverman in response to a Christmas letter that contained Braverman's thoughts about having married a Jewish man and thereby becoming part of a Jewish community. Amy brings Hal into the conversation delicately, almost offhandedly, as part of this larger issue:

My own feelings about Christianity have gone through several more changes, and as a result of one too many encounters with the institutional structure, I've found churchgoing impossible these days—though some sort of belief is still there, winnowed out and diminished but I think the more genuine for that reason. I also feel somewhat closer to Judaism through association—more and more these days—with one of the best, kindest, funniest and most clear-headed of companions, who happens to have been born a

Jew; and although the Polish-shtetl orthodoxy of his parents is something he left behind, it's there unmistakably, and I feel it continually. His name is Hal, and he's a legal scholar who teaches at Columbia, and we first met back in the political turmoil of 1968. We listen to a lot of Mozart and things like the Incredible String Band, have a session of reading aloud every now and then—*Bleak House*, Turgenev, Keats, Milton, Yeats—and since he has an apartment that lends itself to such things, every now and then we give a party. Largely as a result of which I've never, despite everything, been happier.

Companionship and happiness, reading poetry and throwing parties, went together. Late blooming was worth waiting for, especially if it involved someone as clear-headed as Hal.

At concerts of the Incredible String Band, she and Hal were frequently the only people over twenty-two. The woman who never told her age was made young again. For this and for other reasons, the seventies were a good decade for her. For Manhattan they were less good, especially by decade's end, after the resignation of Richard Nixon and the ignominious conclusion of the Vietnam War. Hal's upscale, semi-anonymous neighborhood was certainly the antithesis to the louche, bohemian randomness of Amy's West Village and the street life that Jane Jacobs had made a sine qua non (or at least a myth) of vibrant urban living in *The Death and Life of Great American Cities* (1961), now considered a classic defense of high-density, low-rise urbanism. City life is different on the Upper East Side from what it is on the shaded, meandering streets of old, downtown New York. The numbered north–south avenues are heavily trafficked. Cars and people move quickly. And Hal's full-service building only increased Amy's awareness of economic disparity and social uneasiness. One day after President Gerald Ford refused federal aid to keep New York City from bankruptcy, on October 30, 1975, the *Daily News* broke out a now famous headline: FORD TO CITY: DROP DEAD. In one ironic twist, between 1979 and 1981, Richard and Pat Nixon lived at 142 East 65th Street, a stone's throw from Amy and Hal. It was that kind of neighborhood. This was also the decade when drugs and disco reigned. Studio 54 opened in 1977. It closed, for the first time, in 1980, reopened, and closed again in 1986. Andy Warhol's beloved Max's Kansas City closed in 1981.

An article in *The New York Times* (May 26, 1977) painted a bleak picture of Central Park, the former urban jewel now considerably tarnished: "the once-green lawn of the Sheep Meadow is wearing away, gradually becoming a dust bowl with overuse. At the Bethesda Fountain, drugs are sold routinely and the Duck Pond at night becomes a receptacle for beer and soda cans." During the day, and especially after dark, danger lurked, a complement to ugliness.

On July 13, 1977, a twenty-five-hour blackout hit the city at 9:30 in the evening. A brutal heat wave did not help matters. The economic crisis and high unemployment added fuel to the fire. So did a general nervous fear of the "Son of Sam," a serial killer still at large. Twelve years earlier, New Yorkers had dealt with a similar power loss with relative calm and grace. This time, a thousand fires were set, sixteen hundred stores were looted, and thirty-eight hundred looters arrested.

Throughout the decade, not so much on the Upper East Side, but in other parts of Manhattan and especially in the outer boroughs, graffiti flourished. Crime was up. Still unheard of, AIDS would soon begin its silent incubation period. By the mid-1980s, the scourge of the disease would affect every aspect of city life. Real estate prices were falling, and many dyed-in-the-wool New Yorkers, fearful for the safety of themselves and their children, headed out. Scarsdale and other suburbs enjoyed a renaissance. City living was tougher than it had ever been. On Sunday, April 24, 1977, Amy jotted down some observations in a notebook:

Rain most of the day.

Yesterday a shopping-bag lady appeared in the little plaza in front of the bank under H's bedroom window. She was sleeping, settled back against the raised hedge of the yew that is set into the concrete benches, settled in among the plastic bags that held her belongings, barricaded by a kind of makeshift cart stuffed full of more belongings, with some striped fabric on top, and the lat-

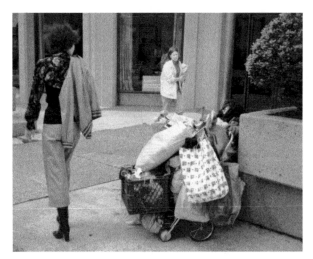

Bag lady's cart, Third Avenue

est Bloomingdale['s] shopping bag, in a red and yellow French-
provincial-print design, sticking up like a kind of banner.

Her venue had changed. Her watchful eye and human sympathy had
not. And she was learning how to turn her observations into poems.
These details simmered in her mind for several months. At some
later point that fall (probably when she enrolled in a poetry-writing
course), she wove them into a sketch that appeared only in a 1990
limited edition, fine-press selection of her Manhattan poems. It is
a poem that shows how she was becoming a poet, even though it
lacks the richness and music of the mature work that would follow.
  "Scavenging" begins:

In front of the bank on the corner
of Sixty-fifth and Third
a shopping bag lady had settled in
with her accumulated belongings. She wore
glasses, and was reading
what appeared to be the Bible.
All day she stayed there
in the lee of the barbered evergreens
like a ship at anchor in an unaccustomed port.

At five in the afternoon, as though leaving her day job, she gets up and moves, along with her shopping cart and its attached bags:

> But lashed
> to the pole that gives the whole thing leverage,
> as yet only half filled
> and bellying out like a pennon, is Bloomingdale's
> latest whimsy: rust, green and gold in a pattern
> scavenged from the French provinces
> (where nothing is ever thrown away)
> and in colors filched from the sail of a dhow—
> one of those tough, overloaded vessels
> that creak up close, smell of oil and rotting bait
> and add romance if you happen to be a tourist.
> Leaving behind not a scrap of litter
> she hove off down Third Avenue
> and was lost sight of.

Clampitt, herself an inveterate scavenger and hoarder, who relished "junking" expeditions later in life in both Europe and the Berkshires, saved this talismanic figure for future use. She did not lose sight of her.

———

The final impetus for Amy's metamorphosis from the chrysalis of anonymous, unpublished novelist into the glorious butterfly of Amy Clampitt, the country's oldest young poet, occurred in the fall of 1977, when she enrolled in a poetry "Creative Writing" course at The New School. The instructor was a young man, almost equally unknown, named Daniel Gabriel (b. 1946), in every way the antithesis of the bookish, gawky fifty-seven-year-old lady—the Village is filled with such earnest types—who came into his class. "When the student is ready," goes the old Buddhist proverb, "the teacher will appear." Amy was ready. Daniel Gabriel appeared. They made for an odd, but oddly productive, couple. One wonders whether another teacher, a poet of a different stripe, would have had the same effect.

My guess is yes: Clampitt had been misapplying her literary gifts, had finally decided to return to poetry, and would, I suspect, probably have flourished under almost any tutelage. She had a healthy self-confidence that underlay her polite, nervous surface. Earlier uncertainties had begun to evaporate. All she required was a push in the right direction. Her teacher provided the push, and set her, if not exactly in motion, along the path to success.

Gabriel, a New Yorker with degrees from City College, taught at The New School from 1976 to 1982. He came from an aesthetic and a worldview (as well as a generation) different from Clampitt's: it was roundly American, infused with large doses of William Carlos Williams and Charles Olson, Black Mountain College and New York avant-gardism. He had studied in college with Muriel Rukeyser, and then with José Garcia Villa at The New School and Joel Oppenheimer at City College of New York while working on a master's degree. These were urban, politically engaged or experimental poets, removed from the canonical Europeans whose work Amy had absorbed at home in Iowa as a schoolgirl and then at Grinnell. Gabriel was the conduit between his shy but confident new student and a reading list of new writers, especially Olson, whose *Call Me Ishmael* he suggested that Clampitt read, and whom she absorbed. She gratefully acknowledged Olson in *The Kingfisher*. Gabriel focused on American artistic exceptionality. Clampitt was committed to the courtly muses of Europe. It is an acknowledged truth that one great drama in American culture has been its ongoing dialogue—sometimes positive, sometimes antagonistic—with the Old World. Clampitt came to bridge the gap between those two worlds. She had confronted Europe first as an eager, dreaming student, then later in her actual travels and her unpublished private writing. Studying with Gabriel forced her to maintain a double allegiance. She never turned her back on Europe; neither did she, from this point on, scant her American heritage. Gabriel may not have made Clampitt a poet, but he certainly reminded her of an alternate, American tradition, thereby adding new resources for her art.

There was another major connection between the teacher and student: they shared a history of religious observance followed by renunciation. Raised in a traditional Catholic family on Staten

Island, Gabriel was in his youth an altar boy. In graduate school he turned away. In an October 1977 journal entry, Clampitt recalled her teacher's reading in class a poem about his rejection of the church. Walking to the subway afterwards, she thought of how a unified worldview can always impose itself on a willing believer, as she had once been. As a younger woman, she had resisted hierarchy and rigidity as obstacles, but she came to accept them for support against chaos and "anarchy of mind," when she tried organized religion in her midthirties. She then dismissed it after a decade in its embrace. Finally, she came to believe that nothing from above could help her. An Emersonian self-reliance welled up inside: "the unity that will satisfy me now . . . comes from seeing things through my own set of experiences and predilections," and she was back with the "continuing autobiography" that her poetry allowed her to articulate, however eccentrically. Many of the things that caused her turn to religion in the first place—the churches of Europe, the masses, cantatas, and oratorios of Bach and Handel, the Renaissance paintings she had first encountered in books when she was in school—remained as sources of comfort and inspiration. It was the church, the theology, and God Himself that she found she could do without. She kept the trappings and the artistic legacy of Christianity. She scrapped its doctrine and the small-minded intolerance of nonbelievers that she found both explicitly and implicitly in many of its practices and adherents. Theology itself was a system, like any other, to be analyzed for its structures and its cultural inspiration. She would henceforth take it metaphorically and seriously, but not literally.

In a correspondence with me, Gabriel recalled Clampitt's student poetry as overwritten, obscurantist, and difficult. He wanted economy, while Clampitt reveled in the "sheer number of words." These are the problems skeptical or hostile readers also noticed once her Knopf books began to come out. Gabriel could empathize: he acknowledged that his own early poems, with their echoes of Dylan Thomas, the favorite of many adolescents in the 1950s and '60s, were equally overwrought and overheated. Both student and teacher were engaging with predecessors, and with tradition, but with different traditions, different predecessors. Meeting with Clampitt over the years after their single workshop course, Gabriel recalled that in spite of her shyness, she later referred unselfconsciously to her "gift." She had gained self-assurance. She knew she had the goods. Could he claim responsibility? "It's possible that my resistance to her work at the time, my reticence, might have spurred her on: a sort of Mephistophelian goading." The genetic strain of Iowa orneriness that Amy shared with her father must have steeled her.

Toward the end of the academic term, Amy wrote to her friend Rimsa Michel (December 19, 1977) about her poetry workshop. She had often considered doing something like this "but never quite dared to" do so. That verb "dared" is significant. For more than a quarter century, she had been both steady in her resolve to write and unclear in her direction. Although sure of herself in many ways, and never shy about expressing an opinion to friends or family, she also suffered from the occasional timidity that made her uncomfortable in groups of strangers. Living with Hal had increased her self-confidence, and standing up for political justice had evidently increased her courage in several ways:

> One is naturally a little uneasy about being cut down or in some way mortally wounded by such a thing; but it turned out not only to be fairly painless but stimulating in a way I never would have predicted. The instructor is a very young poet who is a bit of a jock and who I think disapproves of the kind of thing I do; we argue a lot, but there is enough mutual respect so we may manage to wind up the course as friends. The whole class also went to a poetry reading a few weeks back—Mark Strand was the featured reader; and very good indeed—and I'm wondering whether I may finally get up courage enough to try exposing my own work when there's occasion for it. Anyhow, I've been writing great quantities.

Two weeks later she got up her pluck and appeared at an open-mic event in the back room of a restaurant near Hal's apartment, performing before an audience of strangers. Gabriel, the "established" poet, was the featured reader. Amy was one of the junior nobodies. She practiced in advance with Hal and a tape recorder. Her friend the actor Peter Kybart also helped out with the coaching, urging her to speak loudly, and more slowly. The advice worked. At the restaurant's tiny, crowded bar, she lost her anxiety, read three poems, and was both surprised and gratified by the applause. To Philip Clampitt and Barbara Clark, she wrote virtually identical descriptions of how she had "gotten a taste of becoming a performer." Those years of practicing before the full-length mirror in her cramped apartment three decades earlier obviously had paid off, with both the "heady pleasure" of performing and an explosion of work, "six new poems in the first seven days of the new year." Like Keats, she was about to have an annus mirabilis. More than a year, actually: a decade and a half. The gestation had been long. The following births were comparatively easy.

The heady pleasure she received from performing stayed with her. In all of her readings, some available on the Internet, her voice never sounds old. It is the voice of an eternally youthful poet, not fluttery, but with a "clear, silver, bell-like, gentle sweetness," according to her sometime coach. People who thought they knew her well were surprised: Joan and Dean McClure, and Regina and Stephen Banks, part of the old Village Independent Democrats crowd, had always found her self-effacing, unwilling to talk about herself or announce her latest accolades. But when they came to see her perform, they were astonished: starting with a degree of hesitancy, Amy would gain self-assurance as she warmed to the occasion. Stephen Banks: "When reading, she was transformed, reciting her soul."

Clampitt came to enjoy her public appearances more than she ever might have imagined. Even before *The Kingfisher* was published, and on the basis of her magazine appearances, she began receiving invitations to read her work. The first was at Kenyon College, home of the *Kenyon Review*, a distinguished literary quarterly whose young English editor, Fred Turner, had become a fan and who accepted her poems for his magazine. On October 18, 1981, Clampitt wrote to Barbara Clark. She had been rushing about, maintaining her editing work, which included touching up the memoirs of Lana Turner, and writing notes for David Schoenbrun's New School lectures. Then she dashed out to Ohio, arriving with laryngitis and forced to read in a kind of stage whisper, which she said encouraged people to pay more attention when listening to her than her normal voice would have. The crowd of forty people (she was happy it was no larger) included a woman "who grew up in my home town— metamorphosed from a fluffy, ruffly, ethereal little girl who gave solo piano recitals to a close-cropped, well-tailored type I would never have recognized . . . And there were some darling young people who sort of hovered around afterward." Her New Providence chum was not the only Iowan who had undergone a metamorphosis. The course of Clampitt's public career was set.

Regarding her voice: let's jump forward. In her last important public appearance, at the Poetry Center at Manhattan's 92nd Street YMHA on March 7, 1994—six months before her death—that voice is still crisp, clear, and well modulated. You do not hear a sick woman. Clampitt's diction is precise, her explanations of her poems to her audience helpful but not self-indulgent. She neither lectures nor hectors. She combines the patience of a schoolteacher with the precision of a scientist elucidating her territory. She makes everything clear, in her explanations ("I do seem to write about birds a lot!"), and in her rhythms. She knows how to pace herself: the tempos are fast at first, then they slow down. Everything is controlled without seeming artificial, in order to bring us into, and then out of, the poems' sometimes dense syntactic thickets and their piled-on details. There is a charming naiveté, laced with encyclopedic knowledge of her subjects and herself. ("I'm really a poet of displacement," she says before reading one of the late poems, "Sed de Correr," about any artist's hunger for running away.) Clampitt has taken to heart Robert Frost's pronouncement that "the ear is the best reader." She does not scant on music, clarity, or passion. Just as her poems burst from her, almost miraculously, between 1978 and 1994, so Clampitt's performances of those very poems during these years also sound surprising but natural, even inevitable. Emerson remarked in a different context, "Beauty breaks in everywhere."

———

I have mentioned that Clampitt's poems before the workshop with Gabriel offer little evidence of what was to come later. Political activism and mythology are central to them. "After a Night of Disorders" (dated September 1968, around the time of Hal's arrival on the scene) is eight stanzas of vague mysticism and eroticism:

> I have come home. I have been away too long.
> It was late when I left. And I have missed
> you; all through this darkening Wanderjahr
> I have looked for you, Love, and missed you,
>   missed you everywhere.

The note of anxiety is not one that Clampitt would continue in her maturity, however anxious Amy the person might have felt at any stage. Nor are the simple diction and straightforward syntax.

A decade later, the student work still sounded either effortful or unlike what would succeed it. Take, for example, a long poem called "The Diver" and neatly labeled "Course No. 7295, / Fall 1977 / Daniel Gabriel, / instructor." It begins:

> Bright speed, aureoled encephalogram
> of danger, traveled with him
> as though such stress alone could ease
> the weight of being so winsome
> and so unwilling to win, of
> being loved so to excess
> and by so many, of being so feared for . . .

The syntax is a bit garbled, the focus unclear, but Clampitt is starting to use the repetitions, off-rhymes, and internal rhymes ("encephalogram," "him," and "winsome"; "stress" and "ease"; "winsome" and "win") that she will come to handle better after her course at The New School. Here, however, the result seems labored and unsteady.

Among her papers there are also several overtly political poems in a style she never repeated. One, dated August 9, 1973, "For William O. Douglas," takes the tack of satire, which she swiftly abandoned: "We live in an ugly country, / citizens. But it's our country, after all, / we made it the way it is—yessir, that's right, / we're a self-made country, and if it's ugly, / that happens to be the way we like it." However relevant this small lyric might seem today, decades after its composition, it does not reveal the artistic authenticity that Clampitt was about to achieve. Another poem, from the fall of 1977, presents Amy as a kind of eager graduate student, attending a lecture by Harold Bloom at the New York Psychoanalytic Institute, with Hal and his friends Shale and Rachel Brownstein (the psychoanalyst and the English professor), to whom she dedicated this unpublished piece. She was learning about the latest trends in literary theory and literature's invasion by the Freudians. As someone who had always been skeptical of psychotherapy, she was also coming to see how and why it might be useful. She had recently entered a world in which psychoanalysis, literary study, and Jewish culture seemed to offer resistance to fascism, antisemitism, and the American caste system, which to the academic left represented forces of evil. In the poem, she scans Bloom himself: "in face a half-domesticated howl, in manners / all medieval *courtoise*," lecturing on "catastrophe and the overthrow of fathers." She leans in, listening "as to a difficult piece of music," fearful of missing a word. What she finds is

> history in a cage . . .
> machinery invented to entertain the goyim, stirred up again,
> black as soot from the very ovens of Buchenwald,
> by a grubby kid from the Bronx grown up
> through all the modulations of civility, returning
> like a wind in the leaves, a whirlwind,
> that rainy equinoctial night, of despair
> that sent us away elated.

For the previous decade, Amy had been adjusting to Hal and his heritage, the fact of his Jewishness, and the murders of his mother's family in the Nazi death camps. She had begun to use this as material in her poetry. At the same time, she must have understood that it did not really suit her interests and temperament.

Some of the unpublished work is genuinely affecting and original. One poem, dated 1975, is called simply "FOUND OBJECTS," eight charming quatrains that seem to build up haphazardly. Here are the first three:

DUMPTRUCK
SNOWPLOW
WOODPILE
CELLAR DOOR

BANK BOOK
SLINGSHOT
SNOWSHOE
SEMAPHORE

WINDMILL
LANDMINE
HUBCAP
COOKIE JAR

A kind of Joseph Cornell box filled with ordinary, magical objects, the poem creates associations among items based on their uses and their sounds. Everything accumulates. Amy, who came to relish "junking" expeditions with her friend Karen Chase at the end of her life in the Berkshires, was alert to things found by serendipity and collected by choice. Clampitt the poet, who became a master of lists, of lines of "things," and who turned them into noun-heavy poems, is starting off in a modest, almost imagist mode here, tuning her ear and steadying her eye as she builds to a climax that is also an understatement. The last two stanzas:

DIME STORE
BOX TOP
ROWBOAT
SNOWMOBILE

FILM STRIP
GUMDROP

MOON ROCK
BIG DEAL!

You might say "it's no big deal," and you would be right, but the playful assortment of ordinary items mingling with larger, sometimes more dangerous ones proves that Clampitt's mind has begun to work nimbly with the things of mundane life. She is encouraging us to think of how best to take those things, to examine them as though we had never seen them before.

Who else does this? I think again of Walt Whitman, the quintessential list-maker and optimist. He was a genuine American forebear of Clampitt, original and springing up as if out of nowhere. Having read Emerson's declaration of aesthetic independence—the 1844 essay "The Poet"—with its call for the arrival of a distinct, original, American bard, the author of *Leaves of Grass* announced with combined bravado and gratitude, "I was simmering, simmering, simmering; Emerson brought me to a boil." Clampitt had been simmering since 1956. Hal helped to stir the pot beginning in 1968. Now the flame had been turned up.

The annus mirabilis got a jump-start at the beginning of 1978. Amy came home one day to find an acceptance letter from *The New Yorker*. "The Sun Underfoot Among the Sundews" was finished on January 5. *The New Yorker* accepted it on March 3.

———

How did this acceptance happen? Clampitt's success is, in part, a story of the workplace. What happens in life is owing, according to the old truism, not to what you know but whom you know. Clampitt had the perhaps unique distinction of having work accepted by a revered magazine without ever submitting it herself. Someone else had intervened on her behalf. She was more surprised than anyone to learn what had happened to her work.

Beginning in 1977, Amy had been serving as a freelance but essentially full-time copy editor for John (Jack) Macrae, the editor in chief of E. P. Dutton. By his own admission, he was a preppy WASP.

He was nonchalant and suave, Harvard class of 1954. He said he was raised never to demonstrate expertise or show enthusiasm, or to study hard, but to be a dilettantish jack-of-all-trades, embodying the *sprezzatura*—call it ease, or grace, or coolness—of a Renaissance man. Dutton was the family business. Jack was the fourth Macrae to serve as editor in chief (in 1968) and then as president (beginning in 1969). Over the course of a long career he held exactly three jobs, at Harper, Dutton, and later Holt, at a time when publishing was still a gentleman's profession. One female editor told me that Macrae was universally regarded as the handsomest man in the industry. Things came easily to him. Hiring Amy was a godsend for both of them. Macrae was grateful for her scholarly bent, her accuracy, everything he lacked. They made for a balance of opposites: the worldly patrician dabbler and the birdlike, schoolmarmish librarian. But they also were a good match, as important as the match Amy made with Daniel Gabriel. Although as a writer she tended to prolixity, Amy became an excellent editor, helping her authors refine and prune their work. In 1977, Bonnie Stylides at Dutton quoted Macrae, who called Amy "*the* person . . . for complicated editing," especially in the sciences. Sheaf upon sheaf of yellow foolscap pages in her papers prove the assiduousness and acuity of her work. In a letter from 1984, a science editor named Joanna Stolzar wondered if the "new" poet she was seeing in print was the same Amy Clampitt who, she said, had been "reserved for our most important manuscripts."

However self-effacing she often was in person, Amy was clear in her opinions and never timid about sharing them: "The outline and sample chapter strike me as clever but sloppy and more than a little mischievous," she wrote of one manuscript she had been given. It was later published by a university press. Of another (also rejected), she wrote, "Chapter 1, I have to say, literally put me to sleep." "Maddeningly disorganized," she said of a third. Her authors—the ones whose work was accepted—seemed always grateful for her efforts. Peter Farb wrote thankfully (June 27, 1977), "You really did catch a phenomenal amount of bloopers and inelegancies. And it was marvelous the way you often zeroed in precisely on just the right word that was needed." Do good poets make good editors? Precision counts.

Macrae generally accepted her judgments. In the category we might label "Even Homer Nods," I was intrigued to read a 1977 report on a new travel book submitted to Dutton by a young writer. Amy found it undone by its excesses, "many threads picked up, with such unfailing jauntiness that one begins to suspect a put-on . . . [The author] is always on the go, observing and recording with wit and aplomb whatever the nature of the subject at hand." His "relentless staccato is sometimes fiendishly inappropriate . . . Perhaps his gift is really for fiction, since unlike most travel writers he is better at describing people than at conveying the feel of places."

The critic may unconsciously be describing her own travel writing. But no: this time the writer was Bruce Chatwin. The book: *In Patagonia*. All editors let the occasional gold nugget slip through their fingers.

At some point, Amy must have remarked that she had been writing herself. Macrae asked to see her work. He "suffered" (he said when interviewed years later) through one of the novels, about which he remembered nothing other than its shortcomings. He saw some earlier poems, and about them said Amy wasn't even a "fledgling." But then she showed him more recent work, which he realized was different, indeed better. In my prologue, I mention that Macrae told me he thought the change took place when she was learning ancient Greek, but that was in 1982, when the poems in *The King-fisher* were already rolling out. Instead, it was the trip to Greece in 1965 that helped to turn her away from prose and toward poetry.

But even that trip could hardly explain the twelve years before the major poems came from her. I have already suggested some of the possible reasons for the eruption of poems. Macrae added that she "had no false modesty, but she required someone else to tell her she had the goods." Then the leap took place. Along with Daniel Gabriel, an authority figure because he was a classroom instructor, Jack Macrae was the someone else. He assumed the role of patron, and of enabler or go-between. The poet became, suddenly yet inevitably, herself.

Jack Macrae sent several of Clampitt's new poems to his friend Howard Moss, the longtime, much-respected poetry editor of *The New Yorker*. She had no idea he had done so. In a letter (February 2,

1978), Moss replied to Macrae that he found Clampitt "extremely gifted" but would not accept the three poems Macrae had sent him—"Dancers Exercising," "Deleted Passage," and "Eleusis"—all of which ultimately found homes elsewhere. At some point soon after, Macrae sent "The Sun Underfoot Among the Sundews," which Moss took immediately.

In 1812, with the publication of the first two cantos of *Childe Harold's Pilgrimage*, Lord Byron said he "awoke one day and found myself famous." He was twenty-four, and had another twelve years of a productive and notorious life ahead of him. When "The Sun Underfoot . . ." appeared, Clampitt was fifty-eight and had sixteen more years of life and work remaining. She did not squander her energies. She worked, and wrote, harder and better than she had earlier. She was making up for lost time. Even she was surprised that she was getting paid for a poem. On Easter 1978, she wrote to Barbara Clark with the news of the acceptance, and added, "it appears they must pay by the word: one hundred eighty-two smackers for one little poem! It now becomes clear why everybody wants to get into that magazine." She began submitting more poems, and then more. Some were accepted, some rejected. She sent others. Nothing stopped her. She was becoming a professional.

Her acceptance letter from Howard Moss was the first of many, and it initiated a friendship that lasted a decade, until Moss's death in 1987. Looking back, we see how politeness governed their relationship, and how intimacy succeeded an initial, distant cordiality. Like Marianne Moore and Elizabeth Bishop decades earlier, the two poets addressed each other formally, in writing, until sufficient time had elapsed to warrant greater informality: it was always "Miss Clampitt" and "Mr. Moss." It was almost two years until they met face-to-face, at the Algonquin. In a reminiscence, Amy wrote that at this celebrated literary watering hole, she "didn't look like somebody famous. The fact remains that Howard didn't either." She wrote to Rimsa Michel (November 24, 1979) that she had finally met her editor, and found him "kindly, unassuming, pleasant company, and on the strength of a common fondness for Mozart, especially *Così Fan Tutte*, I'm getting up courage to invite him to dinner with Hal and me one of these days."

Something else was spurring her on. Energy, concentration, stimulation, and satisfaction operate together at the physical as well as the mental and creative levels. Endorphins are related to artistic production and general feelings of well-being. Amy was working on her body as well as her craft during these productive years. In 1978 she and Hal were exercising under the watchful eye of Robert Blue, an actor who doubled as a trainer. They were trying to whip themselves into shape. In October she boasted to Barbara Clark that—not for the first time—she had run two miles along the East River, and she and Hal were meeting with "our angelic exercise guru twice a week for a workout, which gets harder and harder all the time." They expected to cheer Bob on in the New York Marathon the following week. Amy Clampitt was shaping up, in several ways. She and Hal were also taking dance lessons (including a little ballet, which brought out the great balletomane Amy had been in her young days at OUP) at home, a picture difficult and amusing to envision. Bob's girlfriend put them through a series of *pliés*, *relevés*, and *ronds de jambe* at what must have been an improvised barre at their dining table on East 65th Street.

A correspondence with another editor initiated a friendship lasting until Amy's death. Mary Jo Salter was a recent Harvard graduate who in 1978 was working as the "first reader" for Peter Davison in Boston at *The Atlantic*, looking at poems that came in over the transom—the so-called slush pile—most of which received immediate rejection. Salter wrote her first fan letter (May 29, 1979), describing her admiration for the poems, which "unfailingly send me to the dictionary at least once, and although I don't consider this a prerequisite exactly, it does speak for your commitment to precision. You don't write like other people." That assessment is something of an understatement.

The twenty-four-year-old Salter naturally assumed that Clampitt was, like her, a young, aspiring, unknown poet sending her work hopefully into the world. Amy had to disabuse her: she was aspiring and unknown but hardly young. She welcomed the praise and the general friendliness. Most artists need other artists as sounding boards, for support, criticism, attention, rivalry as well as camaraderie. They make their moves, spread their wings, test the waters in the company of others. They require encouragement from their elders and, somewhat differently, from their peers, their contemporaries.

Salter and Clampitt were peers. Were they contemporaries? Clampitt had perhaps another unique distinction among American poets: she belonged to two generations. Born on either side of her, her chronological peers extend from Elizabeth Bishop (b. 1911), Robert Hayden (1913), Gwendolyn Brooks and Robert Lowell (both 1917), through poets born in the 1920s: Howard Nemerov, Mona Van Duyn, Richard Wilbur, Denise Levertov, Anthony Hecht, James Merrill, A. R. Ammons, Allen Ginsberg, James Wright, John Ashbery, Adrienne Rich, John Hollander, Peter Viereck, and Richard Howard. A distinguished group. But her *poetic* generation was composed of the genuinely young poets coming into their own in the late 1970s: Dana Gioia, Salter and her husband-to-be Brad Leithauser, George Bradley, William Logan, Debora Greger, J. D. McClatchy, Gjertrud Schnackenberg, Alfred Corn, David Lehman, Rosanna Warren, and Henri Cole, people decades her junior. Clampitt's chronological allies grew up during the Depression and the New Deal; the younger cohort was composed of Baby Boomers who matured during the Eisenhower and Kennedy years. The former group included men who served in wartime; the latter cluster included men and women who, like Amy and many people of all ages, fought for civil rights and against the Vietnam War.

The Clampitt-Salter friendship was conducted in person once they had met, but Salter and her husband began to spend time abroad on fellowships and academic sabbaticals—in Japan and then Europe—and later were involved raising children in central Massachusetts, so the most productive working part of Clampitt's relationship with Salter was epistolary. At one point (July 2, 1981), Salter, settling into life in Japan, apologized for taking three weeks to answer Clampitt's previous letter. Each poet sent her work to the other, who then replied with praise laced with editorial suggestions

Amy at the wedding of Mary Jo Salter and Brad Leithauser, August 2, 1980

about single words, or lines, or pieces of punctuation. Respectful helpfulness rather than rivalry was the primary tone. Salter's letters from the first year alone extend to tens of thousands of words. The two women were coworkers who became friends. They were equals. They were, also, different. Each bolstered the other.

Salter's mother died young, in 1983. The poet, by her own admission, may have welcomed a surrogate. (Amy, older, was also recently motherless. Pauline Clampitt had died in 1979.) Salter remarked that "Amy did in many ways remind me of my mother, though mine was pint-sized and Amy was tall and lanky. Both were defiantly artistic way back in the '40s and '50s when women were supposed to be Harriet Nelson; both balanced doom-saying with gaiety; both befriended many much younger people. Both were talkers and gigglers." Salter had two brothers; Clampitt had three, plus a sister who was not a reliable equal. Sisterhood was a strong component in the relationship.

Each woman was committed to the life of the working artist. Both were feminists, although of different generations. Salter wrote (December 4, 1979), "I think women (and do I ever include myself) are their own biggest obstacles. I've seen this at the office, over and over—a Stanford graduate who has worked at the Atlantic for three years and has real editorial responsibilities still has to work the switchboard at lunch, and when I told her that she had every right to protest she just sighed, as if I had lost my marbles." Over the course of their friendship, Salter grew unsurprisingly more independent. In an important late letter (February 26, 1992), she replied to an earlier one from Clampitt containing strong objections to certain elements in her new book manuscript. Always polite, but now with firmness, Salter wrote that "this *is*, more or less, the book I wanted to write. I'm grateful for the line editings you offer and will be making quite a few revisions based on your comments . . . It's your larger objection to didacticism that I can't do much to 'correct,' and where we may just have to agree to disagree."

I am reminded again of the relationship between Elizabeth Bishop and Marianne Moore decades earlier. The shy, twenty-three-year-old Miss Bishop from Vassar, eager for a mother figure, and the eccentric Miss Moore, considerably her senior, hit it off. Bishop sent poems, looking for guidance and approval. In 1941, Moore objected to certain vulgarities (like the euphemism "water closets"—hardly offensive to our ears today) in Bishop's antimilitaristic, cunningly feminist poem "Roosters." The younger poet, in an act of polite self-assertion, stuck to her guns. The friendship survived.

The friendship between Clampitt and Salter survived disagreements as well. Shortly after the declaration of independence quoted above, however, Salter moved to Paris for two years with her husband and two small daughters, and was unavailable to Amy in person until the very end, in Lenox. She would become one of her mentor's literary executors.

From Clampitt's side, the relationship with a poet—even a young, untried one—was a godsend. She replied to Salter's initial note with a letter that could barely contain her effusive happiness. She wrote from Maine, where she and Hal had been spending a month each summer beginning in 1974. She rejoices in the new friendship, and apologizes for sending along perhaps more poems than Salter had bargained for. She relates her recent history, the publication of *Multitudes, Multitudes* several years earlier, her first appearance at the open-mic evening in the back room of a restaurant. She then describes her position vis-à-vis the current literary scene: "I don't greatly enjoy the company of literary types—the more literary they are, the more miserable they seem to be as human beings." She acknowledges her gratitude to Jack Macrae, to Hal (whom she cites as "my best-friend-and-severest-critic"), and to Doris Myers, and says she could not have gone on writing without their encouragement.

And then, the greatest gratitude of all: "But I've yearned secretly for a poet I could write to." Editors, she says, are too busy. There are more poets than readers. (This complaint is perennial.) In a 1986 talk, Clampitt—the person who had been toiling for so long alone—remarked, "Writers need company. We all need it. It's not command of knowledge that matters, finally, but the company. It's the predecessors. I for one couldn't be a writer except for them." For her, a living poet was as necessary as the dead ones to help with encouragement and affirmation.

Trying to locate herself in the contemporary literary culture, Clampitt asks Salter:

Is it W. C. Williams who's to blame for the current monotony of manner? This is what Howard Moss says, in a nice thing I just came across in *The American Poetry Review* (where, it strikes me, monotony tends to predominate unduly.) Or is it something more pervasive, a general pulling inside oneself because the environment is so bad out there? The other day it occurred to me that a whole generation has been so deadened by rock music that an ear for the music of words may be obsolescent. "You're in love with words," I was told (by a poet, yet) in a tone of accusation. What he meant, I guess, was that I tend to use too many of them. So you can see why your letter, with its sweet and generous compliments for what in some quarters is evidently seen as a defect, meant so much.

The poet who accused Clampitt of being in love with words was, of course, a man. Why should a poet not be in love with words? With what else should a poet be in love?

Regarding words, especially nouns and other names: Clampitt mentioned in an interview her lifelong attention to birds and bird sounds, and her incredulity that people in New York seemed bemused that someone would take notice of such things. She was thinking of the tufted titmouse, and said that Hal was vastly entertained by the very fact of its existence. She goes on:

> But I don't know that he is any more amused than I am by the language people in his profession . . . use without any notion of how funny it sounds to somebody who isn't. Take *tortfeasor*. I don't know how lawyers can say it with a straight face. I once wrote a poem that ended with the word *tortfeasor*—it was about wild mushrooms, some of which can do harm, presumably without really meaning to, which is more or less the case with tortfeasors—and no editor would take it.

Precision in definition begins with keenness in perception. It ends in sheer delight.

Regarding quantity: it is a truth that every good poet uses the right number of words to express the matter at hand. Clampitt was lavish. She required many words. A more austere poet—Robert Creeley, for example, or Nobel Prize winner Louise Glück—needs fewer. Clampitt was no minimalist. (Nor was Walt Whitman.) The poets decide for themselves. And they decide not only on the number of words they need, but also the kind. Clampitt never wanted to fit in with what she called the "prevailing flatness of diction" in American poetry, which seemed to her forced upon writers by "sheer terror of sounding *like anyone at all whose mother tongue is English.*" Her commitment was to the full range of the English language, not exclusively its American cousin, regardless of other kinds of attachments to her native culture and history.

———

Something else pushed Amy in the direction of becoming Amy Clampitt. The third inspiration for her outpouring of poems, after moving in with Hal Korn, and during and following her New School course with Daniel Gabriel, was a place. This was also an integral part of her relationship with Hal: Corea, Maine. The couple spent a month there almost every summer for twenty years beginning in

1974. Like so much in her life, this new development came about purely by chance. Since his accident, Hal had been seeing a psychotherapist, Sylvia G. Traube. She suggested at one point that he needed a vacation. At a memorial service for Traube in 1989, which Hal missed owing to illness, Amy read a note he'd written for the occasion. Of his doctor, he remembered that "she never took [a vacation] herself, but she had inherited a house there, and it was available. To persuade me, when I objected that I never took vacations, the country didn't interest me, I needed to catch up on work, and for that I needed music, she said I'll see that you have music— and she did. I went, and have gone back to that little town every summer since 1974 (except occasionally when I was in Europe)." Amy then spoke in her own voice: "in my mind our going to Maine in 1974 changed my life forever."

Corea is a small Down East fishing village. Daniel Gabriel helped to shape Clampitt's poetry, but Maine did something equally important, several years earlier. It provided her with a setting and with subjects congenial to her spirit. Amy was entranced by everything: the geography, weather, residents, flora and fauna, and the isolation of the region (the population of Gouldsboro, the main town on the peninsula, has never exceeded 1,700). This is the country of Sarah Orne Jewett's pointed firs, of laconic, self-reliant people and solid families who have made their living from the sea. Amy always said she wanted to escape from Iowa in part because she wanted to live near the ocean. For thirty years she had been within walking distance of the Hudson, and then the East River, but at last she could now actually live, briefly in high season, on the ocean itself. The cottage to which she and Hal kept returning was on a spit of land called Youngs Point. They were one hundred feet from the water on a cove that she looked out on, captivated. It was here, she said, that poetry came most easily from her. It was the prairie in a different material and a different shade, the earth made in another register: water.

Corea is removed from the fanciest Maine spots. On the southeast side of the Gouldsboro peninsula, east of Bar Harbor and the other tony watering holes of Mount Desert Island, it is still today the modest village it has been for more than a century. Like New Providence, Amy's hometown, it has little in the way of tourist attractions: shops, restaurants, bars, even markets are nowhere to be found. During a visit in 2020, I chatted with both the local postmistress and the assistant town assessor. They confirmed that although there has been new residential building in the past three decades—some of it quite smart-looking—little has been torn down. There are no McMansions. Amy would certainly know the place were she to materialize there today. Lobster fishing has always been the primary industry. Marsden Hartley (1877–1943), the native Maine artist who had lived in Europe during World War I, returned to home soil and spent his last years back in Corea. He used the tower of the Baptist church as his studio. The sights and sounds—the fog and the foghorns—appealed to both the visual artist and the literary one. Clampitt wrote to Rimsa Michel in 1975 that "the almost extinguished lights across the inlet reminded me of an Albert Ryder moonscape." That particular summer, the only notable local social activity was the town rummage sale. It was the kind of life in which a major event was going to Ellsworth for a provincial production of Mozart's *Così Fan Tutte* "after not being near the opera in New York for years." Or going to nearby Cranberry Point, or taking an overnight ferry to Nova Scotia for a visit to Grand-Pré, which put the poet-infatuated-with-Greece in mind of Paestum and Samos. Home and abroad became connected, rather than separate, spheres and entities.

Another kind of event didn't even require much of a journey, but a mere pilgrimage on foot to a small uninhabited island reachable only at low tide, and then worrying about getting stuck when the tide returned. That uninhabited island provides the scene for "A Hermit Thrush" (*Archaic Figure*), a poem infused with landscape, love, and danger. It begins at the summer solstice when Hal and Amy scramble along an isthmus for their annual picnic at a site of less than pastoral beauty: "the gust-beleaguered single spruce tree, / the ant-thronged, root-snelled moss, grass / and clover tuffet underneath it, / edges frazzled raw." The previous night, in bed, the couple looked at Jupiter and realized "that no point is fixed, that there's no foothold / but roams untethered save by such snells, / such sailor's knots, such stays / and guy wires as are // mainly of our own devising." From the heavens to the sea, to the "earth's sore surface," everything is tentative, in motion, as capable of being destroyed as being preserved. At the poem's end, Clampitt is remembering "The Darkling Thrush," Thomas Hardy's wintry record of dreariness, fear, and hope. Having stayed too long on their picnic and got their feet wet on the return to the mainland as the tide came in, the picnicking couple feels the oncoming threat of "thunder, rain and wind." Peril seems unavoidable:

> . . . then waiting,
> we drop everything to listen as a
> hermit thrush distills its fragmentary,
> hesitant, in the end
>
> unbroken music.

The poem started with a curt statement of doubt—"Nothing's certain"—but the music is sufficient to restore them to stability, leaving them almost without language to describe their wonder at having participated in "this existence, this / botched, cumbersome, much-mended, / not unsatisfactory thing." This may also put an audience in mind of Robert Frost's "The Oven Bird," which ends with the listener wondering "what to make of a diminished thing." Clampitt affirms a unity—a human relationship, a loved place, a participation in the cosmos—with a kind of British understatement uncommon for this poet given typically to exaggeration. "Not unsatisfactory" sums it all up: we have consolation.

Maine came to be the setting and inspiration for many of Clampitt's poems, especially those in *The Kingfisher* and *What the Light Was Like*. Even more than West 12th Street, where she wrote overlooking the catalpa in the courtyard, Corea fueled her composition for almost two decades. Clampitt wrote more in her annual month Down East than she wrote during the rest of her time in Manhattan or while traveling.

She loved the lobstermen, who, she said, had "a kind of natural courtesy . . . they are not polished people, but they are gracious." The setting and the people finally, and perhaps surprisingly, allowed her to write about Iowa: "I couldn't write about the Midwest until

I'd written about Maine. I wanted to say something about the place I came from but I didn't know how." She needed to be reminded of home by something that was not home but still resembled it. She also made friends with neighbors. One of them was a transplanted Kansan named Donna Murphy. Like Amy, who exclaimed exuberantly in an early letter, "I love weather!," Murphy could be equally vigorous and articulate about meteorology, climate, the minutest registers of heat, humidity, and especially wind. And she called herself—making a nod to Clampitt's beloved Keats—"a full-throated fan" of Clampitt's poetry from the time they met in 1977.

The poet Ryan Harper, another midwesterner, visited Corea in 2019 to pay homage to Amy's village. He also met Donna Murphy and understood immediately the connections between the two women, part-time summer neighbors but never intimate friends. He remarked that "Mainers are the only people I have met who could talk Midwesterners under the table concerning the weather. Midwesterners in Maine, the crash site of the continent's every passing system, become walking almanacs." The weather, in all its mercurial changes, was another reason Amy felt instantly at home in Maine.

It is easy to understand why—almost a decade after her first summer in Maine—Clampitt began *The Kingfisher* with "The Cove." This is a poet's picture, a statement of purpose, a testament to a place, and an aesthetic program. It starts as a still life, then moves outdoors to the landscape, then to the ocean, then to the sky. The poem's expansiveness is also the announcement of an *ars poetica*. Clampitt's eager eye takes in everything, and it brings us into the scene. She begins inside the cozy "snug house," a kind of "*gemütlich* hotel room at Innsbruck," where "we" get comfy by reading Marianne Moore and listening to Mozart by the fire. At dusk, the two observers notice a porcupine, with its "needle-tined paddle tail held out straight" (what a sharply and appropriately alliterative phrase that is!), moving through the trees and then heading back to its underbrush home; they watch the birds from their sundeck. Clampitt sneaks in a reminder of her Iowa childhood, when she sees a turtle, "domed repoussé / leather with an underlip of crimson— / as it hove eastward, a covered / wagon intent on the wrong direction." Looking back at the poet's career we can read this turtle as a stand-in for the poet, who herself headed east years after her forebears headed west. Autobiography comes in many guises, not least of which are the landscape and the life forms it supports.

Illumination strikes at the poem's end. The cove can seem "wrinkling like tinfoil" or like a "sun-pounded / gritty glitter of mica." The pavement of ocean is at times so majestic that it can hardly be looked at, but the eye takes in a panorama extending from down to out to up, from sea to air to sky. The view opens to immensity.

I would like to imagine that when Clampitt was arranging the contents of her first book she was thinking in part of the hierarchy of genres that constituted the ladder of Western painting for almost five centuries: still life occupied the lowest rung; then came portraiture, landscapes, and, at the top, paintings of epic, religious, or historical significance. The poet is saying to her readers: Wait, and watch. You think you are seeing a Dutch interior. You think you are reading a woman's embroidered piece of landscape description. You are wrong. What you are reading is a careful examination of the natural world, its vegetation and animal inhabitants, but it is more, if you are ready for it. Outside there is a blueness so immense that it will blind you. At its apex "there pulses, even / in daylight, a lighthouse, light- / pierced like a needle's eye." Clampitt has brought us outdoors, away from the fireside and into the blazing light of day. Her introductory poem says: My work will dazzle you. You'll see. A needle's eye, like a poet's, has many uses.

Amy came to appreciate Corea in ways that resembled her appreciation of Iowa, once she had been removed from her native soil physically and temporally. In Corea, Amy met another Maine writer, Louise Dickinson Rich (1903–1991), to whom she dedicated the title poem of *What the Light Was Like*. This is an elegy for Ernest Woodward, a lobsterman who died in his boat at sea. (For the local Coreans, this poem helped to cement Amy's honorary status as more than a summer person.) In the introduction to her 1958 book *The Peninsula*, Rich describes her attraction to the cove:

It was beautiful with the only kind of beauty that I was now beginning to recognize as authentic: the great unadorned beauty and strength of the functional. There was nothing anywhere that was unnecessary; nothing, whether the work of man or nature, that existed without a purpose. I was a stranger; but in spite of my strangeness, the country spoke to some inner need of which I had not until then been fully aware, to a need to know who I was and what I was worth.

Beauty allied to usefulness: both the Yankee and the midwesterner could take this combination seriously. What the Latin poet Horace called the essence of poetry—that it be both *dulce et utile*—inspired and confirmed these two writers' sense of their own identity.

———

On July 17, 1978, Clampitt learned that she had won the Bernice Kavinocky Isaacson Award, given annually to a New School student, for her lyric "The Isthmus." It had been written the previous October for her workshop. This prize led to the publication, by the Coalition of Publishers for Employment, of the little chapbook *The Isthmus* (1981), poems written mostly in Maine or set in Corea. They sound only marginally like the other Maine poems that she was simultaneously gleaning from her "teeming brain." (That phrase comes from Keats's sonnet "When I Have Fears," about his terror of dying young before he could harvest all the fruits from the seeds he had been sowing.) She never republished them. She had already moved beyond them. She was working at top speed, like Sylvia Plath (whom she had begun to read with excitement) in the frantic final months before her suicide in 1963.

Clampitt sent three poems to *The Atlantic* on October 12, 1978, noting that her work had appeared already in *The New Yorker*, which had by that point taken an additional three poems, and that something else was to appear in the *American Scholar*. *The Atlantic*'s poetry editor, Peter Davison, showing prescience, wrote to Clampitt on October 31, 1978, returning two of the three, and taking one:

> Dear Miss Clampitt:
> The first time's a charm, I suppose. We'll be delighted to have your "Fog" for the *Atlantic*, and we admire your bright work.

I'd be glad if you could send us more work when you have it, keeping in mind that we are overstocked with long poems at the moment, and understocked with short ones.

"Fog" anticipates what would become Clampitt's signature mature style but without the excesses that would try the patience of some readers later on. She thought sufficiently well of it to place it second in *The Kingfisher* when the book was published in 1983. It has twenty-seven short lines, divided into three sentences, each of which begins as a statement and then opens into a list.

The first:

> A vagueness comes over everything,
> as though proving color and contour
> alike dispensable: the lighthouse
> extinct, the islands' spruce-tips
> drunk up like milk in the
> universal emulsion; houses
> reverting into the lost
> and forgotten; granite
> subsumed, a rumor
> in a mumble of ocean.

"Fog" is a poem of definition, of thesis and proof, of abstraction and specificity, of visibility and accounting. Registering her surroundings, Clampitt makes us realize that fog may distort what we see but that it also allows us to offset "vagueness" with individual details that we might otherwise have taken for granted or ignored altogether. She reminds herself of what is lost, but merely mentioning everything brings it back to her, and her readers', attention.

The poem's expansive last sentence includes two kinds of compensation for loss: a nod to a painting Clampitt remembers, and a proof that loss might encourage sensuous richness, with the audible and the visible coming together in ravishing synaesthetic images:

> Opacity
> opens up rooms, a showcase

for the hueless moonflower
corolla, as Georgia
O'Keeffe might have seen it,
of foghorns; the nodding
campanula of bell buoys;
the ticking, linear
filigree of bird voices.

Acceptances of poems mounted, matching their rapid produc-
tion. At the same time that *The New Yorker* and *The Atlantic* began
to take Clampitt's poems, so did other magazines, quarterlies, and
reviews. Robert Pinsky at *The New Republic* was also an early sup-
porter. The poet who had lived anonymously was becoming a sensa-
tion after almost four decades of writing. By the end of 1978, *Antaeus*
and *The Hudson Review* joined the growing list of her credits. The
editors of sixteen other periodicals then accepted forty-eight of her
poems over the course of the next three years. In Maine for five
weeks that summer, she wrote ten poems.

It did not matter that some people, at least initially, rejected her.
Clampitt moved irresistibly forward, and no rebuff impeded her
energy. She was able to craft honest accounts of her own history, as
in the cover letter for a submission to Eliot Weinberger at *Monte-
mora* (he, of a different aesthetic entirely, returned everything) on
August 16:

> I have been writing poetry as a more than occasional thing for
> the last ten years. Signing up for a writers' workshop last fall was
> a kind of declaration of resolve: I wasn't sure up until then that I
> was quite ready to put on the badge, or the label or whatever it is,
> of Poet—I think because there were other things that seemed to
> need attending to first. I've now concluded that there is nothing I
> can do better, and nothing I want to do more, than engage in that
> craft. I've written sixty new pieces since the beginning of this year.

One of the new poems was a long, rambling thing, part fam-
ily history, part *ars poetica*, called "Crossing the Jersey Meadows,"
which originated in her New School workshop, and which I cited

in my first chapter, "Iowa." It contains a line, something she also quoted in letters to friends, about something she had heard—but never accepted—in Gabriel's class: "You have to explain. / Allusions won't do anymore. Your readers / (if any) can't be expected to know botany / —what's a phragmite?—or to have read / the *Inferno*." Allusions are crucial to Clampitt's poetry. She would not give them up. Her book learning became a major part of her craft.

"Crossing the Jersey Meadows" is a mess, but it gives a foretaste of better things. For one thing, we see Clampitt's efforts to recall and re-purpose her past and her family. In "Iowa" I quoted her, in this poem, as calling her father "the best of men," but "bottled up all his life." Surrounded, hemmed in by the prairie, he experiences a "dread / of emptiness." At the same time, she is attuned to literary precedents: she has turned Roy into an Iowa version of Robert Frost's speaker in "Desert Places," a man who has the capacity within, "so much nearer home / to scare [himself] with [his] own desert places."

Clampitt always thought about the demands placed by an author on her readers, and about how she could help them along. She included endnotes in all of her books from Knopf. Her friend Doris Myers was the one who first suggested that she do so. Alice Quinn and Mary Jo Salter concurred. When Craig Raine accepted *The Kingfisher* for its British publication by Faber & Faber in 1984, he insisted that she remove all endnotes. She complied, unhappily. Clampitt felt, as did Marianne Moore, that a poet could do her readers a favor by giving them some information about the details in her poems. Readers, she believed, are intellectually hungry, and should therefore be grateful for annotations. In a letter to an admirer, she wrote, "I decided quite consciously to cast my vote for helpfulness as opposed to mystification. Not that I expect everything to be explicable of course. But I am persuaded that explication is not to be sneered at . . . I think readers (as opposed to lit-crit professionals, whose needs are different) are entitled to whatever help the author can offer."

Clampitt's idea that readers are entitled to help demonstrates a generosity of spirit most artists lack. In an age of narcissism, of poems as mere cris de coeur, or blunt sudden outcries, such unapologetic testimonies to the life of the mind and to the Groves of Academe were often regarded with suspicion or even derision. In her 1986 interview with Elise Paschen, Clampitt said that poetry "wouldn't be much" if we didn't borrow. Keats, too, was bookish: "He was very young, I'm not but I am incorrigibly naïve." Hostile critics sometimes lambasted Clampitt for her book learning, and her insistence on both allusions and explanations of them. Anti-intellectualism in America has been a long-acknowledged fact of public life in both politics and the arts, and Clampitt, by hewing to her native academic bent, was never going to be a poet for all tastes.

She harbored conflicting aims for her work throughout her creative maturity. The young poet Bill Christopherson reported seeing her at a symposium of poets at New York University in the spring of 1990. One of the other participants was her contemporary Louis Simpson, who said, "I want my poems to be so simple a dog can understand them." In a letter to Christopherson, Clampitt called this "an outrageous remark." Simpson's flip statement deliberately echoes the famous pronouncement of Marianne Moore, one of Clampitt's admired predecessors, who said she wanted to write "in plain American which cats and dogs can read," but Moore was being, at best, disingenuous. Her poems are hardly simple. Regardless of her theoretical preference for easy diction, she knew that her readers might need help with her poems, and so she provided them with explanatory notes.

Clampitt also wrote in exasperation after the panel that she felt that "poets aren't talking to anyone except themselves." She wanted to talk to a wide audience, but she also needed to educate them. Wordsworth had written more than a century before that every great poet creates the taste by which he is to be enjoyed. Clampitt was ahead of her readers but made sure, by glancing back at them, that they could follow her. Book smarts, difficult vocabulary, cultural references: none should, she felt, be an impediment to a poet's direct communication with an audience. Accessibility comes in different registers.

As important to her poems as her voracious reading is a stylistic trait that would become a signature of Clampitt's mature style, something already present in "Crossing the Jersey Meadows": her reliance on lists, on names, on noun-heavy lines in which objects accumulate power and force. Writing of "the dread that dries up sorrow," of the "prairie terrors" of weather and landscape, and their grim toll on the settlers, Clampitt conjures some retroactive solace for her father simply by naming things. Making a list is a way of staving off terror, of rebelling against prairie deprivations and emptiness. Clampitt's verbal and botanical richness—things and the *names* of things—work against the poverty and the human frustrations intrinsic to a farmer's life. If you are a farmer's wife confronting a vast empty prairie, you plant a stake in the ground to have something to look at. If you are a poet, you plant in your work the names of the flowers that grew in your garden. You need something to hold on to.

———

What kind of person might want to write poetry so overloaded with things? Writing rich, as I have mentioned, was a compensation for living poor. It had a parallel in Amy's daily life. She hoarded physical scraps, like pieces of paper and notecards, as well as, in her poems, the names of things. This woman, often living on the brink of poverty in well-off postwar America, could spin verbal riches out of thin air. Collecting, of any sort, is a means of confronting death, of holding it at bay. Hoarding is collecting taken to extremes.

If Amy was a hoarder in her studio apartment, living with Hal only encouraged the habit. He had more space than she, and he was an accumulator as eager as she was. They were both children of the Depression. The East Side apartment had stacks of records, magazines, papers, as well as books everywhere. They seemed to live like students, not adults. A large poster of Bob Dylan looked down from a wall in the living room. Mary Jo Salter referred to a "piling system" that substituted for a more commonplace filing system. The furniture was comfortable, faded, and mismatched. Even the occasional fancier pieces—a newish wing chair with red velveteen upholstery, a better-than-average sofa—seemed to visitors to be old and dusty. Miscellaneous boxes covered the floors. Everything was helter-skelter. The bedroom was even worse, said the few people who ever got to peer inside.

The couple's domestic habits were slapdash. Cooking, for some-
one who had been in her early days a great experimenter, became
a much sketchier enterprise. Dusting and cleaning were scanted in
favor of more pressing creative endeavors. Salter remembers bring-
ing her young daughter Emily to visit Hal and Amy in 1984. The girl,
crawling on the living room rug, was wearing a white dress, which
by the time they left the apartment had turned shades of gray and
brown. Karen Chase called the couple "the two most impractical
people I think I've ever met." They were not bothered by their ad
hoc domestic arrangements.

Housekeeping remained inadequate until the end. In 1989, Hal
became ill with lymphoma and had six months of chemotherapy.
Then he was hit by Legionnaires' disease. When he finally came
home from the hospital, Amy hired as a companion a nurse's aide
named Vivian Banton (who remained helpful when Amy was dying
in Lenox in 1994), whom she described in a letter as a "life-enhancer."
Horrified by the look of the apartment and its clutter of books and
records, with dust everywhere—"'*What a mess!*' was her indelible
response"—Banton "found us Joyce, another Jamaican powerhouse,
who comes three Mondays out of four to keep the dust down and
many other things." They bought new bookcases, clutter came off
the floors, at least for a while, and onto shelves or into closets, "and
though shabby, by now the place is cheerful again." Helping Hal's
recovery, and even with a spell of pneumonia, Clampitt managed
to finish her fourth book, *Westward*, and turn it in to Ann Close at
Knopf.

The Clampitt papers include scraps and notes for poems, jot-
tings on the backs of virtually everything that was at hand: util-
ity bills, envelopes, recycled letters, memos from printing services,
concert programs, invitations to art openings or poetry readings,
hotel notepads, doctors' notifications. Most luxuriantly, there are
lines of poems on dozens of notices printed on the engraved, heavy
stock stationery sent out by legal firms to announce the hiring or the
promotion of lawyers who had been Korn's students at Columbia.
A piece of paper is a thing to be put to use, whether it is from the
gas company or from the law practice of Rosenman Colin Freund
Lewis and Cohen; or Gordon Altman Butowsky Weitzen Shalov

and Wein; or Botein Hays and Sklar; or Mudge Rose Guthrie & Alexander; or countless others. One can imagine Clampitt the poet savoring the names of the partners, the lists of proper nouns strung out across small sheets of embossed stock. Such small economies were no longer necessary for Amy: these accumulations came by force of habit. In her interview with Elise Paschen, she said that once she gave up on prose, she also gave up on keeping a journal: "I just make notes for future reference." These scribbled, jotted-down, random notes—seemingly plucked out of nowhere—would turn into lines and would help her, she said, curb her natural verbosity. (This seems like wishful thinking on her part. We can only imagine what her work would have looked like without such "curbing.") To Patricia Morrisroe, for her *New York* magazine profile, Clampitt admitted to liking the texture of those vellum sheets on which she made her notes: "it's much less intimidating to write on a small piece of paper." The preference for the discarded legal announcements was like her preference for small domestic spaces, and for writing while looking out from a window, ideally with a tree in view.

Like holding on to possessions, naming is apotropaic: perhaps listing common or proper nouns can deflect misfortune. Two impressive poems from *The Kingfisher* can stand for many others that demonstrate what Clampitt did with names. She was by inclination and training an etymologist. She wanted to know the formal as well as the casual names of everything. (She and Hal called his car and also his endless legal treatise "Ralph." Both were means of conveyance.) "Botanical Nomenclature" begins with the ordinary: "Down East people, not being botanists, / call it 'that pink-and-blue flower / you find along the shore.'" The guidebook writers call it "sea lungwort or oysterleaf," and you can hear the delight with which the poet utters to herself those mouth-filling syllables. She proceeds in loving detail to describe the shape and colors of the plant, and its place in a seawall or near the tidelines. Next, she gives us the "learned Latin / handle": *Mertensia*, the name of dozens of North American cousins. The name brings together items separated in time and space, because the poet realizes that back at home, inland, these were the beloved prairie bluebells of her childhood. Etymology joins and layers things. One plant, one proper name, but many recognizable forms: a family comes together. The poem ends:

> spring-bottomland glades standing upright,
> their lake-evoking sky color
> a trapdoor, a window letting in distances
> all the way to the ocean—
> reaching out, *nolens volens*,
> as one day everything breathing
> will reach out, with just such
> bells on its fingers, to touch
> without yet quite having seen
> the unlikelihood, the ramifying
> happenstance, the mirroring
> marryings of all likeness.

The key words are "unlikelihood" (as if she is acknowledging a splendid surprise) and "ramifying" (everything branches out and gathers other things together). And then, the unpredictable last line and a half, that enacts (in "mirroring / marryings") the poem's insight that the making of comparisons, the uncovering of likeness, is what nature and poets do best. One word, a Latin name, can make the whole world kin, *nolens volens*, or, as we say in English, willy-nilly.

Another exemplary poem—one of many—from the first volume that shows how Clampitt could put the facts of her lived life at the service of her imaginative powers is "Beach Glass," which can take its place among important walks-on-the-beach poems in the American canon by Walt Whitman, Wallace Stevens, Elizabeth Bishop, and A. R. Ammons. Like "Botanical Nomenclature," the poem was possible only because of Maine. It begins with a polite reference to the unnamed Harold Korn. As he and Amy are walking along the water's edge, he is "turning over concepts / I can't envision." He's thinking in human terms, and in legal and intellectual terms. She has attuned herself to nature's diurnal rhythms. He belongs to the public, secular world, she to the cosmos. Whereas the scholar turns ideas over in his mind, the ocean literally turns over everything that is tangible. She listens:

> . . . The ocean,
> cumbered by no business more urgent
> than keeping open old accounts
> that never balanced,
> goes on shuffling its millenniums
> of quartz, granite, and basalt.

Any shore is a beachcomber's treasure chest. Not all the items would seem worth noticing, let alone gathering, but Clampitt, always voracious, sees everything: the "driftwood and shipwreck, last night's / beer cans, spilt oil." The ocean is a great democratic phenomenon, for which, as Whitman would agree, "nothing / is beneath consideration."

Clampitt does not turn her concentrated attention to shells, "[t]he houses / of so many mussels and periwinkles," although, having mentioned them, she has brought them alive on the page. Instead, she keeps a lookout for beach glass, random shards:

> amber of Budweiser, chrysoprase
> of Almadén and Gallo, lapis
> by way of (no getting around it,
> I'm afraid) Phillips'
> Milk of Magnesia, with now and then a rare
> translucent turquoise or blurred amethyst
> of no known origin.

Just as the common names for *Mertensia* brought the poet back in touch with her Iowa childhood, so the detritus and treasures of the ocean remind her that glass comes from, and returns to, sand, the world over. She contemplates the eternal process, turning things over in her mind as the ocean turns over its objects. Hal appears again at the end, as the poem turns back to its own beginning: "an intellect / engaged in the hazardous / redefinition of structures / no one has yet looked at."

Korn the scholar approaches the unknown in airy abstraction. Clampitt the poet is tied to the material world and what Hopkins, her early favorite, called its "pied beauty." The poet-critic Christopher Bakken, reviewing Clampitt's letters in 2008, commented that in both "Beach Glass" and the letters, Clampitt's "gaze is entirely devoid of pretension and it takes everything in with an equivalent, oceanic curiosity." Always looking, always curious, Clampitt the poet articulated and clarified what Amy had been doing since childhood, observing her surroundings and appreciating the world's bounty, even when it was cast away by others.

The poems poured out of Clampitt between 1978 and 1982. She was ready to assemble them into her book. Having lived in anonymity for six decades, Amy Clampitt was about to become a public figure with the publication of *The Kingfisher*.

PART 2: 1983–1987

The story of publishing in New York has always been one of connections, serendipity, and pluck. Talent is mandatory, although not paramount. Whom one knows is important, as I have said. Amy Clampitt, would-be novelist, had learned one truth, as she wrote years later to the young poet Ralph Savarese: "Rejection is a river. Let it take you somewhere." Years of frustration had inured her to rejection, but only partly. Karen Chase, who came into her life at the end, said that Amy remembered every detail of every rejection letter and every bad review she received. "Physician, heal thyself" comes to mind. It was easy for her to encourage others to develop a thicker skin than she might have had herself.

Now she was embarking on the years, fewer but more crowded, of acceptance. She embraced whatever good luck came along, knowing that she had earned her success. Her goodwill extended to her dealings with the literary establishment. Savarese told me, "I never heard her gossip about other writers. She just seemed beyond the crassness." Susan Snively, a friend from her period at Amherst College, called her "the very opposite of an egotistical marketeer." Delayed gratification has many advantages. Rejection did not deter her. It spurred her on. Like most professionals, when something was sent back she turned it around and sent it somewhere else. Howard Moss rejected poems. So did Peter Davison, at least three times in 1982 alone. In one letter he wrote that the poems she submitted fell short of the contents of *The Kingfisher* (he had seen the not-yet-published manuscript of her first book), using an analogy that pinpoints a characteristic defect of her style. He said the poems "have the quality of catalogue arias—crammed with event and reference . . . They seem to be managed from the outside, not to evince an inner necessity." The charge of operatic "catalogue arias" (he was thinking of Mozart, Rossini, Gilbert and Sullivan) could also have been made against the beautiful but artistically self-indulgent descriptive passages in Clampitt's novels: her biggest test as an artist was always how to arrange her materials in ways that would allow them to be more than lists, however rich. She needed form.

In late 1981, Clampitt submitted her book manuscript to Knopf, about which she later said:

> The first book with the Borzoi colophon that I distinctly remember reading is Willa Cather's *Death Comes for the Archbishop*, which I found at my grandfather's house when I was a child. Though I had dreams of publishing a book at quite an early age, I don't know that I ever consciously aspired to being a Knopf author—and now that I am one, I count myself a very lucky one . . . There is no one in publishing whom I admire more, or to whom I feel more indebted—as an author, but above all as a reader.

Alfred Knopf, the legendary founding editor, died in August 1984. Clampitt could count herself one of the final new authors to come into the fold under his nominal supervision.

Clampitt's first editor at Knopf was Alice Quinn. The publishing house had begun a poetry series in 1980, designed to launch the careers of "young" poets. Having seen the poems that had appeared in periodicals, Quinn, herself a young editor, eagerly read Clampitt's manuscript. Several other houses (Harper & Row, as well as the Atlantic Monthly Press, headed by Peter Davison) had already rejected it in 1980. Quinn phoned Clampitt with the good news. A contract came from Knopf dated March 17, 1982, and included an advance of $1,000. Because of vanity or shyness—the same part of her that refused to tell her age—Clampitt never allowed an author's photo to appear on any of her book jackets until the final one, *A Silence Opens*, in 1994. At the end, more than silence was opening.

Four years earlier she had returned home to discover that *The New Yorker* had accepted a poem. At least this time, she knew the process was in the works. Quinn's colleague Ann Close, who became the editor for Clampitt's final three books starting in 1987, when Quinn left Knopf for *The New Yorker*, said that she, too, called the apartment, to congratulate Amy. Hal answered the phone: "Amy's not here." Close asked where she was. Hal replied, "You know, Amy is sixty going on three. She's outside skipping up and down the streets." Even Korn managed to slice a few years off Amy's age. When she got her acceptance, she was just shy of sixty-two, but her girlish enthusiasm belied the number of her lived years.

———

Both Quinn and Close shared their memories of Amy the woman in oral interviews. They knew only the new poet, not the young woman who had lived in Manhattan decades earlier. "Tall and thin and gawky," Close called her, "like an adolescent." She was constitutionally nervous. Once she became a public figure, Close added, she was in some ways no longer in charge of her life and her jitteriness became more apparent. A writer is in control at home, while writing; a published author, once successful, must follow the instructions of her editors and marketing people. The new, not-so-young star threw herself into writing more poems, but she was also distracted by the appearances demanded of her. Suddenly she had to learn to manage her time and to husband her resources. Work came first until the very end.

Close ventured an explanation for Amy's self-presentation that none of her other friends and relatives articulated so clearly: "she was kind of sexy when she was younger, but she [had] let herself go a little bit, and I think partly because of Hal." She had decided she would not make herself beautiful and outshine her disfigured partner. But Close added that more than a decade after meeting Hal and after Amy started earning her own money, "she started dressing very fashionably and, with that tall thin frame, she could

Amy, mid-1980s, in front of 354 West 12th Street

wear clothes well." Amy Clampitt: Clothes Horse. This is an image most of her female friends, from all stages, might remember with amusement.

Quinn made another point about Hal and Amy as a couple. She remembered having gone to dinner at the Korn apartment. Hal had one of his migraine headaches, and Quinn, entering, noted "the contrast of Amy's tall, radiant effervescence, just like an incandescent tree with sun and dew," with Hal's "pitched gloom." She, too, was struck by Amy's "remarkable sartorial style":

> I'm not sure that she always had a hat on, but there was always a scarf, there were beads . . . Her blouses always had floral designs or she wore Indian shawls, three-quarter length skirts, beautiful gold boots or old-fashioned, excellent leather, not loafers but sandals, with colored socks.

Amy was "really like a bird of plumage, especially on Third Avenue, in that drab environment." A bird of plumage, but one whose self-created plumage—like that of James Merrill at the opera, in black tie but shod in Birkenstock sandals and purple socks—combined haute couture and thrift shop discoveries.

Quinn again:

> Amy was pretty tall and Hal was not tall. His eyes were very crea-turely. They were always glistening, a little pooled with water and tears, and often very merry. And between her pouncing style and her hand gestures, and Hal's gorgeous smile, they were something to behold. He took complete delight in Amy, and registered his appreciation of her pouncing intelligence in his eyes. He was otherwise quite a still figure. I don't picture Hal moving. Amy was a darter, but Hal was very still.

The picture of Amy the woman dovetails with everyone's sense of Clampitt the poet. She knew what she wanted. She was committed to maintaining as much control as possible over her personal and her creative life. Quinn said "she had a very clear sense of how she wanted to look. And I think she had a very coquettish sense of herself as a sweetly seductive woman. I think she had a lot of confidence, for someone who wasn't in any way an average-looking beautiful woman."

Men as well as women noticed Clampitt's distinctive style, both personal and poetic. Her editor at the *Kenyon Review*, Frederick Turner, remembered her:

> I considered her one of the most important poets in America, but at the time she still felt that she was a sort of editorial mouse in the Manhattan literary woodwork, and she rather liked being taken out by a young fellow for a walk in Central Park and dinner in a nice warm restaurant. We talked about everything—she had the librarian's gift of recognizing every book and author one mentioned, and knowing exactly what was in that odd fifth chapter. Her vocabulary was as large as anyone's I have ever met, and her knowledge of the sciences was astonishing. She was delightful

company and wore her erudition lightly and unconsciously. She was very funny, and liked how I laughed at her unobtrusive wit—wit she seemed quite unaware of, like an instinct. There was a bit of decorous flirtation—I think we both saw it as a sort of Harold and Maude situation and found it ridiculous. She was indeed rather like the Maude character in the movie, eternally young, anciently wise, irreverent, free.

———

The publication of Clampitt's first volume from Knopf increased the admiration of an ever-expanding audience and cemented a fame that had also been growing. The distinguished literary scholar Helen Vendler wrote a fan letter in early 1982, announcing herself as an admirer after seeing the poems printed in *The New Yorker* and elsewhere. Then Vendler took the unusual step of asking to review Clampitt's first book when it appeared. When *The Kingfisher* was published, Vendler was the first major critic to write a detailed and enthusiastic appreciation, in the March 3, 1983, issue of the *New York Review of Books*. She praised the intensity of this "beautiful, taxing poetry." Having read the review before its official publication date, Clampitt answered Vendler's January letter on February 1. The two women maintained a cordial, respectful, mostly epistolary relationship for the rest of Amy's life. Vendler helped her win Guggenheim and MacArthur fellowships, and invited her to serve as the Phi Beta Kappa poet at Harvard's commencement in 1987. In a letter of April 3, 1982, Clampitt wrote gratefully to Vendler. She also sent along copies of *Multitudes, Multitudes* and *The Isthmus* "with some diffidence," knowing now that they were indeed apprentice work, and realizing with self-assurance that "one does write differently in isolation, as I was then. It *is* good to have readers!" Going at her task with an understanding that people like Vendler, Salter, and Moss were paying attention clearly galvanized and inspired the poet in ways she could have formerly only imagined.

In her *NYRB* essay, Vendler set the stage for all the subsequent reviews, mostly laudatory, some critical. From her perch at the top of the academic establishment, she made a daring prediction: that a hundred years later the book would "have taken on . . . the documentary value of what, in the twentieth century, made up the stuff of culture." This was a twentieth-century equivalent of Emerson's proclamation in his letter to Walt Whitman, which the poet published in the 1856 edition of *Leaves of Grass*: "I greet you at the beginning of a great career." Clampitt was not a glittering beginner, in Vendler's eyes; she was already a master. Her poems were exhilarating, both "unpredictable and conclusive," always an ideal blending. Her "liking for mysteries of texture [is] followed by the plain and simple." This is a combination I referred to earlier as a mingling of Keatsian lushness and Quaker austerity. Other critics suggested that Clampitt had wed the verbal density of Gerard Manley Hopkins to the scientific accuracy of Marianne Moore. Above all, Vendler took note of how Clampitt had solved the problem of finding a proper form for her feelings, and her observations of things and other external phenomena: her "words, like neurons, put out branches to other words," through sound, syntax, etymology, or image. Clampitt was articulating connectiveness.

Amy did not much like being controversial, and when negative reviews inevitably appeared, she was not initially thick-skinned enough to ignore or rebuff them. Ironically, Vendler's positive evaluation agitated her even more than the hostile remarks of others. Praise from Vendler was heady stuff. Gratified, Amy also became confused and even depressed. For a brief time, she resorted to pharmacological treatment, even as she threw herself into accepting invitations to read and to lecture. As with the dark period during her years of political engagement, and as with the dark periods that her grandfather recorded in his autobiography, the fog soon lifted and high spirits returned. She had absorbed the truth of an epigrammatic line she admired, from the contemporary poet Naomi Shihab Nye, which sounds like something from Emily Dickinson: "The tear is famous briefly to the cheek." Like fame itself, sadness is merely fugitive.

For the next decade, Vendler remained not only an encourager but also a voice of common sense, offering reassurance as well as commentary on the poems Clampitt shared with her. After a return from the Yeats Summer School in Sligo in 1984, Vendler reported that "they have read you in Ireland." Even more helpful, two years later (April 28, 1986), when Clampitt was smarting from some unfavorable reviews, Vendler offered the wisdom of maturity, and took long views:

> Fear not about the reviews; you will never suit all tastes. All anyone can do is do her work quietly and as well as possible, knowing the centuries sort everything out. Anyone can pick holes in anything, and who should 'scape whipping, etc. I think the people who don't like your verses find them affected, as Elsie Stevens thought Wallace's verse affected. It only means that such people have never felt their minds going in the direction the poet's mind tends to go in. Or that the words used seem to them improbable. We all know that odd directions and improbable words are the very stuff of naturalness when idiosyncracy and idiolect are in question. The more fools they. Relax. Those of us who love your language are not about to desert you. And those who don't love it may love something else, and thereby save their souls in some other direction, or so I hope. After all, Dr. Johnson didn't like *Lycidas*. Odd isn't it, taste.

Odd, indeed, and there is no accounting for it. Vendler's advice is worth repeating to all artists of any age, in any medium. Everyone should post this note above her desk.

———

As Clampitt was assembling what would become *The Kingfisher*, she did something she had long promised herself she would do. It was, in part, a much-delayed homage to her father, the Grinnell Classics major who had first taught her the Greek alphabet. Having studied Greek literature in translation, in school and college, and having finally visited Greece in 1965, she enrolled in Ancient Greek language classes. As early as 1954 she had written about wanting to read Sophocles in a bilingual edition, making use of a newly purchased secondhand Greek dictionary. A decade later, on board ship en route to Greece, she took daily half-hour classes to learn basic conversational phrases. Her intellectual curiosity was, as usual, excited by anything having to do with language, whether native or foreign, contemporary or dead.

She got up the courage—as she had four years earlier when she enrolled in Daniel Gabriel's workshop—to sign on for a weekly class in Attic Greek at The New School in the fall of 1981. She was sixty-one. She took her inspiration from the journalist I. F. Stone, who started his Greek studies at seventy-one in order to learn about Athenian democracy from Thucydides, in the original language. Her classmates ranged from curious young people to a retired physician who read with a magnifying glass. It was the kind of variegated community that had always appealed to Amy, this time in a classroom rather than in a bus or at a protest meeting. "Thrilling though formidably difficult," the course was grist for an intellectual's mental mill, with short selections from Pindar, Aeschylus, Simonides, and the Gospels circulating among the students every Saturday from nine in the morning until one in the afternoon, under the watchful eye of Sam Seigle, a moonlighting professor from Sarah Lawrence, whom Amy adored. He "has the learning and the imagination to bring the entire scene alive, and almost every minute he is striking flint with some new insight, historical or etymological." The material was manna for the voracious student.

Interviewed forty years later, Seigle remembered his student vividly. Coming from the avant-garde precincts of Sarah Lawrence, the professor taught without a syllabus, encouraging students in an elementary course to devise their own paths through new material in a strange tongue. They were forced to think for themselves, he said, especially about the nature of the words and phrases they were learning. "Always curious," he said, Amy took to "the precision of syntax, and the exactitude of the language" with her typical intellectual alertness. She thrilled, her professor recalled, to the difference between an objective and a subjective genitive (e.g., the two meanings of "the love of God"), a concept she had previously not known. After the semester ended, Seigle never saw her again. Nor did he forget her.

The following semester, Amy stayed uptown, at Hunter College, within walking distance of home on East 65th Street. Here she read

Homer with Irving Kizner. She described this to Vendler as "one of the great experiences of my life." And to Salter she recounted the mouthwatering thrill of those famous, ringing and untranslatable Homeric phrases like "polyphlosboio thalasses" ("the muchsounding sea") whose sound is integral to the meaning, regardless how you translate it. She found "it impossible to convey the peculiar excitement that goes with all this: it's like arriving in a place you'd dreamed of all your life."

When she was young, Amy had dreamed of Manhattan, of England, of Greece. She landed, successively, in all of them. She had dreamed, too, of the Greek language, and now was immersing herself in it. She landed in Greek as well as Greece. She traveled both in the flesh and in her mind. One lovely result was a Petrarchan sonnet—"Homer, A. D. 1982"—that appeared in *What the Light Was Like*. It begins with a nod to young John Keats's first great poem, "On First Looking into Chapman's Homer," which conveys the excitement available to both real-life travelers and stay-at-home explorers who experience an original only vicariously, like Keats reading Homer in translation: "Much have I travelled in the realms of gold, / And many goodly states and kingdoms seen." Amy was a traveler of both sorts. Clampitt's 1982 Manhattan is like, and unlike, Keats's 1816 London.

Here is the octave of her sonnet, dedicated to Kizner:

> Much having traveled in the funkier realms of Ac-
> ademe, aboard a grungy elevator car,
> *deus ex machina* reversed, to this ninth floor
> classroom, its windows grimy, where the noise of traffic,
> πολυφλοίσβοιο-θαλάσσηζ-like, is chronic,
> we've seen since February the stupendous candor
> of the *Iliad* pour in, and for an hour and a
> quarter at the core the great pulse was dactylic.

An attentive reader can hear the poet mingling the dactylic rhythms (DUM-da-da) of Homer with the insistent iambs (da-DUM) of English, and alternating in her rhymes between the hard, consonantal endings in lines 1, 4, 5, and 8 and the more mellifluous, liquid sounds of lines 2, 3, 6, and 7. The "great pulse" is a throbbing, bilingual one, Homer's and Clampitt's together. This poem projects the energetic fun that a polyglot intellectual can have, and can share with her readers.

———

The years between 1983 and 1994 constituted a decade of activity that compensated for the previous years of anonymity: accolades, travel, readings, academic teaching assignments, and more informal workshops of shorter duration. Amy seems to have accepted every invitation except when illness, prior scheduling, or conflicts of interest made it impossible for her to say yes.

The poet kept writing. Unlike writers with careers spanning decades, she had neither the time nor the desire to change her style, which remained essentially the same throughout her five Knopf volumes. The subjects changed, slightly, in *Archaic Figure*, her third book, which has more poems about Greece and Greek culture, and more poems about English and American writers and their landscapes (George Eliot, Margaret Fuller, the Wordsworths, Lewis Carroll and his Alice). Clampitt wrote about travel, places, history, family, nature's flora and fauna. Her language, her lists, and the syntax of her sentences were put to the service of her always attentive eye.

Clampitt liked long sentences. She probably wrote more poems that are one sentence long than anyone else of her generation. Of the 193 poems in the 459 pages of her *Collected Poems*, 37 are composed of a single sentence. Many others use an abundance of semicolons where another writer would use periods. Clampitt liked writing "long" as well as "rich."

Why would someone write a one-sentence poem that is lengthier than, say, a sonnet? And what are the effects of such a choice? I'll let one example stand in for many of the others. "Iola, Kansas" (*Westward*) is a bus ride poem. The poem itself is *like* a bus ride, moving on and on, its commas and colons indicating pauses. It reaches a full stop only at the end of its thirty-two lines, after the bus has arrived at a highway "rest stop." Just as the bus contains many passengers, separate but conjoined, so the poem's sentence is another community of parts.

It starts with a noun- and adjective-heavy list of elements in a heavily industrialized surround:

> Riding all night, the bus half empty, toward the interior,
> among refineries, trellised and turreted illusory cities,
> the crass, the indispensable wastefulness of oil rigs
> offshore, of homunculi swigging at the gut of a continent:

The bus moves on from Texas, through Oklahoma and into Kansas. At first, the landscape is anything but attractive, filled with "belch and glare, the alluvium of the auto junkyards," the semis, trailers, and vans of an American freeway. When it reaches Kansas as night falls, our speaker sees the name "Iola" printed high overhead on a water tower. The bus and its human community make their temporary stop. Here they find no vending machines with food for sale, but instead, Wonder Bread sandwiches, and pie, baked by a real person.

The experience resembles the drive in "A Procession at Candlemas," when the poet heads west to visit her dying mother in Iowa, and her bus makes a restroom stop along the highway somewhere in the Midwest. Here is her description, from that earlier poem, of the junk one finds at the cash register in any anonymous turnpike way station along any American interstate highway:

> . . . What is real except
>
> what's fabricated? The jellies glitter
> cream-capped in the cafeteria showcase;
> gumball globes, Life Savers cinctured
>
> in parcel gilt, plop from their housings
> perfect, like miracles. Comb, nail clipper,
> lip rouge, mirrors and emollients embody,

niched into the washroom wall case,
the pristine seductiveness of money.

In "Iola, Kansas," it's not the seductiveness of material things that draws the poet in; it's the shared experience that borders on a kind of secular communion.

The poem's final lines describe a human interchange:

> . . . "It's boysenberry,
> I just baked it today," the woman behind the counter
> believably says, the innards a purply glue, and I eat it
>
> with something akin to reverence: free refills from
> the Silex on the hot plate, then back to our seats,
> the loud suction of air brakes like a thing alive, and
> the voices, the sleeping assembly raised, as by an agency
>
> out of the mystery of the interior, to a community—
> and through some duct in the rock I feel my heart go out,
> out here in the middle of nowhere (the scheme is a mess)
> to the waste, to the not knowing who or why, and am happy.

Like the bus riders in Elizabeth Bishop's poem "The Moose," who are stopped by a giant creature in the middle of the road and then united by a "sweet / sensation of joy" before resuming their journey, Clampitt and her companions join together in a moment of what we can only call "grace."

This is akin to Amy's experience decades earlier at the Cloisters when, in the presence of other people, she felt the sunlight streaming in and over her. Spiritual longing and an awareness of "the strangeness of all there is" prepare her, in spite of her religious and emotional wariness, to be ready to relish such moments when they come. Clampitt's poetic habits matched her personality. As her life began to change, as she moved suddenly and excitedly into the spotlight, she knew exactly how to put those habits to creative use. Rejoicing often takes place in a context of sharing—that is, within a community of other people whose presence assures greater pleasure—and it takes place as well in the syntactic equivalent of community: a long sentence.

———

In August 1982, even before the publication of *The Kingfisher*, but having won two prizes—one from the Academy of American Poets, the other from the Guggenheim Foundation—Clampitt got away from New York and went to Corea to "settle down to the serious business of being a Guggenheim Fellow . . . I discover that I'm more than a little scared, I've never had quite such luxury in the time-to-do-nothing department before. It's a little like stage fright. Even opening up the typewriter entailed a minor struggle." As always, the Maine setting calmed and inspired her. She placed her typewriter on a table in front of the upstairs bedroom window. Hal worked downstairs, also by a window. The view, of course, was an essential fact: "It's wonderful to be breathing sea air again, and to have the luxury of what seems like total quiet—the sound of an occasional engine or a dog barking hardly does more than skim the surface of it." After a month, she returned briefly to Manhattan. She then alit for the Midwest, seeing friends and relatives in Minnesota and Colorado; she returned to Iowa, where she visited Des Moines and gave a reading at Grinnell, discovering friends and former teachers from high school and college. Then Dubuque and Detroit, and, upon returning to Manhattan, she learned from Alice Quinn (December 21) that the first bound copies of *The Kingfisher* had arrived.

The publishing party—an old cultural phenomenon that has now virtually disappeared—took place at the Roosevelt House, 47 East 65th Street, on February 3, 1983, arranged by Knopf but paid for by Amy and Hal. The venue was in their neighborhood but it was hardly part of their daily existence. The event was a very fine celebration of a much-delayed maiden speech, a sort of literary coming-out party. It combined the elegant and the casual, refinement and enthusiasm. Amy described the event in a letter to her friend Rimsa Michel ten days later. Howard Moss was there, as were the poets Marilyn Hacker, May Swenson, J. D. McClatchy, and Alfred Corn, the young novelists Ann Arensberg and Laurie Colwin, as well as David

Schoenbrun, long indebted to Amy for her editorial help. Larry and Jeanne Clampitt came down from Boston. Amy was delighted that her editor Alice Quinn had sent a bouquet containing anemones, stock, delphinium, and freesias, her favorite winter flower. George Gershwin's piano stood in a corner of the big drawing room of Sara Delano Roosevelt's former town house, overlooking the garden. A trio played classical music.

Catering included—appropriately for a poet besotted by English culture—watercress and cucumber sandwiches, little boiled potatoes stuffed with sour cream and caviar, and skewered melon balls topped with a single bead of blueberry. The last especially delighted the honoree, probably because the blueberry made a nod in the direction of Maine, its landscape and its summer fecundity. It may have been a winter day, but the event itself radiated warmth and fine feeling. People had to be shooed from the house. No one wanted to leave. It was the kind of celebration at which people who knew one another mingled happily with strangers, and where pretense and self-promotion were in short supply. Literary eminences shared laughs and stories with nobodies. Regina and Stephen Banks headed to the Upper East Side from downtown with several other old lefties from Amy's activist days. Regina Berry—a neighbor from West 12th Street—said that everyone from the Tenants' Organization who had voted against turning the three adjacent buildings into co-ops also came uptown, a rare occurrence, to rally around their politically active neighbor: "It was the most elegant thing. Amy always knew how to find the best caterers!" Amy's sometime neighbors on West 12th Street were mostly young people who—as she had done decades earlier—also came to Manhattan to make a go at city life. They were songwriters, artists, students, people working in advertising, the usual range of occupations. Downtown blended in with uptown, West Side with East Side. Amy's friends brought along their own friends, who were genuinely glad to meet the latest poetic sensation, and to toast someone who was an ordinary New Yorker as well as a literary luminary. Part of the merriment was due to Amy's own capacity for happiness. As in Greece, she was both easy and eager to please.

From this point on, Amy Clampitt, celebrity and poet, continued

Alice Quinn and Amy at the Kingfisher *party, Roosevelt House, 1983*

both to write and to accept invitations that might have taken another poet away from writing. There was lunch with Richard Howard; a meeting at last with Helen Vendler; a mini reading tour in Boston: all of this while she was involved in trying to prevent her 12th Street landlord from forcing a co-op conversion on his tenants.

In April, Hal and Amy sailed on the *QE2* for two months in England and the European continent. Her greatest desire was to see the Lake District for the first time. As with Greece in 1965, so now, too: something she had known only vicariously, through art, was to enter her life with the full force of something experienced through the senses. On May 4, she wrote to Vendler about her visit to the Keats House near Hampstead Heath, which she had first seen thirty-two years previously: "for most of the several hours I spent in Hampstead, there was the feel of an English spring, with just enough sunshine for it to seem miraculous." The nineteenth century bloomed, once more, in and for her.

Home again, following visits to Venice, Greece, and Yugoslavia, Amy finally left her job at Dutton (Jack Macrae had abandoned Dutton and gone over to Holt, Rinehart). In the fall of 1983, to her amazement, Richard Howard asked her to take part in a homage to W. H. Auden, on the occasion of the tenth anniversary of the poet's death. She found herself onstage beside Joseph Brodsky, who recited his Auden selection from memory and got a storm of applause: "I was pretty scared, but did not trip on the mike wire or spill my water glass or lose my place on the page. I read 'Voltaire at Ferney' and got a small ripple of [friendly] laughter." Her fellow readers included Anthony Hecht, John Ashbery, and Christopher Isherwood. She said she was too shy to introduce herself to Isherwood. Earlier that month she had been in Milwaukee as a writer-in-residence, and she got good mileage out of telling her audiences that Grace Paley, one of her predecessors in that visiting position, had been her chum in jail back in the anti–Vietnam War days.

At the end of October, in a letter to Barbara Clark, she mentioned, in rapid succession, her three weeks in Greece; her offer from Faber & Faber for the British edition of her book; a radio interview; her forthcoming reading at Harvard; meeting at a party the very drunk Kurt Vonnegut, who when introduced to her mumbled, "Oh, old friend of mine," not knowing her at all; the Auden memorial; the Milwaukee residency on Lake Michigan; and her forthcoming— February 27, 1984—reading at the Library of Congress, with a party hosted by Anthony Hecht, then the Consultant on Poetry at the library. In the middle of this expanding account, she asks, "Barbara, do you believe any of this?" The question was directed as much to herself as to her friend. Her response to her newfound celebrity combined gratitude, excitement, and, sometimes, incredulity.

———

In 1984, Grinnell gave Clampitt an honorary Doctor of Humane Letters degree. The American Academy and Institute of Arts and Letters awarded her a fellowship. The Djerassi Program in Woodside, California, offered a residency. During the flurry of socializing and literary appearances, Clampitt was also assembling the contents of her next book. Most of the poems had been written simultaneously with or only shortly after the poems of *The Kingfisher*. The centerpiece of *What the Light Was Like* is "Voyages: A Homage to John Keats." This sequence of eight poems—each a kind of chapter in the life, and about the work, of the young writer who was an early hero of hers—is one poet's testimony to the lifelong influence of a precursor. An author's choice of subjects always opens a window onto her creative process. It is part of her autobiography. In the case of Amy Clampitt and John Keats (and to a different extent, Clampitt and Dickinson, or George Eliot, or the Wordsworths), it is evidence of a life of identification and substitution, using a "predecessor," the very thing she said all writers need, as a model and a mirror for oneself. Clampitt did not need to write about herself in order to let her readers into her imaginative life. She could be revelatory at one remove.

The Keats sequence is beautiful, but not easy for readers with no literary training. It profits from, but does not entirely require, a knowledge of Keats's life and work. Since art communicates on different levels to different audiences, ignorance is not necessarily an impediment to pleasure. Mozart once wrote that two of his middle-period piano concertos contained "passages here and there that only connoisseurs can fully appreciate—yet the common listener will find them satisfying as well, although without knowing why."

Clampitt was a connoisseur. Few people know Keats—the life and the work—as well as she did. She had expertise, even intimacy, in the "field" of Keats. She knew the territory completely, and inwardly. She had been living vicariously through Keats ever since her exposure to him in junior high school, when she read "The Eve of Saint Agnes," his romance about cold and self-denial, and the countering forces of warm love and romantic escape. But even readers without an intimate knowledge of Keats's twenty-five years can appreciate Clampitt's language, her re-creation of Keats's life, and her creation of a new kind of poem. Let's call it a poem of joint ownership. Clampitt is negotiating between traditions: that of her Romantic precursor, and that of some intervening Americans (Whitman, Hart Crane, and Wallace Stevens). America, England, and Europe unite as she combines scattered pieces and absorbs Keats's imagination into her own. She repurposes the life of another person.

On September 7, 1985, Clampitt wrote to Vendler from Winchester, where Keats had composed his ode "To Autumn" in September 1819. It's as if she is experiencing what he experienced. The landscape and the weather are the same. She agrees with him: the town is the pleasantest either of them has ever seen. There is an abundance of footpaths, people walking their dogs, an "ancient and handsome High Street," on which Morris dancers cavort "in scarlet hose with belled and beribboned garters, and funny hats. I have somehow the feeling that even the indigent live in more comfort and dignity than in most other places . . . The window of my hotel room looks out onto a garden where a very old, propped-up apple tree is full of fruit, a fact which the condition of the trunk renders cheerfully improbable." Keats called autumn the "season of mists and mellow fruitfulness" and singled out the apples waiting to be pressed into cider. When she comes upon the same scene, Clampitt is put, however "cheerfully improbable" it may seem, in touch with her tutelary spirit from the past century.

Clampitt's notes to her poetic sequence emphasize "the powerful way in which literature can become a link with times and places, and with minds, otherwise remote." And she quotes the poet's friend, the painter Joseph Severn, who said that Keats would walk across Hampstead Heath and notice the wind passing over a field of grain: "The sea, or thought-compelling images of the sea, always seemed to restore him to a happy calm." Clampitt had dreamed of living by the ocean. She could not resist adding in her notes that she, too, was familiar from childhood with fields of grain. She connects her dreams to poems by Whitman and Crane, from which (in addition to poems by Stevens and Osip Mandelstam) she has garnered the epigraphs to her sequence. Linkage—of minds and places and times—is her governing principle. Her poem is a bridge of connections. Such associations constitute homage.

Of the eight poems, five have titles that locate Keats in space: "Margate," "Teignmouth," "Chichester," "The Isle of Wight," and "Winchester: The Autumn Equinox," all of them places where he wrote, and which got absorbed into the fabric of his life and work. The longest poem, "The Elgin Marbles," details his walking trip from London to the north of England and then Scotland in the summer of 1818. "He Dreams of Being Warm," another title, reminds us of a dilemma Clampitt, who recalled throughout her life how cold she was in winter in her Iowa farmhouse, shared with her predecessor. And the last is a coda, "Voyages," bringing Stevens, Crane, and Mandelstam, writers of the twentieth century, into the panorama of poets absorbed in prairie matters and ocean matters. Some of the poems are rhymed, others not. "The Isle of Wight," in ten-line stanzas, pays homage to the form Keats invented for several of his major odes; and "Winchester: The Autumn Equinox" uses the eleven-line stanza Keats perfected for "To Autumn," his greatest lyric. And throughout the sequence, Clampitt quotes from Keats's poems and letters.

Clampitt's series borrows words and shapes from the work of her precursor, but it doesn't feel drily "bookish." Rather, it attempts to recreate the mind and soul of a dead poet, and in so doing to offer equal access, at one remove, to the soul of the sympathetic, living writer who is following him. Keats and Clampitt both sought ways to escape from unhealthy or unpleasant physical circumstances, and to compensate creatively for absences felt in their hearts. Clampitt emigrated from Iowa, in her school days, through books. Now, past sixty, she is metaphorically leaving New York for another world and an earlier time. Keats, the quintessential young poet, like Clampitt the quintessential late bloomer, longed for other climes. In his case, it was the Mediterranean, which he never saw until the last months of his life when, having shipped off to Italy, he remained in quarantine in Naples before he moved to, and died in, Rome. "Keats's starved stare before the actual, / so long imagined Bay of Naples" is the experience of everyone who has ever dreamed of a place and then arrived at it. Sometimes the reality frustrates or saddens. Clampitt wants us to imagine both satisfactions and disappointments.

Much, if not all, art is a program of sublimation and reimagining. Here are the last two quatrains of "Teignmouth," depicting Keats before the beginning of his miraculous year of creative energy:

an *annus mirabilis* of odes before the season
of the oozing of the ciderpress, the harvest done,
wheatfields blood-spattered once with poppies gone
to stubble now, the swallows fretting to begin

their windborne flight toward a Mediterranean
that turned to marble as the mists closed in
on the imagination's yet untrodden region—
the coal-damps, the foul winter dark of London.

Readers who already know Keats hear the echoes ringing in their inner ear: we recognize images from his odes to Psyche and Autumn, the "Ode on a Grecian Urn," and his pseudo-medieval ballad "La Belle Dame Sans Merci." These enrich the poem. Their absence from another reader's knowledge does not, however, diminish the poem's force or beauty.

One need not know more than what Clampitt tells us, detailing Keats's separation from his brother George and his wife, Georgiana, who sailed for America and fetched up in Kentucky, a landscape that Keats could not imagine. Clampitt imagines it for us, as if borrowing Keats's eyes, in one of her miniaturized lists. How, she asks, could Mnemosyne, the mother of the Muses, herself

> have coped with that uncultivated tangle,
> catbrier and poison ivy, chiggers,
> tent caterpillars, cottonmouths,
> the awful gurglings and chirrings
> of the dark?
>
> ("THE ELGIN MARBLES")

Always a poet of place, Clampitt now places herself into the mind of Keats, sympathizing with his separation from beloved family members and wondering how he could envision the wilderness of the American continent. This was her continent, of course, a century later. She knew what Keats did not.

———

Clampitt attracted attention from the very moment of her appearance on the scene. *The Kingfisher* received considerable praise, as did *What the Light Was Like*. She also became a figure of controversy. Critics like to take sides, pick fights, join in battles. The stakes are high when large egos march into the fray. Harold Bloom and Helen Vendler were on Clampitt's side, her champions. So were many poets: James Merrill, Anthony Hecht, Robert Penn Warren, Howard Nemerov, Mona Van Duyn, Henri Cole, Richard Kenney, Alan Williamson, W. S. Merwin, and Richard Wilbur.

Fan letters arrived from many kinds of grateful literary readers. As early as 1982, even before *The Kingfisher* came out, the poet Gjertrud Schnackenberg wrote to Clampitt that "there are very, very few contemporary poets to whom I can stand to give ear. I am easily dejected by droning, carping, and needless verbal ventilation . . . your voice is now soaring, has given heart, and an uplifted heart at that." That the poems were difficult was no impediment. The English poet Christopher Reid called the title poem of *What the Light Was Like* "an elegy of the highest order, as complex and dignified as 'Lycidas.'" A little later, the Canadian scholar Eleanor Cook had the same appreciative feeling, for both personal and intellectual reasons. Reading "The Prairie" (*Westward*) in 1990, she was reminded of the resemblances between Clampitt's girlhood in a midwestern American terrain and her own Canadian prairie childhood on "root-fattened" lands. She added how much she enjoyed having to look up some of the words in a dictionary—this is what literary scholars love to do—a "pleasure to add them to one's word-hoard." Why should all poems be easy, or accessible, or unchallenging? Clampitt made her readers do their own work, even when she helped with her annotations.

The novelist Edmund White wrote a valuable appreciation, "Poetry as Alchemy," which appeared in *The Nation* (April 16, 1983). He was especially attentive to how Clampitt told a story obliquely, as in "The Kingfisher." Denise Levertov was a poet of a far different stripe from Clampitt. But she wrote to Clampitt in 1984, saying how she "fell in love with" "The August Darks," which came out originally in *The New Yorker* before appearing as the first poem in *What the Light Was Like*. Edward Hirsch, an alumnus of Grinnell, and just beginning to win his own fame, said he felt both "*airborne* and *earthbound*" (these are Clampitt's terms) while reading the poems from *The Kingfisher*. The young poet Rosanna Warren praised "the rampage of language" and the "bravery with which [the poems'] plenty confronts the recognized void." Clearly, readers were hungry for something rich and bountiful, something in a new idiom, a new music. And Clampitt had given them what they didn't know they craved until they read her. J. D. McClatchy said that she did not "follow the latest fads or slavishly imitate what was popular . . .

[She was] interested in structure, rhythm, meter, texture, and not in writing down whatever popped into her head." Brad Leithauser (who had brought Clampitt to the attention of his editor, Ann Close, at Knopf, and then to Alice Quinn) was also struck by the difference between her poems and what other poets at the time were manufacturing: what she "brought to the free verse that served as her customary mode was an all but unmatched sumptuosity. She seemed to work with a larger orchestra than most of the rest of us. It made a wider range of sounds." She matched her incomparable eye for detail with an ear for music, which was—as all of her readers have acknowledged—sometimes mellifluous, sometimes clanging, an inheritance from Gerard Manley Hopkins but, like his "sprung rhythm," a slanted music all her own.

After *The Kingfisher* appeared, it was a finalist for the National Book Critics Circle Award. It came in a close second to the eventual winner. Somehow, the confidentiality that is supposed to attend upon the judges' deliberations was breached, and a newspaper article appeared (I cannot tell what newspaper, but a clipping is included in a letter to Hal from Amy) that described the critical skirmishes at Manhattan's Algonquin Hotel:

The longest and most heated discussion—lasting more than an hour—arose over the poetry award. [The two front-runners were *The Kingfisher* and James Merrill's massive, book-length *The Changing Light at Sandover*.] At first, there seemed no room for compromise. Various board members described Merrill's work as "completely vacuous" and "brilliant"; Clampitt's work was praised for its "generosity of spirit" and condemned as "overwrought occasional poetry." After three hung ballots, one panelist grumbled that Merrill looked like he was going to win "by *droit du seigneur*." But another summed up the general feeling this way: "You couldn't discount the achievement, whether you like the poetry or not." Merrill won a narrow victory on the fourth vote.

This kind of reportage does nothing to establish confidence in the process of awarding prizes. Competition was rife. Clampitt, the new "young" contender, was outclassed by the senior poet, six years her junior. The sheer size of his book, as well as his age, and perhaps gender, triumphed. Merrill himself, however, having been asked in 1983 what contemporary writers might become classics, offered Clampitt's name unhesitatingly. He, too, the gracious winner, was on her side.

Over the course of the next few years, and the publication of the third and fourth books (*Archaic Figure* and *Westward*), some reviewers wrote more measuredly, combining praise and disapproval, not quite knowing how to place Clampitt within the current scene. Mary Oliver reviewed *What the Light Was Like* in the *Kenyon Review*, with an appraisal that might apply to all of Clampitt's work:

> The bounty is large. Few poets have a more dazzling verbal gift. She displays an almost frenzied delight in details; an outpouring of images and adjective-bliss illuminates each page.
>
> This is praise, but only to a point. Clampitt's vigor is precisely her peril. The poems can, and sometimes do, evaporate in a surfeit of sweetness and a lack of arrival.

Dennis O'Driscoll, in *Poetry Ireland Review* (1987), called Clampitt "immensely talented" but found everything she wrote "overwrought and fussy." That was the common charge: she was fancy, not plain, intellectual and fussy, not natural and easy. (I am reminded of a response by Maurice Ravel to criticism that his music was artificial: "Perhaps I'm artificial by nature.") And she was also, somehow, unclassifiable.

In *Poetry*, Sandra Gilbert, one of the founders or godmothers of feminist literary theory, seemed to admire and enjoy much of Clampitt's work, while objecting to its overly allusive nature, especially the Keats sequence, which she glossed as "vapidly" literary. And while she criticized Clampitt for making use of "the old-fashioned resources of rhyme and meter," she also acknowledged the brilliance of her style and the fact that the time had come for a revival of those techniques. It's as though Gilbert liked the poems but felt she should not have, and was trying to cover up a guilty, old-fashioned and perhaps no longer relevant pleasure with a nod to the tastes of the decade. (Clampitt was never a strict "formalist" like James Merrill or Richard Wilbur, but she was frequently associated with them, for no reason other than the fact that her poems, which sometimes rhyme, are often "difficult" as well as allusive.) Gilbert praised the poet's "inventive urbanity" yet attacked that inventiveness when it seemed to go too far. She dismissed "Voyages" as "a Hollywood version of a great and greatly moving life," and played with possible titles for a movie and a musical version. This was a cheap shot, surely, at a poet's lifelong commitment to a literary role model.

Gilbert and her collaborator Susan Gubar did not include Clampitt in their massive *Norton Anthology of Literature by Women: The Tradition in English* (first published in 1985, subsequently enlarged and reissued). Just as Amy was difficult to contain in her native Iowa, so Amy Clampitt the mature poet was sui generis, hard to categorize, or to assign a spot in any predetermined context or tradition. As a woman, she was a model of feminism. As a poet, she would not be a mouthpiece for certain formulaic pieties.

No one would ever claim that all of Clampitt's poems are equally great. How many poets do not have failures, or compose downright stinkers? Many critics were, like Gilbert, measured, trying to separate the wheat from the chaff. About *Archaic Figure*, Mark Rudman called Clampitt and Derek Walcott "poets of excess," but praised "An Anatomy of Migraine" as a poem he loved. Reviewing the same book for *Library Journal*, Frank J. Lepkowski offered praise, but then singled out "An Anatomy of Migraine" as "a self-indulgence as bad as Joan Didion's on the same topic," and called Clampitt's poems about the Wordsworths, George Eliot, and Margaret Fuller "tedious and undistinguished."

Even before *What the Light Was Like* appeared, powerfully negative criticism had also begun to show up, a kind of backlash against the extravagant praise that many early reviewers had heaped upon the newly celebrated writer. In a letter to Doris Myers, with *The Kingfisher* now in its fourth printing, Clampitt notes that the hostile reviews have begun: "a full-page sneer by a disapproving young graduate student in the *Yale Daily News*, a barrage in *The New Criterion*, a sneak attack, which really did upset me, in the *Georgia Review*. But the effect is tonic, I think—much less upsetting in the long run than Helen Vendler's four pages in the *New York Review*, which threw me into a state of depression nobody thought I was quite entitled to: suppressed rage finding its way into the open, or whatever." Thrust upon a national literary scene, the new poet found herself confused by both criticism *and* praise. "I thought I was going to be a person who spent her life in obscurity, and this came. It jolted me. I wasn't ready to have people know about me." Clampitt had dealt with rejection for decades. Success was harder to bear, perhaps because by this point she never expected to confront it.

Some of the criticism was downright nasty, harboring a suspicion of ornament, and preferring plainness to fanciness, the simple to the baroque. In England—where *The Kingfisher* had been commercially and critically successful—Peter Porter reviewed the second book dismissively. He hoped that the poet "had finished with her reports of Nature's seasonal collections, her fondness for accessorizing detail. But she is still at it, overloading poem after poem with clusters of compound metaphors, wagon-trains of adjectives trundling after each tableau."

Another criticism, from different readers, was that Clampitt seemed too besotted with older styles, not in tune with the current modes. Mary Karr, in an essay titled "Against Decoration," said that some of the poems sounded like "a parody of the Victorian silk that Pound sought to unravel . . . [they] could be Swinburne on acid or Tennyson gone mad with his thesaurus." Karr did not like ornament, or the overuse of historical references. (Additionally, she did not much care for Helen Vendler, Harold Bloom, and their preferences, or the work of John Ashbery and James Merrill.) Clampitt got caught in the fury of her outburst. Most of all, Karr railed against "[p]olysyllables, archaic language, intricate syntax, yards of adjectives," all of which "will slow a reader."

The most savage salvo came from poet-critic-scholar Mary Kinzie in *American Poetry Review*. It is filled with phrases like "clumsy pedantries," "lurid brocades," "jagged, lanky, uncouth, obstreperous language," "self-conscious explosions of chatter," and "a bent toward erudite inebriated nonsense." Kinzie, evidently, was not pleased with what she saw.

To which one can say: Vendler was right. Clampitt's poetry is not to everyone's taste. But more important, one might also say, in response to Mary Karr: If poetry should not slow a reader down, what should it do? Should a poem enforce speedy reading? However quickly Clampitt amassed her output, she clearly wrestled with her writing, constantly revising and perfecting it. Her language is anything but "uncouth." And she grappled with ideas as well as with words. In spite of all her encyclopedic learning, absorbed through decades of reading and then editing, she never considered herself an intellectual, let alone an academic. (Her friend Karen Chase, reading the essays that went into *Predecessors, Et Cetera*, once asked her why she didn't write more prose. "I'm not mature enough to write prose," she replied.) Tellingly, she once wrote to Vendler about "ideas": "A barnacle is what I think I really am, seizing on any passing thing that may be tempting, but unequipped to deal with the whole of anything. Ideas do interest me, but I can't hold on to a whole idea long enough to understand it."

Clampitt was attacked from many sides. I wonder whether the critics who opposed her poetry as being too much of the library would say the same about the work of John Milton, Percy Shelley, or Ezra Pound. Were they manifesting a latent anti-British sentiment in American cultural life, a fear of the encyclopedia and the dictionary? Was it because Clampitt wrote, as a drunken James Dickey, seated next to her at a dinner, once chided her, "those nice little poems about flowers"? (She was furious.) Was it simply because she was a woman that she provoked, even occasionally, such hostility, such accusations of pretentiousness? And not just a woman but a *provincial* woman, well beyond middle age, and an unknown? An awkward Greenwich Village beatnik? Not part of any literary movement? That she had not moved through the expected circles but had grown on her own, uncredentialed and on her own time, without paying her dues to the establishment? Was there envy, perhaps, of such sudden celebrity? In some ways she was a sitting target: she was an intellectual who often resorted to recondite—although accurate—scientific terms; she wrote too much like a woman, taking flowers and nature as her subjects; and she was too deferential to her (mostly) male role models. But it is exactly Clampitt's mingling of high and low, big and small, extravagant and everyday that seems— especially in retrospect—a revolutionary achievement.

The charge of an overly wrought, bookish "urbanity" might also be aimed at the poem that follows "Voyages" in *What the Light Was Like*, "The Reedbeds of the Hackensack," a version of the sestina, that most complex of Renaissance forms. It is so jam-packed with literary quotations, echoes, and allusions that only someone with a head full of memories of details from a life of wide-ranging reading can appreciate it fully. It is a poem for scholars, for professional and amateur English majors. Its urbanity is not so much invented as expanded or exploded from Clampitt's combination of book learn- ing, natural observation, and sympathy for a seemingly uninviting physical scene. In her notes, she acknowledges borrowing lines from and making allusions to Dante, Shakespeare, Milton, Keats, and William Carlos Williams.

This is a learned poem, but it is also much more. It is an ecologi- cal and political poem, whose literary references remind us that the tradition of pastoral poetry, even if subverted or otherwise trans- formed, still lives. Clampitt has repurposed old literary forms for new uses. The pastoral now takes root in the garbage of northern New Jersey. "What's landfill but the backside of civility?" she asks. The reeds of the stinking, polluted, ugly meadows of the northern reaches of the Garden State are both the opposite of and the latest version of more benign depictions of nature in Clampitt's predeces- sors. The Hackensack is choking and dying, its reedbeds "a poetry of the incorrigibly ugly." Industrial landfill is no substitute for the beauties of Mediterranean landscapes (even though "Italy knows how to make its rivers ugly"). Still, *Phragmites*, the common reed from which musical instruments like panpipes have traditionally been made, continue to grow there. The scene manages to "subvert the altogether ugly" while never obliterating it. To the discerning eye, beauty and art can flourish under the least plausible condi- tions, in the least likely places. One wonders if this realization is the inevitable aesthetic of a born Quaker: just as the "inner light" can be found in the least promising of human hearts, so nature's bounty, what Hopkins referred to as "pied beauty," blossoms in infected swamps and poisoned meadows.

Clampitt was tarred as having an "elitist" streak as well as being overly bookish. Accusations of this sort usually emanate from within the academy itself, whose denizens take it as their professional obligation to pronounce on what "ordinary" people want and need. The poet-philosopher John Koethe remembered her appearance, at his invitation, in Milwaukee:

> The Center for Twentieth Century Studies at the University of Wisconsin–Milwaukee sometimes invited distinguished poets to spend a week in residency (John Ashbery had been there in 1982), and in part at my urging they invited Amy Clampitt to come for a week in October of 1983. To welcome her, my then wife and I threw an old-fashioned cocktail party at our house, where she seemed genuinely pleased but also somewhat surprised at all the attention she was getting. The next night I introduced her at her reading, which was well attended and received, though I'm ashamed to admit that my main memory of it is the delight my seven-year-old son took at his idea that her name was a combination of the words "clam" and "pit," a pit for clams. But I was struck by how surprised some of my colleagues with a serious though unsystematic interest in poetry, and though a bit jaded by contemporary poetry, were by her reading; and by how they thought that her work was simply of a different order than what they were used to hearing. On the other hand, the English department's creative writing program had a remarked populist bent, and I was told that some of its poets were angered by what they took to be her elitism, though I've never understood that complaint about her work.

In other words, the "professional" poets were appalled or haughtily dismissive. Clampitt and her unclassifiable work were not of the moment, not right for a late-twentieth-century American audience. The ordinary citizens, those who merely loved poetry without having to take sides, and a seven-year-old who loved wordplay, were delighted.

Other beholden, non-poet fans included the polymath physicist Freeman Dyson, and the actor Fritz Weaver, who initiated a correspondence in 1984 that lasted until Clampitt's death. This famous man of the stage was clearly starstruck, and also—perhaps uncharacteristically—a bit tongue-tied. His first letter gave Clampitt at least one impetus to go ahead with a desire to write for the stage. Saying how important the poems in *The Kingfisher* had been to him, Weaver wondered "if you might have somewhere unproduced a play, or a piece for voices ['All my work is for the voice' I hear you saying. Yes! It is wonderfully for the ear and cries for recital] . . . Language has to be given back to the stage, to spoken dialogue, and you have the clearest mandate of anyone to do it . . . Forgive this impudent letter, and accept, Miss Clampitt, my gratitude for hours of pleasure, no, illumination."

Amy answered immediately, and Weaver, courtly and elegant, replied:

> I am awed almost to silence by the thought that my inquiry about a play may have started one to life. I recover my balance when I reflect that poets are birds of paradise, and that any bright object serves their turn. It is clear to me that a play about the Wordsworths already lay as a possibility in your mind, biding its time.

Having read Clampitt's poems about the Wordsworths that were to appear in *Archaic Figure* (1987), Weaver wrote, almost hyperbolically, following a reading of those poems in December 1984 and said that even her "extraordinary utterances" sounded "like normal human speech." This is a response—and from an actor!—strikingly at odds with the critical assessment of Clampitt's poetry as "artificial" by some hostile readers.

Struck by the power of another artist's performance, Weaver was too shy to come forward to meet her afterwards. For him, Clampitt's voice was that of the future, not the past:

... a human voice going in rushes, picking up a hundred things along the way, and moving to small or large climaxes, in which all the separate foregoing thoughts are pulled together—never fancy or "grand," but keeping close to the thought, faithful to it wherever it goes; if it goes sometimes to grandeur, it does not fear to go there, having earned the right by its courage in following the thought so closely.

These are the words of a man in love.

Even six months later (June 1), both fumbling and besotted, he began a letter "Dear Miss Clampitt." He continued:

[I started to write Dear *Amy*, not I hope from presumption, but because, from hours spent with your poems, I have the sensation that I actually know you as a friend]—it's appalling really—but quite *good* for me; I have a new humbled sense of fellow-feeling for some of the shadowy people I encounter outside a stage-door. And you must accept your responsibility in all this, for your art draws us all into your life!

The two artists did not enter upon a first-name relationship for several more years. In their manners, they were Old World to the core, Amy from New Providence, Weaver from Pittsburgh. And if Clampitt's work brought these two like-minded strangers together, Weaver's letters encouraged Clampitt's desire to write for the stage, with decidedly mixed results, as we shall see.

———

During the years of her fame, the responses and the letters from people of prominence were surpassed in number by others from total unknowns. Amy replied to all of them, often maintaining epistolary relationships that extended until her death. A woman from Chicago, identifying herself as "a victim of radical Islam," wrote to say that "Grasmere" (Clampitt's poem about Dorothy Wordsworth) had sustained her: "Unknowingly, you were a companion at a dark hour." A correspondence ensued. Paul Diederich, a septuagenarian Harvard alumnus and a Classics major, initiated another, which lasted for six years: the initial point of contact was a shared interest in bird calls.

The letters poured in from the expected and the surprising: high school students; Episcopal priests; lawyers; bankers; clinical psychologists; migraine sufferers (prompted by "An Anatomy of Migraine," that long, difficult poem in *Archaic Figure*); a senior vice president at Lehman Brothers; a jazz clarinetist; a woman from Estonia; a Harvard senior writing her thesis on Clampitt; a Peace Corps fellow in Africa; an alcoholic, suicidal misfit; people sending copies of their own poems and those of their grandchildren; poets from Colombia, Belgium, and the Netherlands.

The files are an omnium-gatherum of notes from ordinary people hungry and grateful for literary sustenance. All writers receive letters. More often it's the poets, not the novelists, who have the time and energy to respond. (Bernard Malamud once replied to a high school teacher's inquiry on behalf of his students about one of Malamud's books by saying, "Mr. Brady, I write the books. You teach them.") Reading the letters in the Clampitt files, one is amazed at both the variety of those fans and the inevitable similarities in their excited, appreciative responses. The poet was forging bonds with some people she came to meet, and with others whom she never saw.

A philosophy professor from Syracuse wrote that "not since [Robert Lowell's] *Lord Weary's Castle* has a book of contemporary poetry hit me with such a wallop as yours. Your polished absorption of Marianne Moore into your standard repertoire, free of her angularity, is a continual triumph." (Clampitt always bristled at being seen as Moore's descendant.) Unknown poets, young and old, asked for encouragement and advice, and offered their own praise. David Semanki, a student at New York University, wrote saying he loved the work of Leonie Adams and Louise Bogan, whom none of his classmates had ever heard of: what should he do about this situation, and about his projected career? Another correspondence ensued. From Maine, the poet Kenneth Rosen wrote in 1992 that the first time he read a Clampitt poem in *The New Yorker*, he figured she was a recently graduated Yale English major. Like Salter, he heard the voice of a young person.

Amy was seldom not delighted by the attention, and she was attentive in return. A letter to Doris Myers (September 11, 1983) ends, following a description of a European vacation, with this paragraph:

> And I do get the most amazing and delightful things in the mail. My Episcopalian-priest correspondent whose habit is to attach a postcard-sized watercolor to a postcard has sent me four of them in the past month or so. A woman in Beverly Hills [Annette Leo], who noticed "Beach Glass" and has since become a regular-irregular correspondent, sent just lately some amazingly weathered things from the beach at Malibu—altogether different geologically from what one finds in Maine—as well as a manuscript (since I asked her for it) that turns out to be stupendously, unclassifiably vivid and original. (Among other things, she turns out to be acquainted with migraine.) A man in Pennsylvania, having noted the arrowhead in my "Imago" poem, sent me one he'd found in his garden. Did I write about the four poets I went to visit in Scotland? Well, I now hear from *two* of them, both total originals. The four of them meet fortnightly, and after several exchanges of letters with Jimmy Thomson, who started it all, they voted to make me an honorary member. So I *had* to visit them, and they gave me tea in a farmhouse belonging to still another member, and after three hours together, talking incessantly, I [built? had?] another bond forged with all four of them.

Of all the letters from aspiring, unknown poets of all ages, perhaps the most touching, dated December 10, 1987, came from Paul Shuttleworth, a former minor-league baseball player in Winside, Nebraska. Clampitt, who apparently could never turn down a request to judge a contest, had selected his poem "Spring Training" for an honorable mention in a competition sponsored by *Kansas Quarterly*/Kansas Art Commission. He received a fifty-dollar check:

I've been writing poems for exactly twenty years, and this is the most money I've seen out of one poem . . . Over and over, I read the letter from the editors, repeating each time to my wife, "Amy Clampitt chose it. You know, the KINGFISHER poet. The book we got from the book club." And my wife said, "But her poems are so unlike your poems. Hers are beautiful and graceful." Yes, it sure is an odd world. I had to agree. And we both agreed that it was terrific that a stranger could sit down with that poem and find something in it for herself. A kind of miracle only poets and good readers believe in.

It is indeed an odd world. Perfect strangers come to support one another, as they do in Clampitt's travel poems.

Responses from famous and important people probably delighted and impressed Amy no more strongly than one from a minor-league ballplayer. Or the one from Penelope Papailias, who had invited her to read to the students at the Riverdale Country School in the Bronx: "My class is quite excited that you are coming to read to us. They feel unworthy—'A *real* poet is coming to read for *us! Us!*' they keep exclaiming." Thirteen-year-old Janine Purchell, a Bronx middle school student, wrote (June 6, 1993) for help with a biographical sketch she was writing about Clampitt. She added a postscript: "I love your poetry. I like the fact that it is spontaneous and I can sometimes relate to them [*sic*]." The critics who charged her with elitism and fancy circumlocutions would be surprised to learn that a teenaged girl found Clampitt, who responded within a week, spontaneous and relatable.

My favorite may be the letter (one of many of its kind) from Sally Anne Meehan, working at the Eastern Sales Company in Lowell-ville, Ohio. Emily Dickinson began a famous poem (lyric #260) with the timid, excited questions "I'm nobody! Who are you? / Are you nobody, too?" Meehan, a nobody, wrote on April 20, 1989:

> Who are you, Amy Clampitt? I read your poem today—"Nothing Stays Put"—in *The New Yorker*. It's 10:35 a.m. I am sitting at this desk full of have-tos, and I read this poem and begin to cry at the third stanza. I should be selling furnaces and air-conditioners by

the truckload now, but I am soldered to this poem by the truth; the 10-button is *ringing*, the fax is going, and I am trying to brush away tears from the sight of the organized man who will walk into this room in a few minutes.

    If you're ever in Lowellville—please come to my house. It's on route 289 on the Ohio/Pa. border half way between 422 & 224— on the way to nowhere & along the Mahoning River.

Amy replied on May 10. She never visited Lowellville, but had she done so she would have discovered something there—"on the way to nowhere"—to enchant and surprise her. Nobodies like getting together, and even when Amy became a "somebody," she was still the shy, eager teenager who wanted to make an impression, and she welcomed the recognition that came her way from sources humble as well as grand.

———

The whirlwind of activity following the 1983 publication of *The Kingfisher* never stopped. It now began to include classroom ventures. Amy Clampitt became a teacher. In July 1984, she accepted her first assignment, a two-week course at Hofstra University on Long Island about which she wrote to Helen Vendler. Initially, she was fearful:

> My main concern was whether I could distract all those anxious would-be poets from their anxiety about having their work read and torn to pieces, or blandly praised, or whatever, for at least part of the two-and-a-half hour daily session. And this seems to have worked out: the first hour, just about every day, was taken up with very grand or otherwise remarkable examples, including "Lycidas." I had a very pleasant group of students, only one conspicuously talented, but all of them thoughtful, good people who helped one another more than I could have done individually.

Although she was as nervous as a teacher of writing as she had been several years earlier as a student of writing under Daniel Gabriel, she responded to this new challenge with kindness, helpfulness, and a rational assessment of her students' capabilities. In her sixties, at the age when most teachers are winding down, Clampitt was gearing up, entering part-time a new career and a new phase of her own outreach to different audiences.

For the entire 1984–85 academic year, she traveled to Williamsburg, Virginia, once a week by train to teach a poetry workshop at the College of William and Mary. She stayed overnight in an apartment designated for the "writer-in-residence," a ten-minute walk from the train station, a five-minute walk to her classroom. She was pleased with her students and with some of her colleagues. The beautiful campus, with its Georgian architecture, brick walls, sunken gardens, and "magnolia alleys and crape myrtle, its mockingbirds and cicadas," delighted her. The notion of "Jefferson going to classes right there in the Wren building fills me with romantic amazement," she wrote to Vendler.

At the same time, Amy was accustoming herself to life in a modest spotlight. In October, the *New York* magazine profile came out. The following February, she wrote to her friends Libby and Howard Braverman, exhibiting a touch of vanity with regard to the full-color portrait accompanying it: "I'm not sure what to think of it, but it seems my own opinion is of little consequence when it comes to photographs—the ones I think are just too goofy-looking are the ones everyone else likes. Not to mention all those signs of age, which I still resist having to acknowledge." She had been "muffling" her birth date for years, but in her letter to Vendler she came clean, knowing that she was now in the public eye and that the truth would out. She was troubled by the possibility that she would find herself "being asked to assure roomfuls of little old ladies that they can be poets too!" Although she knew she would become something of a role model, she did not want to offer false encouragement.

Yet she rarely turned down an invitation. In 1985, for example, she accepted an offer that even a younger, less well-known poet might find daunting: for eleven days in April she shuffled—or was escorted—from place to place along the Connecticut Poetry Circuit, accepting $150 apiece from fifteen colleges and private schools, each of which provided overnight accommodations and then transportation to the next venue—as close as a writer could come to one-night stands in vaudeville.

———

The William and Mary teaching year expanded Amy's attachments to various people there, and even more strongly to the landscape of the American South, with which she had been mostly unfamiliar. It also sparked an interest in local history. That spark led to something like a modest conflagration several years later, in 1992, when the college invited her to compose, and then return to the campus to perform, a poem on the occasion of its tercentenary. The poem she wrote, one of her keenest political and historical experiments, and the ensuing kerfuffle display both Clampitt's creative instincts and her tough-minded response to rebukes.

The president of the college had decided that it would be an honorable thing to commission a poem as part of the celebrations. The British monarchs had chartered William and Mary in the Virginia colony in 1693. The college would honor Charter Day on February 8, 1993. The choice of poet was put in the hands of a young professor, Henry Hart, who had come to Williamsburg in 1986, after Amy had left, but who knew her work and had published some of it in a small press magazine called *Verse*. The college sent a contract to Clampitt on March 15, 1992. It offered a $2,000 honorarium, another $1,000 for travel expenses and accommodations, and an additional promise of $700 to do an elegant limited edition of her poem. She sent a copy of her poem, as required, before September 15. Then the troubles began.

Someone in the president's office thought the poem unsuitable, and that it might offend what that person deemed the delicate sensibilities of Prince Charles, who was to be the monarchy's representative in England's former colony. The college officials did not know that the Prince of Wales was an outspoken admirer of poetry and poets, or that he had befriended such figures as Seamus Heaney and the more controversial Ted Hughes. Nor would they know that in his speech on Charter Day he would quote from the work of Ezra Pound, not exactly an uncontroversial figure himself. The college wanted to change the venue and the date of Clampitt's performance.

Her letter of reply (September 16), diplomatic enough on the surface, contains some well-aimed barbs. She musters legitimately righteous indignation: "To postpone the public reading of a commissioned work until a month or more after the date being commemorated would be the same as postponing a commencement oration until after the graduates had gone home." She proposes to release the college from its contractual obligations, and ends on a note of surprise and regret: "I have offered the only kind of poem I could honestly write. I am sorry that no one at so distinguished an institution of higher learning has seen fit to reply in kind."

The officials suggested a compromise: Clampitt would read her poem in the library, with the prince not present. And that's what happened. What "kind of poem" did she write? The controversial "Matoaka" (this is the original name of the woman we know as Pocahontas) is in fact too long for an official event. It contains sixty-two quatrains, a total of 248 lines, densely packed with historical and political information, and descriptions of Virginia's landscape. It is a substantial meditation on history, especially those parts and characters that we can never know and never retrieve. Pocahontas— whom Clampitt calls Pocahuntus—herself is the cipher at the center. What she thought, felt, experienced: this, above all, we will never understand. Clampitt touches only delicately on the larger issues— tobacco, money, settlement, the conversion of the heathen, the display of the woman now renamed Rebecca Wolfe when she returned as an Englishman's bride to England—and she never broaches the largest issue of all, slavery in the New World.

Prince Charles might very well have been pleased, or even flattered, by the poem's invitation to understand people and institutions through the lenses of architecture and landscape, two of his great interests. Most of all, just as Clampitt's Keats sequence suggests a possible double biography, so "Matoaka" implicitly urges on its readers a way of understanding the writer through her subject.

Like much of Clampitt's work, it begins outside:

Place names, the names of streams—
the Rappahannock, the Roanoke, the Potomac,
and that commemoration of sometime
     majesty, the James,

its tributary the Chickahominy,
the Pamunkey and the Mattaponi, each
what a people called itself once, subsumed in
     a gazetteer, the names

half-overgrown by the long quasi-
anonymity that is history . . .

History leaves us with names, and in Virginia the linguistic landscape is doubly English and Native American. Clampitt then introduces her heroine, with her "woman's name," albeit not the more common one we know her by, and turns her into a Native American, indigenous version of Homer's Nausicaä, saving the tide-swept hero Odysseus, who has arrived on her shore. What we know about her is only what the conquerors told us about her, first on her native soil and then after her move to England as a newly baptized wife. History has occluded everything else about her. The poem asks questions that it cannot answer.

This woman died at twenty-one, preparing to return to the New World, which was in fact her old world. She was given a Christian burial at Gravesend. History, says the poet, is merely a "shadowy predatory tentshow," from which more is erased than can ever be known. The poem ends with names, again, but now the commemorated English ones,

    Brafferton,

Blair, Wythe, Ewell, past
Crim Dell, down to where
mere water, rippling, preserves
     the name of one—

her true, her secret name perhaps,
but that's surmise—the world has heard of—
of whom we know so little: to stroll thus
 is to move nearer,

in imagination, to the nub,
the pulse, the ember of what she was—
no stranger, finally, to the mystery
 of what we are.

Amy Clampitt, a woman who lived in obscurity for much of her life, found herself for several years on a worldly stage, momentarily in the cultural limelight. Perhaps it is fitting that she tries to understand a much younger woman from a previous century, whose identity cannot be pinned down. Not even fame can clarify the ungraspable mystery at the heart of all selfhood.

———

The 1984–85 year was rooted in, but not limited to, Amy's weekly commitments in Williamsburg. By her own estimate, she had become "more of a nomad than usual," but at the same time more of a stay-at-home, if a somewhat scatterbrained one. Her friend the young writer Nic Christopher remembered heading with his wife, Connie, and Howard Moss to East 65th Street for dinner one evening. They waited, and waited, in the hall. Amy arrived late, laden with shopping bags. She said she was planning to make a chicken fricassee for dinner. She did, but there was a considerable delay before the meal actually appeared. Amy's friends became accustomed to invitations proffered, then forgotten, to plans delayed, then re-begun haphazardly. Improvisation was the order of the day. Little was certain.

Amy and Hal liked movies, but not those one might have expected. Hal, an insomniac, would amuse himself late at night with weird, scary ones. Christopher said that a particular favorite—Amy and Hal had the tape—was Jacques Tourneur's 1943 *I Walked with a*

Zombie. Another of Tourneur's noir films, the 1944 *Cat People*, was also a staple at the Korn household. Margot Honig, the couple's tax accountant, remembered spending an evening watching *The Night of the Living Dead*. These films, not exactly art house fare, were typical ad hoc amusement for the domesticated couple living in dusty comfort.

Amy wrote on February 10 to her friends Libby and Howard Braverman:

> I could almost say that I don't go anywhere, which isn't true— only true about being here in New York, where Hal and I eat large quantities of take-out Chinese food instead of going to restaurants, and go out to a movie maybe once a year, and about that often to the theater (we did see both productions of the Royal Shakespeare Company not long ago), and the rest of the time look at old movies recorded on the VCR, or, in the best of times, read aloud to each other from Dickens—we're on *Martin Chuzzlewit* these days . . .

And then she follows up with reports of travels past and planned.

One month later she participated in a conference at the University of North Dakota on "The Art of Narrative." Fellow panelists included Barry Hannah, Alex Haley, Norman Mailer, and the young Jorie Graham. She described this also to Beth, on May 18, 1985. On a tape of one of two writers' panels, Amy looks almost prim, sitting ramrod straight, where her colleagues (Hannah, Tom McGrath, and the Canadian Sandra Birdsell) are more casual and fidgety. The men are smoking. Asked why she stopped writing fiction, Clampitt replies that she realized she could not make up stories, that what she really "wanted to do was name things."

Her life alternated, but at a more intense velocity, between home and abroad, just as it had done thirty-five years earlier when she left her jobs to travel in Europe. Now, home life was as bohemian as before, but she traveled to Europe under more structured, even pampered conditions.

In June 1985, Amy and Hal went to England, principally for a poetry festival in Cambridge, where she read alongside Seamus

Heaney. The American poets Debora Greger and William Logan, part-time residents in Cambridge who became good friends, helped to host them. Greger remembered:

> When she came to England in spring '85 to read at the Cambridge Poetry Festival, she and Hal took the QE2. William arranged for a taxi to meet them at the dock at Southampton and bring them to Cambridge. Of the Atlantic crossing, she said she was crushed to discover that the room she remembered as a library had been converted to a video game arcade. From Cambridge she made her way north that summer, even as far as the offshore islands, before she turned around. Hal, I think, headed to London & Savile Row to get some of his favorite shirts, then home.

After Hal came home, Amy was on her own for a while longer. And she continued her travels.

She visited her friend Peter Kybart in Berlin. (Two years earlier, she had traveled with him in Greece and the Balkans.) Kybart said that it was she, the consummate tourist, who really introduced him to his new place of residence, where he'd never had the chance to look around because he was working. She went on to Geneva, staying with the bilingual French-American family of the writer Susan

Amy with Seamus Heaney, 1985

Tiberghien, and saw the castle at Chillon and Voltaire's estate at Ferney. In some ways, she had changed. She still loved traveling, but ordinary life, more than high culture and museums, appealed to her now. In Switzerland, for example, "what I liked was going to the market in the little town of Samoens and choosing not only freshly baked bread but also a local cheese and some enormous, sweet local raspberries for that morning's breakfast." Then to Amsterdam to visit the Dutch poet Elly de Waard, and back to England through September, to judge the Arvon Foundation International Poetry Competition, with Craig Raine and the Anglo-American poet Anne Stevenson as her partners. On September 11, the judges attended the ceremony—the £5,000 first prize was given to a young Anglo-Welsh poet, Oliver Reynolds (b. 1957)—and Ted Hughes made the presentation. Amy shook his hand. The ceremony ended. And then she returned to the States.

———

In "Iola, Kansas" we saw how Clampitt used her travels—not only the sights she saw and the sites she visited, but also the actual moving about—to recreate a moment of grace in an unlikely location. Two pieces about foreign travel, "Losing Track of Language" and "Babel Aboard the Hellas International Express," the second almost a grotesque parody of the first, transpose Amy's indefatigable energy, and her openness to even the smallest blessings, to more distant locations and into other tones.

"Losing Track of Language" appeared in *What the Light Was Like* but is based on an episode with an unnamed companion during her European trip in 1951. (The actual incident was recounted in her 134-page book manuscript *Gargoyles, Campaniles, and Clichés*, which, as I have mentioned, no publisher accepted.) Once more, we can see in retrospect what Clampitt did not know at the time: that she was a poet, not a prose writer. In her prose account she tells her story with tact and good humor. Then she moves on to some other subject. The germ of the later poem is here, but none of the poem's impelling energy.

The poem that emerged from the 1951 event is all sunshine and rollicking good spirits. It recounts a train ride crossing between the French and the Italian rivieras. Camaraderie and language are the subjects: to be more precise, camaraderie *through* language, through the words and rhythms of languages. It begins:

> The train leaps toward Italy, the French Riviera
> falls away in the dark, the rails sing dimeter
> shifting to trimeter, a galopade to a galliard.
> We sit wedged among strangers; whatever
> we once knew (it was never much) of each other
> falls away with the landscape.

Words themselves fall away, as the poet and her companion, "all rapport with strangers," flirt with their compartment mates and share cigarettes. One man is Italian, coming from the Vaucluse where Petrarch wrote his sonnets to Laura. Once queried, he begins to recite Petrarch's poems excitedly. We can hear that excitement in the very rhythm of Clampitt's lines:

> A splutter of pleasure at hearing the name
> is all that he needs, and he's off
> like a racehorse at the Palio—plunging
> unbridled into recited cadenzas, three-beat
> lines interleaving a liquid pentameter.

The ongoing movement of the train, the flowing music of Italian verse, and the spirited conversation with her cabinmate remind us that nothing stays put or remains the same. Petrarch's Laura is long gone, and "whatever is left of her is language," and language, like breath, and like leaves, is fragile.

Then she asks her new friend whether he also knows the Greek lyric poet Sappho. Of course he does, and he begins a new recitation:

> . . . The limpid pentameter
> gives way to something harsher: diphthongs

condense, take on an edge of bronze. Though
I don't understand a word, what are words? . . .

More than cigarettes or flirting, words are what a poet trades in.
She recalls the love poems, now reduced mostly to fragments, of
the archaic Greek poet from millennia earlier. She considers Sap-
pho's Timas,

> . . . led before she was married
> (or so one leaf of what's left would have it)
> to the dark bedroom of Persephone, for so long
> nowhere at home, either here or there, forever
> returning and falling back again
> into the dark of these ten thousand years[.]

All is motion; nothing is stable. Clampitt's poem ends:

> The train leaps toward Italy; words fall away
> through the dark into the dark bedroom
> of everything left behind, the unendingness
> of things lost track of—of who, of where—
> where I'm losing track of language.

The poet has not lost track of language. Although she doesn't
understand a word, she intuits meanings through music, through
tones, through a human encounter. She has gathered together bits
of poetic history and woven them into a tapestry of great delicacy
that reminds us that "leaves," "leaving," "losing," and "loss" can be
countered by what we gain—or regain, actually—through travel and
chance meetings.

For Clampitt, language conferred identity, and identity was
always shifting. Writing about her return to France from Italy in
her prose journal that includes the germ of the poem, she says that
she felt like a snake shedding one skin to reveal another, or a sleight-
of-hand artist changing costumes: "The spell of his language still
hung upon me like a beautiful and inappropriate mantle, of which

it was necessary to be divested before I could pull together enough shreds of French to ask for a hotel room." That spinning of similes and metaphors—snake, costume changes, "beautiful and inappropriate mantle," "shreds of French"—tells us that a poet, with her natural gift for metaphor, has been doing the writing, and that she will rediscover herself, but not for a while. She had other mantles to put on and remove, other skins to shed.

I have already mentioned Amy's 1985 visit to Peter Kybart in Berlin. Two years earlier, in 1983, en route from Dodona and other sites in Greece, Amy met up with Kybart, living and working in Berlin, at Saloniki. They took the ferry from Kavala to the isle of Thasos ("Amy knew the names of all the plants and trees," Kybart told me), and then a three-day, two-night train trip from Saloniki up to Munich. The resulting poem (published, along with others based on her Greek trip, in *Archaic Figure*) is "Babel Aboard the Hellas International Express." If "Losing Track of Language" recounts a random encounter with a stranger that opens up a comfortable communion, a moment of grace, through languages not fully understood, "Babel . . ." is its nightmarish, Hieronymus Bosch–like inversion, at least until its ending.

Conditions on the train are more than primitive: they are awful. The passageways and compartments are overcrowded. "No Smoking" signs mean nothing. Toilets and floors are filthy. There is no potable water. Prepared for no food on the train, "we've brought aboard / bread, cheese, wine, olives, peaches." They cross borders. The train stops and starts again. Inspectors terrify them: "We're sots and thralls // of Babel and demography. New ghouls / have come aboard." Passports and papers are repeatedly examined, taken away, and handed back. A passenger is discovered with kilos of contraband coffee. Clampitt's passport is not returned. She takes a Miltown. Her passport reappears. Different hordes of passengers get on in Belgrade. "All Yugoslavia is traveling, / won't be kept out." Cabins are full but the newcomers will not be deterred. A couple barges in with a blind, whimpering child. The washrooms become "a costive-making / hopeless *cauchemar*."

Coalescing crowds fill the car, and multiplying, uncomprehended languages fill the air. Both encourage Clampitt's list-making, which, like the jarring, endless journey itself, seems to have no end that she (or we, her readers) will ever discern:

> . . . The Serbs, Slovenes,
> Croatians, Bosnians, Albanians, who knows what
> else, who swarm the corridors, are civil,
>
> appeal to reason, persist, at last prevail.
> Stout ruddy woman; lean, fair-haired, ruddy man;
> two small dark nondescripts; one human barrel,
> chalk-stripe-tailored, curly-brilliantined,
> Lech Walesa-mustachioed, jovial: with these
>
> till Munich, we're to share what space there is.
> They speak some common dialect, we're not
> sure which.

Wary incomprehension gradually gives way to alcohol-fueled sociability. The dialect that excluded Clampitt and Kybart now draws them in to a joyride that's "untranslatable" except, perhaps, by the final exclamation point that wordlessly combines exultation and relief:

> A bag of prunes is passed.
> We offer olives. The conversation grows
> expansive: we listen in on every syllable,
>
> uncomprehending, entranced. A bottle
> circulates: I hesitate, see what it is,
> and sip. Stupendous. Not to be missed,
> this brew. It burns. It blazes. Anecdote
> evolves, extends, achieves a high adagio,
>
> grows confidential, ends in guffaws. O
> for a muse of slivovitz, that fiery booze,

to celebrate this Babel, this untranslatable
divertimento all the way to Munich,
aboard a filthy train that's four hours late!

The poet was sixty-three years old. Nothing could dim her pleasure. Kybart said she nicknamed the train the Slivovitz Express. Even the literary echo ("O for a Muse of fire, that would ascend / The brightest heaven of invention" begins Shakespeare's *Henry V*) seems perfectly in place. This is a trip we'd probably rather read about than take ourselves.

The pairing of travel and language—the experience of traveling with and in different languages—reminds us that Clampitt was at heart a lover of words, of their sounds and meanings and histories, whatever their origins. She reveled as much in language as in her lived experiences. In "Botanical Nomenclature," she found a flower in Maine identical to one she knew in Iowa, whose name but not whose essence had changed; in "Losing Track of Language," she heard Italian and Greek, and connected with poets long dead and with an accommodating cabinmate. In "Ano Prinios," another poem from her travels in Greece, she arrives (presumably with Peter Kybart) in a pickup truck at a hill village, where the two Americans confront poverty and hospitality at the same time. The poem ends with a lavish display of gustatory and linguistic generosity. One of their hosts brings to the travelers

> dripping as from a fountain, a branch just severed
> from some fruit tree, loaded with drupes
> that were, though still green, delectable.
> Turning to the woman, I asked what
> they were called in Greek. She answered,
> "Damaskēno." Damson, damask, damascene:
> the word hung, still hangs there,
> glistening among its cognates.

"Glistening among its cognates," like the plums just plucked from the tree, a word opens a traveler to a world. Language, which separates people who cannot understand foreign tongues, also unites people who are of the word. An incident from the past "still" retains its clarity in the present.

Clampitt could put into language what Amy experienced in the flesh. She was a poet of meeting rather than parting, of uniting with other people over shared experiences, rather than bidding farewell after a satisfying adventure. Kybart said that Amy hated what he called "those long, heavy Teutonic, lingering farewells." One can see why: there was always the next train or bus to board, the next trip to take, the next poem to write. She wanted beginnings rather than endings.

———

For three weeks in frigid, wet, dark January 1986, Clampitt enjoyed a residency at Yaddo, the fabled artists' colony in Saratoga Springs, New York. Writers, painters, musicians come and go, enjoying solitude, time to work, and one another's company.

Allan Gurganus, about to publish his first novel, recalled their time together:

> My time with her was one long winter at Yaddo and various sightings at the Academy. I knew and admired her work and recall how she was always described as a sudden wunderkind of rare vintage. Knowing she would visit frozen Yaddo, I pictured a virginal stick-thin Emily Dickinson whispering from behind closed doors. When she entered the dining room, she instead had the air of the quiet competent captain of a college girls' soccer team. I felt at once that she was "fair." Her hair was in a no-nonsense bun. Dressed for arctic conditions, she wore Army-Navy layerings suitable for an inveterate bird watcher. At first glance she resembled Popeye's girlfriend Olive Oyl. She soon proved ever ready to be amused, likely to know flora-fauna Latin names. But she was never a pedant. When she laughed her face bunched like a child's sneezing. Her chuckle came in high-pitched squeaks that made others laugh. She took time with everybody, even ones we'd long since decided were proven bores.
>
> It was a brutal winter, even for upstate New York. We ate our

communal meals in the second story library above the garage. Its outdoor stairs were steep, made of cast concrete, blocks of solid ice. Though salt was scattered, the descent felt especially dangerous even for the youngest camper. Amy wore sensible boots with additional metal prongs and grippers on their soles. But I remember fearing for her. She was, in everything, a good sport and would sometimes wait for others before undertaking the climb toward eggs and toast. The more we talked the warmer she seemed and the more physically attractive she became.

After loving Thomas Hardy's novels I had lately discovered his poems, possibly his greatest work. I remember Amy directing me to particular treasures in his work. I memorized "To Lisbie Brown" and once recited it for her. At Yaddo we were all life-boat castaways. It is possible to develop friendships fast. I remember how soon my respect for her ascended to affection. On first sight, Amy seemed a possible figure of fun; but her utter lack of self pity corrected that impression and let you see the heroic in both her survival and achievement. I remember feeling almost mournful the day she left.

The next year my first book, *Oldest Living Confederate Widow Tells All*, appeared. The American Academy of Arts and Letters gave it the Sue Kaufman Prize for best first work of fiction. The citation was wonderfully technical and precise. Praise focused on how an African-American character had been given a ninety-page aria to sing her tale of the Middle Passage. A revered member of the Academy also admired the praise song and when I asked him (James Merrill) who had written it, he said "It was Amy Clampitt, but don't tell anybody I told you."

Gurganus has limned her vividly, if a bit fancifully. No one else has ever confused Amy Clampitt with the captain of the girls' soccer team. She may have been one of the least athletic women of the century, however much she enjoyed vigorous exercise. He's taking artistic license, of course, as though trying to turn her into a secondary character from some great social novel: a sensitive good sport, a woman of great competence and unexpected reserves, odd but kind, generous, and attentive.

From upstate New York's winter ice to the upper Midwest's spring-time: in early May, Clampitt participated in a celebration of "Rural Writers and Writing" at Southwest State University in Marshall, Minnesota, along with Thomas McGrath, Wendell Berry, Carol Bly, her husband the poet Robert Bly, Donald Hall, Ted Kooser, and John Haines. Her sudden rise to prominence had put her on something like an A-list of writers to receive invitations from everyone, from everywhere. She was now prominent as a "rural writer," and she was known equally as a New York (and a *New Yorker*) writer.

——

The 1986–87 academic year found Clampitt settling down at another prestigious liberal arts college. It was here that she began to think seriously about writing a Wordsworth play. In the spring of 1987, she taught a course at Amherst called "The Language of the Stage." It is hard to imagine what the undergraduates thought of it. Her sense of what might actually engage the young people there shows the dis-connect between an eccentric intellectual, decades removed from her own undergraduate years, and the habits and mores of literature students almost a half century her juniors.

In a letter of August 24, she admitted that "writing poems seems safer" than playwriting. For her, "language," rather than character or conflict, was central to an understanding of drama. This was her mistake. In her course, she assigned plays whose language, not people or themes, she found compelling. There was Shakespeare, of course, and, to her surprise, a lot of Irish work (Congreve, Sheri-dan, Wilde, Yeats, Synge, Beckett), followed by some contemporary writers: David Mamet (*Glengarry Glen Ross*), Edward Albee (*The Zoo Story*), as well as Derek Walcott's *Dream on Monkey Mountain* and Lorraine Hansberry's *A Raisin in the Sun*. Class time involved much reading aloud. Stagecraft, blocking, movement, scenery and costumes, even acting, seemed to have held little interest for her. It was language above all, disembodied and on the page, that engaged her attention.

For her first class of the spring semester, January 26, 1987, the new professor told her students that Wilde's *The Importance of Being Ear-*

nest, one of the first plays she ever saw (she had read his *Salome* in New Providence when she was twelve), had impressed her because she had never heard people actually talk like Wilde's characters. People go to the theater, she reminded them, "to hear language as it might be spoken, every line perfectly witty, every sentence perfectly constructed. The way people talk in actuality is pretty embarrassing by comparison." (This is not why most people go to the theater.) Clampitt had ingeniously paired Wilde with parts of the Nixon tapes, to show "that the difference between those recorded dialogues in the White House and the dialogue Wilde wrote isn't an absolute difference at all. The difference is in the *style*. The subject, in fact, is the same: it's lying. More precisely, it's about how to lie and be convincing about it." She might have said the same about Mamet's masterfully explosive rendering of advertising speech.

Clampitt's notes for her lectures and discussions with the students have as many asides, filaments, and reticulations as her poems, with their amassing syntactic snarls. She is trying to put to use her decades of reading, thinking, and theatergoing to get her students to focus on words, sentences, and the very rhythms of human speech. She calls "language a mere invention, like the typewriter or the internal combustion engine." Acknowledging that she is both a non-driver and a bad typist, she goes on:

> I like to think that I'm a little better at the English language; but even though I'm a writer, supposedly, most of the time I'm conscious of not using it very well. At least when you're a writer the point is that if a statement turns out to be meaningless on the first try, you can do some fiddling on the page and *get* it to mean something eventually—if you're lucky.

Whether the students (most of whom were "husky young men") were learning anything about drama, they were certainly learning a truth about writing from a woman religiously committed to her craft.

When it came to making an assignment, Clampitt's educational expectations must have astounded, or at least perplexed, her husky young men and their classmates. Her paper topics are weirdly ambitious, perhaps even nutty; one can barely imagine even the most talented or motivated undergraduate knowing how to deal with them. For their first paper (600–700 words), here is what the teacher requested:

1. Imagine that you are Oscar Wilde reviewing the performance of *Comus* at Ludlow Castle or

2. That you are John Milton reviewing the production of *The Importance of Being Earnest* at the St. James Theater in London on February 14, 1895, OR

3. That you are one or the other of the above, reviewing the opening of [Henry James's] *Guy Domville* on January 5, 1895.

What you should bear in mind, aside from picturing the occasion, are the views of the author you have chosen concerning such matters as vice and virtues, on the one hand, and what has been referred to as the serious business of spellbinding, on the other.

This master of loquacity has commanded her students to compress an encyclopedia's worth of information into a nutshell. She wants compacted brevity.

Clampitt's other course that spring was English 22, "The Writing of Poetry," for which she felt more confident in her own powers—as a poet at least, if not as a teacher: "The bad news about this course: I don't know whether the writing of poetry can be taught. I took a course in it once, rather late in my career, and decided it was more worthwhile than not. What did I learn? I'm not sure. The one thing I do know is that doing the assignments gave me practice in writing verse. And that's what you can expect in this course: practice in writing verse."

The assignments included the composition of limericks, villanelles, and other constrained forms; exercises in prosody (the art of versification); and challenging subject matter: "Think about the phenomenon of doors and thresholds, of inside and outside, the poet as both *outsider* and *insider*, and write a poem, in whatever form you choose, on this subject. At least thirty lines—a sequence of short poems if you prefer." Clampitt was straightforward with her students. Teaching, she said, is a racket: "The key word is 'learning.' And sometimes it occurs simultaneously with 'teaching' but not often. I don't want to give anyone credit for what I know: I found it out myself!" She gave her students a push, just as Daniel Gabriel had pushed her. All credit is shared.

She changed the lives of at least two students.

After studying with Clampitt, Rafael Campo, an Amherst freshman destined to become a physician, opted for an English major as well as his undergraduate pre-med courses, and went on to practice a double vocation, as a prizewinning physician-poet in the tradition of William Carlos Williams.

An impressionable young Emily Todd saw and heard Clampitt read on a visit to Amherst on November 23, 1985. This was one of Amy's first Amherst campus events, the year before she joined the faculty. Todd was a first-year student at the time. Amy would begin her regular teaching the following year. Impressed by the poet's combination of "rareness and immediacy," Todd signed on that fall, Professor Clampitt's first semester, for a course on Wordsworth and His Circle. She was astonished: she had never had a teacher who was interested in the intertwining of writers' lives and their work. (This was the heyday, in American literary studies, of high-minded literary "theory," of the sort Amy had familiarized herself with a decade earlier, and in which she had little interest.) "She wasn't teasing out an argument or applying a theory," remembered Todd. "She was a poet at work on other poets. And she brought poetry into the room. It was a poet teaching. 'Where was this going?' we would wonder, because it was different from all our other courses. Dorothy Wordsworth came alive. I sensed greatness in the room. Amy was never dialing it in. She was vibrant, with no arrogance, and nothing stylized. Her quickness of voice was unforgettable." Elizabeth Bishop had the same effect on some of her students at Harvard a decade before. Like Bishop, Clampitt wasn't interested in anything theoretical, just the nuts and bolts of a poem and whatever we might bring to that poem from a knowledge of its author's life.

After the Amherst course, Todd never again saw Amy in person. In June 1993, she did an interview with her teacher, conducted entirely through the mail. It appeared in Henry Hart's magazine, *Verse*. An impression made in the classroom long outlived the actual teacher-student relationship.

Clampitt came gradually to change her strategies in the classroom. Like any good teacher, she learned by trial and error, and from her missteps. In a letter (February 15, 1990) to a woman whose poems she had agreed to comment upon, she wrote:

> When I find myself in the position of facing a class in writing poetry, I am more and more inclined to fall back on assigning strict verse forms as an exercise: an account of the Superbowl game in the manner of "The Rape of the Lock" is one example.

This is an inspired assignment and a daring challenge. It's as if she is saying to her class, "Take machismo and battle and diminish them to mock-heroic lightness. Alexander Pope, meet American football."

Clampitt learned by doing. She understood what she wanted, what she was good at, and what she wanted to avoid. Planning for an appearance sponsored by the Vermont Arts Council in November 1987, she wrote to the organizers that she wanted to talk about things other than student poems: "I feel strongly that all writers of poetry should be encouraged to read the work of their predecessors. All this is the kind of thing I've brought to my own teaching of so-called writing classes, and the response has been at least astonishing."

Late in her short teaching career, she replied to an invitation from John Williams Gustafson in Duluth (November 11, 1992) to do some teaching at the Lake Superior Writers Series with a letter that shows how much she had learned, how much she had accommodated herself to a new role. (Illness prevented her from finally accepting the invitation.) Clampitt wrote that writing workshops were not her favorite classroom format. She acknowledged the anxiety—hers as well as the students'—that comes from having one's work dissected in front of others, an experience that tends to divide rather than unite the participants. As an alternative, she mentioned the series of "master classes" she had just completed in Manhattan at the 92nd Street YMHA Poetry Center, on the nature of the poetic line, with reference to Dickinson (short lines) and Whitman (long lines, naturally). Everyone had a good time and plans were made "to keep the group going." The Quaker in her must have rejoiced in the fact of a mutually supportive community that avoided conflict and maintained consensus. And the intellectual in her had begun to have second, and more positive, thoughts about a writer whom at the start of her career she had dismissed in her correspondence with Mary Jo Salter. Clampitt could change her mind, which was a flexible, capacious instrument: "I am currently intrigued by William Carlos Williams as a quintessential modern, in contrast to a nearly contemporary figure who was *not* modern (whatever that is anyhow), Edna St. Vincent Millay." She is expanding her view of the poetic landscape to include both an early favorite poet and another, of whom she had not been especially fond.

———

While teaching at Amherst, Amy managed to maintain her peripatetic life. She introduced Seamus Heaney at a Manhattan reading; she talked about Marianne Moore in Philadelphia; she threw a party to mark the publication of *Archaic Figure* in the spring, in Amherst, to which more than a hundred people came, including students, colleagues, and New York friends. The house was filled with flowers from her garden.

William Doreski, a New Hampshire poet, invited Clampitt to come from Amherst to do a reading at Keene State, where he taught. Later in the year, she invited him and his wife to the Amherst book party. When they showed up, Amy could not quite remember who they were: "Then after retreating and scampering around and returning, she brightened up and said, 'Oh, you're Aster's people!' Aster was our orange tiger cat, who came to us at four months and had to be bottle fed. We had told Amy about him, and he stuck in her mind more readily than we did—which, being animal people, we thought spoke well for her."

In June she became the Phi Beta Kappa poet at Harvard's annual commencement festivities. She read "Westward," five pages of almost epic proportions. A travel poem, it describes a trip by train and then boat to the isle of Iona, off the west coast of Scotland.

It spins connections: the sea puts the poet in mind of the prairie; one kind of movement suggests others; the "raw edge / of Europe" calls up the coast of Maine; and all "the routes, / the ribbonings and redoublings" that create and then retreat from empires bear witness to human migrations. This was heady stuff for a university celebration, not a lighthearted "Gaudeamus Igitur." The critic Alfred Kazin gave the featured Phi Beta Kappa "oration." Clampitt described the event in a letter to Barbara Clark. It epitomizes the speed at which she was leading her life, and the gratitude and aplomb that accompanied her energy. She went from Amherst to Boston by bus (of course). Then,

> I was running a temperature when I got off the bus, caught a subway and found my way across Harvard Yard to the Faculty Club, where I had dinner with the Kazins and a couple of Harvard people. There were moments when it seemed to me that Harvard being full of itself was just too much—but the occasion was saved by Mr. Kazin, who went to City College and, although extremely courteous, was clearly not to be overimpressed by all those traditions. The Literary Exercises, so called, took place the next day, and a nice touch was being greeted by William Alfred, he of "Hogan's Goat." I had met him back in the winter, and it was nice to be remembered. So then I found myself in a procession, launched by uniformed fife-and-drummers, in which I walked side by side with President Derek Bok himself—there is a snapshot to prove it, with me beaming all over and looking perfectly healthy. In fact, the reading went quite well, and I got through the reception afterward, and things wound up merrily in a café called the Algiers, with three graduate assistants whose attitude toward Harvard, or maybe toward academia on the whole, bordered on the derisive. Then I caught the Boston subway back to the bus station, and the bus back to Amherst, where I phoned Hal in New York—he had been laid low by the same cold, or its twin, or he would have been there—and crawled into bed.

Neither fever nor illness nor academic pomp and pretension could stay her from the completion of her elected rounds. A decade before,

Amy with president Derek Bok, who is looking at the camera,
Harvard commencement, June 1987

she was a nobody. Now she was celebrated. She still used the bus and the subway.

PART 3: 1987–1991

It is time to broach more fully the complicated matter of Amy Clampitt, the Wordsworth circle, and her attempts to manufacture a theatrical piece out of a fascination with these English predecessors, especially Dorothy Wordsworth. Her curious, noble efforts were misguided, but they tell us something about the workings of a literary mind. When she was younger, Clampitt had for decades thought mistakenly that she could write novels. (In an interview, she said she finally accepted that this would never happen when she read Thomas Pynchon's *The Crying of Lot 49* and realized she simply did not know what he knew.) So also, at the end of her career, she assumed that she could create a stageworthy play. On April 17, 1984, during a residency at the Djerassi Program in Northern California, she mentioned a new project in a letter to Hal back in Manhattan:

"an idea came to me for a *play*, with a part in it that Fritz Weaver could be right for. How about that?" That jaunty three-word question shows her partial incredulity as well as her enthusiasm. The play idea became an obsession that bore dubious fruit, and it lasted for the final decade of her life. Her courses at Amherst—on the Wordsworth Circle in the fall of 1986, and on the Language of the Stage in the spring of 1987—braced her determination to continue along a path that was not congenial to her natural talent. And yet she persisted, with an iron will, until the end.

Her stubborn commitment to the project was a vocational error that showed how even an artist in full control of her powers can, thinking to wander into a new arena, go far astray. The Wordsworths themselves were not the problem. Clampitt was able to deal with them sympathetically in a handful of poems that appeared in *Archaic Figure* and *Westward*. Anthony Hecht, a fan from the start, was probably thinking of those poems when he wrote a letter (March 25, 1987) in which he praised their precision and detail. He added that the poems' "human dimensions are surely the most powerful and moving qualities about them." Clampitt could create characters in poems. What caused her trouble was her feeling that she could "do" them in a drama. Encouraged by Fritz Weaver's insistence that she had a play in her, she went ahead with the idea, in the same way that many of her nineteenth-century literary "predecessors"—Wordsworth, Coleridge, Keats, Tennyson, and especially Henry James—thought that they might do something for (and make money from) the stage, at a time when London's West End was the equivalent of Hollywood for writers eager for a wide audience and some financial security. Clampitt was not interested in the money, but like her models, she, too, failed thoroughly in her attempt to write anything for the stage.

In 1986 she sent Helen Vendler a copy of her poem about Dorothy Wordsworth ("Grasmere," which was published in *Archaic Figure*), with the addendum that she was contemplating a play. Vendler replied with wonder and acuity: "a *play*? My goodness! I have never learned to box, wrestle, or whatever the kinesthetic equivalent of drama is; walking is novels; singing is poems. I sing, but I walk not, neither do I wrestle." Clampitt was vigorous, hardheaded, and simply confused about her own gifts. Like fiction, drama is a social genre. It requires a special understanding of people, and how they function within themselves and with one another. This kind of knowledge was never Amy's strong suit, as her friend Phoebe Hoss knew at the start when they were both beginning their careers in postwar Manhattan. Amy was attuned to principles. She found an appropriate outlet for them in her political activities, struggles for social justice, welfare hearings, protest marches, and, for a while, religious structures. She made poems out of her alertness to nature and her obsession with language. Although she said that one goes to a play to hear language purified, she was wrong. Most people go to plays to watch the action, to understand the characters. Drama is conflict followed by resolution. And Amy, still and always a Quaker at heart, resisted conflict, especially at the personal level. In art, as in life, real people presented her with difficulties and problems that she could not deal with.

Her efforts to rework her play seem like a repetition of the decades of work on her novel, or novels. In both genres, she kept circling around the same people, her ever-changing cast of characters imagined or real, trying to bring them to life. She had visited the Lake District for the first time in the summer of 1983. Dorothy Wordsworth—eighteen months her brother's junior—became vivid to Clampitt then, and she remained increasingly so for the rest of the poet's life. We can understand why. In a 1993 letter, Clampitt described her as "quick, responsive and eager" and quoted from Thomas De Quincey's assessment that she was "the very wildest (in the sense of the most natural) person I have ever known." William Wordsworth and Samuel Taylor Coleridge, whose *Lyrical Ballads* (1798) ushered in Romantic poetry as we know it today, are the two other major characters in the play. William is his sister's opposite, "phlegmatic and introspective, unbending except when (and this is central to his genius) he is deeply moved." Coleridge "is all air and quicksilver—a windbag of moods, exaggerating everything, given to self-pity but to self-mockery as well." Clampitt could identify with Dorothy, and find sympathetic ties to both of the other characters. She could see in William traits she would have known from her father and grandfather. And Coleridge's extravagance and enthusiasm would have engaged her equally. The question was: how to bring them alive on the stage? She never succeeded in doing this.

Clampitt offered a tantalizing but mysterious explanation for her interest in the Wordsworth-Coleridge trinity to her friend Sister Mary John in a letter (August 23, 1986), as she was about to begin her term at Amherst College:

> . . . the one thing that fascinates me above all is the idea of the threesome, as compared with the more usual couple: I suppose I'm partly intrigued because of the experience I've had, a couple of times, of belonging to a threesome in which the participants balanced somehow, in an intimation of a perfect trinity. Which of course sets off certain mystical overtones, some of them having to do literally with tones—with whatever happens when a string vibrates at certain intervals, and with such matters as the way, say, that a fern grows, by a kind of tertiary progression.

With what kinds of threesomes had Amy been involved? Something with her friends Mary Russel and Peter Marcasiano comes to mind. Or her pre-wedding trek with Doris and Tom Myers. Or her participation with Doris and Anne Marshall, the trio of potential religious converts to Episcopalianism. Or perhaps random and fleeting moments of camaraderie on her long-ago European travels as a young, romantic Jamesian heroine in search of adventure.

Just as relevant to our understanding of her mind is the way she moves immediately from a human arrangement to a metaphysical one ("a perfect trinity"). This transition is certainly appropriate for the woman to whom she is writing, and with whom she shared a religious commitment decades before. And from metaphysics she moves to matters of music and botany. This associative method indicates why her dramatic project will fail. She takes something personal and immediately shuffles it aside in favor of something spiritual, or aesthetic, or scientific. This is a poet thinking. She will not reveal what she does not want an audience to know.

The play's title, length, structure, and chronology were all constantly in flux. Few things stayed put. Clampitt called her play, variously, *Friends: A Play in Three Acts*; *Dorothy: A Romantic Drama*;

The Three of Us; *Mad with Joy*; and *Mad with Joy or "A Guilty Thing Surprised": A Chronicle in Two Acts*. "Mad with joy" is a phrase from one of Wordsworth's letters about the French Revolution, "in consequence of [which] the whole nation was mad with joy." Clampitt took a statement about a collective, national mania and turned it into a formula for the personal relations among three creative souls. Some versions of the play have two acts, some three. Scenes shifted around. The author kept toying with the ordering of events. One version is set in 1836–41, with an extended flashback to 1797. It then depicts events from 1802 and 1806, and it contains "two spoken interludes" not directly related to the action. One version has a scene set in 1854, four years after William's death, with his disembodied voice reciting poetry. Another adaptation has a straightforward chronology, beginning in 1797 when Coleridge and Wordsworth (along with Dorothy) were at the start of their most creative, energetic collaboration. In this version, Act I, scene 1 opens with De Quincey, a kind of choral figure throughout the iterations, introducing himself: "I am the Opium-Eater." It continues with William and Dorothy discussing Coleridge's dietary preferences. The action shifts among the places the Wordsworths and Coleridge lived (which Clampitt visited and recorded in her poems): in the Lake District, Racedown in the southwest of England, and London. At one point, the scene moves to France, where Wordsworth spent several months in his early twenties. He was caught up in the political fervor of the times. He may have engaged in subversive political activity. He fell in love with a woman named Annette Vallon, by whom he sired a daughter, whom he always acknowledged within the family circle.

Additional people from the Wordsworth circle move in and out of the iterations of Clampitt's play: William's wife, Mary Hutchinson Wordsworth; the Romantic writers Henry Crabb Robinson and De Quincey; the Wordsworths' daughter Dora and her husband, Edward Quillinan; William Cookson, a Wordsworth uncle; and some miscellaneous companions and housemaids.

The play lacks conflict, and it also (ironically) lacks the vivid spoken language that Clampitt, as poet and professor, wanted so enthusiastically to reproduce. Transitions between speakers are awkward: Coleridge asks at one point, "Have you forgotten the days at Racedown and at Nether Stowey, when the three of us, you and Dorothy and I, went rambling?" To which William replies, "We were young then, and quite mad, all of us." The characters "do" their poems with seemingly offhanded nonchalance. One stage direction reads: "Enter WORDSWORTH in the throes of composition." He then recites part of the opening of his epic poem *The Prelude.* The playwright has injected, sometimes awkwardly, excerpts from her characters' diaries, letters, and other writings. Much of the dialogue seems stiff or wooden, not heightened and purified. Coleridge says, "'The Ancient Mariner' was never anything more than a fool's attempt at sublimity." To which Sara Hutchinson, Wordsworth's sister-in-law, the woman with whom the unhappily married Coleridge was hopelessly infatuated, says, "You are quoting Robert Southey. Shame on you." William chimes in, "My genius. If genius is indeed the name for the unmanageable goading, lumbering, ungainly, fearful prospect, the palsy of anxiety." In one of her notes, Clampitt deludes herself: "I have modified existing language for dramatic purposes. In my own mind, those I have depicted live on as actual persons. As depicted, they are to be regarded simply as characters in a play." She has not "modified existing language" sufficiently for any twentieth-century audience to believe that the characters are truly alive.

These plays, all variations on a single theme, show Clampitt trying to understand and then reproduce the lives of geniuses who encouraged and supported one another. The action is rife with pathos but short on energy. One version of *Mad with Joy* ends with a touching posthumous scene. De Quincey has announced the death of Coleridge (1834). The scrim reveals Mary, leading Dorothy ("in her right mind but feeble") onto the stage:

MARY: Come, dear, we must not tire him.
DOROTHY: I believe I am happiest when there are three of us.
WORDSWORTH: Coleridge? Did you say Coleridge?
DOROTHY: Oh, no, William. Coleridge is dead. They say he died happy.

This is followed by an epilogue, a paragraph by De Quincey on Wordsworth's genius:

For a time, each of us lived in his shadow. Whether his need for any of us was greater than his sister's daily need for him, or the need of Coleridge for his daily opium, or I for mine—oh, we are needy creatures, all of us!—I would tell you if I knew. But what is an opium-eater's opinion worth? I have told you my story. Thank you, and good night.

In all versions of the play, everything ends as elegy.

Clampitt takes Dorothy as her focus, not as a sister or a hand-maiden to her brother but as a major figure in her own right, a writer of more than mere talent. (The recuperation of her reputation and an appreciation of her creative accomplishments resulted from the burgeoning interest in women writers that occurred in Britain and the States during the 1980s and 1990s.) Throughout her life, Dorothy had dedicated herself to her brother, perhaps denying her own creativity by submitting to his needs. She lived with him, his wife, and their children, assuming the role of aunt and helper. (Amy, too, was an aunt.) William died in 1850, and she five years later. She had episodes of madness, and lived her last years in a mental fog. Her writing about her brother has encouraged speculation among recent scholars about her possibly incestuous feelings for him (she refers to him in her journals as "my beloved"). On the day of his wedding to Mary Hutchinson in 1802, Dorothy was stricken with one of her migraine headaches, which made it impossible for her to attend the service. Genius repressed? Another woman destined to submit herself to the power of a man? Or victimized by structures of the patriarchy? Ignored by history and then reevaluated upward and re-restored to her proper place? One sees why Clampitt would take an interest.

Malcolm Lowry once called his literary obsession with Melville and Conrad Aiken "a hysterical identification." Clampitt's connection to Dorothy Wordsworth was milder and more reasoned, but one appreciates how one woman writer needed to find "predecessors" of her own gender as well as—more generally—any masters of style who would inspire and guide her. One wonders about the importance of sibling relationships to Amy Clampitt, woman and poet. She could identify doubly with Dorothy: first, as a talent who was, for a variety of reasons, unable to express her native genius; and second, perhaps, as a version of Amy's talented younger sister, Beth, ruined by mental illness, but stalwart until the end.

Over the years, Clampitt showed excerpts and versions of the work to friends. People tried to be kind but they were also realistic. Her biggest supporter, Fritz Weaver, decided in 1987 that this was neither a well-made play nor a commercially viable one, but that it should be published. After thirty years on the stage, he said he had come to realize that the public requires "one or two events set in motion and *shown happening.*" He had a palpable condescension toward hoi polloi, and he realized that Clampitt would not be able to reach them. He was softening his criticism in part by blaming the potential audience, not the writer herself. He correctly saw the work as all talk and no action, even though Dorothy's madness is, or could be, "a powerful dramatic tool." The novelist William Kinsolving, also seeing that Dorothy was the primary focus, urged Clampitt not to quote so much from her characters' letters and to get rid of exposition and offstage developments. In other words: this was not, at least yet, anything like a play. Ben Sonnenberg, editor of *Grand Street*, a Clampitt admirer and publisher of many of her poems, observed in a letter that the play "smells, as they say, too much of the lamp." Like Weaver, the poet Alfred Corn suggested that it might be what used to be called a "closet drama," something to be read, not watched. Clampitt's recent English friend and admirer David, Viscount Eccles, married to an American book collector and living in New Jersey, asked in 1991, "Is the whole actable?" clearly implying that it was not. Several years earlier, he'd sent the play to John Gielgud, who wrote promptly and candidly to Amy and suggested that it would be better on the radio. Both Mary Jo Salter and the young poet George Bradley doubted the wisdom of dealing with Coleridge's constipation, which in one version takes up an entire scene. Bradley wrote to Clampitt, "there's a reason why the Greeks always confined physical agony to the wings. Poor humanity, even its suffering so often seems silly!" And Salter, who dutifully read many versions, suggested delicately that "certain problems remain . . . such as Coleridge's long speech on his constipation, which is both funny and miserable in real life but may turn only funny on stage."

Because of connections, favors requested and granted, and a general respect for the author herself, the play finally received a performance. In October 1988, William Wadsworth from the Manhattan Theatre Club wrote to Amy saying the play was not for him, but he suggested writing to Andreas Teuber at the Poets' Theatre in Cambridge. Clampitt made an inquiry. Teuber said yes. On Sunday, February 12, 1989, the play, now called *The Three of Us* and reduced to two acts with three scenes each, was given a reading at the Lyric Stage on Charles Street in Boston. Afterwards, Teuber wrote a thoughtful note to Clampitt saying that it was really two plays, the first about the relations among the three central characters, and the second about Dorothy's decline into madness.

The play and its life—or at least its creator's hopes—continued. Clampitt received grants from the Lila Wallace–Reader's Digest Fund in 1991 and 1992 to continue her work on it. In May and June 1991, Amy and Hal went to the Villa Serbelloni at the Rockefeller Foundation's Bellagio Center, near Lake Como, where she had been given a residency, according to her notification from the foundation, "to work on your play, *Dorothy*." (This place had been the setting of her visit more than thirty years earlier with her young friend Anne Marshall, soon to become a nun.) Then it became *Mad with Joy*. She gave a reading from the play to the other Bellagio guests in mid-May. That she was tinkering with the title is a sign that she continued to be unsure of the work as a whole. On November 1 of that year, having returned stateside with a new revision, Clampitt appeared at a benefit at the Tsai Performance Center in Boston for the Playwrights' Theater. Billed as "An Evening of Poetry and Drama," it featured a dazzling group of participants reading from their work: Joseph Brodsky, John Guare, Jamaica Kincaid, Galt MacDermot, Gregory Mosher, Robert Pinsky, Charles Simic, Mark Strand, Derek Walcott, and August Wilson.

Clampitt refused to give up on it. She even dreamed about a film version. On March 1, 1993, just before her cancer diagnosis, Clampitt attended another reading, also sponsored by the Poets' Theatre, this time at Agassiz Theater on the Radcliffe College campus in Cambridge. Helen Vendler and other local fans were in the audience. Everyone was embarrassed by the mediocrity of the product.

Even as a closet drama intended to be read on the page rather than performed on the stage, the work never found a publisher—in any of its multiple versions. John Herman, director of Ticknor & Fields in New York, wrote, "I can't see publishing *Mad with Joy* to any good purpose. The play seems to me too specialized to weather the heavy winds of general trade book publishing."

After the author's death the play lived on, however briefly, a seemingly unkillable revenant. We find in the Clampitt papers a flyer for a reading of it at the Edward-Dean Museum in Cherry Valley, California, sponsored by the San Gorgonio Pass Poets Society, on Saturday, November 19, 1994. That notice refers to "the late Amy Clampitt."

———

Clampitt failed at what she was trying to do, but she had not entirely wasted her time and energy. Her fascination with the early generation of English Romantic poets, like her commitment to Keats's life and work, bore fruit in the form of several poems that appeared in *Archaic Figure* and *Westward*, the two books that were contemporary with her obsessive dramatic efforts. Blocked on one front, she simultaneously moved forward on another one, this time the lyric genre. We may apply the phrase "poem of joint ownership"— my label for her Keats sequence—to the new poems she wrote as a means of paying homage to artists she admired. These included Margaret Fuller and George Eliot, but it was, inevitably, Coleridge and the Wordsworths who most engaged her attention.

What Clampitt could not do in a play she managed to deliver in these shorter poems, which are part narrative, part lyric, and always filled with descriptive passages. Some reviewers, as I have pointed out, hated these poems. Other readers found them moving. There is a trio of them in *Archaic Figure*—"Grasmere," "Coleorton," "Rydal Mount"—named for places associated with her three main characters. At the beginning of the first, a kind of prelude to a scene about to happen, she places herself in the action:

Rainstorms that blacken like a headache
where mosses thicken, and the mornings

smell of jonquils, the stillness
of hung fells thronged with the primaveral
noise of waterfalls—contentment
pours in spate from every slope; the lake fills,
the kingcups drown, and still it rains,
the sheep graze, their black lambs bounce
and skitter in the wet: such weather
one cannot say, here, why
one is still so happy.

Cannot say, except it's both so wild
and so tea-cozy cozy, so snugly
lush, so English.

As she often did, the poet uses the place to stand for, and to prepare us for, the people who occupied it years earlier. In the Lake District now, she feels the livingness of the past as she did at Winchester in 1985 when she retraced Keats's steps there, and as she had in 1949, visiting England for the first time. Landscape and weather have remained constant. And the music of her phrasing—the redundancy of "cozy cozy," the internal rhyming in "snugly/lush/English"—alerts us to the pleasures the visiting poet is experiencing. The poem's repeated sounds suggest repeated events in the lives of the poets.

She then engages us with the history of William and Dorothy, of William and Mary Hutchinson, and with the communal life at Dove Cottage. She quotes from letters, journals, and poems, less awkwardly than she did in her play, reminding us of her characters' actions and feelings. She laces the narrative with more details from the observed landscape. Dorothy's headaches and William's nervous stomach, which acted up whenever he put pen to paper, all the maneuvers of life and work, come into clear focus.

The poem ends by returning to the landscape:

> . . . To ail, here in this place,
> this hollow formed as though to be the vessel
> of contentment—of sweet mornings

smelling of jonquils, of tranquillity
at nightfall, of habitual strolls
along the lakeshore, among the bracken
the old, coiled-up agitation
glistening: birds singing, the greening
birches in their wedding veils,
the purple stain of bluebells:

attachment's uncut knot—so rich, so dark,
so dense a node the ache still bleeds,
still binds, but cannot speak.

The landscape, and the poet's rich reproduction of its clotted dense-ness, represent her "cast of characters" and also keep them to one side. Amy the woman might have had throughout her life difficulty understanding how people actually lived and felt, but Clampitt the poet can let us into these people's lives obliquely. "Here in this place," mystery and clarity remain together, because the poet has shown us the people through, and in, a specific locale.

The narrative grows more intense in the following poems-of-place. By 1805, Coleridge had gone off to the Mediterranean to escape his failed marriage, and to try to cure his drug habit; he returned weakened; John Wordsworth, William and Dorothy's sailor sibling, had drowned; Mary had given birth to several children; William had composed *The Prelude*. Time moves on. "Coleorton" ends with foreboding, as William and Dorothy "wait. Together, / as the older stars come into bloom / above the coal-pits, they look up / and feel the prospect darken." And "Rydal Mount," named for the poet's final home, purchased in 1813, and inhabited through his almost marmo-real final phase as a national institution, brings us forward through the decades. Coleridge has died, as have two of the Wordsworth children; William, a radical in his youth, has hardened into a con-servative Tory and has become, as of 1842, the poet laureate.

This poem ends with the poet and his sister, watching and remembering. At the close, they return to their years of glory in the previous century: "a doddering pair, like / gypsies camping out, the way they'd camped / one night at Tintern, the untended grandeurs /

of a time gone dim gone dim behind them." The American poet has brought her dying English characters to life. Repetition is her key tactic: "gone dim gone dim" is a stroke of lyrical genius.

———

At the same time that she was reworking her play, Clampitt was writing the reviews and essays that she accumulated in *Predecessors, Et Cetera*. Some of these throw light, implicitly, on why she failed on some fronts and succeeded on others. The best criticism is always—both Oscar Wilde and Harold Bloom knew this—autobiographical, even if it never mentions its author's life. Clampitt found herself drawn to gestures of theatricality in Emily Dickinson and Henry James, writers she had long admired. And in both cases, she understood the imbalances between their engagement with and their withdrawal from the greater world.

Clampitt wrote that Dickinson (like Margaret Fuller, George Eliot, Dorothy Wordsworth, Alice James, and other nineteenth-century women) was acutely aware of "the problem of feeling in excess of any available object." She seems to be slyly revising T. S. Eliot's famous theory that a playwright—indeed, any writer—must find an "objective correlative" by which to harness strong feelings in a work of literature. Dickinson, says Clampitt, "is all extremes," charged by a "skittish insecurity": it is as though she is describing herself. Her essay "The Theatrical Emily Dickinson" reminds readers that her subject, often accused of ignoring the realities of contemporary history while retreating to the spare redoubt of her bedroom, was a covertly political poet. Over half of her poems were composed between 1861 and 1865, and many of them are filled with a consciousness of carnage and bloodshed. The poet did not have to mention the Civil War to acknowledge its force. Clampitt could also be political, as well as theatrical, at one remove. And she could identify with her American predecessor on another front: both women grew up in an age of evangelical revivals, which they both resisted. Both came to spurn any organized religion that relied on public—one might say "dramatic"—displays of faith as proof of spiritual feeling and salvation.

The identification with James is subtler, more surprising and more original. Like Clampitt, the novelist wanted to write for the stage. The debacle of *Guy Domville* in 1895 proved how he had mistaken his gifts. Again, what we see is a not-so-hidden autobiography: Clampitt might as well be thinking of herself as of Henry James when she writes that he was a social animal, "but it was in stillness that his own, and his characters' insights came alive." James was "a poet's novelist" in part because so many of his greatest scenes take place in stillness. Her favorite James novel was *The Ambassadors*. She would have been drawn, of course, to the theme of the American in Europe, the collision and collusion between the Old and New Worlds. Even more, she is struck by James as a writer of weather, one of her signature subjects: *The Ambassadors* "is suffused with the meteorological sense of Paris," and in *The Wings of the Dove* "the weather becomes literally a character in the drama." It's all "a protracted tribute to the poetry of appearances." This, from the woman who could register on her pulse and then duplicate with her pen the minutest meteorological shifts.

Weather cannot become a character in a play. It can, at least a little, in a poem or a novel.

Reading James is like listening to a piece of music, she says, or "it is maybe a bit more like what exercises at the barre are for a dancer." The complications of personal and social life are represented in the thickets of James's intricate, even convoluted sentences, with syntax always branching out, extending, getting qualified and modified. Does this sound like the poetry of Amy Clampitt herself? She does not say, but her reader will make the association.

———

Clampitt's Wordsworth poems appeared in her third Knopf volume, *Archaic Figure*, dedicated to Mary Jo Salter, Peter Kybart, and Howard Moss, who died that year. Ann Close had taken over from Alice Quinn as Clampitt's editor. The new book also contains "An Anatomy of Migraine," which is at once a scholarly and intimate poem. It comes with the longest series of endnotes in Clampitt's collected works. Its subject is nothing less than an investigation of the history of consciousness, the brain, and the nature of pain and suffering. Amy's father and grandfather suffered from migraines, as did Hal Korn and Annette Leo, a recent friend, whom Clampitt met only once, corresponded with, and to whom she dedicated the poem. It mingles considerations of the poet's genetic inheritance with references to and quotations from various philosophers and scientists as well as poets and novelists. It is deeply personal without being confessional. It is also very much of the library, without being oppressively freighted. It struck a sympathetic chord in many readers: the Clampitt files contain fan letters of gratitude from migraine sufferers.

Because the human brain has twin symmetrical hemispheres, the poem is also appropriately bifurcated: two halves, each containing twenty-five quatrains, one hundred lines. What exactly is "the self"? Where does it reside? These are heavy questions, for which scientists, philosophers, and artists have sought answers, all of which are just guesses. "The old conundrum," she calls it: "*Who am I / where did / I come from*?" Both halves of the poem balance the speculative and the personal. The second part touchingly relates Annette Leo's story. A migraine sufferer—"*You too!*" the poet exclaims—Leo becomes part of "a gathering of shades." Clampitt labels these victims, in a list of course, "an elite / vised by the same splenic coronet." They include

> Dorothy Wordsworth, George Eliot, Margaret
> Fuller, Marx, Freud, Tolstoy, Chopin, Lewis
> Carroll, Simone Weil, Virginia Woolf

and Clampitt endearingly calls them "forebears and best friends who'd all gone / to that hard school." She has constructed a noble fraternity of sufferers, composed of many of her cultural idols and ordinary people as well. They come together in a harmony of disharmony, of unity in suffering. She addresses "Anny, friend by mail," acknowledging how letters both separate and join writers and readers, making correspondence itself a symmetrical occurrence.

Anny Leo died in her sleep. Her widower sent Amy the news. The poem, so full of philosophical conjecture, and rife with Clampitt's signature syntactic tangles, ends tenderly and simply:

I miss her. Though our two lives just touched,
the torn fabric of some not-yet-imagined
prospect hangs there, streamered, splendid,
    vague: well-being rainbowed

over a lagoon of dark: all that I'm even
halfway sure of marked by that interior cleft
(black, white; sweet, sour; adazzle, dim), I
    live with shades of possibility,

with strangers, friends I never spoke to, with
the voices of the dead, the sunlight like gold
water on the wall—electron-charged, precarious—
    all tenuously made of consciousness.

A literary reader hears the echoes of Dickinson ("I Dwell in Possibility") and Hopkins ("sweet, sour; adazzle, dim"). A reader who does not hear these echoes can still be moved. Friendship, selfhood, indeed all of life is defined by connections, some of which we can miss, others of which hit us with brute force. Clampitt is well aware of the delicate precariousness of the whole complicated tangle. "Well-being" is always "rainbowed over a lagoon of dark"—a conjunction of opposites both inevitable and provisional.

———

For the next six years, after Amherst, the rhythm of Amy's life alternated between public acclaim and her need to carve out private time for poems and other kinds of writing. On December 14, 1987, she wrote to Rimsa Michel that New York had become a place "without either soul or manners," a universal complaint, it seems, when people grow complacent, weary, or as overwhelmed by the city as Amy had recently become. But she made an exception for one event that evidently gave her substantial pleasure: a reading at the Morgan Library, before an overflow audience "consisting partly of directors of the library and the Academy of American Poets, who appeared in black tie, and a fair number of friends of mine, who mainly didn't." She bought a new dress for the occasion and before the reading had dinner at the venerable Colony Club on Park Avenue with the black-tie crowd, where she met David, Viscount Eccles. The Iowa Quaker was now hobnobbing with a member of the English House of Lords. After dinner a limousine delivered the poet and Seamus Heaney—who was to introduce her—to the Morgan Library. "Having been seen emerging from a limousine in those circumstances, and having it reported to friends in other parts, is a bit peculiar. But I did have fun . . . it's been downhill ever since." Earlier in the year she had gone to Harvard with a cold. Now she returned from the Morgan Library and came down with another cold. She was pleased equally by the limousine and the high society event on Manhattan's East Side, and by the bus-and-subway ride from Amherst to Harvard Yard. Everything was an occasion for gratitude and surprise.

In 1988, she gave readings in the South and the Midwest, served as Fannie Hurst Visiting Professor at Washington University in St. Louis, and participated in T. S. Eliot centennial celebrations there and back in Cambridge. Befriended by Viscount Eccles and his wife, the former Mary Hyde, she went with Hal to the Eccleses' New Jersey sheep farm for lunch. Mary Hyde was a major collector of books and memorabilia by and about Samuel Johnson. She also collected plenty of other things. She brought out, for Amy's inspection, items connected to the Wordsworth circle, as well as an original typescript of *The Importance of Being Earnest*. To a friend in the South, Amy admitted that "such experiences only confirm me in my bohemian ways; but I won't deny that they're fun, in extreme moderation if you know what I mean." There's "fun" again, now experienced as an oxymoron, moderate in its extremity. A springtime celebration for Joseph Brodsky—with whom she bonded over a mutual love of cats, but of whom she claimed to be terrified—brought her back to central Massachusetts, where she saw friends and former students from her Amherst year. She read in November at the Library of Congress alongside May Swenson and her fellow Iowan Mona Van Duyn, in a tribute to Marie Bullock, the longtime president of the Academy of American Poets, who had died two years earlier. As she wrote to Barbara Clark, "otherwise I'm staying pretty much in the vicinity for the foreseeable future." Her "vicinity" was, however, always expanding.

That summer, Hal and Amy spent part of June and July in England and in the Netherlands, where he led a legal seminar in Leyden. Lunch at an Oxford college (Brasenose) took her back almost forty years to her first visit to Oxford in the company of Charles Johnson. The excursion resulted in a reminiscent poem, "Having Lunch at Brasenose," both reticent and confessional like "The Kingfisher." There's not a first-person pronoun in the entire lyric. Decades before, "one was very young," and everything one saw was

>   . . . lit up by the dazzling
> gaze of him with whom one was, of
>   course, at once in love
>
> overwhelmingly, cravenly half aware
> even then it was no merely erotic
> trap one had fallen into, it was
>   centuries of enclosure,
>
> it was the walls, not the riotous
> break-in of all that was happening,
> mainly, in one's own imagination[.]

It wasn't only Charles Johnson, it was Oxford and its spires, it was England, it was the livingness of the past, that brought out in young Amy what her older self calls, at the end of the poem, "the airy / indignity of being young."

Not only Oxford's history, architecture, and consummate beauty but also smaller, inconsequential things appealed to her, like being able to walk to the train station without asking for directions, and feeling "very very worldly," or, in other words, that she actually belonged to the place after all these years. That worldliness, tinctured as usual by incredulity rather than entitlement, was boosted by a visit with her new friend in Parliament:

> One evening, in the midst of all those snacks-in-the-room, we were picked up by a driver named Whiting, who took us to a house directly across from where John Gielgud lives, not far from the Houses of Parliament, where we had champagne with (get this) a member of the House of Lords! . . . his name is David Eccles, he's married to an American, and they're both book collectors. While we had champagne, he showed me his three first editions of *The Waste Land*, among other things.

"Get this" means "I'm pinching myself here, not showing off."

In between such gallivantings and hobnobbings, Clampitt kept receiving invitations to read, teach, and, occasionally, to judge. To one request at least, she finally had to say no. In a 1989 letter to David Lehman, the poet-critic and longtime editor of the annual volumes of *Best American Poetry*, she explained why, having first accepted his invitation to do that year's judging, she would have to decline. She allowed that she often enjoyed finding something to say when asked to write a jacket blurb for someone else's poems. What she did not "find illuminating or valuable is having to say, This is the best . . . Who can say what is best? . . . One responds to a piece of work, or else one doesn't." And she concluded that she just didn't feel "tough enough." She was tough enough to know her own mind about politics and her predecessors, just as she was tough enough to have announced decades before that she "could write a whole history of English literature and know just where to place everybody in it, with hardly any trouble at all. The reason being, apparently, that I feel *I am in it*." Now that she was in fact in it, she did not wish also to become a keeper of the gate, or the kingmaker for the following generation. She would not take on the role of a Bloom or a Vendler. The unwillingness to judge others was part of her Quaker legacy, as were her reluctance to compete, and her willingness to lead others only as *prima inter pares*, part of a community but not of a hierarchy.

Later that year (November 1989), the New York Public Library named her a "Literary Lion," along with seventeen other notables including Edward Albee, William Arrowsmith, Lucille Clifton, Tess Gallagher, Robert Giroux, Elmore Leonard, and Garry Wills. Patience and Fortitude, the guardian stone lions at the Library's Fifth Avenue entrance, must have been smiling when they learned that the institution was honoring someone who exemplified their virtues. Amy was at that moment, indeed, *in* the nation's literary culture, if not the entire history of English literature. The following year, Knopf published *Westward*, her fourth book in less than a decade. On April 26, Hal threw a cocktail reception for a hundred guests. Five months later, in mid-October, the poet herself managed a trip westward to New Providence to speak at the Honey Creek Meetinghouse. The semi-prodigal daughter made a temporary return to acknowledge her Quaker heritage. The following month she received a letter from a pair of writers who were translating poems from *The Kingfisher* into German (they included their version of "Sunday Music"), with the surprising appraisal that "the seemingly casual, sometimes colloquial tone of much of your writing is not easy to transport into German, with its often pon-

Amy with other literary lions, New York Public Library, November 9, 1989

Amy and J. D. ("Sandy") McClatchy, New York Public Library, 1989

derous syntactic structures." Hostile American critics had chastised Clampitt for her meandering list-making and pretentious diction. Read through the lens of another language, her diction and syntax appeared offhanded, casual, even easy.

Also in 1990, Clampitt was named a Chancellor of the Academy of American Poets, one of the few women in an otherwise male and somewhat staid organization. William Wadsworth was the new director, and he recalled her enthusiastic engagement in poetic activities throughout the city. She was a full-time New Yorker, of course, and had the advantage of proximity, but even so she threw herself into action with unprecedented gusto. Wadsworth said she was more fully involved than others, and her "unaffected generosity and open curiosity" impelled her to dart around the city, participating, for example, in a panel and reading by Filipino poets at the Chinatown branch of the New York Public Library. Glamour did not entice her. It's hard to imagine her more mandarin colleagues among the Academy's chancellors, like Anthony Hecht, John Hollander, James Merrill, and Richard Wilbur, doing the same. Just as she was intrepid in her European jaunts, so she thought nothing of hopping on the Number 6 subway and heading downtown to survey what was, for her, new poetic territory. Clampitt was as committed to the great traditions of English and American poetry as her fellow chancellors, but she was more vigorously populist in her political activities and her willingness to branch out to non-European cultures. Two years later, she wrote to the English critic and journalist Jim McCue of her delight in meeting five Chinese poets living in exile around the world. Gathered in Manhattan and accompanied by interpreters, they discussed and read from their work: "I found them very lively and thrilling to hear." Curiosity kept her going. I think of Frank O'Hara's buying "NEW WORLD WRITING" and his casual desire "to see what the poets in Ghana are doing these days" as he walked around Manhattan on a hot Friday in July ("The Day Lady Died"). Clampitt would have approved.

In the spring of 1991, Amy and Hal visited the Rockefeller Foundation's Villa Serbelloni on the shores of Lake Como, where they both had monthlong residencies. Hal was still working on "Ralph," his endless legal article. Amy was fussing with the newest version of her Wordsworth play, writing poems, and working on translations from Dante's *Inferno*. She was now no longer an anonymous American tourist as she had been decades earlier, but a celebrated American poet. Following their Italian stay, the couple went to England, where they paid a visit to Anne Marshall, now Sister Mary John, and officially "Reverend Mother" since 1990, in her Anglican convent in Kent. That year also saw the publication of *Predecessors, Et Cetera: Essays*, Clampitt's considerations of various touchstone authors who had influenced her, especially Dickinson, Moore, James, and, of course, the Wordsworths.

Clampitt sent the book to Sister Mary John. Her friend replied (the letter, undated, is probably from April 1992), offering special thanks for the essay on Paul's Epistles to the Thessalonians, and apologizing for not quite having understood Amy's personal reason—her attachment to Hal—for souring on Christian doctrine decades earlier:

No wonder that you rejected what you encountered as Christianity then, and little wonder that you turned away in sorrow when you later encountered the blindness, callousness and amazing rejection of the Jews in a body that owes its historical life to the Jews. For all that, I don't believe that your seed of faith has quite perished, and surely God watches over it with tenderness—if I may speak anthropomorphically in Semitic style.

The two women understood each other, although time, space, and cultural preferences now separated them.

———

The Bellagio residency produced a new friendship, with the writer Karen Chase and her husband, Paul Graubard, a psychologist turned painter, Americans from Lenox, Massachusetts. It was Bob Dylan who, at second hand, brought the two women together. On May 24, when the residents were seated at dinner around a well-appointed table, Chase remembered that it was Dylan's fiftieth birthday. She suggested an impromptu celebration, produced a cassette of one of his records, and put it on a tape recorder. Amy, wearing a red linen blazer and leaning against a door, said nothing, but began "swaying her shoulder, in the most awkward way, to the rhythm of the song. I looked at her. I was just shocked, and I thought, Oh, maybe she

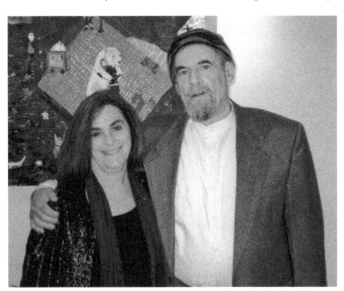

Karen Chase and Paul Graubard

Nettie Korn

could really be a friend! And she looked at me and said, 'Bob Dylan has been very important to me.'"

Having forged an initial bond over Dylan, Chase and Clampitt deepened their friendship in those weeks at Bellagio. Later in the summer of 1991, after they returned to the States, Hal and Amy were planning their annual getaway to Corea, with Hal's mother, Nettie, in tow. An Orthodox Jew, Nettie would not travel on the Sabbath, so the Korn trio arranged to spend a Friday night in the Berkshires with their new friends. Lenox impressed them. They did not realize at the time how important the place would soon become to them. At year's end, Amy spent the month of December at Smith College as the Elizabeth Drew Professor.

PART 4: 1992–1994

Years later, Chase recalled shopping expeditions with Amy. Even at the Villa Serbelloni, the two made occasional escapes to go "junking," as they called it. They were never looking, or shopping, for anything specific. They waited with eyes open for things to catch their attention. It hardly mattered what. Shopping of this sort always relies on the principle of serendipity. (In Clampitt's case, so did the writing of poetry.) Near Lake Como they found themselves in an actual junkyard: "Amy was in heaven, and I remember her looking . . . her eyes got so huge and she said, 'I love . . . *junk*!' There was a huge pause between 'love' and 'junk.'" ("I do have a fondness for discards, human and otherwise," she remarked in an interview.)

All the random detritus in Clampitt poems like "Beach Glass" begins to make sense in the context of its author's life. Amy collected. I have pointed out that collecting, like list-making, is an art of accumulation for self-protection as well as pure pleasure. Chase offhandedly observed, as a general truth but with special relevance to her new friend, that "the good thing about junk: it's easy come, easy go. You have your junk, you give it away or you give it back to the junk store, and then you get other junk. So, it just sort of moves around." Amy appreciated what Wallace Stevens, in the title of a poem, called "the pleasures of merely circulating." Amy accumulated objects trivial and talismanic. Sometimes they became stays against disorder and homelessness. But she could part with them easily. When her parents died, according to her neighbor Regina Berry, she took a few pillows Pauline had embroidered and let the rest go. Her feeling for material things extended to her relationship with money. Whether she had it or not—for most of her life she didn't have it—she gave it away, to political and charitable causes that appealed to her, or to friends like Peter Kybart who were occasionally in need. Clampitt could find beauty in junk, just as she could imagine a modern pastoral scene amid the rank and stinky reedbeds of the polluted Hackensack.

We can associate the movement of material things in her life with her own movement through life, her travels, and her sensitivity to the movements and travel of others: what she calls "transhumance" in "A Procession at Candlemas" (*The Kingfisher*). She also wrote two poems about avian pilgrimage, and the fullness one can find in vacancy: "Vacant Lot with Tumbleweed and Pigeons" (*What the Light Was Like*) and "Vacant Lot with Pokeweed" (*Westward*). Abundance flourishes everywhere. One person's junk, one person's bed of weeds, can be another's poetic garland. There are different ways of establishing a homestead. Like so many squatters, the pigeons in one poem return annually to the same lot with its roofless building, dispossessed but still desperate to find a home in the "soon-to-be obliterated stations / of nostalgia." And pokeweed manages to seize a foothold in its own deserted lot, making its home within "the season's frittering, / the annual wreckage."

Amy Clampitt, inveterate traveler and happy stay-at-home nester, was about to get the first nest she ever owned rather than rented or borrowed. Like her acceptance from *The New Yorker* in 1978, a much larger benefaction, this one in the form of a large sum of money, came to her unexpectedly.

———

When she was in Maine, Amy seldom bothered to check the messages on her Manhattan telephone's answering machine. One day in June 1992, the phone rang in Corea. It was Karen Chase, telling her that the year's list of MacArthur award winners included her name. On June 19, 1992, four days after her seventy-second birthday, and a week after receiving an honorary degree from Bowdoin College, Amy wrote to Rimsa Michel with the news. She was of course incredulous. The foundation's official letter was dated June 11: the prize was $375,000 ($773,000 in 2022 dollars), with no strings attached, to be paid out over the next five years. In addition to calls from well-wishers, a producer for the television newsman Ted Koppel phoned her with a plan for a two-minute *Nightline* segment about poetry. Nothing came of it. "That's showbiz," her friend Peter Kybart reminded her.

Two weeks later, Amy and Hal bought a house in the Berkshires. This was speedy work. Amy had already told Chase at the end of their phone call that she intended to use her money to buy a house. Karen looked around, and found some houses for the couple to visit. They loved one of them and made an offer. It was accepted. The modest, charming but otherwise architecturally undistinguished three-bedroom cottage occupies a nearly one-acre site on a cul-de-sac right off the main road between Lenox and Stockbridge. "Downtown" Lenox is a half mile away, a bracing uphill walk. The cottage is also close to Tanglewood, the Boston Symphony's summer home

Amy and Hal in their Berkshires cottage

and America's most beautiful lawn. A couple of miles in the other direction, there's Edith Wharton's impressive country place, The Mount. The near-fatal sledding accident in her 1904 novel *Ethan Frome*, based on a real Lenox event, occurred nearby, on the Old Stockbridge Road.

The house was the only home Amy ever owned. It was also the first actual house, rather than a New York City apartment, that Hal ever lived in. Gray shingle, with deep green shutters on its windows, the house appealed to Amy and Hal in part for its backyard landscape, wilder and more secluded thirty years ago than it is now. A gigantic Rose of Sharon practically covered the small garage; a lilac bush adjoined the mailbox; some large evergreens grew in front and back. Violets bloomed in late April, an apple tree in May. Then, as now, the back lawn in summer was a lush carpet of an emerald green hue. Today, the landscape looks tamer and more manicured. Shapely hostas have replaced the Rose of Sharon; and the large backyard birch tree under which Amy's ashes were buried has been felled, replaced with its hardier relative, a river birch. Some years after her death, a catalpa tree was planted in the yard: a testimony to, and a reminder of, the apartment on West 12th Street.

That nature, like everything else, changes, is a truth that was never lost on this poet, whose awareness of transience became more acute as she aged, even as she was setting down new roots. I mentioned in my second chapter that Amy's early life in Manhattan partook equally of staying at home and going abroad. The interplay of stasis and upheaval, of home and abroad, became a major motif in poems from her final books. "Nothing Stays Put" (*Westward*), for example, presents movement as our common destiny, not just for people but for nature's bounty itself. The fate of this bounty is the result of natural process and also of commerce and politics. The poem begins as an updating of Wordsworth's sonnet "The World Is Too Much with Us":

> The strange and wonderful are too much with us.
> The protea of the antipodes—a great,
> globed, blazing honeybee of a bloom—
> for sale in the supermarket! We are in
> our decadence, we are not entitled.
> What have we done to deserve
> all the produce of the tropics—
> this fiery trove, the largesse of it
> heaped up like cannonballs, these pineapples, bossed
> and crested, standing like troops at attention,
> these tiers, these balconies of green, festoons
> grown sumptuous with stoop labor?

It's as if a Wayne Thiebaud painting of lavish, colorful stacks of fruit has come to life, but with a reminder that nature's gifts do not arrive like manna, or grace, from God directly. They require human intervention and hard work. We can now eat fruits out of season: it's a kind of miracle. An orange in December is no longer a rare gift to be placed in a Christmas stocking. We can enjoy exotic flora from everywhere, all the time. Everything is available, "opulence by the pailful," at the corner greengrocer's market: orchids, "slightly / fatigued by the plane trip from Hawaii," and freesias "fattened a bit in translation from overseas."

Having seen the domestication of the foreign, and the losses entailed in travel, she notices stems of cobalt blue bachelor's buttons.

These put her in mind of and send her back to her Iowa homestead and her grandmother's garden, "sown with immigrant grasses." Especially when it is repeated, "sown" makes a homonymic pun with the unstated word "sewn," and the poet remembers the embroideries of her native landscape created "by a love knot, a cross stitch / of living matter, sown and tended by women, / nurturers everywhere of the strange and wonderful, / beneath whose hands what had been alien begins, / as it alters, to grow as though it were indigenous." "Beneath whose hands" also means "within whose hands," as the laying down of seed outdoors becomes synonymous with women's indoor work: stitching and sewing.

Everything alien eventually comes to seem almost homegrown. Iowa and New York, space and time, can expand and contract. Strolling through Manhattan side streets on an April afternoon, looking up at hybrid pear trees in bloom, Clampitt is reminded of "the indigenous wild plum of my childhood." Who can say what, or who, belongs where? What does "indigenous" even mean? Everything came originally from somewhere else. Hybrid pears and wild plums: nothing is pure, and nothing stays put, especially in the human mind. At the end, as sometimes happens in poems by this artist given to long lists, long sentences, and strings of items, we get a pared-down conclusion that covers all activity, internal and external: "All that we know, that we're / made of, is motion." Although we are made of motion, the poet's language here exudes calm rather than the verbal whirlwind that so often defines her style.

———

In her 1992 interview with Emily Todd, Clampitt said, "I'm not a poet of place, but of *displacement.*" She was both. The person who had been a renter, a member of the Coalition for the Homeless, a fighter for the housing rights of welfare families, a sometime protesting squatter in vacant Manhattan buildings, now owned real estate. Over the span of seven decades, she had essentially five residences, all differently but equally important: the two Iowa farmhouses; the West 12th Street studio; Hal's Manhattan one-bedroom apartment; and, finally, the Berkshires cottage, furnished with throwaway stuff accumulated on her junking expeditions with Karen Chase. Her friend Doris Myers said that buying her first house made Amy "jump with joy" and that "for someone who was as much of a tumbleweed as she was, she did have a sense that it would be good to be rooted."

The rooting in Lenox occurred almost simultaneously with an uprooting. Amy's West Village apartment, after almost a half century, would soon be emptied. As early as October 1980, the tenants in the three adjacent buildings on West 12th Street had received a survey asking whether they had an interest in a co-op conversion. A meeting was held at the Village Nursing Home. Thirty-one people were opposed, eleven were undecided. No one was in favor. More than a decade passed. Things changed. The conversion was approved. On April 23, 1993, Amy received her landlord's proposal. By this time, she was ill. Everyone in the complex was similarly notified. They had no choice. The purchase figures seem today unbelievable: Apartment 5C was offered for $21,890 (with Citibank financing) or $21,014 without. Monthly maintenance was calculated as $267.41.

Amy's neighbor Regina Berry, who came to know her in 1979 when Amy was living mostly uptown with Hal, said she could never forgive Amy for persuading her not to buy her studio apartment, which would, decades later, have made her both self-sufficient and real-estate-rich. She said buying real estate somehow violated Amy's socialist principles, at least during this phase of her life. For perhaps the same reason, or perhaps simply not wanting to bother with ordinary real estate transactions, Hal continued to rent his 65th Street apartment until the end. Berry said they both had seen and could remember what happened to people during the Depression, and they had no desire to be involved with money. On November 9, having moved her remaining things uptown to 65th Street or out of state to Lenox, Amy wrote to Philip that "Twelfth Street is finally altogether a thing of the past." Things were heading toward closure. Amy herself had less than a year to live.

———

At the start of 1992, before the contretemps at William and Mary over her Matoaka poem and before the purchase of the Massachusetts house, Clampitt went to the Atlantic Center for the Arts in New Smyrna Beach, Florida. For three weeks, she was the "Master Artist" in charge of ten poets in mid-career, who shared space with musicians and visual artists, all eager to spend much of January in the warmth and sunshine of Florida. By this point she had gained confidence and settled comfortably into teaching. Amy assumed her role as leader "with a lightness of touch," according to Katherine Jackson, one of her students. Clampitt had begun to feel that American poets, including herself, were "too constrained by certain well-wrought urn notions of the lyric," and urged her students against "tidy" and "polite" short lines, pushing them toward longer lines "to follow the vagaries of consciousness, the unruliness of the world." She wanted them to move into greater untidiness and to break the bonds of poetic mannerliness.

Jackson's recollections coincide with Harold Bloom's characterization of Clampitt as always on the lookout for something new. Nothing was not interesting. One evening, one of the student poets mentioned "Heavy Metal." Amy had no idea what that was, but she wanted to learn. The words alone piqued her curiosity. For Jackson, this eagerness exemplified "a lifetime of such forays into whatever [struck] her at the time as *terra incognita*. So, too, with her anxious, staccato, self-interrupting lines: who can say what extra-poetic sounds underlie them? And she was, again, foraging for new sounds, new rhythms." "Foraging" is like "junking" or "seeking": Clampitt was always bent on exploration. She came to her classes with no predetermined program. She was more interested in "following the stutter-step of tangential discussion" than sticking to a lesson plan. She relished the unexpected and the random just as, years before, she had made a poem out of found objects.

One evening she read to the group a long poem by the avant-garde Charles Bernstein, created entirely out of real or imagined junk mail. This led the group into a discussion about noise. In her life as in her work, Clampitt worked associatively as well as cumulatively. Ideas and things piled up. They then led on to other ideas and things. Jackson wrote, "Amy's speech tends to dart like a waterbug, here and there, and light briefly on a word, usually a verb, which thereby acquires special emphasis. Then she is off, never less than lucid, but airborne, darting. Soon we were talking about certain poets' use of four-letter words, and explicit sexual imagery. 'Well,' said Amy, matter-of-factly, 'that's fine if you aren't a prude. I happen to be a prude so I don't use that sort of thing, but a lot of poets aren't prudes and they do.'" She had come to know herself. The young woman cruising through Europe at the age of thirty-one in search of sensuous adventures, sometimes random, had settled into what was probably her most authentic self, a kind of curious but prim, solitary onlooker. One night before a communal dinner, someone put on a Grateful Dead tape. Amy went off to the sidelines and danced happily, by herself, for twenty minutes.

Especially in her maturity she could be like Whitman who, by his own estimate in "Song of Myself,"

> Stands amused, complacent, compassionating, idle, unitary,
> Looks down, is erect, or bends an arm on an impalpable certain
>   rest,
> Looking with side-curved head curious what will come next,
> Both in and out of the game and watching and wondering at it.

Clampitt, the poet and the person, could always maintain that double stance, becoming part of a group while simultaneously remaining apart from it. Jackson recalled her at a reading: "Amy's way of listening—rather as a fox listens, head cocked to one side, eyes abstracted . . . attuned to sound as an entrée to understanding."

Another of the students was Kurt Leland, fledgling poet and serious astrologer. He remembered Amy:

> I found it difficult not to regard her simply as a curiosity. Unruly salt and pepper hair, deep owl-like rings around the eyes, a perpetually astonished expression, the clear though warbly high soprano of her voice, the prim elegance of her dress—she struck me as a turn-of-the-century spinster, the polymathic librarian of a small Midwestern town. There was something schoolgirl-like in her fits of giggles, her tendency to rock back and forth in her chair when excited. If the face seemed ravaged, elderly, the body was lithe and the level of energy in conversation so enthusiasti-

cally intense that it would have been hard to place her age with accuracy. Though born in 1920, she could easily have passed for fifty or even younger. Seeing her in shorts one day, a woman in our group remarked, "Imagine showing off your legs at that age!" And there they were, as slender and shapely as a thirty-year-old's.

Amy had mastered the art of give-and-take in the classroom. She clearly had progressed as a teacher. She was no longer nervous. Leland continues:

> Amy conducted a conversation as if she were directing a musical ensemble. Once the theme was announced, she drew people out and wove their remarks together, intruding her own opinion only to carry the argument from one solo voice to the next. She orchestrated the flow of information and kept it focused on the theme with the skill of a conductor, creating a genuine feeling of community. There may have been passionate outbursts but there was rarely conflict. When someone offered personal details meant to impress, Amy's pained expression let us know that wrong notes had been sounded. We learned to avoid such moments, experiencing that rarest of realities, a non-egocentric gathering of artists.

The Quaker spirit of listening-within-a-community prevailed in her. And she had learned to maintain in public the equilibrium between self-exposure and self-hiding that also balanced her poems. In her letter about the residency, Amy said that she'd found herself "mulling the contraries of spontaneity and withholding, of the cryptic as opposed to the discursive approach to language."

To an intellectual like Amy, everything in the world is potentially attractive and remarkable. Another of the poet-guests, Barbara Jordan, recalled that one of the first things Amy did when arriving at the center was to seek out the library, in order to learn from books about the local flora and fauna, and the region's original inhabitants. The weeks in residence included local hikes, and trips to wildlife refuges and a prehistoric Indian midden. But also: some of the musicians, Jordan wrote, "may have coaxed Amy once to the Sit 'n Sip, a bar with a leather? fake grass? counter and a friendly local clientele who'd look stunned by sunlight each time the door opened." She was as much at home here as anywhere.

Outer space also beckoned. With Jackson and several others, Amy drove to watch the January 22 launch of the space shuttle *Discovery* from nearby Cape Canaveral. This is not the kind of subject we are used to in her poems. But the aptly titled "Discovery" (dedicated to Jackson) looks around from Blue Spring, a state park along the St. Johns River. The poem begins with a pod of "lolling, jacketed, elephantine" manatees; then reaches out to a mention of nearby Disney World; the Florida myths of "sun-kissed nakedness" and "year-round, guilt-free / hibiscus and oranges"; and to the Spanish conquistador Ponce de León in search of his own fountain of youth. The poet looks up to the ship lifting off, shedding its jackets as "a snake does its husk, / or a celebrant his vestments." The seven astronauts in the belly of the ship become like the earthbound manatees, "jacketed, lolling / and treading . . . clumsy in space suits." And then they are released from the earth.

As she does in other poems, Clampitt finds kinship in the unlikeliest of venues, and between the strangest of creatures. She ends the poem with a question that she then implicitly answers:

> What are we anyhow, we warmth-
> hungry, breast-seeking animals?
> At Blue Spring, a day or so later,
> one of the manatees, edging
> toward discovery, nudged a canoe,
> and from across the wet, warm,
> dimly imaginable tightrope,
> let itself be touched.

Clampitt traces those "vagaries of consciousness" that she wanted her students to explore. We animals seek connections, even tenuous ones, and in unlikely arrangements.

———

In the fall of 1992, Clampitt received a contract from Smith College to become the first Grace Hazard Conklin Writer-in-Residence for the spring term in 1993. She would receive $30,000 plus housing and benefits. She would not, however, finish out the term. In April 1993, she learned that she had cancer. The poet William Doreski remembered an appearance at Keene State early that month:

> All seemed to be going marvelously well for her. When the women's studies people asked me if Amy would be a good poet to invite for a reading I said, "Of course." This turned out to be a grim occasion, though. Halfway through the reading, Amy felt a sharp, unfamiliar pain, so severe that she couldn't continue. Although in obvious distress, she refused to be taken to the local hospital, so we drove her back to Northampton. This turned out to be the first serious symptom of the cancer that killed her.

Cancer took up much but not all of her energy for the remaining eighteen months. She spent the rest of 1993 working and trying to persevere. Katherine Jackson said that Clampitt was furious when she received her diagnosis: she wanted more time for more writing. At the beginning of her fame, she had remarked to Patricia Morrisroe that she didn't think "you have to suffer in order to write. Intensity doesn't always have to be centered on unhappiness. I realized at some point that if I was going to be a poet then I'd have to be a professional and treat it like a business. I couldn't sit around and wait for the muse to strike. I had to accept that writing is hard work, and it will *always* be hard work." Now she was suffering, but working hard and not unhappy.

In the fall of 1992, she had also arranged for another teaching gig, this one something unofficial, without grades, and for adult students, at the Poetry Center of the 92nd Street YMHA. The focus alternated between Whitman and Dickinson and their respective poetic lines (long versus short), and then the work of the student poets themselves. The course was such a success that the students suggested continuing informally. One of them, Patricia Carlin, volunteered her apartment, and in the spring of 1993 the group reassembled. The experience was festive as well as instructive. Always willing and eager to look at things from many angles, and trying to do justice to the opinions of the students, Amy would respond, Carlin recalled, with her "overriding integrity." If she was not sure of something, she would say, "Oh, I don't know—I'm not sure." Amy observed that the future of poetry in America would be in small groups like this one, lovers of poetry gathering informally to discuss matters. She feared that literacy was declining along with the quaint custom, going back centuries, of families reading aloud from Shakespeare and the Bible.

Carlin paints a picture of Amy, right before her cancer diagnosis and then during the early stages of therapy, that resembles those of people who knew her fifty years earlier:

> She seemed tiny, perched on a large armchair in my living room, but with great tensile strength, like strung-out steel wire. Her movements and bursts of speech were rapid, staccato. She'd cock her head to one side in a birdlike way, and her movements were somewhat birdlike. Her manner was girlish. When something delighted her, which was very often, she'd clap her hands together with a kind of girlish glee.

Amy's costume for their first meeting included a pair of leather boots and a flowered skirt, suitable for a party. The experience of poetry, and talking about it with others, was in fact a party, especially now, because her teaching career and her days of renown would be brief. She learned by doing, in as well as out of the classroom.

———

Ann Close said that Clampitt submitted the manuscript of *A Silence Opens* in early 1993, before she received her diagnosis of ovarian cancer. The book, in many ways Clampitt's most accessible, both revisits old poetic themes and territory and forges new paths. Close also recalled her "spooky feeling" that this would be the poet's final collection, as if Clampitt herself had some eerie presentiment of mortality. Especially in retrospect, it seems haunted by death. Close singled out "Syrinx," which Clampitt had placed deliberately at the start, as the reason for her odd premonition. This lyric summons up Homeric ghosts from the underworld; it describes the "syrinx, that reed / in the throat of a bird," and the music of birdsong and opera singers; it mediates between the meanings created by language and the ways pure sound can rise "past saying anything" and moves "above the threshold, the all- / but dispossessed of breath." Achievement and release are the poem's central concerns.

It says something about the vagaries of taste and fame that Clampitt's star may have begun to decline—temporarily, or just a little?—almost as soon as it had risen. A decade earlier, *The Kingfisher* had sold more than 10,000 copies. In England, it went through four printings, selling 8,000 in the first year alone. In November 1993, Christopher Reid, who had succeeded Craig Raine as the editor at Faber & Faber, wrote to Clampitt and said his house would not publish *A Silence Opens* because her previous book, *Westward*, had sold only 934 copies in Great Britain. Clampitt's last book remained unpublished in the country she had adored since her youth.

A Silence Opens shows that Clampitt knew her own mind, and was continuing to hone her craft. She was moving ahead and simultaneously looking back. "Discovery" is one of several poems that came out of the three weeks she spent in Smyrna Beach. "Matoaka" represents the politically engaged Clampitt, as do "Hispaniola" and "Paumanok." "Brought from Beyond" repeats things from "Nothing Stays Put." A real kingfisher appears in "Bayou Afternoon." "Manhattan" is Clampitt's reminiscence of her salad days and the fates of her friends from the forties and fifties. "Homeland" and "Cadenza" recall the Iowa of her girlhood. Maine, England, and the Villa Serbelloni are all revisited. "Handed Down" and "'Eighty-Nine" are elegies in the manner of "What the Light Was Like." The second of these concerns the tragic death of Andrew Myers, son of Amy's old friend Doris Myers, in a car crash at the age of twenty. It alludes to Tiananmen Square, the 1989 Velvet Revolution in Prague, and Amy's own days of protest in the 1960s. The terrifying angels in Rilke's *Duino Elegies* of 1923 also make an appearance. Botany figures heavily in poems set in Maine and the American South. Clampitt was deepening, not merely repeating, her investigations.

There are wholly new things here as well. Clampitt had been invited by the poet and editor Dan Halpern to translate some cantos from Dante's *Inferno* for a book by many hands. She chose Cantos 9 and 10, about the Heretics in the sixth circle of Hell, and included her sturdy translation of the former in her last book. Perhaps deliberately, she was drawn back to issues of religion that, in her life, she had more or less abandoned or transcended. She read from her Dante at an event at the 92nd Street YMHA Poetry Center on April 14, 1993. Nancy Crampton's photograph captures the distinguished company: Clampitt surrounded by Alfred Corn, Deborah Digges, Jorie Graham, Halpern, Robert Hass, Seamus Heaney, Richard Howard, Galway Kinnell, Cynthia MacDonald, W. S. Merwin, Susan Mitchell, Sharon Olds, Robert Pinsky, Stanley Plumly, Mark Strand, Richard Wilbur, C. K. Williams, and Charles Wright. These were stars of the poetry world. Rebecca Pepper Sinkler, a *New York Times* journalist, described the four-hour event in the *Times Book Review* the following month (May 9), observing that the hall was packed. No one left even after the intermission.

Philip Clampitt said intriguingly that "Amy talked about love as a kind of silence before the unknown." This comment explains her silences about many subjects, and it also explains why she was beginning in her fifth book to counter the verbal exuberance of so much of her earlier work, and to write in new registers.

"Sed de Correr," for example, is a poem in one of those new registers, a meandering and terrifying piece about the "thirst" for running away, an authentic Clampitt subject. It recalls writers on the move: César Vallejo, Federico García Lorca, Virginia Woolf, Franz Kafka, Rilke (again) and his angels. Exile and the search for refuge are leitmotifs. Movement was always a poetic topic for Clampitt, but here she makes dramatic shifts between her life and the lives (and deaths) of other writers. It is also the only poem in which Clampitt recalls her earliest days in New York, when she was briefly a Columbia graduate student, living in Morningside Heights above Harlem. She had just recently arrived from Iowa, where "the botch of being young" was something to run away from. In her previous books, Keats, George Eliot, the Wordsworths, and Dickinson were precursors who fascinated and stood in for her. But the artists in the later poem are mostly continental, not English, as well as desperate and suicidal, not merely neurotic. Clampitt is a full character in her poem, as hungry to escape as any unhappy European artist. Self-hood and otherness mingle. "Sed de Correr" is another autobiography, both actually and also partly at one remove.

One detail that makes its way puzzlingly into the autobiography is a reference to a German-born painter named Jan Müller (1922–1958), a man she never mentions elsewhere in letters, journals, or poems. As a young student in Manhattan, Amy once toured Harlem with him. But he appears here. How did she meet him? What did they do? As with other mysterious details in her life, we shall probably never know. He was a student of Hans Hofmann, and might have been hanging around the Jane Street Gallery where Amy's likely fiancé Howard Mitcham was the director. Why does she name Müller here, while throughout her work she elides or otherwise ignores other friends and even relatives? (She never names Hal in her work.) Because he, a refugee, was, like her, a transplant? Because she loved him? Because she originally wanted to be a painter?

She portrays her youthful self as both hopeful and fearful, comparing herself to the Puerto Ricans, a new batch of refugees to New York, or to the arrivals like Müller, displaced during and after the European war. She offers vignettes: one night, by a window overlooking an airshaft she "stood awed / at the sight of two men making love. I'd not / known how it was done." Here was a young woman, fresh from the farm and working through the odd adjustments and accommodations of any newcomer in the city. Looking back, the now mature, sophisticated New Yorker can admit to her naiveté.

Her poem begins with a reference to an ash tree on the Iowa farm. The thirst for movement had brought her to Columbia and Morningside Heights. She moved away again, fetching up on West 12th Street. At its end, the poem returns to the Iowa ash tree, and also to things that gave solace and stability in her Village studio apartment during her Manhattan years: the catalpa tree in the backyard, and—an important detail for a person who often sympathized more with birds and beasts than with people—"the fluttering fan / of a warbler on the move." Hope gives way to an acknowledgment of mortality and also to anxious, unanswerable questions:

> On West Twelfth Street, the tree is dying:
> the rough, green-napped, huge heart shapes,
> the cigar shapes, the striations at the throat
> of the ruffled corolla, year by year, are
> expiring by inches. The axe is laid
> at the root of the ash tree. The leaves of dispersal,
> the runaway pages, surround us. Who
> will hear? Who will gather
> them in? Who will read them?

The bird, "all but inaudible" and now long gone, and the tree now dying toward the end of the poet's life, followed by the plangent echoes of Rilke's *Duino Elegies*, tell us there will be no more running. Clampitt seems presciently aware of many kinds of endings.

"Sed de Correr" is a sad poem, full of terrors brought up from decades past. Other poems in the book are equally sober but more subdued and, especially considering the self-described "garrulous creature" who made them, laconic. Silence is a major theme, announced in the book's title. Clampitt has begun to move away from words and toward a tacit understanding of meaningless sound, inner light, and the kind of grace she experienced at the Cloisters more than three decades earlier. The opening "Syrinx" has already prepared the reader for these tropes. It explores birdsong, music without meaning, or without meaning for human listeners: no meaning, no syntax, not saying anything, as the wind—just pure breath—says nothing.

And the volume ends with "A Silence," unpunctuated, short lines with no capital letters other than for God and George Fox, the English founder of the Society of Friends. At the end of her life, Amy is returning to her Quaker roots, to the experiences, and the words for those experiences from different religious traditions, that offer an escape from ordinary consciousness. She lists the not-quite-synonymous terms—"revelation," "kif," "nirvana," and "syncope"— for whatever gift might give rise to a vision of "the infinite / love of

God" and produce "great openings." Fox appears three times in the book, a reminder of Clampitt's past and a partial symbol of everything she seemed to be working toward.

At a posthumous tribute to Clampitt at The New School (May 18, 1995), Harold Bloom read and discussed the poem. He mentioned the "canonical splendor" of Clampitt's last two volumes, containing "the uncanny authority for which we thirst." These were always terms of praise in the vocabulary of this high priest of canon-making, who here put Clampitt in the company of Marianne Moore, Elizabeth Bishop, and May Swenson, and also—referring specifically to the last poem in her last volume—placed her "in converse with T. S. Eliot." Bloom's ex cathedra pronouncements indicate how far Clampitt's star had risen in the few years of her presence on the scene.

Bloom, the august and exuberant, larger-than-life scholar, could also display a reverential—or disingenuously modest—side when dealing with an artist he genuinely admired. He wrote Clampitt a letter (July 16, 1994) two months before her death, offering admiration and hope for a social meeting, which of course never occurred. "Dear Amy Clampitt," he begins with polite formality:

> We met a few times in 1990–91 at meetings of the Awards group at the academy [the American Academy of Arts and Letters], but I was feeling shy and awkward and did not tell you how much I loved your poetry. But that was only the first three volumes—*Westward* seemed to me the best poetry since Ms. Bishop's *Geography III*, and I write to thank you now for *A Silence Opens*, which is as powerful. "Manhattan," "Homeland," the magnificent last verse [paragraph] of "Sed de Correr" and "A Silence" haunt me in particular, as does nearly all of *Westward*.
>
> I don't know if your husband is the Harold Korn I have missed badly these many years, or not. If he is, please give him my continued affection. My wife and I tend to be in New York City every weekend from September on, and I would like us all to meet.

The magisterial Bloom has become—like Fritz Weaver, David, Viscount Eccles, and other eminent *personnages*—a modest, even tongue-tied admirer, waiting at the stage door for an autograph from a star.

————

The turn toward something mystical in her poetry was not entirely replicated in Amy's secular life in 1993. She wrote an apology to George Bradley in June for not responding to an earlier letter with her customary alacrity. Landing in the hospital for surgery, and then chemotherapy, she found she was too weak to pick up a book, but enjoyed being read to, "a marvelous lifeline . . . the letters of Diana Cooper and Evelyn Waugh, of all people, and recently a new biography of Ottoline Morell." This is light reading for someone about to head to Lenox "equipped with a Diana Cooperish Italian straw hat." It is what one would imagine for a woman eager for amusing diversion, not a person preparing for death. Perhaps lightness offered the best solace; perhaps she still entertained hope for recovery. She may have been too weak to hold a pen, but a notebook entry (April 28, 1993) contains lines that she later reworked into "The Equinoctial Disturbances," the last of her poems to appear during her lifetime in *The New Yorker*:

> Pain Management arrives
> dressed all in green
> a rosebud in (can morphine
> have invented this?)
> its buttonhole

That same lightness is evident in a poem written around this time, but not published until after Amy's death, in *The New Yorker* (May 22, 1995). The language of "Pot Nomads" refers both to the three potted primulas given as a gift to a sick woman, and to the sick woman herself. "Peripatetic, rooted nowhere really," it begins, appropriately for the woman who called herself a poet of displacement, and who now finds herself "mortgage-bound / to a plot of ground, a hideaway / in the conifers of the Berkshires." A kindly colleague has brought the plants to cheer up the apartment, while Amy is in chemotherapy ("while I / gallivanted elsewhere," she calls her trips to the hospital). She takes them with her to Lenox in March, hoping to plant them but then defeated by a two-foot snowfall. Back they go with her to Manhattan, stranded again but still hardy. In June, the nomadic poet and her trio of primulas return to the Berkshires. She puts them, previously pot-bound, into a flower bed and forgets about them until autumn. Then she rediscovers them. The poem conjures a common destiny for plants and poet:

> . . . in October—windfalls
> thick in the grass, a glory inhabiting
> each of a thousand maples—a feeble
> grubbing at late weeds uncovered
> three stubborn leaf-rosettes, greenly
> holding on. Hothouse origins behind
> them, travels over, roofed under
> by a thatch of mulch, a hood of snow,
> out there, will they (I shiver, thinking)
> make it through the winter?

Perhaps lightness is not quite the word for the tone: chiaroscuro is better. Reading the poem after the author's death, we understand that she is foreshadowing her end, "holding on" and shivering, not knowing whether she will last another season. The flowers may be perennials; the woman is not.

In November, she felt a bit stronger after her seventh round of chemo. She wrote to Philip about her ten-minute appearance at the Poetry Center the previous month. She also felt well enough to do a half-hour reading at the Dia gallery in SoHo with the poet Donald Justice. With other writers, she participated at a Scandinavian Poetry Festival, reading English translations of work by Karl-Erik Bergman, a Swedish poet and fisherman. And she was translating the story of Jason and Medea from Ovid's *Metamorphoses*. She and Hal moved books from West 12th Street to Lenox. All told, they made three short visits to the Berkshires, in June, August, and October, in between her cancer treatments and while awaiting the results of more tests. She was slowing down, but she was not stopping.

———

I found, by serendipity, a copy of *A Silence Opens* in the poet's cottage. It contained a sheaf of five brief pages clearly meant to introduce a reading of poems from the book. To whom? When? Where? We do not know. My guess is that she was appearing before an audience of high school students, and before she read her own work she said a few words about a poem not her own, but one that she was sure her audience knew: "The Road Not Taken." She recalled how much she had liked it as a girl, "the way it sounded. I liked the rhymes." She then worked her way from sound to picture or image, stressing Frost's economy of means and the way that he "withholds a lot" in his coy way. (I was reminded of how much Clampitt withheld of her life from even her first-person poems.) Next, she branched out, considering Michael Ondaatje's *The English Patient*, which she had been reading recently, and the character of a "sapper," the man who defuses unexploded bombs, and who must follow "the different paths of wire" as his mind "travels the path of the bomb fuse," turning and cutting one way and then another. Only after this divagation did Clampitt return to Frost and his paths, reminding us that he was perversely tricky, that he was the last person to give or take inspirational advice, that he was "fooling [his] way along." Before (I assume) the speaker launched into a reading from her own work, she gave a final piece of salutary advice. She told her youthful audience "not to worry too much about what you don't get. And above all, don't look for a message." Clampitt was never a maker or deliverer of messages.

Nor was she interested in symbols that represent other, let alone higher, conditions. She was interested in the things of this world, and how they look, not what they mean. Her last poems clarify something that had been present in her work from the start: her indebtedness both to the prairie of her childhood and to the idea of flatness that it represents. She could never shake off her memory of the prairie despite her interest in other landscapes. The critic Bonnie Costello has observed that Clampitt, like Marianne Moore, often "replaces depth with an at times almost rococo surface." This connects her to Whitman as well as Moore, with both of whom she shared a watchful eye and a listening ear. Whitman's surface was far from rococo, but he, like Clampitt, gazed far and wide in order to notice everything, to take it all in. Another scholar, Angus Fletcher, in his original *A New Theory for American Poetry* (2006), says that most Western religious and philosophical traditions, beginning with Plato, ask us to think transcendentally and vertically, to consider things in nature inferior to, or inadequate representations of, things higher and more important in the spiritual realm. Dante, Milton, and many other religious poets are Platonists through and through. Fletcher proposes another paradigm, represented by the English Romantic poet John Clare, the twentieth-century American poet John Ashbery, and, right between them, Whitman. These writers reject the notion of a great chain of being, or any cosmology that locates perfection in heaven or an afterlife, that relegates the things of this world to a condition of damaged imperfection.

Clampitt honored both paradigms, but ultimately it was the democratic, not the hierarchical, that commanded her allegiance. One remembers her early attachment to Gerard Manley Hopkins, the Jesuit priest who praised God, but primarily for the "pied beauty" and "dappled things," mottled and impure, to be discovered all around us. Like Hopkins, Clampitt rejoices in the things of this world. Like Moore, she sticks happily to surfaces. In "The Spruce Has No Taproot" (*What the Light Was Like*), she favors horizontal, not vertical, movement:

Depth isn't everything: the spruce
has no taproot, but to hold on
spreads its underpinnings thin—

a gathering in one continuous,
meshing intimacy, the interlace
of unrelated fibers
joining hands like last survivors
who, though not even neighbors

hitherto, know in their predicament
security at best is shallow.

This observation has a religious component, and it derives from Clampitt's inherited Quakerism. The inner light is gathered, enmeshed, and spread everywhere. Security may be shallow, but depth isn't everything.

The contest between the horizontal and the vertical has a social analogy. In "The Poet's Henry James," Clampitt quotes the novelist's objection to "the great religion of the elevator," which he discovered on his return from England to his home country in 1904–5. He recorded his impressions in a series of journalistic postings that he gathered together in *The American Scene* in 1907. James was offended by the ubiquity of the elevator—he called it "the sempiternal lift"—which he took as a symbol of secular aspiration and of the gregariousness that seemed the motivating force of his countrymen. Amy had moved from a fifth-floor walk-up to an elevator building in 1973. She understood what high-rise living meant. She accommodated herself to it, but she probably never approved of the great religion of the elevator, any more than she approved of living in a high style.

Whitman again comes to mind. He was happy to be lost in a crowd. He wanted the privacy and loneliness that E. B. White called the great gifts of living in Manhattan. And he remained committed to the horizontal quality of urban living. He was also gregarious and egalitarian in ways James never could be. They make for an unlikely trio: the poet who celebrated ordinary American life, the Anglo-American novelist who depicted the vexed relations between his native soil and his adopted home, and the twentieth-century poet, trying to negotiate a middle path.

One might imagine a different configuration of writers, one that replaces Whitman with Marianne Moore. I have already mentioned Clampitt's refusal to be considered a mere epigone or imitator of Moore, but both poets shared a strong appreciation of James, one of many things that connect them. And I have also observed that all literary criticism is a form of self-analysis. Earlier in her career (May 20, 1986), Clampitt had summarized her thoughts on Moore in a talk at the Chicago Public Library Cultural Center. She expanded them into a 1988 essay that eventually made its way into *Predecessors, Et Cetera* three years later. One sees that paying homage can be a complicated matter. Clampitt could identify with Moore in terms of "natural reticence," and the "aesthetic rigor" and "merciless discipline" (that phrase is borrowed from Anna Pavlova's reminiscence of exercises at the School of Imperial Ballet in St. Petersburg) that each brought to her art. Both poets maintained an ambivalent relationship to Puritanism, a stance of principled removal: "a Puritanism so frankly obliging must by now be almost extinct—which is not to say that the more rankling and troublesome forms of it have ceased to operate." Clampitt admired Moore's combination of "gusto" (a Keatsian quality) and sternness. And, like James, both women were averse to the vulgarity they found in American life, and both were committed to what Elizabeth Hardwick, in an essay on Sylvia Plath, termed a "greed for particulars . . . the true mark of the poetry of women in our time." Moore termed those particulars "observations" in her poems. Clampitt, who called herself "by nature an unruly person," needed, perhaps unconsciously, a similar focus on particulars, as well as the discipline of attention to create her authentic work.

———

A Silence Opens contains a quartet of poems about the seasons, in which Clampitt focuses her eye on the particulars of weather and the palette of nature's colors. These four lyrics are sharply observant, bookish, but they are also, perhaps obliquely, personal. They refer in passing to Dickinson, Thomas Hardy, Chaucer, Dante, and the American biologist George Wald. They also gently echo Robert Frost and James Joyce, but they are not fussy "literary" poems. They are contemplations of seasonal change and they are visual renderings— as if coming from a painter's eye—of scenery. Everything is dealt with equally and equitably. The poems acknowledge change but do not mourn it. They make for a kind of musical offering, each with a different form. "White" is structured in unpunctuated quatrains; "Green" in delicately rhymed quatrains; "Thinking Red" in tercets; and "Nondescript" in six-line stanzas. "White" sounds like an updating of Clampitt's unpublished "Found Objects" from two decades before, repeating the leitmotif of falling snow that covers everything. "Green" is for spring, but it contains reminiscences of the "white" of the preceding poem, and foretellings of the "red" in the following one. (This is one reason that it rhymes: to bring things together.) "Thinking Red" is autumnal. "Nondescript" records the New England Indian summer, "a season / no one would call the fall" whose "gold dust / of pollen and petals" looks back and ahead to spring. Indian summer is itself a Janus-like moment: it is possible only after the first frost has been temporarily succeeded by deceptively warm days. "Nondescript" is a poem of "in-betweenness," of a moment when the "camphor trees' untimely / crimson keeps on coming down, coming down / in the midst of the green."

These are mature poems that, on the one hand, seem to exclude personal references. On the other hand, they cunningly acknowledge the seasonality of human life, one phase merging almost invisibly into the next, and all stages both sequential and blended together. They are Clampitt's equivalent of Keats's "To Autumn," in which the time of harvest is also the occasion for backward and forward glances. Moving beyond the merely personal, as Keats did, Clampitt made her poems even more touching.

———

Amy's health was in serious decline by the end of 1993. In December she wrote to Sister Mary John in England that she was reading and that she enjoyed being read to. She was happy that her Jamaican companion Vivian Banton had come with her and Hal to Lenox, where she cooked for the couple. Mostly her tone is one of gratitude, her usual register: Vivian "is one of those great people who make one feel better just by being there. Hal is well. I can't but consider myself generally lucky in spite of everything."

She attended the annual meeting of the Modern Language Association in Toronto in December, in order to participate in a discussion of Edgar Allan Poe. "Good poet or bad poet or what?" was her assignment, and she accepted the invitation in order to think of him in connection with Dickinson, "another isolated phenomenon." Hal, more fretful than usual, didn't want her to go. They were in Lenox. It was snowing. "I just want to appear somewhere," she said. Karen

Chase inferred that Amy knew this would be her last public appearance. Although the trip was physically hard, Hal and Amy mustered their energy and managed it.

She described the trip in greater detail in a letter to Barbara Clark at the beginning of February. In her writing, at least, she retained her characteristic good humor, in part because Hal was "just so comfy to be domiciled with" and because she was occasionally "able to go out and Make an Appearance fortified by some fantastic piece of millinery (since I have lost all my hair), the latest being a velvet beret with coq feathers. People come to me, totally strangers, to say they love it—it's *that* outrageous." The couple, she writes, has cast their lot with New England's wintry mode: they love the snow and the fireplace by which they sit, and they read aloud "or just beam at each other." The place is homey. Indeed, it is home. For the first time in her life she has her own study, not borrowed, not temporary, and she and Karen Chase have resumed their hunting excursions, one day coming up with a good rug, which she calls—as Dorothy Wordsworth had done almost two centuries before—"a *Turkey carpet*!!!! . . . a kilim in hot colors, along with a nineteenth-century cherry wood table by way of a desk, and a chair that turns out to be Jacobean—if one believes the dealer, and all that carving persuaded me he was to be believed." She is repeating, with similar energy and excitement but with a slightly larger budget, the decorating of the West 12th street studio a half century earlier.

———

By April, things had taken a turn for the worse. But there was still time for a final road trip, to Key West. Amy described it briefly in an April letter to Eileen Berry, one of her students from two years earlier at the Atlantic Center for the Arts. She called it "a delicious few days of exploring, eating fish and absorbing the wonderful light and air." Chase accompanied her on the trip, first by car to New York, then by train to Fort Lauderdale, and finally by car once more, along the length of the Keys. The traveling itself took as long as their three-day stay at the Marquesa Hotel in Key West. Chase painted a picture of a more complicated trip than Amy did. It was the journey, not the arrival, that was the occasion for excitement, the two companions in individual sleeper compartments looking out of their windows and alerting each other to sights on the road: "Kudzu!" or "Iris out!" At one point the train was halted for more than an hour owing to mechanical problems. Amy's response: "I love trains. I can forgive them anything."

Once arrived at their tropical destination, Amy had energy for only several hours of gentle morning activity, after which she rested. Much of the time, Chase found her tentative, even haunted. The two women sat in their room and read Wallace Stevens to each other. His line "The imperfect is our paradise" ("The Poems of Our Climate") resonated in the heat of the Keys. So did "The Idea of Order at Key West," "The Man with the Blue Guitar," and "Of Mere Being," whose evocations of sensuous pleasure warmed and chastened Amy. She knew that such pleasures would not come again, that she was slipping away from all attachments:

> A gold-feathered bird
> Sings in the palm, without human meaning,
> Without human feeling, a foreign song.

Chase also read "Farewell to Florida," about the speaker's desire to leave the South and return to the frozen North. Amy replied, "It's horrible, it's tragic. It's something else, not Florida," trying to understand Stevens's responses to landscape, more complicated than her own. Chase observed, "Her face clouded over, darkened, and then the cloud passed." Amy, always fascinated by water, now refused to go into the ocean, or even into the hotel's swimming pool, "as if the sensuality would have been too painful," Chase conjectured. Amy wanted only to see the ocean and the sky. Looking was enough. She sat still at a picnic table at Fort Taylor Beach, gazing out but going no farther along the shore. At a tourist place to which they had gone in search of Key lime pie, Amy was struck by the whirring fans indoors, and the gentle winds outdoors. She said, "The breeze makes me feel like I'm being made love to." This was a brief moment of solace, of southern comfort.

She had always wanted to live near the ocean. In her interview with Elise Paschen, she said that water had engaged and tempted her from childhood on: "The Greeks associated water with the source of inspiration. Life came from the sea. Being in sight of it puts everything into perspective." In Maine, she had made this dream a reality for at least part of each year, and she turned it into poetry. In Florida, she sat in a window seat at her hotel, wearing a scarf and a flowing white dress. She looked out at the sea; she wrote in her journal. Chase remembered that several days before Amy died, five months later, she said, "The water. There's something complicated about water, and I don't know what it is." She would have agreed with Melville's Ishmael, who says that "meditation and water are wedded forever." At the end, she was still meditating on water, captivated and mystified.

Clampitt had always admired Elizabeth Bishop's poems. Now, given the opportunity to see the house at 624 White Street that Bishop owned from 1938 to 1946, she remained at her hotel and sent Chase on ahead. The sick poet asked her friend to report back to her. "She would want to hear about the world from me," Chase said. For a woman so given to close observation, the decision to experience something vicariously was at least partly a result of fatigue. But in this case, there was something else, a disapproval of Elizabeth Bishop as a person: "She's very elitist and snobby . . . She sold books autographed by friends of hers." (Bishop's biographer Langdon Hammer said he doubted that Bishop ever sold anything except out of dire financial need, and that she probably sold only books by poets she did not particularly like, not those of her friends. Amy had a set, stubborn idea, albeit a misguided one.) As Phoebe Hoss had noticed from their youthful days in the world of Manhattan publishing, Amy could be fiercely judgmental, not necessarily with family and close friends but with people in the public eye, or others whom she didn't know. Mary Jo Salter wrote that she disapproved of people who disapproved of other people, but was often unaware of the paradoxes in her judgments. Familiarity always bred kindness and forgiveness, not the opposite, in her, but strangers could provoke nervousness, or at least wariness. She held celebrities to the highest standards: given their prestige and power, they ought to be, she thought, ethical as well as professional models.

The contradictions in her personality were lifelong. She had once seriously considered becoming a nun; she wanted to be removed and protected from the world. Then she became passionately engaged with political involvement on both the local and the national scenes. Interviewing Karen Chase, Revan Schendler neatly summarized Amy's paradoxes: "She was too sensual to embrace the church and she was too otherworldly to feel completely comfortable in the world."

Other contradictions and reconciliations came alive at the end, when Amy and Hal brought marriage into the equation of their lives together.

———

For most people, slow dying means a gradual closing down and a series of farewells, but Amy also clung to her ongoing work. In June, she signed on to give a reading at Amherst in November, perhaps thinking, according to Salter, "that agreeing would make it more likely she'd live that long." It is as though, at the end, everything she did and said might constitute one of the "great openings" that she mentions in the final poem of her final book. The eager, inveterate traveler was coasting into new territory at home. Once it became clear that chemotherapy and other medical interventions would be of no use, she and Hal settled into the Lenox cottage. In what was probably her last letter, to Eileen Berry in April, Amy mentions her final round of chemo in New York. It left her "very tired—but still hopeful." She spent her last months in Lenox. Spring blossomed into full summer. Then came the faint early touch of autumn, Keats's "season of mists and mellow fruitfulness." Amy watched all of this from her hospital bed, set up in the dining room and overlooking the spacious backyard of her Lenox cottage.

There was also a new development in her personal life.

Parents and children—in this case a mother and her son—can make for a dangerous, perhaps fractious bond. Thus it was for Harold and Nettie Korn. Doris Myers said in an interview that Nettie was always more important to Hal than Amy was. (This was not meant as a compliment to either mother or son.) He was dutiful but, as an only child, often resentful, especially after his father died in 1987. He phoned his widowed mother every day. In a dark moment of rage, he once said Nettie had ruined his life. Sooner or later, a boy grows up or is forced to do so by circumstance. He declares his independence. He asserts himself, but not necessarily by rejecting the mother entirely.

Like all of Amy's friends, Peter Kybart noted the similarities between Nettie and Amy. They were both energetic, enthusiastic, and full of "ardor and fire." Amy became close to her ersatz mother-in-law, and an affectionate bond developed between them, independent of the man who had brought them together. Nettie never got the Jewish daughter-in-law she had wanted. She never got grandchildren. Accepting, she was grateful for what Amy did and was.

Chase said that one day in May, Amy brought up the subject of marriage. It had been on her mind. Karen thought Harold had been afraid to propose marriage for decades because he was still under his mother's thumb. Queried, Amy worried, "Well, I think it's too late," and "I don't know if he would." Ever hopeful, Karen assured Amy it was not too late. A little later that day, Hal came into the room. He did not make a public declaration of fidelity. He did not kneel. Karen stepped aside and watched the event unfold. Conversation between the prospective bride and groom was plain, not dramatic. He made a proposal. It seemed scripted and, simultaneously, spontaneous.

Phoebe Hoss said that the couple always got along like two children. I like to picture their engagement, although inspired by the knowledge of impending death, as a stage comedy starring two nervous, giggling teenagers (that's how Ann Close described them in the short period before the actual ceremony), rushing in and out awkwardly from the wings. It's a delicious image: the meticulous legal scholar beloved by generations of students and the award-winning poet head over heels in giddy adolescent uncertainty. And Karen remembered that they made up their minds on the spot: a precipitous decision following years of successful cohabitation "without benefit of clergy," as an old expression puts it. They now made a stab at the kind of legitimacy they had always possessed in everything but name.

The engagement brought out Amy's girlish side, which had surfaced at other key points throughout her life. When *The Kingfisher* was published, the sexagenarian celebrity poet developed an adolescent crush on an admiring young writer, according to Karen. Maybe this was Fred Turner, her supportive *Kenyon Review* editor, or maybe someone else. Over the years, there were several starry-eyed but probably unrealized, nonexistent romances. Amy flirted; Amy had rich, mostly unrealized erotic phantasies. Remember Bill, "the authentic flower child," who came briefly into Amy's orbit in 1968 and just as abruptly left it? Hal came into her life but he never left it.

The couple made their decision almost twenty-six years after meeting. They wed two weeks later, attended only by the local justice of the peace, Karen, her husband, Paul, and Vivian Banton.

The ceremony had been planned for outdoors, in the garden, but the day was wet and chilly, and the bride found it difficult to stand, so everyone moved inside. The newly married couple mailed out a printed announcement: "Amy Clampitt and Harold Korn /

Vivian Banton, Karen Chase, and Paul Graubard with the bride and groom

Were Married in Lenox Massachusetts / June 2, 1994." A photo captures the jaunty, grinning groom with an open-necked shirt and a boutonniere, standing beside his new bride. She is sitting in their Jacobean chair, smiling broadly beneath the wide brim of a floppy white hat that covers a head made bare by chemotherapy. Karen had bought a dress for her from a local shop. It was made in Nepal, composed of squares of rayon with off-white weavings. Flowers are everywhere: on Amy's hat, in her lap, and behind her in a large vase. Karen had assembled random buttercups, phlox, white astilbe, wild geraniums, yellow globeflowers, honeysuckle, lilacs, miscellaneous wildflowers, and lots of wild grasses picked by the side of the road. The floral miscellany was appropriate for a woman who relished random "junking" expeditions. By her own admission Karen was hardly a cosmetics expert, but she also brought along some makeup for the bride's use. This was Amy Clampitt's final "public" appearance, however intimate and small the audience. The woman who had been ambivalent about the institution of marriage became a June bride, fifty years after many of her classmates had celebrated their nuptials.

By mid-August Amy's health had declined precipitously. Tumors blocked her intestines, and despite three surgeries she could no longer eat. She decided to stay at home in Lenox to die. Karen had gone on vacation to Amsterdam, urged on by the hospice workers who told her that Amy could linger for a long time. She spoke to Amy by phone on August 16. Amy said that, for the first time, she and Hal had talked, the night before, about her death and what might follow it. On September 1, she discussed what music she wanted played at a memorial service—Beethoven's last piano sonata (the Opus 111), subject of her early poem, and some Mozart. She said to Karen, who had by then returned to Lenox, "I can't move. I want to run. Run into the flowers . . . There's so much I want to do, and I don't know if I can do it. What will become of me? I'm in a fog all the time. I can't communicate." The voluble creature was now dependent on others. Always curious, she told Karen, "You look so beautiful. Tell me about the world. Tell me everything."

Phoebe Hoss had also come in August to help out, staying for most of a month in the Chase-Graubard house. Back in New York, on September 5 she wrote to Barbara Blay, Amy's host from her first trip to England forty-five years earlier. She described Amy's decline and her inability to write. The letter continues:

> She's at home, essentially starving to death with no big pain, only occasional discomfort. Her situation is lovely; she lies downstairs in a hospital bed looking out over a long receding landscape of green lawn (the back lawns of several houses) and trees; in the foreground is a busy bird feeder, and a cat occasionally ambles, or stalks, by. Her care is wonderful—the local nurses—and Hal is bearing up . . . So sad as the occasion is, Amy couldn't be in better hands and is slipping away easily and peacefully.

Doris Myers also visited in August with her husband, Tom. She asked Amy if she was in pain. "I don't have pain," she replied, "I have discomfort." Her only nourishment was licks from a popsicle.

The day before Phoebe wrote her letter to Barbara Blay, Amy was strong enough to be wheeled outside, bundled up in a blanket, to enjoy a few hours in the natural world that had always inspired her. Then she began to move in and out of lucidity. Mary Jo visited twice, once with Brad Leithauser and Cynthia Zarin, once with Ann Close. Close had sent Amy the galleys of the latest book by Alice Munro, an author Amy admired, and with whom she said she had "certain things in common . . . Trees. Rivers. Rain. The names of things that grow."

Salter remembered "that was always Amy's special forte, a novelistic one—the amassing and remembering of detail, enjoyed for its own sake . . . On my first visit, with Cynthia, she weakly described for us her circle of local friends, helpers, nurses—and mentioned that a neighbor, 'a retired engineer,' cuts their lawn. Surely I will not, on my deathbed, expend any extra energy in mentioning that a neighbor is a retired engineer."

Phoebe and Mary Jo both said that, at least some of the time, Amy remained alert to her surroundings. The vast yard had many trees in full leaf, a birdbath and a bird feeder, and sometimes a squirrel. "That's what I like about it. There's always something going on," the poet spryly observed. Mary Jo was right: "Only the naturalist she is could have said *that.*" Amy, the born naturalist, remained a curious observer until the end.

The phone rang frequently. Hal fielded the calls, deflecting most of them. He read to his wife a bit from favorite novels. Mary Jo recited Hopkins's "Pied Beauty" and Wordsworth's "A Slumber Did My Spirit Seal." Katherine Jackson drove from Boston with her friend Emily Hiestand several days before the end. They walked into the makeshift downstairs bedroom, and Amy, lying down, excused herself for not getting up. She chuckled: "I always made an awkward bow."

It was meant as a witty, composed gesture. It came from a woman whom her Amherst friend Susan Snively recalled for her "joyous husky laugh," and for the way she clapped her hands "to celebrate a lovely quotation, a joke, or a bit of literary ridiculousness." But the words will bring tears to the eyes of someone who knows their source. Amy was quoting someone else, as she so often liked to do in her poetry. These had been Keats's final written words, in a letter from Rome in November 1820, three months before his death. At the end, Clampitt was paying homage to her first hero, using him to guide her out of life.

That lifelong homage then took a surprising turn. A few days before Amy died, Karen asked her whether she wanted something by Keats read at her service. Her reply was immediate and forceful: "Keats, Keats, I don't want Keats! I don't want to be anywhere near Keats!" This is tantalizing. One wonders what she meant, and why she said this. Keats was the one poet whose work she refused to have read at her burial service. Ann Close suggested that she may have been angry that her first poetic love—who had died so young— could not save her now. Perhaps she identified with him, because she thought that she, too, was dying too young, even at seventy-four, and the identification disturbed her. Her executors also honored this request at the subsequent memorial service in Manhattan. Per- haps, paradoxically, she wanted to take Keats, by herself, with her to the grave. We can only speculate. The last moments of life, the acknowledgment of mortality, required a giving up, and a turning aside. Amy was shedding layers from her past. On her deathbed, she called out to Karen, "Take away all the flowers." Amy, who during her life loved both Keats and flowers, now banished them both. Karen removed the flowers.

No one can predict what he or she will say or do at the end, but we like to think that deathbed words have epigrammatic meaning or existential value, and that the best of them—whether of real or imaginary persons—offer exquisite summaries, or keys to open certain doors. Sometimes they do: "Thomas Jefferson survives"; "*Mehr Licht*"; "The sadness will go on forever"; "Tell them I've had a wonderful life"; or "The horror! The horror!" and "Rosebud." These give the survivors something to hold on to. They add to a legacy; they help with a myth. For the lucky, they may contribute to the appearance of a "good death."

Amy's last words were "I can't breathe." The nurse opened the window. It was as if Amy was revisiting the final lines of "Syrinx" (the first poem in *A Silence Opens*): "the all- / but dispossessed of breath." Language had abandoned this woman of many words. Then her breath gave out. She, too, was dispossessed.

In the "Ode to a Nightingale," Keats had asked for a rich and easy death: "to cease upon the midnight with no pain." This was not his lot in Rome, nor was it Amy's in Lenox. The following day, the death gurgles and hellish sounds began as her lungs filled with fluid. The nurse asked Hal and Karen to leave the room. Hal, already exhausted, took a nap. Karen and Paul went out for supper but then returned, a bit after the death occurred. The hospice workers described the end as anything but peaceful. It came at 8:33 on the evening of Saturday, September 10.

On September 16, the following Friday, a service and burial took place in the backyard. A funeral party paid homage. Between sixty and ninety people attended; accounts vary. Larry Clampitt greeted the guests, and Ann Close acted as an informal emcee. The day was hot but the backyard was shaded. Amy had requested an event held in the spirit of a Quaker meeting, with people speaking spontaneously and from the heart. She asked for readings from the Old Testament (the twenty-third psalm, a passage from Isaiah), poems by

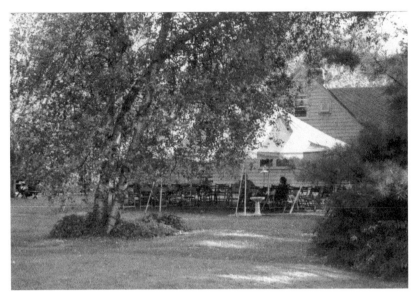

The backyard setting for the service

Wordsworth and Hopkins ("A Slumber Did My Spirit Seal," "Pied Beauty," "The Windhover," "God's Grandeur"), but nothing by Keats. She encouraged people to read anything that they had written themselves. Mary Jo read "Amherst," Clampitt's poem about Emily Dickinson, only to give some context to the Dickinson poems that other people then read at the service. (Clampitt had quoted from ten of these in her particularly dense poem, which is as much Dickinson as Clampitt, and even more convoluted and referential than her Keats sequence.) She forbade all other readings from her own work, a command that Mary Jo obviously ignored. Others may have as well, during the impromptu time of homage and recollection. (Memory plays tricks.)

Philip Clampitt told the story of two-year-old Amy crossing the Mississippi, looking down at it, pointing and exclaiming, "Big drink!" Jeanne Clampitt recalled her children's adoration of Amy Aunt. Larry sang, a cappella, the "Libera me" from Fauré's *Requiem*. To honor Hal, Paul Graubard recited the Hebrew kaddish, the prayer for the dead that never mentions the name of the deceased. Alice Quinn, who shepherded Amy at Knopf, and then at *The New*

Yorker, shouted with gusto and alphabetical precision, "Clampitt, Clare, Coleridge, Crane—Amy, you are there!"

Admirers had come from New York, Amherst, Boston, and the Midwest. There were friends and also luminaries from the literary and publishing worlds. There was a sprinkling of Lenox and Stockbridge neighbors who had become recent friends. It was like a repeat of the publishing party for *The Kingfisher* at the Roosevelt House in Manhattan a decade earlier, but this time the mood was elegiac as well as celebratory. Amy's old boss Jack Macrae, who had negotiated her debut in *The New Yorker*, recalled for the assembly how he had known, after reading Amy's unfortunate attempts at fiction decades earlier, that she was always a poet, not a novelist. He told this story often over the years, taking partial credit for her success. The oldest friends, Phoebe Hoss and Joe Goodman, remembered Amy's early Manhattan days. Phoebe summoned up memories of the 1940s in the West Village when it "was juicy with possibility," and summarized Amy's special gifts: "ardor, a capacity for rapt attention, and unflagging devotion to the life of the mind." Joe, who had met the Clampitt family via the American Friends Service Committee in Mexico in 1944, recalled thinking—like Jack Macrae—all along that Amy was a poet after hearing her read from her never-to-be-published fiction. One of Amy's nurses from the last months said that "Amy giggled when she told me she was getting married."

The larger group dwindled to a smaller one of fifteen people who stayed on to bury Amy's ashes under the birch tree that she had designated. They took turns with the spade: Larry Clampitt, then Jeanne, their daughter Martha, Hal, Marty Townsend (an Amherst friend), Mary Jo, Ann Close, Alice Quinn, Mary Russel, Cynthia Zarin, Brad Leithauser, Karen and Paul, and Phoebe. Hal emptied the ashes from the urn into the ground, and everyone scattered over the ashes rose petals sent by William Logan "for the late bloomer." People then took the spade again, and according to Mary Jo "covered Amy's ashes with the earth. When the intact piece of sod was replaced over it, there was a curious, wonderful sense of *protecting* Amy—as if putting her to bed."

Then it was finished. She had returned to the earth, escorted and honored by friends and family.

THE POSTHUMOUS LIFE

The informal, Quaker-inspired backyard burial in the Berkshires was not the end. A more formal, public event followed three months later. Mary Jo, in conjunction with Hal and Cynthia Zarin, made the arrangements, trying to do justice to what they thought Amy would have liked. One irony would not have been lost on Amy. The site of her memorial on December 5 was the grand Cathedral of St. John the Divine in upper Manhattan, near Columbia University, where she had begun her New York life more than a half century earlier. This had been the church of Bishop Paul Moore, the left-leaning cleric whose refusal to lean even further left infuriated the politically engaged Amy in her days of anti–Vietnam War activism, and caused her to break fully and finally with the Episcopal establishment. That establishment now welcomed her back.

The lengthy service in the massive cathedral was a heterogeneous mix of music, poetry, and religious rituals suitable for the woman whose work and life consisted of a similar blend of traditions, interests, and intense, often self-contradicting passions. Much was a repetition of the more informal Lenox gathering. As a prelude, the choir sang "I Am the Resurrection and the Life." Anglican chants of Psalms 23 and 121 and a reading from "Lamentations" followed. Other prayers were supplemented by Paul Graubard's second recitation (for Hal's benefit) of the kaddish. There was music by Purcell, Fauré, Mozart ("Ave Verum Corpus") and Beethoven, including again the adagio from his last piano sonata, the one that occasioned Clampitt's "Beethoven, Opus 111."

There were poems: Wordsworth's "Intimations Ode," the same trio by Clampitt's beloved Hopkins ("Pied Beauty," "The Windhover," "God's Grandeur") that had been read in Lenox, and six Dickinson lyrics, as well as six Clampitt poems: "Beach Glass," "Amaranth and Moly," "The Sun Underfoot Among the Sundews," "Syrinx," "The Horned Rampion," and "Gooseberry Fool." The organizers knew that the audience would expect to hear the poet's own words, which would gratify and soothe them. Whereas only a single poem of hers was recited in Lenox, in the more public memorial a half dozen, these more accessible, were heard. Some words, some debts, remained unspoken: as in Lenox, Keats was notable by his absence.

The makeup of the lengthy list of readers was no surprise. People wanted to offer homage. Literary eminences, family, and friends all took part. There were the closest relatives: Larry and Jeanne Clampitt, their children David and his sister Martha Merrill, as well as David's pianist friend Norman Carey. Phoebe Hoss represented the stalwart pals from the Old Crowd in the early Village days, when "to be young was very heaven." Mary Russel and Peter Kybart, later additions to the inner circle, joined her. And newer friends, the latest born in Amy's world: Karen and Paul. Naturally, the poets came, like symbolic pallbearers, gentle muses bidding fair peace with lucky words to one of their own: Nicholas Christopher, Henri Cole, Alfred Corn, Anthony Hecht, J. D. McClatchy, Paul Muldoon and his wife, the novelist Jean Hanff Korelitz, Mary Jo, Grace Schulman, and Cynthia Zarin. And the literary figures who helped to pave Amy's path to renown: Lyn Chase, president of the Academy of American Poets, Ann Close, and Alice Quinn. Helen Vendler was prevented at the last minute from participating, by a bomb scare as she was boarding a plane in Boston. Hundreds of mourners, admirers, and fans, people known and unknown, crowded into the church.

Emily Dickinson might have noticed a "certain slant of light" pouring through the windows that winter afternoon. The memorial began at four. It was dark when the cathedral emptied. At least one literary maneuver may have occasioned surprise. Everyone knew Amy's fondness for Hopkins and Wordsworth. Their poems were readily absorbed. But the six poems by Dickinson, none of them among her most famous or accessible, must have sounded new to many people in the pews. Alice Quinn thought Amy had chosen them herself, and she was partly right. The poems are all part of the group contained in Clampitt's Dickinson poem, "Amherst," which Mary Jo Salter had read in Lenox. This particular sestet reveals, at second hand, implicit resemblances between the twentieth-century poet being mourned and celebrated and the recluse of Amherst, a virtual unknown until she was discovered, or resurrected, long after her death.

I like to imagine the six Dickinson poems as Clampitt's final autobiography-at-one-remove, figuring her life in the words of a much-loved predecessor. There's birdsong ("To hear an Oriole sing," Dickinson #526), but the tune is in the listener, not in the bird. In #530, there's an irrepressible inner fire ("You cannot put a fire out") and a congruent outpouring ("You cannot fold a Flood— / And put it in a drawer"). Like Dickinson, Clampitt knew that "fold" is already folded into "flood," and she would have appreciated her predecessor's serious playfulness when describing containment and explosion. In poem #593 ("I think I was enchanted") Dickinson commits herself to the transforming power of poetry when she hears a new voice, in this case Elizabeth Barrett Browning's. Amy had many such revelations, beginning when she was a schoolgirl coming to poetry for the first time. Dickinson's language would also have appealed to her for how it prefigures her experience at the Cloisters when she was touched by grace and had lost all sense of self. Dickinson:

> Whether it was noon at night
> Or only heaven at noon
> For very lunacy of light
> I had not power to tell.
>
> I could not have defined the change—
> Conversion of the mind
> Like sanctifying in the Soul—
> Is witnessed—not Explained

Thus, the first Dickinson trio, two shorter lyrics building to a third, longer, more excited one.

The pattern repeats itself in the next three poems. "The battle fought between the Soul" (#594) reminds us how both Dickinson and Clampitt internalized the language of warfare and struggle, aware of contemporary political and historical currents, and were able to portray an internal "bodiless campaign" as turbulent as any actual battle. It is as if Amy wanted the world to remember that she, too, was involved in great actions, protest marches on the street and emotional upheavals within. "Like mighty footlights burned the red" (#595) applies the language of stagecraft and theatricality to religious revelation. And last, the longest, and most mysteriously erotic, "Again his voice is at the door" (#663). An unidentified, almost spectral suitor, a familiar figure throughout Dickinson's poetry, returns, a lover both bodily and celestial. For Amy, he is perhaps the sum total of all the men who courted her, or whom she flirted with as a young woman before she settled into domestic comfort with her partner of a quarter century. These are the men whom we barely know—sometimes only by their first names, or through references in Amy's journals, or in the letters and memories of family members and friends. The suitor may also shadow the men on whom, as an adult, she had her passing crushes. I like to think he also embodies young John Keats, the first poet whom she loved and whom, at the end, she sent packing.

Clampitt tells her own story, often guardedly, in her poems. At her memorial service—at both of them, rather—she had arranged for a retelling of that story through the words of another poet. And the words, articulated, came through the actual voices of living poets and other friends. In a posthumous collaboration with her executors and survivors, Amy left a reminder of herself, but she also subsumed her individual identity into a commitment to our common lot. This is what funerals, as well as poems, should do. They produce what she had called in "Botanical Nomenclature" "the mirroring / marryings of all likeness." For Clampitt, it was the mirroring of and with Dickinson that best brought out her likeness. An unpublished essay, parts of which she folded into "The Theatrical Dickinson," includes a list of qualities that seems as much a description of herself as of her predecessor: "Hyperbolic extremes: maidenly timidity and the brandishing of the loaded gun; the desire for fame and the retreat into obscurity; the archly cute and the sublime." The sentence makes for a double epitaph as well as a double, mirrored, homage.

———

Peter Kybart recalled that throughout the summer before her death Amy kept scanning newspapers and journals for reviews of *A Silence Opens*, and was disappointed to find none. Like Keats, she was perhaps afraid that her name would be writ in water. She need not have worried. The poetry world is not committed to timeliness. The reviews came, most of them too late for the author to read the words of praise. A few short ones did appear while she was alive, but perhaps she missed them. Others came later still, acknowledging her death or recognizing, as her editor Ann Close had a year earlier, that death itself haunts the volume, just as silence seems to triumph over speech.

In *The New York Times* (May 15, 1994), Patricia Hampl wrote, presciently, that "silence is an entrance to poetry, not its absence. And here, at the hinge of silence and song, Ms. Clampitt ends her quest, having gone as far as language can go." In the summer 1994 issue of the *Southern Review*, Robert Hosmer praised the "exquisitely sensitive exploration of where and how the mysterious intersects with the ordinary . . . mortality weighs heavily on her poems [but there's] nothing morbid." That fall, other notices appeared: one by Clampitt's British supporter Jim McCue in the *Times Literary Supplement*; another by Robert Shaw in *Poetry*; a brief mention in *The New Yorker*.

Most interestingly, a piece by the poet-scholar John Hollander appeared in *The New Republic*, on September 19. Amy might have seen this before it was published, said Salter, who was the poetry editor of *TNR* at the time. She thought she might have shown her dying friend a copy right before it was published. Hollander awkwardly tried to ally Clampitt with W. H. Auden, who was never a real stylistic influence, but he hit on something more important that unquestionably connects the two poets: "the life of the mind as the life of the heart," and "cultural and historical fact" as "authentically part of nature." For three bookish, intellectual poets—Auden, Clampitt, Hollander—reading and thinking are the essence, not the antithesis, of what Keats called "the true voice of feeling."

Three years after her death, Knopf published Clampitt's *Collected Poems*. Her reputation was still secure. It is a rare thing for *The New York Times Book Review* to put a poet on its front page, but the lead article on November 9, 1997, was Christopher Benfey's glowing appraisal of the book and of Clampitt's career. He was well aware of her tics: "She is in love with hyphens, parentheses, dashes—anything that melts words together. She likes parts of words, even individual letters, to drip into the waiting dish of the next stanza." He specified where he thought she had failed, especially in "the stiff-necked . . . well-researched biographical tributes" to the Wordsworths, George Eliot, Margaret Fuller et al. (Other readers, like me, would disagree with him here.) In a wonderful phrase, he called her helpful scholarly notes "a commonplace book of magpie reading, a nomad's roaming of the library," and categorized the final poems in *A Silence Opens* as "a perceptible scaling back, a renunciation." The review was enthusiastic and fair. Benfey's enumerating of what he took to be Clampitt's stylistic flaws in no way impeded his appreciation of her strengths.

Benfey was not alone in his enthusiasm. Equally favorable notices appeared in *The Economist*, *The Nation*, *Poetry*, *Sewanee Review*, and elsewhere. A lengthy essay by the poet Daniel Hall appeared in *Parnassus: Poetry in Review* (1999), and it's worth quoting from, not least as a careful riposte to the attacks that had been leveled at Clampitt over the previous two decades:

> She has been dismissed as an embroiderer, a versifying beach-comber, when a list of her obsessive concerns would include war, poverty, environmental devastation, the oppression of women, and the clash of individual and culture. She was in the truest sense a political poet, the likes of which we haven't seen since Lowell; that is, a poet deeply engaged with the world and with history, but whose first and last loyalty is to language. The famous "weaknesses"—the gushing and redundancy, the baroque convolutions—turn out to be a small price to pay; some readers even allow themselves to take pleasure in them.

Few other reviewers had commented on the depth of her political engagement that accompanied her loyalty to language. And Hall announced her stand-alone eminence:

> She's been called regressive, but what period do people imagine she's a throwback to? She is one of a small group of poets who are maddeningly unplaceable, freaks of time, alumni of no known

school—in a word, unique. It may have been her oddity that kept her searching the world, and the world of art, for a niche, or at least a place to stand.

In England, a bit earlier, Blake Morrison had reviewed *Westward* and suggested that Clampitt was the first American poet since Robert Lowell to provide continuities between America and the United Kingdom, to bring two artistic communities back to speaking terms with each other, to offer a "hopeful version of the relationship between Old World and New." He was grateful for an American poet whom the British could finally take to, if only because she was an Anglophile at heart. In *The Observer*, the British psychologist and cultural critic Adam Phillips also offered a positive review of the *Collected Poems*. He was especially attentive to her echoes and borrowings: "You can hear Clampitt so distinctively among the jostle of voices, partly because her pleasure in being influenced is palpable. Undaunted by being so possessed, her poetry is remarkable for its subtle self-possession." (Still, as I have mentioned, no British edition of *A Silence Opens* ever appeared.)

Extending the transatlantic commerce, Vendler wrote appreciatively about the *Collected Poems* in the *London Review of Books*. And cementing his own quirky commitment to an American aesthetic, Bloom expatiated in *The Yale Review*. He was never shy about inventing or revising his own canon. Clampitt was now part of it:

> Between Elizabeth Bishop and the generation of John Ashbery, A. R. Ammons, and James Merrill, the principal American poets are Wilbur, Swenson, and Clampitt—in my judgment . . . Clampitt is a poet who at her best joins Marianne Moore, Elizabeth Bishop, and May Swenson as a great maker in the tradition that includes Emily Dickinson and Wallace Stevens.

Clampitt had taken a seat in Bloom's visionary company of poets in the high Romantic pantheon.

Literary critics and historians seek, and also create, connections. They want to figure out who leads on to, or away from, whom. They want to see lines of influence, of order, of originality and swervings. Unacademic readers are probably more in tune with Daniel Hall's estimation of Clampitt's odd originality. Another young poet, Tess Taylor, wrote on the Poetry Foundation website in 2011 (almost two decades after Clampitt's death) that she feared Clampitt had been forgotten. But Taylor also acknowledged the "secret devotion" of some of her contemporaries, people afraid to admit their guilty pleasure: "it's a shame to think of her as forgotten, forgettable, or less than remarkable. It's too quick, as some do, to dismiss her flights of syntax as some kind of doilied grandmotherly festooning. In fact, Clampitt is exactly the kind of grandmother we all might learn from."

In my prologue to this biography, I quoted a friend who long ago said that reading lots of Clampitt's work was like eating a meal composed entirely of desserts. In other words, *de gustibus non est disputandum.* The motif of reading as nourishment goes back, in English at least, to Francis Bacon's 1625 essay "Of Studies" and his much-quoted aphorism that "some books are to be tasted, others to be swallowed, and some few to be chewed and digested." Bacon was not as interested in the substance of the meal as he was in its quantity. Images of food and nourishment have always worked their way into the language of Clampitt's reviewers. Discussing *The King-fisher*, mostly favorably, Peter Stitt allowed that "reading it is a bit like eating a gallon of bouillon at one sitting; you are filled up and feel heavy, but an hour later wonder where all that substance has gone" (*Georgia Review*). In another positive review (of *Westward* in *Poetry*), Alfred Corn observed that Clampitt's large vocabulary can sometimes have an overwhelming effect: "Now and then it seems excessive, smothering the content as a thick sauce can ruin a nice piece of fish." Robert Shaw called *A Silence Opens* "a cornucopia out of control," although he meant this as a compliment. And even Tess Taylor admitted that Clampitt can feel precious, "her velouté-filled poems like a fetishized carrot on a 1980s dinner plate." That last image suggests why Clampitt's gifts were out of step with certain aesthetic trends of her decade. The big dinner plate with an exquisite scallop covered in foam with a garniture of a dainty, well-placed piece of greenery, or a single raviolo topped with a drop of caviar and a soupçon of crème fraîche was a haughty dismissal of the large, rich French meals American tourists like Amy had rushed to the Continent to experience decades earlier. Nor was her poetry the equivalent of a health-crazed macrobiotic, vegetarian, or vegan diet. If anything, it was a hearty boeuf bourguignon, transforming ordinary ingredients into a substantial, perhaps noble creation greater than the sum of its parts, and guaranteed to satisfy. She took the words of the English language—some of them ordinary, some of them borrowed or unusual—and arranged them in ways no one had ever thought of before.

———

Other deaths followed. Amy's sister, Beth, confined for decades to health facilities, died in November 1994, two months after her sister. Nettie Korn died five years later. Hal hung on for seven years after Amy's death. He continued to use the Lenox cottage as a retreat from New York, sometimes for extended periods. Weijia Li, a Chinese professor at Amherst College, befriended him in his last years, seeing him in Manhattan and Lenox. She had met him through his Columbia Law School colleagues. She recalled to me his utter devotion to Amy's memory, and also his ongoing compulsion to listen to jazz on his cassette tapes. He required music in the living room in Lenox. And even in summer, he wanted a fire. He would ask Li to run into town to buy copies of *The New York Times* on a Sunday morning, and having read the news, he then used the paper as kindling for the fire they would sit in front of during the afternoon and evening, Miles Davis streaming from the (even then) antiquated cassette machine.

In his last year, a young Lenox woman "of slight acquaintance" proposed marriage to him: "You know, it's not every year I am proposed to. I really need time to think about it," he said with a grin. He died of esophageal cancer at seventy-one on March 27, 2001. A paid death notice appeared in *The New York Times* the following day. It mentioned his parents and Amy, and continued, "Lover of life, learning, work and the arts. He worked on his groundbreaking articles until the day he was admitted to the hospital." On April 14, a formal obituary appeared in the same paper, and it specified his ongoing, never-ending work: "At his death he was finishing a book, 'Modern Conflicts of Law and Jurisdiction' that discusses revisions of law necessitated by changes in modern life, like lightning communications technology, a global economy, and major toxic spills." Ann Close, Alice Quinn, Mary Jo Salter, and Cynthia Zarin attended his memorial service on May 21 at the Columbia Law School. Judge Weinstein spoke, as did one former student, along with Hal's old colleague Hans Smit and his first cousin Helen Korn Atlas. Hal was buried in a plain pine box according to the strict Jewish custom, beside his parents, in a Jewish cemetery in Queens. In death, he honored his father and his mother, respecting their religious beliefs, which he did not necessarily share. He and Amy went their separate ways, he to his forebears, with the kaddish being chanted, and she to the earth, with flowers scattered over her after an informal Quaker meeting.

Hal's final legacy was the creation of a fund in Amy's name. He deeded the country cottage to the use of other writers. This was the home in which he and Amy had lived briefly but contentedly as a couple, and which he visited as a widower. Since 2003, writers—most of them poets—have been granted residencies at the house. Clampitt's books are still there, as are the Turkey carpet, the Jacobean chair, and other random objects, the accumulated "junk" Amy had assembled from her improvised shopping expeditions. Like a protective spirit or a nomadic transplant from West 12th Street, a catalpa tree stands in the backyard, offering shade and protection.

Most people leave material possessions to their heirs when they die, through which they live on, at least for a time, in the memories of those who survive them. Artists leave their work as well. If the maker is lucky, these bequests will communicate a human presence to an audience that extends beyond an immediate circle of friends and family. Clampitt fans still exist, usually older people who remember having read her during her years of prominence. In November 2019, visiting London, I found myself on a drizzly afternoon in one of the quirkily intimate, dusty bookstores—now rapidly disappearing—near Charing Cross Road, which often contain obscure items or things one never knew one wanted until coming upon them. The proprietor was a tall woman in her early eighties, with piercing blue eyes, white hair tied up in a chignon, and a complexion we call English Rose. I was looking for a copy of the English edition of *The Kingfisher*. The woman lit up. Although she didn't have the book, she exclaimed, "Amy Clampitt? I named my cat after her."

Amy Clampitt's legacy is her poetry, not "improbable and perfectly natural," like her life as we look back on it, but inevitable and dazzlingly wrought. As we've seen, the poems are often self-portraits at one remove. In "The Horned Rampion" (*A Silence Opens*), a late and especially poignant autobiography-by-proxy, Clampitt uses a flower as a stand-in, presenting herself, we might say, botanically. In seven six-line stanzas—in which the word "I" appears only twice—the poet describes coming upon something she'd never seen before, in the "entrancingly perpendicular / terrain" of Bellagio, during her 1991 stay in the Italian Lake District. She is susceptible to the opening of some new "marvelous / thing." And she finds something previously unknown to her, which piques her always intense curiosity:

> ... spurred,
> spirily airy, a sort of
> stemborne baldachin,
> a lone, poised,
> hovering rarity, hued
>
> midway between the clear
> azure of the rosemary
> and the aquilegia's
> somberer purple,
> that turned out to be
> named the horned rampion.

One day the flower is singular, alone and poised; the next day it has multiplied and become so ordinary that she calls it "the mere horned rampion." Then it passes entirely from her mind.

This little plant, *Phyteuma scheuchzeri*, a member of the campanula family, thrives in rock gardens. It has spiky purple clusters of violet-blue flowers. (In a 2002 interview, Amy's student, the poet Patricia Carlin, used "spiky" to describe her teacher.) Low to the earth, it reaches up out of the low mounds of its blue-green leaves. An Alpine plant, it grows in crevices, and would be easy to overlook in isolation. The Smart Seeds Emporium (found online) calls it "bizarre, but charming."

What follows in the poem should not come as a surprise. The woman who was always committed to etymology, nomenclature, research, and libraries has temporarily forgotten all about the little rock plant she chanced upon, until a later day when she pulls down from the shelf a volume of the *Encyclopaedia Britannica*. It falls open, at random, to one page . . .

> . . . and there was
> the horned rampion, named
> and depicted, astonishing
> in memory as old love
> reopened, still quivering.

Everything happens, and then happens again in a different register, first in life and then in writing. "Named and depicted" is the surprising phrase. For centuries, people, Amy Clampitt among them, used to press dried flowers between pages in books. A different kind of poet might have offered the experience of finding nature brought indoors this way. Clampitt goes in a more unexpected direction: she finds not an actual flower but only its name and its picture. But for her, nature at one remove is nature still.

Stéphane Mallarmé, the French symbolist poet, proclaimed that "le monde est fait pour aboutir à un beau livre": the world is made to end up in a beautiful book. We might say something similar. Amy Clampitt created "un beau livre" out of her life and out of all the phenomena she witnessed and read about. A flower may offer an occasion, however fleeting, for a self-portrait. Like her newfound plant, Amy, too, was "spirily airy . . . a lone, poised, / hovering rarity." She saw the horned rampion first outdoors, a serendipitous experience.

Its color alone would strike her, perhaps because it reminded her of the violets she had seen on the family farm when she was not quite three and her brother Larry had just been born. (She may also have been thinking of Wordsworth's "violet by a mossy stone, / Half hidden from the eye," something easily overlooked but, once encountered, unforgettable.) Then she found it again, and also by chance, indoors, in a massive encyclopedia tome, "named and depicted." We might call these revelations "firsthand" and "secondhand" were it not that, for Clampitt, a library was as rich and fertile, as natural as a mountain rock garden. Her fortuitous encounters with a flower, and then with a book, end in an erotic charge. It is as if the poet has been provoked by the memory of an old love to give herself up, once more, to the occasion, and to him. Like all the flowers she saw, loved, and remembered as a child, and then used as poetic material, and like the primulas she carried with her from Manhattan to Lenox in "Pot Nomads," the horned rampion becomes an object for description that allows her to recover, viscerally, an earlier part of her life.

In her 1991 review of *Westward*, Helen Vendler wrote that landscape was "the refuge to which, for its serenity, its visual variety, its biological laws, [Clampitt] turns" in order to resolve the troublesome questions she faced in her social, familial, and personal life. Almost as a secondary consideration, Vendler mentions the importance of reading in the poet's life, but added that nothing "ever gave her the pure wordless solace of the earth's changing sights and sounds . . . Landscape was for Clampitt the first aesthetic realm." Landscape probably came first—in the child's earliest years—but we know that she was also a very young reader; if the indoor activity was second chronologically it was never second in importance. Nature was an early teacher. So was the library. Both were partners in the poet's imaginative life, right from the start.

As is true for many writers, we can best take the measure of this poet's life by reading what she read (and how she read, or what she did with her reading), and then reading what she wrote (and studying how she wrote). The writer who had said in 1985 that what she most wanted to do was "*name* things" rather than tell stories, spent her creative maturity accumulating such names and things—often arranging them in lists—and occasionally forgoing the verbs that might help a reader hear a narrative constructed along conventional lines. But for those readers who, schooled by Clampitt, learn to follow stories told obliquely, the *Collected Poems*, her "beau livre," grants equal access to the writer and to her world. These poems are the writer's best biography.

Informants

The following individuals are the most prominent of the people whose testimony I have relied on in my book. Some of them were interviewed by Revan Schendler in 2007. A few years earlier (2002), Clampitt's actor friend Peter Kybart conducted another handful of interviews. Her Lenox friend and neighbor, the poet Karen Chase, conducted several others. And in preparation for this book, I had discussions, meetings, and correspondences with still other individuals. I am offering their names and some information about them here.

HAROLD BLOOM (1930–2019): Literary critic and Sterling Professor of Humanities at Yale University who, along with Helen Vendler, was one of Clampitt's earliest and most enthusiastic champions. In an appreciative essay in *The Yale Review*, Bloom called "A Hermit Thrush" "certainly one of the great American love poems of this century" and named Clampitt, along with Richard Wilbur and May Swenson, a "principal American poet" of her generation.

RACHEL BROWNSTEIN (1937–): Professor of English, Emerita, at Brooklyn College, CUNY. Clampitt dedicated an unpublished poem ("The Ordeal of Civility") to her and her husband, Shale (1933–2018), a psychiatrist friend of Hal's, on the occasion of attending a lecture by Harold Bloom.

PATRICIA CARLIN: Poet and professor, Emerita, at The New School who studied poetry with Clampitt at the Poetry Center of the 92nd Street YMHA. In an interview, she recalled Amy's "somewhat birdlike" movements and "girlish" manner.

KAREN CHASE (1943–): Poet, essayist, and fiction writer who met Clampitt in Italy in 1991 and became a close friend. Chase introduced Clampitt to Lenox, Massachusetts, where the poet bought a summer house and spent her final years.

NICHOLAS CHRISTOPHER (1951–): Poet, novelist, Columbia professor, and friend of Clampitt's. One of the many notable poets who attended her memorial at the Cathedral of St. John the Divine.

DAVID CLAMPITT (1951–): Clampitt's favorite nephew, the eldest son of Lawrence and Jeanne Clampitt. A musician and musicologist, professor in the Music Department at the Ohio State University.

LAWRENCE (1923–2017) and JEANNE CASWELL CLAMPITT (1926–2018): The eldest of Clampitt's three (younger) brothers, Larry was an electrical engineer, an accomplished tennis player, and a sailing enthusiast.

PHILIP (1930–) and HANNA DEUTSCH CLAMPITT (1933–): Clampitt's youngest brother, an academic zoologist and peace activist. In a letter to Philip, Clampitt recalls her baptism "of light" at the Cloisters, one of the defining events in her development as a poet.

ANN CLOSE: Clampitt's second editor at Alfred A. Knopf. She oversaw Clampitt's final three books, beginning in 1987 when Alice Quinn left Knopf for *The New Yorker*.

DANIEL GABRIEL (1946–): Poet, playwright, and Clampitt's teacher at The New School in the fall of 1977, who introduced her to the work of Charles Olson.

ALLAN GURGANUS (1947–): Novelist who met Clampitt at Yaddo, where they bonded over the poetry of Thomas Hardy in January 1986.

JANET HALVERSON: Along with Phoebe Hoss, an important friend from Clampitt's early days at Oxford University Press, where she worked as a book designer.

PHOEBE HOSS (1926–2017): Author, editor, translator, and Clampitt's oldest and longest-standing New York friend, who worked at the Oxford University Press. Clampitt dedicated the poem "Manhattan," from *A Silence Opens*, to her.

KATHERINE JACKSON (1943–): Poet and artist who studied with Clampitt in 1992 at the Atlantic Center for the Arts. She remembered her "lightness of touch" in the classroom, and they remained close until Clampitt's death.

JEAN HANFF KORELITZ (1961–): Novelist, playwright, and poet married to Irish poet Paul Muldoon. In an interview, Clampitt told Korelitz that her "first ambition was to be a painter."

PETER KYBART (1939–): German-born American actor—known for his roles in *Inside Man*, *The Good Shepherd*, and *Miracle at St. Anna*—who was one of Clampitt's close friends and traveling companions. He coached her before her first open-mic poetry readings and was with her on the train trip from Saloniki to Munich that inspired "Babel Aboard the Hellas International Express," in *Archaic Figure*. Kybart remembered, "I don't think I ever saw Amy in bad spirits, never in a bad mood."

JOHN (JACK) MACRAE (1931–): Editor at E. P. Dutton, where he was Clampitt's boss, and later at Henry Holt. Without telling Clampitt, Macrae sent her poems to Howard Moss at *The New Yorker*, which led to the publication of "The Sun Underfoot Among the Sundews" in that magazine and sparked the poet's career.

SISTER MARY JOHN (née Anne Marshall) (1940–): The former Mother Superior at St. Mary's of Kent, in West Malling, England, who met Clampitt in 1956 at a Sunday service at St. Luke's Chapel. Marshall, Doris Thompson Myers, and Clampitt comprised a trinity of friends during the poet's religious period in New York.

PATRICIA MORRISROE (1951–): Journalist, novelist, and biographer known for her biography of Robert Mapplethorpe. For a 1984 profile in *New York* magazine, Clampitt told her, "Intensity doesn't always have to be centered on unhappiness."

DORIS THOMPSON MYERS (1934–2019): Along with Anne Marshall (later Sister Mary John), one of the Manhattan trio of friends during Clampitt's religious period and the dedicatee of "Rain at Bellagio," in *The Kingfisher*. The death, in a car crash, of Myers's twenty-year-old son, Andrew, inspired Clampitt's poem " 'Eighty-Nine," in *A Silence Opens*.

MAXINE PHILLIPS (1947–): Journalist, social worker, and friend of Clampitt's from political circles. They were both booked into the 100th Street Precinct House for taking part in a 1971 protest (in which they were the only white women present) by the Village Friends of Welfare Rights. She stayed with social activism, serving as national director of the Democratic Socialists of America, and later as executive editor of *Dissent* magazine.

ALICE QUINN: Editor of Clampitt's first two books at Alfred A. Knopf (where she worked from 1972 to 1987), and former poetry editor of *The New Yorker* (1987–2007), where she succeeded Howard Moss. Additionally head of the Poetry Society of America (2001–2019).

MARY JO SALTER (1954–): Poet and Krieger-Eisenhower Professor, Emerita, at the Johns Hopkins Writing Seminars. She became a longtime friend of Clampitt's when, in 1979 and at the age of twenty-four, she wrote the older poet a fan letter while working as a poetry reader for the *Atlantic Monthly*, to which Clampitt had submitted poems. The two maintained a close correspondence until Clampitt's death, and Salter edited both the *Collected Poems* and *Selected Poems*.

EMILY TODD (1967–): One of Clampitt's students at Amherst College, where she took the new professor's course on Wordsworth and His Circle. She remembered sensing "greatness in the room" and years later conducted a mail interview with the poet for *Verse*.

She became a professor of English and a dean at Westfield State University in Massachusetts.

FREDERICK TURNER (1943–): Anglo-American poet and editor who published Clampitt's poems in the *Kenyon Review* and considered her "one of the most important poets in America."

HELEN VENDLER (1933–): Literary critic and Arthur Kingsley Porter University Professor, Emerita, at Harvard. Along with Harold Bloom, one of Clampitt's fiercest early supporters. In her influential review of *The Kingfisher* in the *New York Review of Books*, Vendler praised Clampitt's "beautiful, taxing poetry" and predicted that the book would be read for centuries to come for "its triumph over the resistance of language."

FRITZ WEAVER (1926–2016): American actor known for his roles in *The Legend of Lizzie Borden* and the miniseries *Holocaust*. In 1984, Weaver wrote Clampitt an enthusiastic fan letter, beginning a correspondence that lasted until the poet's death.

Notes and Sources

The quotations in this biography come from both published sources and, equally, from unpublished ones.

The preponderance of Amy Clampitt's poetry appears in *The Collected Poems of Amy Clampitt* (New York: Alfred A. Knopf, 1997). This book brings together her five earlier Knopf volumes: *The Kingfisher* (1983), *What the Light Was Like* (1985), *Archaic Figure* (1987), *Westward* (1990), and *A Silence Opens* (1994). I have quoted generously from these poems without specifying page numbers in the body of my text.

Three previously uncollected Clampitt poems, "The Equinoctial Disturbances," "Pot Nomads," and "The Winter Bird," along with excerpts from an earlier, never-published poem, "The Sun on the Stone," appeared in *Selected Poems*, edited by Mary Jo Salter (New York: Alfred A. Knopf, 2010).

In addition, there are two early Clampitt chapbooks: *Multitudes, Multitudes* (New York: Washington Street Press, 1973); and *The Isthmus* (New York: Coalition of Publishers for Employment, Inc., 1981). I have quoted from these poems in the text, without specifying page numbers.

Other Clampitt works from which I have quoted are:

Love, Amy: The Selected Letters of Amy Clampitt, edited by Willard Spiegelman (New York: Columbia University Press, 2005), hereafter *Letters*. I have repeated, revised, and modestly repurposed some sentences from my introduction to the *Letters* in the opening section of this biography.

Predecessors, Et Cetera: Essays (Ann Arbor: University of Michigan Press, 1991), hereafter *Predecessors*.

Two privately printed family memoirs are:

Frank T. Clampitt. *Some Incidents in My Life: A Saga of the "Unknown" Citizen.* 1933.
Roy Clampitt. *A Life I Did Not Plan.* 1966.

I quote from these throughout, without page numbers.

As I mention in my prologue, all of Clampitt's papers are or will be housed at the Henry W. and Albert A. Berg Collection of English and American Literature, New York Public Library, Astor, Lenox, and Tilden Foundations. In addition to the eighty-six boxes of organized material already there, there are many other things in the thirty-two boxes that were stored in Adams, Massachusetts, from 2001 until 2021. These have yet to be catalogued. In the following notes, quotations from the catalogued materials are cited as "Clampitt Papers. Box X, Folder Y." Anything not yet in the files is cited as "Clampitt Papers. Additions."

Throughout these pages I have quoted from interviews conducted by Karen Chase (1996, 2002), Peter Kybart (2001–2), and Revan Schendler (2007–8). These, too, will all come to the Berg Collection. Unless otherwise noted, all quotations attributed to the following people are taken from these interviews: Regina and Stephen Banks, Patricia Carlin, Karen Chase, David Clampitt, Lawrence and Jeanne Clampitt, Philip and Hanna Clampitt, Ann Close, Janet Halverson, Margot Honig, Phoebe Hoss, Peter Kybart, Sister Mary John (née Anne Marshall), Doris Thompson Myers, Alice Quinn, Mary Russel, Mary Jo Salter.

PROLOGUE: ASSEMBLING A LIFE

10 "the happiest times": "Amy Clampitt: The Art of Poetry, XLV," *Paris Review* 126 (Spring 1993): 80. Interviewed by Robert E. Hosmer. Hereafter *Paris Review*.
10 "I believed": *Paris Review*, 83.
12 "What I see": *Paris Review*, 91.
12 "the dangerous qualities": Quoted in Karen Chase's interview with Sister Mary John, née Anne Marshall, in England (1996).
16 "I feel as if": *Letters*, 53.
17 "a writer is what": *Letters*, 88.

17 "I've yearned secretly": *Letters*, 199.

18 "solitude": *Letters*, 103.

18 "I made a real try": *Letters*, 99.

19 "hair is neatly tucked": Patricia Morrisroe, "The Prime of Amy Clampitt," *New York* magazine (October 15, 1984), 46. Hereafter Morrisroe.

20 "There were several": *Letters*, xvii.

21 "It is out": "Openhearted: Stanley Kunitz and Mark Wunderlich in Conversation," Poets.org (October 11, 1997), https://poets.org/text/openhearted-stanley -kunitz-and-mark-wunderlich-conversation. Originally from *American Poets*, published by the Academy of American Poets (1997).

23 Jack Macrae: Author's interview with Jack Macrae (July 9, 2019).

23 "the delight": *Paris Review*, 101.

23 In another interview: Jean Huesgen and Robert Lewis, "An Interview with Amy Clampitt," *North Dakota Quarterly* 58, no. 1 (1990): 119–28. Hereafter *NDQ*.

IOWA

33 "the mentality": "Providence," in *Townships*, ed. Michael Martone (Iowa City: University of Iowa Press, 1992), 33. Hereafter "Providence."

33 "Everybody who is ambitious": "What Amy Clampitt Was Like: An Interview with Jean Hanff Korelitz," *The Honest Ulsterman* (Spring/Summer 1986): 41–51. Hereafter Korelitz.

34 "She was like": Author's interview with Cynthia Zarin.

39 "as one of the fortunate": *Letters*, 224.

39 "shy eminence": *Letters*, 247.

39 "not so much because": Clampitt Papers. Box 16, Folder 2.

39 "I'm afraid I have": Clampitt Papers. Box 30, Folder 5.

40 "It is the twenty-sixth": "Providence," 32–33.

41 "By the time": "Providence," 32.

41 "There had been a drought": *Letters*, 216.

43 "What I most enjoyed": *Paris Review*, 80–81.

45 "Martedì il dicianove": Clampitt Papers. Additions.

47 "we must greet him": Clampitt Papers. Additions.

48 "Since I first encountered": Clampitt Papers. Box 21, Folder 3.

48 "O cold": Clampitt Papers. Additions.

49 "I think the reason": *NDQ*, 120.

49 "It may be": Clampitt Papers. Box 19, Folder 2.

50 "had no ambition": Clampitt Papers. Additions.

51 "Last evening I went": Clampitt Papers. Additions.

51 "The time is ripe": Clampitt Papers. Additions.

52 "it was / the youngest": Clampitt Papers. Box 8, Folder 9.

52 "When I am gone": Clampitt Papers. Additions.

55 "I feel best": Clampitt Papers. Additions.

55 "I grew up": *NDQ*, 127.

55 "I'd rather read": Video recording from the University of North Dakota Writers Conference (1985). Clampitt Papers. Additions. Hereafter, *UND* Writers Conference.

57 "When there were rehearsals": Clampitt Papers. Additions.

59 Amy's music teacher: Clampitt Papers. Box 43, Folder 7.

60 "a voice out": Clampitt Papers. Box 29, Folder 3.

60 Her brother Philip: Letter from Philip Clampitt to the author (May 7, 2019).

60 Shirley Mayo: Clampitt Papers. Additions.

60 "I seem to recall": "Providence," 35.

62 "The Great Revival": "Providence," 36–37.

63 "would memorize poems": Clampitt Papers. Additions.

63 "from the most forbidding": *Out of the Garden: Women Writers on the Bible*, ed. Christina Büchmann and Celina Spiegel (New York: Fawcett Columbine, 1994), 252–53.

65 "For sheer inanity": "Epistles to the Thessalonians," *Predecessors*, 95.

66 In a letter: *Letters*, 248.

69 "I didn't think": Clampitt Papers. Box 44, Folder 1.

69 "There comes a time": Clipping from Silletto Papers, courtesy of Philip Clampitt. Clampitt Papers. Additions.

69 "Self-consciousness is": Clampitt Papers. Box 16, Folder 2.

70 "I was wondering": Clampitt Papers. Additions.

71 Another soon-to-be roommate: Clampitt Papers. Additions.

71 "Write again": Clampitt Papers. Additions.

72 "O innocent wickedness": Clampitt Papers. Box 30, Folder 1.

72 "I talked about": Morrisroe, 48.

73 "I ask": Clampitt Papers. Box 30, Folder 1.

74 "In the work": "Two Cheers for Prettiness," *The New Republic* 106, nos. 1–2 (January 6–13, 1992): 44–46.

74 "This is very fine": Clampitt Papers. Additions.

75 "I saw your picture": Clampitt Papers. Box 24, Folder 4.

75 "Do you know": Clampitt Papers. Box 29, Folder 1.

75 "directed a one-act play": Clampitt Papers. Box 27, Folder 7.

76 "Since I lived": Clampitt Papers. Additions.

77 "Dear Miss Frazier": Clampitt Papers. Additions. Further quotations about Clampitt's time at Cummington come from the same papers.

81 "My earliest ambition": Korelitz, 44–45.

81 "the livingness": *Predecessors*, 3.

82 "I saw the warm": Clampitt Papers. Additions.

83 "Then suddenly the universe": Clampitt Papers. Additions.

84 "For an American": Quoted in Michael Luick-Thrams, *Out of Hitler's Reach: The Scattergood Hostel for European Refugees, 1939–43* (Ames: Iowa State Press, 1997), 127.

85 "We all wore": Morrisroe, 47.

85 "I don't myself feel": Clampitt Papers. Box 21, Folder 4.

86 "I think / of my father": "Crossing the Jersey Meadows." Unpublished poem. Clampitt Papers. Box 10, Folder 4.

87 "You gave of your time": Clampitt Papers. Box 33, Folder 3.

89 "a little space": Clampitt Papers. Box 5, Folder 5.

90 In a kind of reverse irony: *NDQ*, 128.

OBSCURITY

93 Decades later: *Letters*, 208.

95 "the Midwest may": Clampitt Papers. Box 21, Folder 4. Clampitt conducted an epistolary interview with Elise Paschen on October 3, 1986. A severely redacted version appeared in *Oxford Poetry* and was reprinted in *Predecessors*; quotations are from the complete, unpublished interview. Hereafter Paschen.

97 She helped with: Clampitt Papers. Additions.

97 "getting out of": Clampitt Papers. Additions.

97 "It is no excuse": Clampitt Papers. Additions.

98 "Howard may be": Clampitt Papers. Additions.

99 "Your love slave": Clampitt Papers. Additions.

101 "This is volume 1": Clampitt Papers. Additions.

103 "a soggy and frowzy tale": *Letters*, 44.

104 "All over town": Clampitt Papers. Additions.

105 "This was going": Clampitt Papers. Additions.

106 "We saw one another": Clampitt Papers. Box 47, Folder 3.

106 "I may never": Clampitt Papers. Box 49, Folder 3.

107 "I've just taken": *Letters*, 226.

110 "Why are people": *Letters*, 10.

110 "Situated on a cobblestone": Description by Christian Emanuel for StreetEasy .com (2022).

111 "I'd open all": Letter from Karen Chase to the author (December 6, 2019).

112 "at least I did": *Letters*, 4.

112 "You do have the makings": Clampitt Papers. Additions.

113 In her interview: *Paris Review*, 89.

115 "Death, death, death": Clampitt Papers. Additions. Further quotations from Clampitt's travel journal come from the same papers.

121 "You asked about England": Clampitt Papers. Additions.

123 "it was a relief": Clampitt Papers. Additions.

125 "I wanted a great romance": *Letters*, 24.

127 "an exquisitely handsome": Clampitt Papers. Additions.

129 "a literary agent": Clampitt Papers. Additions.

129 "It would be nice": *Letters*, 5.

130 "holes in my shoes": *Letters*, 7.

130 "I can bother": Clampitt Papers. Additions.

131 "There's no place": Clampitt Papers. Additions.

131 "there's the matter": Clampitt Papers. Additions.

132 "the pressures of prestige": Clampitt Papers. Additions.

132 "For instance": *Letters*, 39.

133 "He keeps oysters": *Letters*, 31–32.

133 "Scribner's turned it": *Letters*, 43.

134 "Did I tell you": *Letters*, 128.

135 "still in the same": Clampitt Papers. Additions.

135 "My agent entered": *Letters*, 143.

135 "the article is not": Clampitt Papers. Additions.

136 "that dangerous": *Letters*, 25.

137 The first: Clampitt Papers. Additions. Further quotations from Clampitt's unpublished fiction come from the same papers.

137 Clampitt's initial letter: Clampitt Papers. Additions.

139 "it's pretty much": Clampitt Papers. Additions.

144 In a letter: Clampitt Papers. Additions

145 Three months later: Clampitt Papers. Additions

145 In an extraordinary letter: *Letters*, 48–57.

147 A 1956 Easter letter: *Letters*, 58–63.

148 In May, again writing: *Letters*, 63–7.

149 Looking back: *Letters*, 214–15.

149 "We can't be friends": *Letters*, 70.

149 In a late letter: Clampitt Papers. Additions.

150 "feeling so cheerful": *Letters*, 104.

155 Two entries: Both journal entries that follow come from the Clampitt Papers. Additions.

157 "I am not a born": *Letters*, 88.

157 "I felt like a misfit": Morrisroe, 47.

158 In January 1959: *Letters*, 91.

158 "a little secret": Clampitt Papers. Additions.

158 She wrote to Mary Russel: *Letters*, 103.

159 "We are living": *Letters*, 107.

159 "I never ate": *Letters*, 109.

163 Secrecy, as she once: *Letters*, 67.

165 "elfin, serene presence": Clampitt Papers. Box 24, Folder 1.

165 "Twelve years compounded": Clampitt Papers. Additions.

166 "wedding trip before": *Letters*, 129.

166 "By now I could": Clampitt Papers. Additions.

166 She kept notes: Clampitt Papers. Additions.

167 "We have a delightful": *Letters*, 131–32.

168 She obliges: *Letters*, 133.

168 Two years earlier: *Letters*, 99.

169 "English country dancing": *Letters*, 134.

169 "one of the most": Clampitt Papers. Box 21, Folder 2.

170 "and someone gave me": Clampitt Papers. Box 21, Folder 2.

170 She writes to Rimsa Michel: *Letters*, 140–41.

171 "Her idea of really challenging": Letter from Mary Jo Salter to the author (July 29, 2021).

171 "The penalty": *Letters*, 145.

172 Art has given way: *Letters*, 144.

172 In June 1968: *Letters*, 149.

174 Bloom could recall: Author's interview with Harold Bloom (September 2019).

174 "resolving conflicts of laws": Letter from John Sare to the author (November 26, 2020).

175 "should not really be depressed": Clampitt Papers. Box 47, Folder 3.

175 In a memorial note: *Columbia Law Review* 101, no. 6 (October 2001): 1219–26.

175 Elizabeth Bernhardt: Letter from Elizabeth Bernhardt to the author (July 20, 2021).

176 "Hal studiously": Letter from John Sare to the author.

177 "once you noticed": Letter from Rachel Brownstein to the author (July 20, 2021).

178 "the gentlest and most unflappable": Clampitt Papers. Additions.

178 "never to exert": *Letters*, 23.

179 Clampitt inscribed: Clampitt Papers. Additions.

180 "How to categorize": *Letters*, 172.

180 "There was a small flurry": *Letters*, 205.

182 "At the end": *Letters*, 150.

183 "The accretions": *Predecessors*, 106.

183 "I think we've all": Clampitt Papers. Additions.

184 One letter to Barbara Clark: *Letters*, 159–62.

185 "It was like a vision": *Letters*, 151–52.

185 Describing the same event: *Letters*, 155.

186 The Clampitt files: Clampitt Papers. Additions.

188 "to be arrested": Clampitt Papers. Additions.

189 The previous fall: Clampitt Papers. Additions.

189 In her 1968 Christmas letter: *Letters*, 149.

192 "From what Jennette": Letter from Amy Clampitt to her family (October 8, 1971). Clampitt Papers. Additions.

193 "my life of crime": Clampitt Papers. Additions.

195 "for the time being": Clampitt Papers. Additions.

FAME

200 "My own feelings": Clampitt Papers. Additions.

201 At concerts of the Incredible: Letter from Jim McCue to the author (December 4, 2019).

202 "Rain most of the day": Clampitt Papers. Additions.

203 At some later point: *Manhattan: An Elegy, and Other Poems* (Iowa City: University of Iowa Center for the Book, 1990).

206 In an October 1977: Clampitt Papers. Additions.

207 "One is naturally": *Letters*, 182.

208 "gotten a taste": *Letters*, 184.

208 Those years of practicing: *Letters*, 185.

209 "who grew up": *Letters*, 217.

210 "I have come home": Clampitt Papers. Box 5, Folder 1.

210 "Bright speed": Clampitt Papers. Box 6, Folder 4.

210 "We live in an ugly": Clampitt Papers. Box 6, Folder 6.

211 "in face a half-domesticated": Clampitt Papers. Box 7, Folder 7.

212 "DUMPTRUCK": Clampitt Papers. Box 6, Folder 6.

213 By his own admission: Author's interview with Jack Macrae (July 9, 2019).

214 "*the* person": Clampitt Papers. Additions.

214 In a letter from 1984: Clampitt Papers. Box 44, Folder 7.

214 "You really did catch": Clampitt Papers. Additions.

215 "many threads picked up": Clampitt Papers. Additions.

216 "it appears they must": *Letters*, 190.

216 "didn't look like somebody": *Predecessors*, 138.

216 "kindly, unassuming": *Letters*, 200–201.

217 "our angelic exercise guru": *Letters*, 194.

217 "unfailingly send me": Clampitt Papers. Box 42, Folder 2.

219 "Amy did in many": Letter from Mary Jo Salter to the author (March 5, 2020).

219 "I think women": Clampitt Papers. Box 42, Folder 2.

220 "this *is,* more or less": Clampitt Papers. Box 42, Folder 7.

221 "Writers need company": *Predecessors*, 5.

221 "Is it W. C. Williams": *Letters*, 199–200.

222 "But I don't know": *Predecessors*, 2.

222 Clampitt never wanted: Clampitt Papers. Box 17, Folder 2.

223 At a memorial service: Clampitt Papers. Additions.

224 "the almost extinguished lights": *Letters*, 174.

224 "after not being": *Letters*, 181.

225 "a kind of natural courtesy": *NDQ*, 128.

226 "I love weather!": *Letters*, 74.

226 "Mainers are the only": Letter from Ryan Harper to the author (June 3, 2020).

228 "Dear Miss Clampitt": Clampitt Papers. Box 10, Folder 1.

230 "I have been writing": Clampitt Papers. Box 10, Folder 1.

230 One of the new poems: Clampitt Papers. Box 10, Folder 4.

231 "I decided quite consciously": Clampitt Papers. Box 21, Folder 4.

232 In her 1986 interview: Paschen.

232 "an outrageous remark": Letter from Amy Clampitt to Bill Christopherson (May 11, 1990). Courtesy of the recipient.

234 "life-enhancer": *Letters*, 270.

234 The Clampitt papers: Clampitt Papers. Box 9, Folder 5.

235 "it's much less intimidating": Morrisroe, 48.

238 "gaze is entirely": Christopher Bakken, "Nothing Is Beneath Consideration," *Contemporary Poetry Review* (March 23, 2008).

238 "Rejection is a river": Letter from Ralph Savarese to the author (September 5, 2020).

238 "the very opposite": Letter from Susan Snively to the author (August 5, 2020).

239 "have the quality": Clampitt Papers. Box 23, Folder 7.

239 "The first book": Clampitt Papers. Box 33, Folder 1.

242 "I considered her": Letter from Frederick Turner to the author (July 2, 2019).

243 When *The Kingfisher* was published: Helen Vendler, "On the Thread of Language," *New York Review of Books* (March 3, 1983), 19–21.

243 "with some diffidence": *Letters*, 225.

245 "they have read you": Clampitt Papers. Box 46, Folder 5.

245 "Fear not": Clampitt Papers. Box 46, Folder 5.

245 As early as 1954: *Letters*, 26.

245 A decade later: *Letters*, 131–32.

246 "Thrilling though formidably difficult": *Letters*, 219.

246 "Always curious": Author's interview with Sam Seigle (November 18, 2021).

247 "one of the great experiences": *Letters*, 226.

247 And to Salter: *Letters*, 222.

251 "settle down to the serious": *Letters*, 228–29.

251 "It's wonderful to be breathing": Clampitt Papers. Box 21, Folder 2.

253 "for most of the several": *Letters*, 238.

254 "I was pretty scared": *Letters*, 242.

254 At the end of October: *Letters*, 243–44.

256 "ancient and handsome": *Letters*, 255.

259 "there are very": Clampitt Papers. Box 43, Folder 2.

259 "an elegy of the highest": Clampitt Papers. Box 70, Folder 2.

259 A little later: Clampitt Papers. Box 26, Folder 6.

259 But she wrote: Clampitt Papers. Box 34, Folder 5.

259 Edward Hirsch: Clampitt Papers. Box 31, Folder 2.

259 The young poet Rosanna Warren: Clampitt Papers. Box 47, Folder 1.

259 "follow the latest": Morrisroe, 44.

260 "brought to the free verse": "Amy Clampitt: Poems, Essays, Tributes," *Verse* 10, no. 3 (Winter 1993), ed. Bonnie Costello, 76. Hereafter *Verse*.

260 "The longest and most heated": Clampitt Papers. Additions.

261 Merrill himself: *UND* Writers Conference.

261 "The bounty is large": "Gathering Light," *Kenyon Review* 8, no. 3 (Summer 1986): 129.

261 Dennis O'Driscoll: "The Muse with an American Accent," *Poetry Ireland Review* 20 (Autumn 1987): 78.

261 In *Poetry*: Review of *What the Light Was Like*, *Poetry* 147, no. 3 (December 1985): 156–58.

262 About *Archaic Figure*: "Voluptuaries and Maximalists," *The New York Times* (December 20, 1987), section 7, page 12, column 1.

262 Reviewing the same book: Review of *Archaic Figure*, *Library Journal* (March 15, 1987): 80.

262 "a full-page sneer": Clampitt Papers. Additions.

263 "I thought I was": Quoted in *Times Record* of Brunswick, Maine (July 20, 1990), 15.

263 "had finished with": Clampitt Papers. Box 35, Folder 3.

263 "a parody of the Victorian": *Parnassus: Poetry in Review* 16, no. 2 (1991), 277.

263 The most savage: Mary Kinzie, "Thick And Thin," *American Poetry Review* 14, no. 6 (November/December 1985): 7–15.

264 "I'm not mature enough": Letter from Karen Chase to the author (October 10, 2020).

264 "A barnacle": *Letters*, 252–53.

264 "those nice little poems": Letter from Patricia Carlin to the author (July 10, 2020).

266 The poet-philosopher: Letter from John Koethe to the author.

267 His first letter: Clampitt Papers. Box 47, Folder 3. Further quotations from the correspondence between Clampitt and Weaver come from the same folder.

268 A woman from Chicago: Clampitt Papers. Box 24, Folder 6.

269 Bernard Malamud: Letter from Michael Brady to the author (April 25, 2020).

269 A philosophy professor: Clampitt Papers. Box 24, Folder 1.

269 From Maine: Clampitt Papers. Box 41, Folder 7.

270 "And I do get": Clampitt Papers. Additions.

271 "I've been writing poems": Box 43, Folder 7.

271 "My class is quite excited": Clampitt Papers. Box 44, Folder 7.

271 Thirteen-year-old: Clampitt Papers. Box 40, Folder 4.

271 "Who are you, Amy Clampitt?": Clampitt Papers. Box 36, Folder 1.

272 "My main concern": Clampitt Papers. Box 46, Folder 5.

273 "magnolia alleys": *Letters*, 246.

273 "I'm not sure": *Letters*, 248.

273 "being asked to assure": *Letters*, 247.

275 Her letter of reply: *Letters*, 280.

277 "more of a nomad": *Letters*, 252.

278 "I could almost say": *Letters*, 249.

278 "wanted to do": *UND* Writers Conference.

279 "When she came to England": Letter from Debora Greger to the author (May 2, 2019).

280 "what I liked was going": *Letters*, 253.

282 "The spell of his language": Clampitt Papers. Additions.

286 "My time with her": Letter from Allan Gurganus to the author (September 2, 2019).

288 "writing poems seems safer": *Letters*, 260.

289 "to hear language": Clampitt Papers. Box 53, Folder 1. Further quotations from Clampitt's notes about "The Language of the Stage" come from the same folder.

289 "husky young men": *Letters*, 259.

290 "The bad news": Clampitt Papers. Box 53, Folder 3. Further quotations from Clampitt's notes about "The Writing of Poetry" come from the same folder.

291 An impressionable young: Author's interview with Emily Todd.

292 It appeared: *Verse*, 5–8.

292 "When I find myself": *Letters*, 272.

292 "I feel strongly": Clampitt Papers. Box 46, Folder 6.

293 "I am currently intrigued": Clampitt Papers. Box 27, Folder 5.

293 "Then after retreating": Letter from William Doreski to the author (June 18, 2020).

294 "I was running a temperature": *Letters*, 260.

295 In an interview: *Predecessors*, 2.

296 "an idea came": Clampitt Papers. Additions.

296 Anthony Hecht: Clampitt Papers. Box 31, Folder 1.

296 Vendler replied: Clampitt Papers. Box 46, Folder 5.

297 In a 1993 letter: Clampitt Papers. Box 13, Folder 4.

298 "the one thing": This letter, cited here courtesy of Sister Mary John, will be housed in the Clampitt Papers.

298 Clampitt called her play: The various versions of the play are housed in Boxes 11–13 of the Clampitt Papers.

300 "I have modified": Clampitt Papers. Box 11, Folder 1.

302 "one or two events": Clampitt Papers. Box 11, Folder 1.

302 "smells, as they say": Clampitt Papers. Box 11, Folder 1.

302 Like Weaver: Clampitt Papers. Box 11, Folder 1.

302 "Is the whole": Clampitt Papers. Box 11, Folder 2.

302 Several years earlier: Clampitt Papers. Box 49, Folder 4.

302 "there's a reason": Clampitt Papers. Box 11, Folder 2.

302 "certain problems remain": Clampitt Papers. Box 11, Folder 2.

303 She even dreamed: *Letters*, 262.

304 "I can't see publishing": Clampitt Papers. Box 13, Folder 4.

308 "but it was in stillness": *Predecessors*, 71.

308 "is suffused with": *Predecessors*, 63–64.

308 Reading James: *Predecessors*, 69.

311 "Having been seen emerging": *Letters*, 262.

311 "such experiences only confirm": *Letters*, 264.

312 "otherwise I'm staying": *Letters*, 267.

313 "One evening": *Letters*, 266.

313 In a 1989 letter: *Letters*, 269–70.

313 "could write a whole": *Letters*, 53.

314 "the seemingly casual": Clampitt Papers. Box 33, Folder 2.

315 William Wadsworth: Letter from William Wadsworth to the author (September 13, 2020).

316 "I found them": Letter from Amy Clampitt to Jim McCue (May 16, 1992). Courtesy of the recipient. To be housed in the Clampitt Papers.

316 "No wonder": Clampitt Papers. Box 35, Folder 7.

319 "I do have a fondness": Emily Todd, "Amy Clampitt: Interviewed by Emily B. Todd," *Verse*, 7.

320 "That's showbiz": *Letters*, 277.

323 "I'm not a poet": *Verse*, 7.

324 Thirty-one people: Clampitt Papers. Box 1, Folder 3.

324 The purchase figures: Clampitt Papers. Box 69, Folder 7.

324 "Twelfth Street is finally": *Letters*, 282.

325 "too constrained by certain": *Verse*, 78.

325 "a lifetime of such forays": *Verse*, 79.

325 "Amy's speech tends": *Verse*, 79.

326 "I found it difficult": Letter from Kurt Leland to the author (June 29, 2020).

327 "mulling the contraries": Letter from Amy Clampitt to Kurt Leland. Courtesy of the recipient. To be housed in the Clampitt Papers.

327 "may have coaxed": *Verse*, 32.

329 "All seemed to be going": Letter from William Doreski to the author (June 18, 2020).

329 "you have to suffer": Morrisroe, 48.

331 In November 1993: Clampitt Papers. Box 28, Folder 5.

335 At a posthumous tribute: Amy Clampitt Tribute, audiotape. Clampitt Papers. Additions. Bloom's tribute seems to have inspired his later review of Clampitt's *Collected Poems*: "The Achievement of Amy Clampitt," *The Yale Review* 86, no. 1 (January 1998): 179–84.

335 He wrote Clampitt: Clampitt Papers. Additions.

336 "a marvelous lifeline": *Letters*, 262.

337 She wrote to Philip: *Letters*, 283.

338 It contained a sheaf: Clampitt Papers. Additions.

338 "replaces depth": *Verse*, 40.

340 "the great religion": *Predecessors*, 69.

341 Clampitt could identify: *Predecessors*, 35.

342 In December she wrote: *Letters*, 285.

343 She described the trip: *Letters*, 286.

343 "a delicious few days": *Letters*, 288.

345 "The Greeks associated": Paschen.

346 "that agreeing would make": Mary Jo Salter, journal entry shared with the author.

346 "very tired": *Letters*, 288.

350 "She's at home": *Letters*, 288–89.

350 Salter remembered: Letter from Mary Jo Salter to the author (May 28, 2020).

350 "That's what I like": Mary Jo Salter, notes shared with the author.

351 It came from a woman: Letter from Susan Snively to the author (August 5, 2020).

353 Clampitt had quoted from ten: In her notes to the poem, when it appeared in *Westward*, Clampitt uses the numbers for Dickinson's poems from the 1960 edition of Thomas H. Johnson.

354 "covered Amy's ashes": Mary Jo Salter, journal entry shared with the author.

359 Most interestingly: John Hollander, "The Art of Memory," *The New Republic* 211, nos. 12–13 (September 19/26, 1994): 51–53.

360 A lengthy essay: Daniel Hall, "Pure Astonishment," *Parnassus: Poetry in Review* 24, no. 1 (1999): 63–75.

361 "hopeful version": Blake Morrison, "The Cross-Country Poet," *The New Republic* 203, no. 1 (July 2, 1990): 29–32.

361 "Between Elizabeth Bishop": Harold Bloom, "The Achievement of Amy Clampitt," *The Yale Review* 86, no. 1 (January 1998): 179–84.

362 Another young poet: Tess Taylor, "What Tries to Stay Put," Poetryfoundation.org (May 11, 2011), www.poetryfoundation.org/articles/69691/what-tries-to-stay-put. Hereafter Taylor.

362 "reading it is a bit": Peter Stitt, "Words, Book Words, What Are You?," *Georgia Review* 37, no. 2 (January 1983): 428–38.

362 "Now and then": Alfred Corn, "Review of *Westward* by Amy Clampitt," *Poetry* 157, no. 1 (October 1990): 41–44.

362 "a cornucopia": Robert Shaw, "Review of *A Silence Opens* by Amy Clampitt," *Poetry* 165 no. 3 (December 1994): 161–65.

362 "her velouté-filled poems": Taylor.

367 "the refuge to which": Helen Vendler, "Books: Imagination Pressing Back," *The New Yorker* (June 10, 1991), 103–11.

Acknowledgments

For assistance of many sorts—biographical, critical, scholarly, historical, financial, editorial, and personal, or some ineffable combination—I am grateful to the following individuals, many of whom may have already forgotten the favors they did for me. I offer assurance to all of them that I have certainly not forgotten their services:

Crystal Alberts, Emily Katz Anhalt, Neil Astley, Mark Atlas, Jennifer Banka, Elizabeth Bernhardt, Csilla Bertha, Matthew Bevis, Lorna Blake, Ric Bogel, George Bradley, Michael Brady, Ralph Buultjens, Rafael Campo, Bill Christopherson, Kay and Les Clampitt, Peter Clampitt, Philip Clampitt, Henri Cole, Jennifer Crewe, Margaret Cruikshank, Belinda DeKay, Yi Deng, the late Richard Deppe, William Doreski, Sam and Wanda Estes, Muki Fairchild, Robert Freedman, Laura Furman, Gabriella Gage, Jonathan Galassi, Kelly Garwood, Jan Huesgen George, Matthew Gilbert, Roger Gilbert, Dana Gioia, Warren Goldfarb, Michael Gorra, Debora Greger, Randall Griffin, Judith Hallett, Langdon Hammer, Ryan Harper, Jeffrey Harrison, Henry Hart, Thomas Heacox, Roberta Korn Helft, Edward Hirsch, Margot Honig, Robert Hosmer, Sheri Huber-Otting, Anthony Kemp, Karl Kirchwey, Ann Kirschner, James Kissane, Caroline Knox, John Koethe, Danielle Kovacs, Cheuk Lee, David Lehman, Brad Leithauser, Hilary Leithauser, Weijia Li, William Logan, Cindy Lowe, Christopher MacGowan, Colombe Marcasiano, Jim Martin, Jim McCue, Martha Clampitt Merrill, Terry L. Meyers, Joel Minor, Polly Morris, Donald E. Morse, Ben Moser, Donna Murphy, Cynthia Nadelman, Anton Nemirovski, Elise Paschen, Robert Pinsky, James Richardson, Dwight Rogers, Kenneth Rosen, David Rosenwasser, John Sare, Ralph Savarese, Lloyd Schwartz, Sam Seigle, David Semanki, Vijay Seshadri, Joe

Small, Susan Snively, Margaret Soffer, David Sofield, Alec Spiegelman, Jane Spinack, Kathy Starbuck, the late Anne Stevenson, the late Richard Stone, Tony Stoneburner, Peter Strauss, James Tatum, Andreas Teuber, Julia Turansky, William Wadsworth, Nancy Webb, Lisa Westkaemper, Christy Williams, Baron Wormser, Cynthia Zarin.

———

Other people, and several organizations, deserve more than simply being named.

I am lucky and grateful that Southern Methodist University, where I taught for forty-five years, has continued to support my creative and scholarly work in the form of grants for travel and for manuscript preparation. Tom DiPiero, dean of Dedman College; Jim Quick, dean of research; and Brad Cheves, director of development, have offered generous assistance. My former student Bob Bucker has been a part of my life for more than forty years, most recently as my point man with the SMU administration. My last department chairman, Darryl Dickson-Carr, put in a good word or two when I needed them.

In the bleakest days of the Covid pandemic, Betsy Maury at the Berkshire Taconic Community Foundation, which supervises the activities of the Amy Clampitt Fund, was a breath of spring. She offered warmth as well as patronage. A gracious host and a good sport, she uncomplainingly, even cheerfully, helped me cart dozens of heavy boxes of Clampitt materials from the gloomy solitude of an industrial storage shed in Adams, Massachusetts, where they had sat undisturbed for two decades gathering dust, back to her office in Sheffield. There I was able to examine their contents. Her enthusiasm and professional efficiency eased my work, lifted my spirits, and made possible the wonderful serendipity that every researcher welcomes when, groping around in the dust or the darkness, he comes upon a scrap of paper, a letter, or a picture that he never knew he needed until he found it. And under Betsy's leadership, the Clampitt Fund authorized a grant that helped to underwrite my work and travels.

It was the officers of that fund—Karen Chase, Ann Close, John Hennessey, Todd Portnowitz, and Mary Jo Salter—who in 2018 asked whether I might be interested in writing a Clampitt biography. In 2005, when I edited Clampitt's letters, I had suggested that there could be no biography of a woman who became famous too late in her life to have left sufficient information, and whose friends and relatives had mostly died off. I was wrong. More than a decade later, having retired from my long-held academic post, and perhaps in need of a new focus, I gave the idea of a biography a second thought, and said something like, "I've never written a biography, and I have no idea how to go about it. Let me reconsider." I have always believed that a person with a steady, rational outlook on life should base his important decisions on impulse. I paused for a while and then replied, "Yes. I think I'll do it." I hope that my efforts have repaid the confidence placed in me by the Clampitt trustees.

When I was a bookish child, libraries offered stimulation and security in equal measure. Decades later, my younger self came alive again. In pre-pandemic days, from the spring of 2019 through March 2020, I had a reassuring reminder of the reason my life has followed an academic path. I conducted the bulk of my research in the tranquil, wood-paneled Berg Collection at the New York Public Library. Carolyn Vega and her staff rolled out for my perusal box after box, folder after folder of materials from the Clampitt files. I sat in quiet splendor taking notes under their supervision. Their polite but vigilant reminders also ensured that I did not crease or otherwise damage any of the pages I was turning.

Another point of contact with my earlier self is Martha Kaplan, a high school classmate in suburban Philadelphia sixty years ago, and more recently my calm literary agent, who has performed countless professional favors for me since 2007.

The words "professional favors" don't even begin to describe the benefactions on my behalf committed by Ann Close and Todd Portnowitz in the offices of Alfred A. Knopf. They have guided my manuscript through various iterations, and served as trusted advisers and overseers. Thanks also to Chip Kidd, Rob Shapiro, Nicholas Latimer, Victoria Pearson, Maggie Hinders, and Roméo Enriquez.

My manuscript has profited from the keen eyes, intellects, and pencils of several people. Karen Chase, my official host in the Berkshires in 2003–4, and an ongoing source of light, shared details about Amy's life (and death) without which this book would have been less accurate, and less lively. Mark Oppenheimer gave a working journalist's appraisal of my book's contents, pacing, and style. Alice Quinn, always attentive to nuance, provided astute suggestions during the early stages of composition, and even more sensitive ones as the book neared its completion. Mary Jo Salter, the prime mover behind this entire project, read everything several times, acting as both an editor and a fount of information about events and people from long ago.

Over the years on the home front, Doreen, Lucy, Norma, and Ollie have offered much appreciated companionship, distraction, and pleasure.

Kenny Martin has helped as research assistant, fact-checker, and computer whiz, offering his literary intelligence and technical expertise when I was preparing the manuscript for publication. During my years at SMU, I taught many superb students. Kenny was the last of this impressive group, and also the only student to whom I ever said (after one month in class), "I have nothing more to teach you."

Amy Clampitt would smile, I hope, to read that I make my final acknowledgment in phrasing adapted from John Keats. I have dedicated this book (in part) to the other Ken, the one who swam into my planet in 1968, and who has improved my prose, and my life, for more than fifty years.

Index

Page numbers in *italics* refer to illustrations.

A NOTE ABOUT THE AUTHOR

Willard Spiegelman was for many years the Hughes Professor of English at Southern Methodist University in Dallas, and the long-time editor of the *Southwest Review*. Since 1987 he has written about books and the arts for *The Wall Street Journal*. A recipient of fellowships from the Guggenheim, Rockefeller, and Bogliasco foundations, and the National Endowment for the Humanities, he is the author of eight books of literary criticism and personal essays, and the editor of *Love, Amy: The Selected Letters of Amy Clampitt*. Spiegelman currently lives in Stonington, Connecticut, and New York City.

A NOTE ON THE TYPE

This book was set in Minion, a typeface produced by the Adobe
Corporation specifically for the Macintosh personal computer, and
released in 1990. Designed by Robert Slimbach, Minion combines
the classic characteristics of old-style faces with the full complement
of weights required for modern typesetting.

Composed by North Market Street Graphics, Lancaster, Pennsylvania
Printed and bound by Berryville Graphics, Berryville, Virginia
Designed by Maggie Hinders